W9-DFT-260

CIVIL DISOBEDIENCE

AN AMERICAN TRADITION

Lewis Perry

Yale UNIVERSITY PRESS

New Haven and London

Published with assistance from the foundation established in memory of Calvin Chapin
of the Class of 1788, Yale College.

Yale University Press books may be purchased in quantity for educational, business, or
promotional use. For information, please e-mail sales.press@yale.edu (U.S. office) or
sales@yaleup.co.uk (U.K. office).

Designed by Mary Valencia.
Set in Minion and Franklin Gothic types by IDS Infotech, Ltd.
Printed in the United States of America.

Library of Congress Cataloging-in-Publication Data

Perry, Lewis, 1938–
    Civil disobedience : an American tradition / Lewis Perry.
       pages cm
    Includes bibliographical references and index.
    ISBN 978-0-300-12459-0 (cloth : alk. paper)   1. Civil disobedience. I. Title.
    JC328.3.P444 2013
    303.6'10973—dc23
                                                                    2013015092
A catalogue record for this book is available from the British Library.

This paper meets the requirements of ANSI/NISO Z39.48–1992 (Permanence of Paper).

10 9 8 7 6 5 4 3 2 1

This book is dedicated to Bond Elston Perry, my brother,
and to the memory of our sister, Diantha Louise Perry Gross

CONTENTS

PREFACE

Hannah Arendt pointed out in 1972 that civil disobedience was "primarily American in origin and substance" and "quite in tune with the oldest traditions of the country." I agree, but add that one dimension is generally missing in public controversy that ebbs and flows over civil disobedience: history. Although there are studies of individuals and events, no one has examined long-term patterns, influences, and discontinuities. In this book I aim to recover that missing history.

How far back can we go in the search? Although advocates and practitioners of civil disobedience have accorded to the so-called Boston Tea Party of 1773 and more broadly to the revolutionary movement an inspirational place in its history, we must look at that claim with a little skepticism. To be sure, the destruction of the tea in Boston harbor has retained a symbolic importance, in the United States and abroad, for resistance movements against British imperial power and other political insurgencies. But the destruction bore little resemblance to the openness and nonviolence that has usually characterized the practice of civil disobedience. We will find more relevant precedents in the actions of men and women who opposed state-enforced religious authority in their colonies, especially New England Baptists who on the eve of the Revolution organized what has been called "massive" civil disobedience against what has been termed unfair taxation by the Puritan state church.

Law breaking and rebelliousness were common enough in early America, but the earliest plausible instance of civil disobedience, as we understand it, did not occur until 1829, and again it was based on religious dissent. In that year over a dozen Presbyterian-Congregationalist mission-aries refused to cooperate with Georgia laws aimed at removing the Cherokees. Two of them served jail terms at hard labor until the U.S. Supreme Court upheld their claim that state law was invalid in the Cherokee territory. That was only a temporary victory in the fight against removal, but it deserves notice as a milestone, perhaps even the starting point, for civil disobedience in the history of the American nation. Because the missionaries served their time in a test of law, some might call it a model of how civil disobedience should work. But it did not stop the Cherokees and other nations from being removed, and the case had little enduring influ-ence on the making of a tradition.

Of more lasting consequence, we will turn to the deeds and writings of men and women who escaped from slavery, often in the lands from which Indians had been expelled. We will find the origins of civil disobedience in their accounts of resistance to their masters while they were held as slaves and of the illegal aid they received from black and white abolitionists when they were fugitives. National controversy over laws to impede their flight led to confrontations in northern cities, and in the 1840s and 1850s white abolitionists, ministers, and lawyers also provided arguments justifying disobedience. Those decades were the time when civil disobedience entered fully into American tradition, later to be popularized by Mahatma Gandhi in India and, in turn, by interpreters of Gandhi in the United States. Those arguments have been adopted, down to the present, by champions of woman suffrage and by opponents of foreign wars, racial segregation, and, more recently, abortion. The best remembered (but by no means best understood) civil disobedient of the pre–Civil War era is Henry David Thoreau, though he was not the best known in his own time. Especially in the twentieth century, it became a firm conviction that disobedience and resistance to injustice should never be passive, that it must be active. That teaching came from Thoreau, but even more from Gandhi and his American interpreters, and it has had firm critics, as well as champions, in the decades since Arendt identified the American tradition. It is a thread that will run through this book.

ACKNOWLEDGMENTS

First I wish to acknowledge the importance of the family I grew up in. Both my brother Bond and my sister Diantha, to whom this book is dedicated, were civil disobedients. Bond did his jail time in Crawfordville, Georgia, in 1965 while he was working for SCLC's Summer Community Organization and Political Education program (SCOPE). In that program, modeled on the previous year's Freedom Summer, northern college students assisted local communities in the southeastern states with voter registration, school integration, and legal rights. He also recruited students from northern colleges and lived as a community organizer in an isolated black community in Lisman, Alabama. In 1967 Diantha, a twenty-year-old student at Bard College, was arrested with twenty-eight others for blocking access to navy and marine on-campus recruiters in New Paltz, New York. In a good book with a terrific title, *Don't Shoot—We Are Your Children,* J. Anthony Lukas noted that she was one of only two who refused to pay the fine of fifty dollars and served her ten-day sentence. Years later, my mother told me that my father, who was a Universalist minister, had driven up to New Paltz to get Diantha out, but she would have none of it. If he really did try to spring her, that would have been out of character for him. When I came into possession of many of my father's sermons and newsletters, by then a little moldy and water-stained, a few years after he died, my wife and I sat on a porch in New Hampshire refoldering them in new boxes. At one point she announced, "You're going to like this," and handed me a folder on civil disobedience with a sermon from 1973 and notes for lectures in 1966 at a junior college and in 1968 at a high school in Rhode Island. During his time in Rhode Island, my father joined vigils and protests with the Brown University historian William McLoughlin, who wrote extensively on civil disobedience as an important theme in early American history.

A grant from the Harry Frank Guggenheim Foundation supported research that was the essential groundwork for this book. I spent the academic year 1991–92 at Rutgers University in New Brunswick, New Jersey, where the chair of the History Department, Rudy Bell, arranged for me to borrow a faculty office and a desktop while using libraries in New Brunswick and New York. At the year's end, I gave a seminar on civil disobedience to a lively, challenging group of Rutgers Americanists. (It was from one of their number that I learned that his radical groups usually just spoke of "CD.") An essay titled "Black Abolitionists and the Origins of Civil Disobedience," which appeared in a volume on *Moral Problems in American Life* that I coedited with Karen Halttunen, was the first published outcome of the Guggenheim support. This book completes that project.

In subsequent years I received research support associated with the Andrew Jackson Professorhip at Vanderbilt University and the John Francis Bannon Chair at Saint Louis University. Vanderbilt is not famous for student radicalism, but early in my tenure anti-apartheid protesters erected shanties on the quad. Every year students and faculty benefited from the stimulation of week-long programs, planned under the guidance of the university chaplain, Rev. Beverly Asbury, on the legacy of Martin Luther King, Jr., and the civil rights movement and on issues raised by the Holocaust. Like many of my colleagues, I feel a special debt to Bev. At Saint Louis University antiwar and social justice traditions were stronger. I first saw student "die-ins" there. When I spoke at SLU I received feedback from philosophers, theologians, even a mathematician or two, who had thought carefully on issues relevant to civil disobedience. Conversations with Jim Fisher, who was working on labor priests, were especially memorable.

At both institutions I had the help of graduate research assistants, several of whom have moved on to accomplished careers. At Vanderbilt these assistants included Lisa Pruitt, Amy Stanley, Brad Lambert, and Bruce Harvey; at Saint Louis, Steve Hardman, Jennifer Medeiros, Ken Mueller, Matthew Sherman, and Marcus McArthur. For part of my year at Rutgers, I was able to enlist the assistance of Grace Elizabeth Hale.

Before I ever imagined writing anything substantial on civil disobedience, I accepted an invitation to write a brief article in the *Encyclopedia of American Political History* (1984), edited by Jack P. Greene. That was not the start of a book, but it was an occasion to learn that the subject was scantily explored. A couple of years later I presented the lecture "Civility, Disobedience, and the Constitution," with stimulating discussions afterward, at Indiana University, Bloomington, and at Ball State University. The lecture was published by the Poynter Center, Indiana University, with support from the Ball Brothers Foundation (1986).

In summer 1986 I was invited to lecture for a month in India for the AMPART program of the United States Information Service. The invitation called for lectures on American intellectual life, a subject on which I had recently published a book, for a conference in Udaipur, but I was requested to provide a list of additional topics from which sponsors in other cities might choose. And so my records show that I lectured, from notes, on "Civil Disobedience as a Problem in American Society" at U.S. Cultural Centers at Bombay (Mumbai), Calcutta (Kolkata), and Madras (Chennai), and the Universities of Goa and Hyderabad. Each audience was different, questioning was always sharp, and I learned a lot. Among the many persons who saw me through the experience, I am especially grateful to the late Subir Das Gupta of the American University Center in Calcutta for introducing me to the intellectual excitement of that great city. Most memorable were a visit with the faculty at the Nataji Institute for Asian Studies (and women's studies) and an Indian dinner that Subir and his wife Boudi hosted in their apartment as an opportunity for me to meet informally with Calcutta intellectuals.

I still did not turn directly to a book on civil disobedience. I had just moved to Vanderbilt as Andrew Jackson Professor, teaching in the "middle period" of a history much shorter than Kolkata's, and was committed to a book centered on Nashville, a city with a great story but nothing like Kolkata's, though with its own special relation to nonviolent civil disobedience. Hopes for another, longer stay in India were never realized, as funding on cultural priorities changed, but I did begin to sketch some thoughts in my mind and then to present papers and lectures on civil disobedience.

In addition to the seminar at Rutgers, previously mentioned, I presented my general ideas about civil disobedience in American history at a meeting of the Columbia Faculty Seminar on American Civilization organized by Eva Moskowitz in 1995, at a Madison Day dinner at Belmont University in the same year, to a seminar at Binghamton University in 1992, and to the History Department at Washington University in St. Louis in 2000. I presented my thoughts on reform traditions and civil disobedience in a

William O. Douglas Lecture in the Humanities at Central Washington University in 2001 and in a presentation at Washington University's 2007 School of Law symposium on the *Dred Scott* case. I tried out ideas on woman suffrage and civil disobedience at conferences on Women and Public Life (University of Wyoming, 1994), and with particular reference to Abigail and Julia Smith at a conference on Women's Friendship, University of Southern Maine, 2002, and at meetings of the British North American Historians (BrANCH), Cambridge University, 2005, and the Women's History Network's annual conference at Durham University, 2006. I presented formal convention papers on the antebellum origins of civil disobedience at the annual meeting of the Organization of American Historians in Memphis in 2003 and later the same year, and once more in Memphis, on American interpreters of Gandhi at the Mid-America History Conference. On all of these occasions I benefited from feedback from those who heard me. I think especially of questions posed at Columbia by the late Michael Wreszin. Critical reactions led to some corrections, but more important, they helped me find my voice, not critical enough for some, too disrespectful for others, on a paradoxical tradition. I am especially grateful for the thoughtful comments of the respondents Norrece T. Jones, Jr., and Julie Jeffrey at the OAH, and James Lanier and Robbie Lieberman at the MAHC.

I did research for this book at the Swarthmore College Peace Collection, the American Antiquarian Society, and the Massachusetts Historical Society. The help of librarians and the availability of databases and statewide services at Saint Louis University libraries have proved invaluable. Special thanks go to Sarah Elbert of Binghamton and Ithaca who sent me a videotape of a film she made in Chicago in summer 1968 and on the basis of which she testified in the notorious Chicago Seven trial. I also appreciated encouragement in brief encounters along the research trail from two participant-authorities on American civil disobedience: Homer Jack and Mary King.

Conversations with friends and colleagues have helped me throughout this book's long journey to completion. I would like to thank Melvyn and Phyllis Leffler, Kitty Sklar and Tom Dublin, Linda Kerber, Hendrik Hartog, Howard Brick, Valarie Ziegler, Iver Bernstein, Thadious Davis, David Oshinsky, Mary Kelley, Michael Frisch, Ron Giere, Barbara Hanawalt, Joan Bertin, Helen and Dan Horowitz, David Brion Davis, Michael Kammen, Don Critchlow, Doug Mitchell, James B. Stewart, Drew and Mary Cayton, Michael Bess, Laurence Schneider, Rafia Zafar, Julian Long and Kathleen

Farrell, Susan Wiltshire, Jeff Clymer, and Karen Manners Smith. Not long before the sad news of his death reached me, I had a stimulating conversation with Paul Boyer, with comparative reflections on our pacifist parents and new research leads.

Other persons whose assistance must be acknowledged include my literary agent, Geri Thoma, for help in clarifying the project; Christopher Rogers, editorial director at Yale University Press, for his belief in the book and his patience; and Elaine Marschik, instructional technology coordinator at Saint Louis University, for expert, cordial help in preparing the manuscript for delivery. My greatest help came from Elisabeth Israels Perry, the scholar who is my traveling companion in life, who guided me through the completion of this long project.

1

The Drama of Civil Disobedience

This book examines the practice, justification, and criticism of civil disobedience in the United States from its pre-revolutionary backgrounds to the present. A distinctive American tradition of civil disobedience originated in the eighteenth century, took shape in the antebellum decades, and persisted, and sometimes flourished, from that time forward. Although it has been most clearly discussed in the twentieth century, especially in the early 1970s, changing attitudes toward law and government may have blurred some of its once-central implications, such as nonviolence, respect for law, and commitment to democratic processes. At the same time, awareness of the tradition among activists who practice civil disobedience has never been stronger. As the tradition is likely to endure, one of my hopes in writing this book is that clarification of its origins and history will contribute to further discussion and public understanding. Thus, the book does more than narrate the history and trace connections between periods and movements. It highlights some recurrent problems as experienced by those who have violated laws in the name of a higher morality and as observed by critics concerned that any law breaking undermines public order. Especially, it focuses often on the underlying paradoxical feeling of wanting to respect the law and institutions of civil society while being unable to acquiesce in or ignore immoralities in those laws and institutions.

Civil disobedience appears in the news almost daily. In springtime the stories often originate on campuses. These may concern local issues. In 2001, for example, Penn State students staged a sit-in and disrupted the Blue-White football scrimmage in order to "call attention" to death threats against a black student leader. Wesleyan students, angry that a popular teacher was being let go, conducted a hunger strike and then occupied the university president's office. Harvard students took over a campus building for three weeks to press the university to pay a "living wage" to janitors and other workers. In 2005 a similar sit-in and hunger strike took place at Washington University in St. Louis and in 2006 at the University of Miami. In 2006, protesters from Evergreen State staged a "die-in" as part of an effort to delay the departure of a navy cargo ship and "call attention" to an immoral war in Iraq. Of course, civil disobedience is by no means restricted to campuses in springtime. In recent years protests against abortion clinics, police brutality, nuclear armaments, marriage laws, and world trade policies have featured dramatic and well-publicized acts of civil disobedience. These are late instances of a long-standing tradition, and even amid heightened concern about terrorist threats there has been relatively little public talk of suppressing Americans' recourse to sit-ins and other expressions of civil disobedience. If the past is any guide, there may in the future be greater criticism, more repression, and new lulls in the practice of civil disobedience. But it seems likely that civil disobedience will continue to have an important place in American public life.

Contemporary disobedients (and journalists who comment on their actions) show awareness of the tradition when they refer to precedents in previous eras. In spring 2004 advocates of same-sex marriage compared events in New Paltz, New York, and San Francisco to the woman suffrage protests during World War I, bus boycotts of 1955, and lunch counter sit-ins of 1960. For years, anti-abortion leaders have called themselves the "new abolitionists" and linked their blockades of Planned Parenthood centers with abolitionist defiance of laws supporting slavery. In the 1960s the Student Non-Violent Coordinating Committee (SNCC) also called its campaigners against segregation in the rural South the "new abolitionists." In addition, SNCC's actions had links to the Congress of Industrial Organizations (CIO)'s sit-down strikes of 1936–37 as well as to the free speech fights and "jail, no bail" tactics of the Industrial Workers of the World (IWW) a generation earlier. In 1948 A. Philip Randolph and the March on Washington Movement (MOWM) pointed to the Underground Railroad as a forerunner, proving that nonviolent civil disobedience was not alien to American society or black culture. Leaders of the woman suffrage movement in the 1870s appealed to memories of the defiant deeds of antislavery heroes. Abolitionists, for their part, held memories of Quaker and Baptist civil disobedience against established churches in the eighteenth century. Nearly everyone raises the Boston Tea Party as a precedent for civil disobedience, and though we will find the analogy faulty in some respects, its repetition signifies a belief in a national heritage of resistance to unjust laws that underlies the civil disobedience tradition. Though defiance of law is an important part of this heritage, it is not so much a heritage of violent rebellion as one of moderate protest.

The creation and continuation of a tradition through lulls and periods of intensity is a major subject of this book. But there are important contrasts to note and recurrent disagreements to understand. A look, at the outset, at two fairly recent events will identify themes that will prove of recurrent interest throughout these pages. Both events occurred at Gallaudet University, the nation's foremost educational institution for the deaf, sometimes called the "Deaf Mecca," in Washington, D.C., and both had to do with conflict over the selection of the university's president. In March 1988, when trustees, meeting at a downtown hotel, named a president who, like all her predecessors, was not deaf, angry students, who had expected the choice of one of two deaf candidates, marched to the hotel in protest. On several occasions during the week that followed, joined by alumni and students from other schools for the deaf and by representatives of organizations for the deaf, protesters closed down the campus by forming human chains and deflating the tires of cars and buses in front of the gates. They held numerous rallies, won faculty support, met with congressmen on the board of trustees (Gallaudet receives substantial funding from the U.S. government), and received much attention from the news media. Before the week was out, the new president had withdrawn, the "Deaf President Now" (DPN) movement had prevailed, and I. King Jordan, a professor of psychology and dean of arts and sciences, was named Gallaudet's eighth president. Also, the board accepted the resignation of its chair, agreed to increase the numbers of deaf trustees to at least 50 percent, and granted amnesty for all student demonstrators. In short, the victory was complete. In the following years Jordan proved to be a notably successful educational leader—raising the endowment, adding new programs and buildings, and serving as a symbol inspiring deaf persons around the world to accept no limits to their aspirations.

The DPN movement drew on parallels with the civil rights movement of the 1950s and 1960s. Marchers carried a banner to the Capitol that read

"I Have a Dream," and protesters sang the anthems of the earlier move-ment, "We Shall Overcome" and "We Shall Not Be Moved."[1] Jordan has been called a Martin Luther King for deaf people, and the 1988 triumph has been called a Selma or Stonewall for the deaf—that is, the start of a new era in achieving civil rights for the deaf and, some would add, all persons with disabilities. Jordan himself spoke of such milestones in the history of civil rights as "Rosa Parks' refusal to relinquish her seat on a bus, women suffragettes demanding the right to vote, and Martin Luther King's 'I have a dream' speech" and added, "I honestly believe that the success of DPN ranks among these memorable moments."[2] These events became central to the historical memory of the university, recorded and celebrated on its Internet site and in a book by Gallaudet professors published by the univer-sity. Some of the most influential writings on nonviolence and civil disobe-dience depict the creation of a "beloved community" where differences are reconciled, justice achieved, and people progress through cooperation. DPN often sounds like a realization of such a vision of overcoming differ-ences for the common good. One of the protest leaders, the Arizonan Tim Rarus, recalled how he received help in hotwiring a bus and blocking a gate from a student who, though deaf, was "oral" and not proficient in American sign language (ASL) and who, to boot, was long-haired, wore a black leather jacket, and came from New York City: "I tell this story because before DPN, I was not one to interact with deaf people who were not culturally deaf like myself. Deaf people have a history of fighting among themselves. Yet, during DPN, we all worked together for that common goal: a deaf president. Never mind the mode of communication our presi-dent would choose or his background, as long as he was deaf. And together we accomplished that goal."[3]

In May 2006, Gallaudet's trustees announced that Jane K. Fernandes, a professor and administrator at the university, would be Jordan's successor and Gallaudet's first deaf woman president. The announcement set off angry protests resembling a reenactment of DPN, but this time no one could claim that the confrontation unified the campus community. To outside observers, the reasons for conflict were confusing. Every finalist for the presidency was deaf. Protesting students voiced complaints about Fernandes's personality and administrative style and about a selection process in which their views, though heard, went unheeded. Some faulted Fernandes's fluency in ASL and claimed her strong interest in technolog-ical advances—cochlear implants and improved hearing aids—threatened what they called "Deaf culture." Students set up a tent city on campus and, with support from some alumni, teachers, and activists in the deaf community, protested the trustees' choice. The excitement subsided after commencement, when many students left campus, but a summer's respite did nothing to cool off angry emotions.

In the fall, a coalition of students renewed opposition to the new president. During an embattled October, tents went up again, demonstrations resumed, the main classroom building was occupied, and most normal activities on campus were interrupted or shut down. The extent of student support for and opposition to the protests was bitterly contested, but marches and rallies drew thousands of participants. Members of the football team blocked the gates to the campus. The volleyball team sat in the president's office. The administration's response—calling in police, dispatching heavy equipment (a front-end loader) to remove the tents—often seemed brutal. The arrest of 134 protesters, who "went limp" as they were carried off, on "black Friday" (October 13) gave the movement a new demand: as in 1988, there should be no penalties or reprisals. The protesters, communicating electronically through group e-mails, hand-held messagers, and laptops, generally projected a wholesome, peaceful image of themselves. "Wear Black Tomorrow," instructed Elisa Abenchuchan, one of the first and most influential bloggers, in preparation for Friday, October 26:

Dress all in black.
7 AM: Be at the 6th street gate to do a human tunnel and greet people
8 AM: Hunger strikers will do a sit-down at the President's Office
9:59 AM: Drop what you're doing wherever you are and drop on the floor for 10 minutes
Noon: Meet at the front gate—and create a human chain around College Hall
5 PM: Those arrested meet at the front gate to march to the President's House
8 PM: Community meeting. . . .

Only one of these actions seemed to require a bit of explanation. Abenchuchan gave a little more detail on what was called for at 9:59. "Sit down and relax" was her message.

For the past three weeks, Gallaudet and its community has been thrown in disarray. Often, it feels like people on all sides have been subjected to frustrations similar to the Chinese water torture method. But, here's something we can all do to address this.

If you are for a better, healthy, united Gallaudet, do this. At 10am on Friday, wherever you are, whatever you're doing, drop everything and sit on the floor for 10 minutes. Sit for better educational standards. Sit for social justice. Sit for unity for Gallaudet. Sit for the future of Gallaudet. Our future.

What seems peaceful to one person may strike another as coercive. And one person's unity may be another's divisiveness. Consider a flyer that Abenchuchan reproduced a few days earlier: "Call Jane Fernandes tomorrow!" it read, and it gave the president-designate's phone number. "Ask for her resignation!" it continued. "We want her phone ringing off the hook all day!" It concluded with a postscript: "Important: We are peaceful protestors. When you call, PLEASE be pleasant. No swearing or crude language. Kindly ask Jane to resign in the best interest of Gallaudet University and the Deaf Community worldwide."[4]

Despite considerable criticism of the protesters' harassment of those who did not join them, there was no doubting the growing strength of the opposition to Fernandes. On October 16, the faculty by a large majority called for Fernandes's removal and voted no confidence in the board of trustees. They also voted no confidence in Jordan, whose standing on campus steadily eroded as he staunchly supported Fernandes. At the end of October, the trustees backed down, "terminated" the new president, and prepared to find an interim president and launch a new search. Exultant protesters greeted the news by shredding and burning an image of Fernandes. Some commentators called this an expression of "hatred bordering on very serious mental illness," but defenders of the protests denied any intent to humiliate her. It was nothing personal; "it was to close her down, more of a symbolic thing." Martin Luther King, in the opinion of one supporter, would have been proud of the commitment to nonviolence.[5] It is hard to think of any previous campus protest in which the demonstrators succeeded so completely in winning—"win" was a much-used word, in fact—their demands for a large share in campus governance.

They won a strong voice, but no amnesty. In December the administration announced that those who shut down the campus would in fact face punishment through campus disciplinary proceedings. Still, some observers were shocked that the board by ousting Fernandes had "caved in" to "mob rule." The trustees' chair and Senator John McCain, who served as a congressional representative, resigned from the board. In contrast with the ebullient feelings of unity and progress following the DPN protests of 1988, thirteen university administrators addressed the community on November 6 on the personal despair and shared horror they had passed through and their hope to join with others in a healing process.[6]

Throughout the media reports on these events and the profusion of blogs documenting the feelings of demonstrators and their critics, a recurrent issue was civil disobedience. "Nothing could enrage the entire Deaf world more than ordering the arrests of peaceful protesters who are practicing noble acts of civil disobedience," warned one blogger. Anyone who prevented students from attending classes deserved their punishment, others replied. One blogger insisted that the protesters' "commitment and dedication alone" should suffice to gain respect in a city that is "populated by people who won civil rights through civil disobedience." To another writer, such a comparison with the civil rights movement was "insulting to black folks . . . and their REAL struggles." Could anyone point to "hearing only" water fountains and lunch counters? When Fernandes described the campus situation as "anarchy and terrorism," a group called Stakeholders for a United Gallaudet replied: "Civil disobedience activities on campus have been quiet and peaceful. Laws are not being broken. Peaceful candlelight vigils by the faculty are not terrorism. Students sitting on the campus walls and sleeping in tents is not terrorism. Comparing your students to the words of 9/11 is reprehensible. There is no terrorism nor anarchy at Gallaudet University. There is only a peaceful protest." Discussion of civil disobedience almost never reached a general or theoretical level of justifying or analyzing what was legitimate or why.

Allusions to the civil rights movement were frequent enough, but casual as in the example quoted. No doubt one could find references to Henry David Thoreau or Mahatma Gandhi buried in blogs and records, but for the most part protesters seem to have resorted to a familiar scenario of campus disobedience. Perhaps there was general confidence that in a confrontation between "civil disobedience by the majority" and law and order represented by the board and administration, success was inevitable: "The USA has a long history of seeing civil disobedience eventually succeed."[7]

In a thoughtful posting to the Gallaudet community, Jane Hurst, chair of the Philosophy and Religion Department, denied that the protests could accurately be called nonviolent civil disobedience. Nonviolence, she wrote, was based on "the idea that each person has the power to change things not by inflicting suffering on others but by being willing to undergo suffering for a cause." Threats, retaliatory attacks, and the angry, vindictive "feeling tone" indicated that the Gallaudet protests were not in keeping with the classic tradition of nonviolent resistance as taught by Gandhi and King. Civil disobedience she defined as "a technique of breaking the law and being arrested to achieve a goal." The Gallaudet protesters' complaints about being arrested were "ridiculous," according to Hurst, "since being arrested is the point of civil disobedience." By breaking the law, the students, acting their part in "the drama of civil disobedience," had in effect "requested" campus authorities to have them arrested. The continuing disrespect, intimidation, and vindictiveness of student protesters and faculty supporters showed that "this protest is NOT civil disobedience and it is NOT nonviolent." Protesters could not hide behind those labels while engaging in personal attacks on their opponents and demonstrating no confidence in their own ability to achieve change peacefully.

In other writings, Hurst described herself as a lifelong protester who had come to Washington in 1969 to demonstrate against the Vietnam War and had participated in many demonstrations for women's rights and gay rights and against the war in Iraq. Having spent decades working personally to cultivate within herself "generosity, self-acceptance, loving kindness, and forgiveness," she could not support a movement that expressed so much hatred: "Though physical attacks did not occur, it has been surrounded by death threats, stalkers, anonymous hate mail, and what to me felt like, well, a really bad vibe. It was so full of anger at Dr. Fernandes that she was stalked on her family vacation and vilified on a 'Wall of Hate' put up during a building takeover, to say nothing of the death threats, obscene websites and blogs. All this anger directed at a person is not something I could support." After the protesters had "won"—a word used often on the student blogs—Hurst joined "a group of faculty, staff, and students urging mediation and peaceful respect for all. . . . What we must do is encourage change in the hearts of the people who harbor such hatred. I know that such angry protesters have issues that need to be resolved before they can live peacefully in community with those who disagree with them, so there is much individual work to be done."[8]

It is not clear, from the flood of documentation generated by the Gallaudet protests, whether Hurst's analysis received much respect or attention. It is doubtful that many protesters were studying or applying Gandhi; more likely, they were reenacting the DPN protest and deploying tactics familiar in the scripts of campus protests of the 1960s and in recent years, such as events that closed down the University of Miami in 2006, with additional reminders that deaf people have a deeper claim of ownership of Gallaudet than most students have concerning their campuses. Some deaf protesters, linked by ASL and electronic communication, looked for unity in memories of the past different from the thread of American history featured in this book. After the arrests of the courageous comrades who "made a lot of sacrifice to stand up for what is right and the best for Gallaudet," a blogger known as Ridor, who prided himself on being "arguably the most controversial deaf blogger in America," inserted a panel from New Titan comics to explain "exact[ly] how I feel right now." The scene is a moment of defeat at Armageddon, with dark smoke billowing in the background as a group of superheroes and changelings hang their heads while one proclaims, "HONEY, I'M AFRAID IT'S JUST BEGINNING." Events had reached "rock bottom," one reader responded. "We are MORE THAN EVER determined to press on," wrote another. Ten days later, Ridor included a panel of "my favorite villain in a D.C. Comics, Mordru," expressing defiance in response to threats. "What you see on the image is the exact response that the protesters have for the administration." Despite all the threats and repression, the students stand up bravely against the injustice and divisiveness sown on campus by Fernandes and Jordan.[9]

At that point Ridor set down thoughts on civil disobedience utterly different from Jane Hurst's. In his vocabulary, civil disobedience was the opposite of politeness, sportsmanship, and trying to be "nice" in order to open up dialogue with the authorities (he refers to the Gallaudet administration as the "Axis of Evil"). Civil disobedience was analogous to grabbing I. King Jordan's testicles in a fight to improve the university. It had to do with power, effectiveness, forcing the "silly putzes" in the administration and trustees to act. The protesters were trying to defend the school and improve the lives of deaf people, and civil disobedience—"blocking roads, seizing the offices/buildings, going on a hunger strike" and any other "drastic" measures—was justified as including all means necessary to "rattle and pressure" the administration and trustees to reverse bad decisions, institute a more accountable search process, and find a better choice for the presidency. Ridor's professions of love for Gallaudet and his wish to save it from harm, however impatiently, cannot be dismissed.[10]

Can we argue that one of these contrasting views of civil disobedience is the right one? Of course, individuals can take their choice and find precedents for it, but the truth is that arguments like the one at Gallaudet recur throughout the evolving discourse on civil disobedience that this book examines. That history includes both Hursts and Ridors, those who eschewed anger and violence and others contemptuous of their opponents and interested in pressuring authorities to act or perhaps resign. Both types recognize, at least to some degree, limits to how far they can go; both profess respect for democracy; neither aims to overthrow authority. It should be noted that Hurst testified to her own long journey to overcome anger. Neither Hurst nor Ridor refers directly to the other's viewpoint (by name),[11] but I would like to suggest that the point-counterpoint implicit in the dialogue at Gallaudet can be taken as identifying my core subject. Historically, there have been two periods (before the Civil War and in the 1960s) of intense discussion of civic obligation and limits on disobedience, and during other periods many groups and leaders have addressed issues of law breaking and nonviolence. Certain movements with well-thought-out positions have sought to influence or prevail over others. At times, perhaps especially in recent decades, civil disobedience has spread in a kind of imitative ritual. In those versions, words and actions may be based on study of previous instances, but there may also have been unexamined enthusiasm for doing what has been done elsewhere with a sense of tradition that is relatively vague. Connections to an ongoing movement may not be restrained by theory, training, or historical knowledge. Yet certain themes have been recurrent. We may call some core issues in the evolving discourse of civil disobedience *Definition, Justification, Punishment, Community, Audience,* and *Discipline,* as we take a first look at them here at the start.

Definition. Regarding civil disobedience as "a technique of breaking the law and being arrested to achieve a goal," Hurst referred to the online, reader-created encyclopedia *Wikipedia* for a definition that emphasized renunciation of physical violence, an attitude of "respectful disagreement" with authorities, and an expectation of punishment, perhaps even brutal retaliation. *Wikipedia,* in turn, relies on the words and example of the great leader of India Mohandas K. Gandhi. It notes, however, that the American author Henry David Thoreau "pioneered the modern theory behind this practice" in the 1840s.[12] And what was Thoreau's definition? We will see that Thoreau did not think of himself as practicing "civil disobedience"— the term did not yet exist—and thus gave no coherent definition of it. But his writings had a strong influence on Gandhi's early adoption of civil disobedience. In 1907 Gandhi, seeking to detach his countrymen living in South Africa from their "deep-rooted superstition that a law cannot be disobeyed," urged them to read Thoreau and discover that "there is no obligation imposed upon us by our conscience to give blind submission to any law, no matter what force or majority backs it."[13] This negative contention that governments cannot demand unreserved obedience is at least part of a definition, but as Mary King explains in her excellent book *Mahatma Gandhi and Martin Luther King, Jr.*, for Thoreau "civil disobedience was a form of remaining true to one's beliefs" that was applicable to "individuals and groups who had little intention of producing broad political transformation." King herself defines civil disobedience as the practice developed in later times of "deliberate, peaceful and open violation of statutes, laws, orders, decrees, or military or police directives, accompanied by willingness to accept all of the penalties."[14] That is an excellent basic definition, though it may not fit every example.

Why do discussions of civil disobedience so often dwell on issues of definition? For one thing, civil disobedience is an odd and elusive concept. In 2008, National Public Radio reported on a class of Long Island teenagers who after studying Thoreau's essay engaged in principled protest against high gasoline prices by leaving their car keys at home and going to school on a rainy day by foot or on bikes and scooters.[15] A few years ago, the managing editor of the *National Review* encouraged applicants for college admission to pledge to lie about their race as "an act of civil disobedience" in protest against affirmative action. Could lying really be counted as an instance of civil disobedience?[16] Sometimes in ordinary speech the term is used as a synonym for violence and disorder. One example is a 1993 comic book involving the X-Men (the publishing rival of Ridor's favorite Titans) with the title *Civil Disobedience!* which I purchased with curiosity to see whether it might make some comment on nonviolent responses to evil. It includes one hero, said to be misled by pacifist teachings, who has renounced blood letting and gone back to the land, and it depicts a devastating uprising of oppressed "genetic deviates" who have been manipulated to seek more rights from the humans who exploit their labors. In other words, it does deal in a distorted, magnified way with issues of resistance, emancipation, public order, and justice that are relevant to our subject. But "civil disobedience," in this instance, refers to carnage and destruction on a massive scale.

Even when used more positively to denote a category of law breaking that is not the same as ordinary criminal behavior, there can be something incongruous about claiming a right to break a law. Yet this claim is made often enough by demonstrators justifying acts of defiance or by their attorneys claiming for those acts enough legitimacy to lighten or eliminate punishment. Indeed, it is probably not just at Gallaudet that there have been protesters who saw blockades and sit-ins as legitimate parts of an American tradition of minority rights that should not, by definition, be met with more than token punishment.

When the case is made that *civil* disobedience is a special category of acts deserving special treatment, the two words often function as a contradiction in terms—an oxymoron—with the word *civil*, connoting politeness, decency, respectfulness, joined to a word, *disobedience*, associated with violations, law breaking, even sin. Gandhi's writings furnish many examples to show that, whatever was intended when the term was invented, it frequently has been used deliberately as an oxymoron. Gandhi defined it as "outlawry in a civil, i.e., nonviolent manner," and in order to be "civil," he insisted, it had to be "charged with goodwill" and respect for law. According to Mary King, a veteran of the civil rights struggle in the American South, the effectiveness of sit-ins and freedom rides came from the protesters' "courteousness in the face of obnoxious cruelty. Civility was synthesized with disobedience." Advocacy of civil disobedience redounds in paradoxical terms like "peaceful rebellion" or "quiet battle." But sometimes it still is used simply for protests whose participants expect to get arrested, as distinguished from "direct action" referring to "disruptive action without arrest."[17] These oxymorons and distinctions constantly need definition and explanation.

Justification. Some law breaking may be innocuous enough, especially if done by individuals. Sometimes, but not always, the state will exempt or provide accommodation to individuals whose religious upbringings or private ethical convictions lead them to refuse to obey laws respecting religious observances, diets, even military service. Some group actions— for example, the disobedience of racially discriminatory laws by Indians in South Africa led by Gandhi and later by American civil rights activists— are commonly remembered as heroic, though at the time they had many critics. But group actions like those at Gallaudet—occupying an office, blocking traffic, barraging an official with phone calls—have victims who are barred from attending classes or conducting business, and since these actions are not directed at unjust laws, the inconvenience or hardship might require more justification than the claim, whether convincing or not, that they are pursued civilly or peacefully. To say that they are guided by individual conscience might not suffice to make these actions more acceptable.

After defining civil disobedience, Mary King noted that "such action originates from a conviction that there are circumstances when the moral responsibility to disobey illegitimate laws must be adhered to out of obedience to higher laws."[18] This was a lesson taught by Howard Zinn as a young political scientist to student civil rights protesters, including Mary King, in the 1960s: natural law took precedence over the legal apparatus of segregation.[19] References to "higher laws" recur throughout the history we are tracing. Postures of obedience to higher laws were especially prevalent, as we shall see, in the early years of the American republic when civil disobedience originated. In that era, many spoke of earthly government as a divinely approved institution and of obedience to the laws as a sacred obligation. Antislavery critics of the Fugitive Slave Law appealed to divine truth, voiced reverence for law, and spoke of the sacredness of government and, sometimes, of their willing acceptance of its punishment. They did not appeal to majority rule.

By the end of the nineteenth century there was less certainty in using words like "sacred" to describe government. By the 1940s those who contemplated civil disobedience were likely to be suspicious of religious absolutism. To A. Philip Randolph, an atheist and a labor leader who led the March on Washington Movement protesting segregation in the military and war industries, government was "an accommodative and repressive organism which is constantly balancing pressures from conflicting social forces in the local and national communities, and without regard to the question of right and wrong, it inevitably moves in the direction of the pressure of the greatest challenge." Methods of protest must be "revolutionary, unusual, extraordinary, dramatic and drastic in order to be effective in placing the cause of a minority into the mainstream of national and international public opinion."[20] Despite an analysis of government as insensitive to right and wrong, Randolph based his own justification for disobeying the draft laws and laws of treason on a "higher law of righteousness."[21]

In the 1950s and 1960s, Martin Luther King, Jr., and other black Southern Baptist ministers reintroduced the language of divine justice into the civil disobedience tradition, and more recently, the anti-abortion movement has praised the abolitionists' fidelity to the law of God in justifying its own actions on behalf of "the unborn." Some writers on religion and the law argue that believers have an "obligation of witnessing the absoluteness of God" in an all-too-secular world. The precedent of the post–World War II trials of war criminals supports a defense of civil disobedience as obligatory for citizens when orders of their government violate principles of justice.[22] It is still doubtful that many political activists would call government sacred. The *Oxford English Dictionary* defines civil disobedience as refusal to obey certain laws "of a government as part of a political campaign," and to Howard Zinn it was simply "the deliberate violation of a law in pursuit of a social goal."[23]

Punishment. "Being arrested is the point of civil disobedience," wrote Hurst, and demanding "amnesty" was therefore "ridiculous." Her point of view seemed exceptional at Gallaudet. "No reprisals" was a principal demand of the DPN movement in 1988, and it was granted along with the selection of Jordan as president and the resignation of the chair of the trustees. The call for amnesty was well remembered during the protests and blockades in 2006. The assumption that penalties would be light was part of the appeal to protesters. "Remember, to get arrested, you'll be out in two hours' time and $150 bail," Ridor wrote on "black Friday," October 13. The actual fine reportedly turned out to be $50, and 125 or more students then had an unlawful assembly arrest record to be explained on future application forms. Months of bitter protest followed the administration's failure to follow the 1988 precedent of amnesty.

We will see statements on both sides of the issue of whether civil disobedients must accept the penalties of the law. Hurst's view has been prevalent in what might be called the "classic" strain of civil disobedience that cites Gandhi and Martin Luther King, Jr., as major inspirations and holds that the law breakers should go courteously to their punishment, however unjustified or cruelly administered. We submit, some say, to the sacrifice of going to jail to show that we are respecters of law and order even though we defy one unjust law. That was the stance of some opponents of the Fugitive Slave Act and, a century later, of segregation. In his now-famous "Letter from the Birmingham Jail" (1963), Martin Luther King, Jr., asserted, "One who breaks an unjust law must do so openly, lovingly, and

with a willingness to accept the penalty." An individual who accepts imprisonment "in order to arouse the conscience of the community ... is in
reality expressing the highest respect for law."[24] This position is still familiar
in discourse on civil disobedience.

To some civil disobedients, assertions like King's may be inspiring
pieties, but they are not binding requirements in confronting a law or order
that does not deserve obedience. King himself did not always stay in jail for
long. It is common for student protesters, like those at Gallaudet, to expect
a kind of amnesty as their communities seek to rebuild good will after a
time of disruption. The same is true after some civil rights protests, and
negotiation over punishment may be an issue in settlements. In the 1960s,
with increased attention to law breaking as a means of creating a test of a
law's constitutional legitimacy, some commentators stressed the need for
the disobeyers, however noble their intentions, to "serve their time."

Still another view of punishment was held by Industrial Workers of the
World and, later in the twentieth century, by the Student Non-Violent
Coordinating Committee (SNCC) and freedom riders. "Jail, No Bail" was
the motto for a tactic of "jail-ins" that imposed the pressure of increased
costs and shortage of prison space on communities that refused to grant
civil rights. Operation Rescue later went even further in imposing heavy
expenses on cities that arrested anti-abortion activists. In recent decades,
zealots in the anti-abortion and forest defense movements searched out
the most difficult locks to break open in order to tie up maximal time and
energy from officers assigned to remove and arrest them.

I do believe that a willingness to be identified and to accept punishment is definitive of civil disobedience in the American tradition. I have
been asked whether hackers who seek to disrupt the programs and businesses of corporations they detest could claim to belong to that tradition. If
they do not try to escape detection and are prepared to accept punishment,
perhaps the case might be arguable. There is, after all, the precedent of
Daniel Ellsberg's 1971 release of the massive "Pentagon Papers," showing
that the public had been misled about the war in Vietnam; but Ellsberg
clearly took responsibility for his actions and accepted the legal consequences. "Electronic civil disobedience" sounds more analogous to breaking
and entering or sabotage, which at least one authority on civil resistance
recommends against.[25]

Community. After the DPN's triumph, Gallaudet portrayed itself as
a harmonious community transformed by the good will of all parties

involved in conflict: the protesters, the trustees who gave in to them, students and faculty, even the rejected president. Scholars have argued that among the reasons for the DPN's triumph was that it always was linked to the advance of civil rights rather than the interests of one narrow group.[26] No one claims that the 2006 protests had such a happy result. Hurst and others called for mediation and a purging of hatred from a fractured community. Announcing that they had terminated Fernandes's appointment as president-designate, the trustees called for a time of healing in "our beloved community."[27] Soon they appointed a new interim president, and conversation on campus switched to new topics—shrinking enrollments, funding threats—with occasional eruptions of bitterness over the importance of ASL in the curriculum. Hurst voiced concern about hostility on campus to "us hearing folks who have dedicated our professional lives to the success of deaf students." A poster on Ridor's blog called for firing "any remaining audists and lousy-signing professors." By late fall 2007 Ridor, concerned about invasions of his private life, had suspended or closed his blog and moved on.[28] Quiet and distraction are not the same as "beloved community."

That phrase, which originated in the Progressive Era among intellectuals concerned about the effects of industrialism on human personality and social relations, was familiarized in a later era by Martin Luther King, Jr., to describe an ideal of harmonious integration brought about through nonviolent resolution of conflicts and inequalities. Speaking from a utopian vision that has appeared frequently in writings on nonviolent civil disobedience, King did not underestimate the sacrifices necessary to reverse a history of oppression and inequality, but he saw the willingness to go to jail as a key to "the good of the community" rather than as a zero-sum game in which one side advances at the expense of the losers.[29] Integration, rather than merely desegregation, was "the ultimate goal of our national community." By the time of King's death, however, many civil rights activists had less confidence in the power of nonviolent civil disobedience to create a beloved community. They were willing to use it as a tactic when no other recourse seemed practical, but the results seemed disillusioning.

The anti-abortion movement in the early 1990s presented similarly divergent views of community and nonviolent tactics. Operation Rescue protesters who blockaded clinics that performed abortions adopted tactics of other movements—sitting-in and going limp, for example—not in order to integrate an activity but to stop it. They spoke of their duty to use any means available to stop an atrocity and believed communities like Buffalo, Little Rock, and Wichita, far from East and West Coast influences, would give Christian support to their actions, as to some extent proved true. But they created issues of public disorder that angered many in the community and led to new regulations, and in the following years the talk of resorting to "any means possible" led to threats of violence and murders of obstetricians that dampened religious and political support. Even before the escalation toward violence, West Virginia University law professor Charles R. DiSalvo, writing as an opponent of abortions, argued that "the disobedient who has no love" and no respect for the welfare of the community, "who hurls epithets at the other side, who has to be dragged away from the arrest site, who refuses to identify himself, who defiantly pleads not guilty, who complains of imprisonment—this disobedient generates no public sympathy." Instead, a type of disobedience associated with King and Gandhi and "characterized by sacrificial, redemptive, suffering" would be much more effective. The lesson that Operation Rescue needed to learn was that "arrogance alienates. It is love that converts."[30]

Similar debates have been heard over controversial tactics adopted in recent times in the environmental and antinuclear movements. As in the anti-abortion debates, these movements are not always motivated by deeply held beliefs in nonviolence or by visions of beloved community. Respect, or disrespect, for the community's values may be determined by practical calculations of effectiveness for the cause. Even earnest advocates of the power of redemptive suffering—DiSalvo is a good example—tend to be concerned about projecting a favorable image of their actions.

Audience. To whom are the acts of disobedience addressed? The community—in hope that its members will address problems, expand opportunity and participation, and strengthen the institution and democratic society? Perhaps in theory, but in the twentieth century an external audience almost always has been a critical concern. At Gallaudet, DPN sought and gained tremendously favorable attention in the media. The 2006 protesters angrily complained that the *Washington Post* and other news outlets were biased against their actions, and some called for the firing of certain reporters. For their part, some journalists saw at Gallaudet a reenactment of the intolerance and disruption on American campuses in the "bad old days" of 1968.[31] A year after the conflict subsided, Gallaudet officials complained about the media's continuing depiction of the campus as a site of "cultural war" over sign language and spoken English.[32] The concern about good or bad public relations is understandable enough, but is it incongruous with the idea of redemptive suffering?

It has not always been clear whether the goal of civil disobedience is to be true to private conscience, to demonstrate morality, or to exert power. Is it to convert or coerce? Though nineteenth-century civil disobedience often was justified in terms of private conscience, in the twentieth century disobedience was increasingly linked to power. In fact, one influential work, first published in 1935 and entitled *The Power of Nonviolence*, described the combat between a nonviolent protester and his opponents as a form of "jiu-jitsu" conducted in view of a circle of spectators.[33] That image recurs throughout modern advocacy of civil disobedience.

Sometimes civil disobedients have been indifferent to local opinion. Sometimes their acts have aimed to arouse press attention and exert pressure on authorities outside the local community to force the state or national government to intervene and insist on change. That was the intention of many civil rights protests in the 1960s. It was a goal echoed in one Gallaudet blog that emphasized congressional oversight of the college and hoped the protests would send "a wake-up call to the proper legislative, executive and judicial officers, so that proper investigations and proper lawful remedies may be implemented. This is intended . . . to put pressure on Jordan and Fernandes to step down, in order to accelerate the process of justice so that, as one protester put it, we may 'get on with our lives.' "[34]

Randolph's March on Washington Movement made it clear that it was trying to use leverage gained in wartime. (The same had been true of women suffragists who protested in Washington during World War I.) If marches and strikes offended observers in government or the press, that was immaterial. Embarrassment for America in the world would be a source of power.

In 1961 news photographs of a burning bus in Anniston and of brutal beatings in bus stations in other Alabama cities were published around the world and moved the Kennedy administration to put pressure on the state's authorities and on the anti-segregation freedom riders to stop causing situations that embarrassed the United States overseas. The pacifists who carried out the initial freedom rides did not anticipate the scale of the violence their actions would provoke or the national and international publicity that ensued. In the years that followed, however, the dramatic audiences looking at newspapers or sitting before television sets became important witnesses to many acts of protest. The antiwar movement of the

1960s had a strong sense of performance before an audience, as seen in the large-scale draft card burning in Central Park in New York and demonstrations at the Pentagon in 1967. "The whole world is watching"—that chant is associated with demonstrators in Chicago at the 1968 Democratic Convention as scenes of streets filled with tear gas and police clubbing young protesters appeared on television sets around the world.[35] Some of the theatricality was the work of a Yippie faction that professed little interest in the history of nonviolence while it exploited the absurdity of public life. There were also factions of protesters after 1968 who spoke and acted as revolutionaries and saboteurs. These stood almost completely outside the tradition of civil disobedience.

Expressions of protest, including acts of disobedience, often take a dramatic form. Demonstrations can be ways of "acting out," especially if carried out by or on behalf of groups who are unenfranchised, as when abolitionists stood up in church to protest slavery or interposed themselves between marshals and a "fugitive" slave. Dramatic protest had an important history among women's rights reformers who entered the polls and insisted on their right to vote, a tactic contributing to grand moments of pageantry in the twentieth century. Some advocates of woman suffrage criticized what they called disgraceful and ineffective "stunts" which, in their view, impeded progress in persuading legislators to enact suffrage for women. This has been a recurrent division in the history of civil disobedience.

The theatrical side has become especially noticeable among radical environmentalists. In July 1985, for example, members of Earth First!, an organization of "fundamentalist nature lovers," donned bear costumes and demanded rooms and trout dinners at a Yellowstone hotel. For their protests against man's incursion into the bears' habitat they were arrested and fined $50 each.[36] Tree sitting provides less comical examples. In 2002 a woman called Remedy lived almost a year 130 feet up in an ancient redwood in Humboldt County, California, where she received food and water from a network of activists opposed to the destruction of these ancient trees. Remedy and other tree sitters, perhaps dozens at some times, received little publicity for dramatic actions in remote locations. To a spokesperson for the lumber company impeded by these actions, including protesters who chained their bodies to loaded lumber trucks, the campaign was "basically eco-terrorism."[37] Sometimes celebrities join other activists and attract widespread publicity, as when the cinema actress Daryl Hannah spent three weeks forty feet high in a walnut tree in an effort to prevent the demolition of an urban farm in South Central Los Angeles.[38]

In recent times the Republican and Democratic Party conventions, increasingly staged events in their own right, have become the occasions for dramatic protests. As the invasion of Iraq was about to be launched in 2003, some protesters advocated "showy" acts of disobedience to catch public attention, while others were concerned that disruptive tactics would "alienate the public that they were trying to sway."[39] These concerns echoed debates over stunts versus earnest approaches to the public in earlier times.

Similar debates have recurred throughout the history to be studied here. They were visible in the differences between the thinking about disobedience of northern African American abolitionists and white reformers in the 1840s and 1850s. They returned in the different versions of disobedience advocated and practiced in post–Civil War women's rights movements. They were central to the advocacy and practice of civil disobedience in the civil rights and antiwar struggles of the twentieth century. Though I emphasize conflicting views, it should be recognized that they have in common the search for some kind of leverage to create change on the part of people whose ultimate goal is to remain, or to gain inclusion, in the community of citizens. Whether they volunteer to go to jail or demand "no reprisals," they seek a middle way that will bring real change without creating chaos. For the most part, they have not been terrorists or revolutionaries (although the techniques of civil disobedience—or "CD"—are in recent years sometimes contemplated and adopted tactically by some who are willing to consider more violent acts of protest).

In fact, there has been some ambiguity over whether there should be rules or even codifiable issues in dispute. Civil disobedience often is presented as the action of brave, stubborn, or fed-up individuals behaving spontaneously. Henry David Thoreau's night in jail was not, as he related the story, a planned protest against slavery or the Mexican War but something the state forced on him as a moral individual at the spur of the moment. A familiar example in the modern era of civil disobedience is Rosa Parks, whose refusal to move to the back of a bus in 1955 in Montgomery, Alabama, has been celebrated as the start of the great boycott that launched a new era of civil rights. It doesn't matter how carefully scholars have detailed the organizing carried out by Montgomery men and women or Parks's own participation in nonviolent integration movements beforehand, the moment of spontaneous, individual heroism is what public memory holds onto to explain what incited change.

It is not wrong to think that civil disobedience comes down, or should at least, to individual decision and commitment, to ethical choice. Liability before the law is individual, not collective as with a corporate "person." Protest actions may be collective or even called "massive," but decisions to break the law are made by individuals, regardless of whatever influence or inspiration comes from others. If violent repression follows, it will be experienced, in the first instance, by individuals as individuals (though perhaps next by families and communities) if they are jailed, injured, or killed. For some of us today, as in earlier times, there may be an agonizing weighting to be done by individuals who value social order but are intolerant of prolonged injustice or immorality, but when is disobedience in order? Recent writings on the Nazi atrocities against European Jews before and during World War II have accentuated the urgency of individual moral choice not to be a bystander when a massive injustice looms.[40]

A bystander is a highly individual image. Yet in these same writings the most heroic examples of individuals who embraced and protected fugitives from the Nazi Holocaust are the people of Le Chambon, whose history and religious leadership had already made them a community of resistance. So the individual moral choice is made easier by group ethics of "disruptive empathy"[41] (an oxymoron deeper perhaps than civil disobedience). We may note, in fact, that Hannah Arendt, one of the most thoughtful and influential students of Nazism, has in other writings contended that civil disobedience is always a group action. Why did she say this, since there certainly are spontaneous individual instances of what would easily fit most definitions of civil disobedience? Perhaps because she had learned from Alexis de Tocqueville to appreciate the vital importance of nongovernmental associations in American society, the tradition of voluntary organizations in American social history, and the accommodation to these groups in American legal history. "Civil disobedients," she wrote, "are nothing but the latest form of voluntary association, and . . . they are thus quite in tune with the oldest traditions of the country."[42]

Some inspirational calls to civil disobedience place high demands on the faith of its practitioners, and at the point when that happens, the individual/group distinction seems unimportant. Take, for example, an article written by the Trappist monk Thomas Merton (who both lived in austerity/isolation and enjoyed popularity as an author) in 1967. The first condition he identified for "relative honesty in the practice of Christian nonviolence" runs as follows: "Nonviolence must be aimed above all at the transformation of the present state of the world, and it must therefore be free from all occult, unconscious connivance with an unjust use of power. This poses enormous problems, for if nonviolence is too political it becomes drawn into the power struggle and identified with one side or another in that struggle, while if it is totally apolitical it runs the risk of being ineffective or at best merely symbolic." Other conditions include evidence of altruism or selflessness as well as avoidance of "facile and fanatical self-righteousness" and of expectation of quick results. The goal is not to overcome an adversary but to discover through dialogue "the common good of *everyone*"—a goal that Merton, following Gandhi, presented as "truth." The "test of our sincerity" is our willingness to learn from adversaries who are presumably just as interested in "being right" as we are.[43]

Many will feel that this is an admirable position, but the humility and willingness to learn from adversaries that Merton praised have been relatively unusual in the American practice of civil disobedience. Especially in the twentieth century, civil disobedience was often planned to get publicity and exert political pressure. If the conditions Merton stated were strictly required, the history of civil disobedience would be much shorter.

Consider news accounts of the Berkeley-based Ruckus Society's Democracy in Action camp in the Malibu hills, where activists trained newcomers in the skills of nonviolent resistance in preparation for the 2000 Republican National Convention. There was instruction in disguises and reconnaissance, the best locking devices to bind protesters' wrists together, and the importance of picking "spots for actions that will look good in a television or newspaper picture." Students role-played a "mass action" with some taking the parts of infiltrators and the police. News stories carried sensational photos of climbers on elaborate scaffolds practicing skills they would need in order to unfurl banners from buildings or trees. Some reports emphasized official alarm at this training camp for a troupe of law breakers. But the activists pointed out that they were skilled in reducing tensions and threats of violence. They placed themselves squarely in the tradition of Gandhi, Rosa Parks, and Martin Luther King, Jr. "What have you been up to?" one Ruckus Society veteran asked another as they gathered. "Keeping up with my court dates." In the end, the two major political parties and the police kept these protestors from getting much attention; the protesters kept their actions reasonably peaceful; and there were a good many arrests. But there was not much evidence of the humility and willingness to learn from adversaries that Merton praised. To overcome the massive advantages of "large corporations who can afford to hire public-relations companies and have most of our politicians in their back pocket," said one instructor, "we have to be savvy."[44]

"Although the phenomenon of civil disobedience is today a world-wide phenomenon," Hannah Arendt wrote in 1970, "it still is primarily American in origin and substance; . . . no other country, and no other language, has even a word for it, and . . . the American republic is the only government having at least a chance to cope with it . . . in accordance with the *spirit* of its laws." Some may object to describing this tradition as "primarily American."[45] Other nations have histories of extralegal and reasonably nonviolent protest, and American practice has at times been influenced from abroad. Black and white abolitionists justified defiance of law by evoking courageous examples of religious martyrs and revolutionary nationalists. Advocates of passive resistance referred to Tolstoy. Radical leaders of the National Woman's Party witnessed new kinds of militance in Britain. Some twentieth-century civil disobedients honored the example and studied the philosophy of Mohandas Gandhi (who in turn praised the American example of Henry David Thoreau). Yet Hindi newspapers use the English term *civil disobedience*, and an Indian academic once told me he could not translate the term into his native Marathi. Admittedly, the development of a tradition is not justification for treating civil disobedience in the United States in isolation from events in other societies. But there is still validity in suggestions of its distinctiveness, as this book will demonstrate.

What made American civil disobedience distinctive? The growth of republican and democratic institutions made it inadvisable for reform movements to promote the breaking of specific laws without also signifying respect—sometimes even reverence—for law in general. Civil disobedience became a distinctively American via media between revolution and submission to majority rule. It has been most acceptable when presenting an alternative to intolerable threats to democracy from insurrectionists, from revolutionary anarchists, or from terrorists. While professing commitment to principles that impelled them to violate laws, civil disobedients sometimes, but not always, have accepted the necessity of punishment as a sign of respect for both the will of the people and social order. Over time "civil disobedience" became for Americans (as for Gandhi) an oxymoron joining together the traditionally opposed ideas of civility and disobedi-ence. A few decades ago, religious and legal organizations sought to estab-lish ground rules to ensure the civility of the practice of civil disobedience. More recently, the arrests of students, clergy, or Hollywood celebrities sometimes occur in an unmistakably American nonviolent ritual that reporters characterize as "exceedingly civil" disobedience.

But the boundaries are elusive. Did California's "barstool rebels" appeal to a higher law when they defied state antismoking laws? Can we differen-tiate civil disobedients from animal rights activists arrested in 1999 for climbing the scaffolding around the Washington Monument? The law they violated had nothing to do with their protest against funding of primate research by the National Institutes of Health. What about acts of violence and destruction? Probably all of us would exclude protesters in the same cause who sent letters booby-trapped with razor blades to univer-sity scientists and the ecoterrorists who have burned down ski lodges and Hummer dealerships. But what about the chopping down of genetically engineered corn at the University of Maine? Or Philip Berrigan's attempt, with his Plowshares comrades, to damage navigational equipment by squirting his blood while onboard a missile-launching naval destroyer on Ash Wednesday 1997?[46]

In presenting and analyzing an American tradition of civil disobedi-ence, I do not contend that it comes, or should come, with an unvarying dogma or a uniform code of behavior. The tradition exhibits abundant contest and variation. Proponents of civil disobedience have not always agreed on how civil law breakers should dress, whether they must go to jail, how deeply held their pacifist convictions ought to be. The practice of civil disobedience in America has by no means been restricted to progressives. In a famous image of passive resistance, two soldiers in 1944 carry Montgomery Ward president Sewell Avery out of company headquarters for defying pro-union directives of the War Labor Board. In 2003 I heard the almost unclas-sifiable radical leader and perennial presidential candidate Lyndon LaRouche defend his supporters, who shouted protests at his exclusion from a debate, by appealing to "the civil rights tradition of civil disobedience." The tradi-tion also has many critics who claim that it endangers civil order and indi-vidual liberty to impart to anyone, especially students, the idea that they have any right to disobey "indispensable social rules" or to violate laws without "accepting punishment openly and respectfully."[47]

2

A Heritage of Civilly Disobedient Acts

In a free verse dramatization of his trial for destroying Selective Service records in 1968, Father Philip Berrigan explained to his attorney that he was "in direct line with American democratic tradition . . ."

> From the Boston Tea Party
> through the abolitionist and anarchist movements
> through World War I and World War II
> and right on
> through the civil rights movement
> we have a rich tradition
> of civil disobedience.[1]

Others have also claimed that the American republic was founded in acts of civil disobedience, which are a fundamental part of our heritage. Such claims were not stated so clearly before the 1960s—before, that is, civil disobedience began to seem almost ubiquitous in American protest actions, and attempts to justify it frequently reached the courts. One of the most influential historians of working-class radicalism, Alfred F. Young, observed that the civil rights movements and countercultural upheavals of the 1960s helped him and others to perceive in the revolutionary era what previous generations had neglected—"the most successful campaign of civil disobedience in American history," one in which the leader of the Sons of Liberty, Samuel Adams, played a leadership role parallel to that of Rev. Martin Luther King in a later era.[2]

With the adoption of civil disobedience tactics by anti-abortion activists, some writers and attorneys commonly thought of as belonging to the

25

Christian political right also began to honor a tradition of civil disobedience going back to the origins of the nation. John W. Whitehead, founder of the Rutherford Institute, best known for representing Paula Jones in the sexual misconduct suit that led to the impeachment of President Bill Clinton, is an excellent example of a widening recognition of civil disobedience as an American tradition. Whitehead in 1991 wrote indignantly that the failure of courts to extend to blockaders of abortion clinics the same protections that sit-inners and other civil rights advocates received was not only unfair but reflected a misunderstanding of American legal tradition. "Civil disobedience is an important part of the American heritage," he contended; throughout the nation's history it provided "a means for significant changes in the laws and policies of the United States without a need to resort to armed rebellion or anarchy." Among the "series of acts of civil disobedience" leading to the American Revolution he stressed resistance to the Stamp Act and especially the drafting and ratification of the Declaration of Independence, which placed a "high value" on "individual conscience." The claim may go too far, even if we pass over the burning and looting of HMS *Gaspee* (1772) and other extreme acts, often approved by local leaders. Setting fire to effigies, tarring and feathering imperial authorities, and trashing their houses are several steps removed from most definitions of civil disobedience, and the Declaration of Independence was a step away from professions of loyalty to established rule. An argument can indeed be made that "a succession of civilly disobedient acts" led to the establishment of a new governmental system, but few prominent political leaders had tolerant attitudes toward law breaking in the new order. Whitehead was on sound ground in alluding to the legal struggles of abolitionists and advocates of women's rights and, more recently, the civil rights and antiwar movements, all of whom claimed descent, and some right to violate immoral laws, from revolutionary traditions of resistance. In complaining that while civil rights protesters had succeeded in overcoming legal repression Operation Rescue had not, he raised serious issues about a revolutionary heritage for activist dissenters.[3]

Discussion of anti-abortion movements belongs in a later chapter, but the issue of the revolutionary origins of civil disobedience will be explored here. Does my claim that a tradition of civil disobedience has developed in the United States require that its origins be located in the founding acts and governing documents of the nation? Hardly, but the tradition is affected by the system of government and laws that has followed from the

Revolution, the Declaration, and the Constitution. The very fact that civil disobedients in later times have claimed that lineage is important to understanding the Americanness of the tradition. But this chapter will show antecedents of the civil disobedience tradition in the pre-revolutionary religious history of America. In the constitutional founding it will show significant deterrents to what would later be called civil disobedience. In many reform activities in the early republic it will still find important origins for civil disobedience as a contested tradition.

Boston, December 16, 1773. About thirty men, well disguised as "Mohawks," are joined by fifty to one hundred volunteers. Their faces blackened with coal dust, they divide into three parties and, at the sound of a whistle, row out to three ships that have been held in the harbor for three weeks. The ships are loaded with chests of tea that leading Whigs have prevented from being unloaded because the English Parliament has imposed a tax to be collected when local merchants receive them. A deadline is imminent. At a meeting of the whole people—that is, without property limitations—to discuss what to do with the tea before troops arrive to protect it, the plan is set. The three parties take one chest after another, 342 in all, carry them on deck, smash them open so that they will surely be ruined by sea water, and throw each one overboard. The sound of hatchets splitting open wooden chests can be heard for hours. On the docks a large crowd watches quietly; the orderliness of the boarding parties impresses observers. The destroyers of the tea are never identified, though many clearly were master mechanics, and most of the less-well-disguised were apprentices and journeymen who, though trustworthy, were less likely to be familiar to the authorities. The significance of these events was dramatic. John Adams praised their act in his diary as "the most magnificent Moment of all" in the struggle of patriots against unjust imperial taxation. "This destruction of the Tea is so bold, so daring, so firm, intrepid and inflexible . . . and so lasting, that I can't but consider it as an Epocha in History."[4] Eventually, the patriotic meaning of the events would be enhanced by writers like the great Democratic historian of the Jacksonian era, George Bancroft, who ranked that December 16 in Boston as "a day by far the most momentous in its annals."[5] In American history the "Boston Tea Party" continues to be commemorated as a show of resistance to imperial oppression and unjust taxation and as an expression of colonists' aspiration for independence.

"The destruction of the tea," as Adams called it, was the term commonly used for a half century after the Revolution. Though the destroyers of the tea joked about turning the harbor into a teapot, no one spoke of the events as a party. As Alfred Young has shown in a fascinating work of historical recovery, "tea party" replaced "destruction," and the event began to be celebrated about fifty years after the Revolution. By that time few survivors were around to remember it, and fears of working-class acts of violence no longer seemed too threatening, and suggestions of more decorous resistance were consistent with the creation of a sanitized public memory. Bancroft quoted John Adams to indicate that the destroyers were not a riotous mob and did nothing immoderate, uncivil, or anarchic: "All things were conducted with great order, decency, and perfect submission to government"—but not to Parliament's illegitimate claims of power to tax the colonials.[6]

In time the tea party also received a place at the origin of a tradition of civil disobedience. We are told, for example, that Adams justified the "civil disobedience" of destroying the tea as a last resort when other measures had failed.[7] Adams did not use the term *civil disobedience*, however, and its use to describe those actions is anachronistic since the concept did not really exist in the 1770s. The "destruction" was too violent to fit definitions of civil disobedience that gained familiarity later on; the actors concealed their identities and demonstrated no willingness to accept punishment or go to jail. It has more accurately been called "one of the most celebrated examples of violent civil disobedience in our history"[8]—it was violent, carried out by civilians, and defiant of a law—but it does not fit well with most familiar definitions of civil disobedience or provide close parallels with acts of peaceful resistance made familiar in later times by sit-inners, freedom riders, or draft resisters.

When proponents and defenders of civil disobedience cite the Boston Tea Party as a meaningful precedent, they may be anachronistic, but they are not wholly off the mark. The tea party does summon up images of popular resistance to unjust acts of government in the name of the welfare of the whole people. It is the best-remembered expression of the revolutionary transition of an American populace to feeling part of, rather than excluded from, political society. Organized boycotting has often accompanied later campaigns of civil disobedience. And mobilized defiance of laws carried out with "perfect submission" to government certainly bears some of the contradictoriness of later expressions of civil disobedience.

In any case, links to the Boston Tea Party are ubiquitous in writings on civil disobedience. It would be easy to compile a long list of books and articles linking together references to "the Boston Tea Party, the suffragette movement, the resistance to British rule in India led by Gandhi, the U.S. civil rights movement led by Martin Luther King Jr., student sit-ins against the Vietnam War," as "instances where civil disobedience served as an important mechanism for broad social change."[9] American reporters often compared Mahatma Gandhi's actions—particularly the 1930 march to the sea in protest against the imperial salt tax that demonstrated the effectiveness of civil disobedience to the world and popularized the term itself—to the Boston Tea Party. Britain, they predicted, would lose India over salt as it had lost its American colonies over tea.[10] Gandhi himself often mentioned the Boston Tea Party, especially in relation to what has been called his own "famous Tea Party" when he was invited to negotiations with the English viceroy, Lord Irwin, after a stay in jail at the conclusion of the Salt March. At this meeting he opened a small pouch and sprinkled its contents into his teacup: this was, he said, "a little salt for my tea, to remind us of the Boston tea party." Both men are said to have smiled.[11] In 1948 the League for Nonviolent Civil Disobedience against Military Segregation, a successor of the March on Washington Movement, defended the legitimacy of draft refusal by claiming the Boston Tea Party as a prominent early example of civil disobedience.[12] Martin Luther King appealed frequently to the precedent of the Boston Tea Party, which he described as "nothing but a massive act of civil disobedience" through which our nation came into existence. There was no way to "scorn" civil disobedience "without canceling out American history."[13] In modern Boston, as interest in the tea party has grown along with improvements to the Freedom Trail, the link between the tea party and civil disobedience has acquired curricular status. At Old South Church a program called "Resisting for Justice" annually hosts thousands of elementary and high school students who participate in debates on civil disobedience and take roles in reenacting the tea party as well as conflict over the Fugitive Slave Law of 1850.[14]

Early in Barack Obama's presidency, a number of tea parties—some called "well financed"—were staged in American cities by protesters angry at the taxation and stimulus measures the U.S. government had passed. No civil disobedience was reported in these reprises of the tea party motif by American protesters. In 2010 a burgeoning "tea party" movement among Republican Party voters resulted in significant changes in the House of

Representatives and in nominations for several U.S. Senate races. Though it included a march on Washington imitative of the legacy of Martin Luther King, Jr., it has not been much, if at all, identified with civil disobedience or nonviolence, and so it may be viewed as parenthetical to our discussion here.[15]

To launch discussion of the origins of civil disobedience with the Sons of Liberty and the Boston Tea Party, as many have done, is to emphasize themes of popular resistance and working-class radicalism, some inherited from England (the blackened faces) and some emphasizing the rights of Americans (the Indian garb). These themes are certainly relevant to the organized, efficient disobedience of the Sons of Liberty. But in many parts of British North America, and preeminently in New England, questions of obligations to obey government were often expressed and understood in religious terms. If rulers were reasonably just, then people were obliged to obey them, to be nonresistant even when they suffered injury—such was God's command—but rulers also were confined by divine command, and when they misruled, as the example of the Puritan revolution and Glorious Revolution always reminded, obedience reached its limit. The place of the church in the just and good order that God required was a persistent issue in the development of American political obligation. In early decades Puritan governments jailed, banished, or executed Baptists, Quakers, and others who disturbed good order by public insistence on different beliefs and practices. A later Baptist leader, Isaac Backus, noting how the Puritans had complained that Protestant churches of the Reformation, in flying from Roman Catholicism, had carried too much of "the spirit of *imposition* and *persecution*" with them, complained of the Puritans' determination to establish "worship that was supported by violent methods" without recognizing its similarity to the coercion they had experienced in England.[16] To Quakers, Baptists, and many others, especially after the religious revivals of the Great Awakening, it was essential to salvation that individuals renounced sin on their own without the coercion of the state.

The earliest instances of American civil disobedience took the form of expressions of conscience in which strongly felt personal motivations were based on religious conviction and collided with the state. Such conflicts were not limited to Puritan New England. Every colony except Pennsylvania and Rhode Island had an established church, and opportunities to defy religious compulsion on grounds of religious principle were widespread.

One excellent documentary collection on civil disobedience in America begins with a "Remonstrance" (1657) in which settlers of Flushing defied the edict of Governor Peter Stuyvesant of New Netherland prohibiting any hospitality or encouragement to Quakers who might pass through and seek to gain converts. The remonstrance's thirty-one signatories appealed to a charter that accorded them liberty of conscience and to their understanding of the Golden Rule and other biblical admonitions against unkindness and harsh judgment of others. Those who drafted it were threatened, jailed, fined, and by other means forced to recant; one who did convert to the Friends shortly afterward was sentenced to solitary imprisonment and then deported, though his eventually successful appeal advanced public recognition of the principle that "people's conscience should not be forced by anyone but remain free in itself." This action by "ordinary citizens *against* government" has been celebrated for planting "the seed of freedom of conscience" in America.[17]

Conflict between faith and law often centered on taxation to support established churches and more particularly to maintain their clergy. Instances of the most common version of disobedience—tax refusal—occurred, among many other places, in Flushing. When disputes in New York were brought up in a Boston paper as proof that other colonies treated religious dissenters "worse than New England has," Backus's retort was that Baptists never depicted "the fathers of New England as the worst of the colonists; we believe the contrary." But acts of persecution in earlier times were hard to forget so long as related offenses persisted.[18] There were issues concerning recognition of the Baptists' churches as churches and of their clergy as "settled ministers." In one significant case in 1769, for example, decades after Puritan government had supposedly relaxed old restrictions, assessors and the constable came to the house of Nathaniel Green, a Baptist pastor in Leominster, Massachusetts, demanded a tax payment, and when he replied that "he would never pay," because he deserved the same exemption from all taxes that other "settled ministers" enjoyed in Massachusetts, they "took his body, carry'd him about 10 miles to Worcester, to put him in Gail." After spending six hours as a prisoner, he accepted advice to pay up under protest and take the issue to court. At trial John Adams argued on behalf of the assessors that exemptions were meant to apply only to "learned, orthodox" ministers, not to upstarts and separatists. A jury found in Green's favor, recognizing his status as minister and returning taxes taken from him under duress. The case was hailed by Backus as an important "check to oppression" and in later histories as a "symbolic turning point" on the path toward religious toleration and recognition of the civil legitimacy of marriages and other rites performed in Baptist congregations.[19]

Baptists were dissatisfied with the workings of the so-called certificate system, in effect since the 1720s, by which individuals could be exempted from paying taxes to maintain the established church by presenting an annual certificate signed by their minister and affirming their financial support of an approved alternative. Supposedly this was an advance over earlier oppression, but those who filed certificates were frequently denigrated and harassed, and tax assessors looked for ways to invalidate their certificates and compel payment to support an establishment that they rejected. Some New England Baptists refused to cooperate with the certificate system as an unscriptural violation of liberty of conscience. Even if it exempted some individuals, the state exacted an acknowledgment of its claim to power to establish one religious sect above others. Laity who practiced what has been termed "individual civil disobedience"—that is, they refused to pay—were jailed or watched their property being seized ("distrained") or auctioned.

In 1773, after amassing information on the many individual and local grievances, Baptist leaders sought a united way of asserting their right through collective refusal to submit certificates even if it meant jamming the court dockets and filling the jails. Though some local spokesmen were more cautious than others—all agreed that God ordained civil government, and none accepted the right of human government to establish a particular sect—the great majority voted for what the historian William G. McLoughlin called, perhaps with a little exaggeration, a policy of "massive" nonviolent civil disobedience. In fact, it was left to individual churches to decide whether to defy the law en bloc or leave the decisions to individuals; and there is no record as to whether or for how long they held to anything like a common stand. Massive or not, the plan was never tested or executed fully because the events of the Revolutionary War meant that enforcement of the certificate system fell by the wayside. (It returned, however, in a new version in 1780 and remained controversial until the Massachusetts constitution was amended in 1833. As late as 1838, as we shall later see, a young Henry David Thoreau, no Baptist, faced a jailing for failure to pay his town for support of his parents' church.)

Since 1773, when Baptists adopted their stance of concerted disobedience, was also the year of the tea party, one might ask how the Baptists responded to the revolutionary ferment. They were not, as their opponents charged and may have actually have suspected, Loyalists, though they had appealed, successfully, for the Crown to overturn a law that would have compelled Baptists to pay taxes to support Puritan churches.[20] Backus had contemplated another appeal to the Crown before the intensification of revolutionary sentiment in the 1770s made that a bad idea.[21] Baptists commented bitterly on the hypocrisy of "our fathers and brethren who inhabit the land to which our ancestors fled for religious liberty" and who were now "accused with being disorderly and rebellious." Why were they not more sympathetic toward the Baptists' stance? How, they asked their revolutionary contemporaries, could they justify their rebellious behavior by complaining: "You are taxed where you are not represented. And is it not really so with us? ... [H]ave we not as good right to say you do the same thing?"[22] The so-called Sons of Liberty, said one Baptist, "ought rather to be called Sons of Violence," as they trampled on their Baptist neighbors' "sacred right to religious liberty."[23] Does this comment imply criticism of the violence of pre-revolutionary protests against the Stamp Act and Tea Act? Perhaps. Though the Baptists were not a peace sect like the Friends or Moravians, their criticism of the Puritans' coercive religious order was related to their emphasis on faith and rebirth in the realm of the spirit. They were outsiders, remote from the main centers of politics, some-what conservative in outlook, and certainly not preoccupied with "state affairs" or familiar with street violence in the cities, as illustrated in Backus's detached recollection of news of the "wild conduct" of anti–Stamp Act rioters in Boston. He was thankful when the act was repealed, the "commotion ended," and colonial liberties restored.[24]

Backus and the Baptists of New England were not Tories, however. They did not take the Patriots' side (which they associated with their Congregational antagonists) until choice was inescapable, but when the time came they sided with revolution (unlike the Quakers, Moravians, and other sects that stayed neutral). In 1774 Backus attended the First Continental Congress in Philadelphia, where his advocacy of religious freedom was viewed as divisive. After fighting broke out at Lexington and Concord, he preached in opposition to "the doctrine of passive obedience and non-resistance to kings," which led to "the brink of popery and slavery," and in support of the revolutionary cause.[25] In 1788 Backus was elected to the Massachusetts ratifying convention for the Constitution, which he supported. (He praised in particular "the great advantage of having religious tests and hereditary nobility excluded from our government.")[26]

The Baptists' protests focused on why people who believed in the necessity of a second birth and adult baptism should be taxed to support clergy in churches that insisted on infant baptism. Their arguments went beyond simple fairness, and they were not presented as defenses of indifference to the spread of Christian faith; they pointed to issues of fundamental religious conviction in which disobedience of the law of the state could be justified by a holy imperative as surely as the church establishments believed in a religious mandate to enforce their system. They objected to religious taxation in the name of the conscience, over which the Massachusetts charter acknowledged that "God alone is Lord."[27]

The Baptists, as much as their antagonists in the Standing Order, were people of a tolerant time. They were willing to go to jail to defend church practices that they had no intention of enforcing on anyone else. It might surprise some perusers of the arguments over Nathaniel Green's tax exemption that it was his counsel, not John Adams for the other side, who set the dispute in the broadly reasonable context of the English philosopher John Locke's influential "Letter Concerning Toleration" (1689), defining a church as a voluntary society worshipping in their own way and choosing their own minister.[28] The prolific and Calvinistic Backus marked this definition in his copy of Locke[29] and went on to present in many works and hundreds of pages his reconciliations of religious truth and progress with social and political toleration. His belief in the church as a voluntary society unsupported by the state did not imply a minor role for religion in social progress. To the contrary, he held millennial expectations that religion would transform society—but without interference from a theocratic state. In addition, his sermon topic when war broke out—nonresistance and passive obedience to kings— referred to issues current in liberal circles in England and was influenced by a text widely circulated in the pre-revolutionary colonies—Jonathan Mayhew's "A Discourse Concerning Unlimited Submission and Nonresistance to the Higher Powers" (1750)—a work that John Adams reported was "read by everybody."[30] This was not designed as a revolutionary pamphlet, except as a defense of the Puritan revolution and execution of King Charles and an attack on the Anglican elevation of Charles to sainthood and perceived threats to impose an Anglican establishment in America. Opposition to establishment stands as a counterpart to the defense of toleration. Intellectually, what gave Mayhew's "Discourse" fame and influence was its rejection of the rule long derived from the book of Romans—that the powers that be are ordained of God and must never be deposed, rebelled against, or disobeyed.

There were at least two clear instances, according to Mayhew, in which disobedience was not only legitimate but glorious: disobedience to commands that pervert and violate "the divine religion brought from Heaven to earth by the Son of God," and disobedience to a government that overturns "the sole end of all government—the common good and safety of society." Even children and servants may legitimately disobey in such circumstances without raising the fear of anarchy.[31] Bernard Bailyn has said of Mayhew's "Discourse" that it enlarged the public audience for "the extreme radical position on the subject of civil disobedience" as never before in America.[32] Obviously applications of this use of *civil disobedience* would not meet all criteria for later definitions, but they did point to something indispensable to the origins of an emerging tradition. As applied by Baptists in the 1770s, by persecuted evangelical movements in other colonies, and by Quakers refusing tax support for war, it afforded glimpses of new uses of civil disobedience to improve the church and society. The radical position might grow even more extreme when it turned from protections of religious freedom to liberation of those most subservient or excluded from society's protections.

Civil disobedience is invisible in the Constitution. Occasionally someone has tried to argue that the First Amendment protects civil disobedience. This takes ingenuity even today, since a claim that the law protects law breaking is illogical. As far as the Founding Fathers are concerned, we can say without qualification that the mere thought of disobedience alarmed them. The prevailing view was expressed by Alexander Hamilton in *The Federalist* No. 15:

> Government implies the power of making laws. It is essential to the idea of a law, that it be attended with a sanction; or, in other words, a penalty or punishment for disobedience. If there be no penalty annexed to disobedience, the resolutions or commands which pretend to be laws will, in fact, amount to nothing more than advice or recommendation.[33]

He proceeded to argue, in brief, for a government strong enough that its courts and magistrates can effectively penalize infractions of law rather than a loose confederacy where "every breach of the laws must involve a state of war; and military execution must become the only instrument of civil obedience."

That view runs throughout the *Federalist*, through Madison's essays as well as Hamilton's. It might be objected that the *Federalist* was merely a Federalist propaganda effort, not an authoritative explication of the Constitution.[34] That is undoubtedly true. But on the simple point I am making, it *was* representative of pro-Constitutional thought. On this point there was little, if any, disagreement at the Philadelphia convention, in the state ratifying conventions, or in the pamphlet battles between Federalists and Anti-Federalists. A search of those sources reveals absolutely nothing spoken in favor of anything resembling civil disobedience and much spoken on the importance of civil obedience. Charles Pinckney voiced fears held by many others when he told the convention:

> Our government is despised—our laws are robbed of their respected terrors—their inaction is a subject of ridicule—and their exertion, of abhorrence and opposition—rank and office have lost their reverence and effect— . . . our citizens loosened from their obedience. We know neither how to yield or how to enforce.[35]

One might conclude from these debates that the influence of Jonathan Mayhew had been much abated. Or perhaps that it was so rampant that the framers sought to hem it in.

For a good illustration of the prevailing mood, we can turn to the discussion in Philadelphia of the "guarantee clause," eventually article 4, section 4, of the Constitution. The committee-proposed language was "that a Republican Constitution & its existing laws ought to be guarantied to each State by the U. States." Gouverneur Morris of New York objected: he was "unwilling that such laws as exist in R. Island [laws favoring debtors over creditors] should be guarantied." Another delegate made a similar point about the unwisdom of perpetuating Georgia's constitution. James Wilson of Pennsylvania countered that the committee's sole object was "to secure the States ag[ain]st dangerous commotions, insurrections and rebellions"; and Virginians George Mason, Edmund Randolph, and James Madison and Daniel Carroll of Maryland all voiced agreement. Predicting that rebellions against the general government would originate in the states, with monarchist factions, most likely, spreading their snares from one state to the next, Mason contended that without such a guarantee the general government might be simply "a passive spectator of its own subversion." Particularly apt was the remark of Nathaniel Gorham of Massachusetts: "With regard to different parties in a State; as long as they confine their disputes *to words*, they will be harmless to the Gen[era]l Gov[ernmen]t & to each other." If they turn "to the sword," he went on, the general government might well have to "interpose & put an end to it." These were not abstract issues. The specter of Shays's Rebellion in Gorham's state was never far from mind. The convention swiftly moved to wording that retained the guarantee without promising to perpetuate all state laws.[36] We might stress that no one contested the distinction between disputes confined "*to words*" and those which went beyond. What was missing from these two categories was any sense of actions that reached beyond words yet upheld law rather than subverted it.

One delegate, Luther Martin of Maryland, spoke against empowering the general government "to suppress Rebellions"; he favored leaving that power in the hands of the states.[37] His example reminds us that many opposed the Constitution. Whether these Anti-Federalists took a more tolerant view of factional activity, even if it went beyond words, is an interesting question. Anti-Federalists usually did not take the alarmist view of the "loosening of obedience" that their Federalist opponents put forward. They were more likely to speak pathetically of liberty trampled by "consolidated" government. Nevertheless, their opposition to the Constitution did not signify a view of the world wholly at odds with the Federalists' view, and it is not clear that the two sides disagreed in any fundamental way over the importance of authority or, for that matter, liberty.[38] Few Anti-Federalists would have dissented from the contrast that James Monroe, in a major speech opposing the Constitution, drew between European and American history: "In all the nations of that quarter of the globe, there hath been a constant effort, on the part of the people, to extricate themselves from the oppression of their rulers; but with us the object is of a very different nature—to establish the dominion of law over licentiousness."[39] One after another, Anti-Federalist speakers pleaded the importance of obedience to law, but they preferred the kind of voluntary obedience that arose from loyalty to free government. They shuddered at the image of a centralized, unpopular government compelling obedience by force of arms.[40]

Beyond question, it was the proponents of the Constitution who spoke most ardently on the limits of freedom and necessity of restraint. Sometimes they remind us of seventeenth-century Puritan John Winthrop's famous distinction between the "natural" liberty of vicious animals and the "civil or federal" liberty to obey the law.[41] The most likely source, if there was a single source, of their much-repeated terminology was William Blackstone's immensely influential *Commentaries* (1765–69; first American edition, 1771). There one could find the notion that every man " 'when he enters into society, gives up a part of his natural liberty as the price of so valuable a purchase,' receiving in return 'civil liberty,' which is natural liberty 'so far restrained by human laws (and no farther) as is necessary and expedient for the general advantage of the public.' "[42] James Wilson was the most notable rhapsodist on this theme, telling the Philadelphia convention that "Federal Liberty is to States, what civil liberty, is to private individuals." States ought to be as anxious to acquire "federal liberty" by the "necessary concession of their political sovereignty" as "the savage is to purchase civil liberty by the surrender of his personal sovereignty, which he enjoys in a State of nature."[43] Wilson also reminded Pennsylvania's ratifying convention of "the dissensions and animosities" that made "civil restraint" more desirable than liberty in a state of nature.[44] Very similar speeches were made by others, including Fisher Ames and William Phillips in Massachusetts and Edmund Pendleton in Virginia, the latter referring to the authority of "the most respectable writers—Montesquieu, Locke, Sidney, Harrington, &c."—for the view that "firm" execution of the laws is even "more necessary" in a republic than in a monarchy.[45]

Not everyone agreed with this view of obedience and authority. Jefferson rejected it as "toryism." Rather than stressing the indispensable protection that firm government afforded genuine liberty, Jefferson spoke tolerantly of "a little tempest now and then, or even . . . a little blood."[46] But Jefferson was away in France, and this much-quoted remark on Shays's Rebellion was more a rhetorical flourish than a reasoned principle to be applied to his own practice. At home, where the Constitution was being framed and debated, there was so little controversy over obedience that we are in more danger of underestimating than of overstating the consensus regarding its necessity.

The Founding Fathers were well aware of traditions of dissent and protest that went "beyond words." They were themselves revolutionaries who had witnessed use of an entire arsenal of methods of resistance to

British law. Many of them were also veterans of religious conflict, aware that evangelicals in America had repudiated the authority of the state over questions of conscience. The Constitution may have been ratified in the name of social restraint, but there was good reason to anticipate future resistance to government in the name of political autonomy and religious conscience. In addition, Anti-Federalists expressed fears that government would squash rights of opinion; those fears forced adoption of the Bill of Rights to tether central authority. Though none of the Founding Fathers exactly foresaw the development of civil disobedience, they did recognize the possibility of conflicts between government and religious imperatives, between government and minority opinion, conflicts that could take the form of moral opposition to coercive power.

There were no early national precedents for civil disobedience as it came to be known later. The boundaries enclosing permissible dissent from governmental policies were altogether uncertain in the 1790s, when civility and candor were in short supply and specters of sedition stalked throughout Federalist and Republican imaginations. In the absence of much acceptance of loyal opposition within political chambers, we search vainly for the more novel concept of civil disobedience outside the doors. The concept was clearly missing in moments, actual or exaggerated, of "rebellion," such as the resistance to the whiskey excise or the land tax. It is true that the historian Mary Tachau put forward an argument that the failure of Kentucky whiskey makers to pay the excise was a "significant contribution" to the history of civil disobedience. Tachau showed that Kentuckians' tax refusal was accompanied by violence and threats of secession; it gave voice to no moral leaders; it succeeded because "almost the entire population" quietly supported or tolerated it, and the federal government, preoccupied with what it took to be direr threats, particularly in Pennsylvania, was powerless to suppress it. Tachau herself differentiated the Kentuckians of the 1790s from later civil disobedients who aimed not to evade the law but to change it.[47]

One way to understand the political worldview that left no middle ground between domination and submission is to think of the years between the Revolution and the Jacksonian era as a hiatus between the colonial era, when constituted authority was clear enough even though protest and rebelliousness were familiar facts of life, and later eras when the precise boundaries of agitation and dissidence were open to experiment and negotiation. Peter Gay has credited the entire bourgeois nineteenth century with the invention of politics, in which opposition to the government in power was tolerated and ritualized because it was no longer confused with sedition.[48] But in post-revolutionary America, the tendency sometimes veered in an opposing direction as political leaders sought to blunt the radical potential of notions that had justified revolution: the ideas that governments were human creations and could be changed, that the people were sovereign but governments often served the interests of the few, that all people were citizens and possessed natural rights that could not justifiably be abridged or denied. "It is authority against authority all the way till we come to the divine origin of the rights of man at the creation," wrote Tom Paine.[49] While remembering that revolutions were occasionally justified—Hamilton, after all, had served in a revolutionary army—American leaders usually emphasized the need for obedience. In a government based on the people's consent, justifications for revolution must be rare indeed—and even then, the government was justified in seeking to put them down with whatever ruthlessness was requisite. And make no mistake—an unsuccessful revolution was just another name for treason against the people.

If malcontents could violate national law with impunity, Andrew Jackson reflected in 1832, the nation would long since have fallen apart over the whiskey excise, the carriage tax, the embargo, or another of those measures that had caused a firestorm of protest in one section or another. The War of 1812 would have ended in disgrace instead of vindicating national honor. Since Jackson believed more strongly in democratic government than did many other leaders, his response to South Carolina's threats to nullify and resist the tariff was a striking illustration of the Thermidorean logic that turned the revolutionary origins of the United States into a theory of compulsory obedience. South Carolinians were mistaken, according to Jackson, in thinking they retained "the revolutionary right" of resisting laws they deemed "unconstitutional and intolerably oppressive" and that nullification was "a peaceable remedy" based on that right. They were in no sense comparable to the revolutionary generation as an oppressed people. To the contrary, they were "free members of a flourishing and happy union." Better still, they lived under a constitutional government, uniting the states and "giving to all their inhabitants the proud title of *American citizen*, protecting their commerce, securing their literature and their arts, facilitating their intercommunication, defending their frontiers, and making their name respected in the remotest parts of the earth." We may look ahead and see that this use of citizenship to disallow the right of revolution was double-edged: eventually in fact it would furnish the crucial justification for civil disobedience on the part of those whose citizenship was being curtailed. The immediate point was, however, that for Jackson as for many others in the new republic attempts to foment disunion or provoke disobedience to the nation's laws amounted to treason.[50]

In a message to Congress a few weeks after the Nullification Proclamation, Jackson clarified points that are so important to our inquiry. First, people suffering under oppression have "a natural right" to break their "obligations to the Government." But second, this is "the last resort," the "*ultima ratio*," and is improper unless all remedies are exhausted. Natural this right may be, but it is "necessarily subjected to limitations in all free governments," which provide means for peaceful changing of the laws. At the least, misrule, in order to justify disobedience must be "great and lasting," much more intolerable than South Carolina had experienced. Third, to be faithful to the memory of the "fathers" and preserve the "rich inheritance" they bequeathed us in the form of a government of laws based on popular representation, open resistance to the laws must be put down and punished. Free institutions tended to substitute peaceful persuasion and negotiation for armed conflict, but this process depended on repression of extralegal protest that endangered liberty's continued existence.[51]

One way to account for the origins of an American system of civil disobedience is to remember this republican response to resistance to hated laws. It may help us to understand versions of protest that distanced themselves from the political process, that took up the cause of those whose participation in free institutions was at best ambiguous, and that insisted that their intention was to strengthen free institutions, not to subvert them. Jackson's remarkable claim that all inhabitants were citizens was untrue in his time (as it remains in our time). We might even link the origins of civil disobedience to individual and organized campaigns to convert that claim into truth. In the short run, however, Jackson voiced a view of democratic society in which overt resistance to government was intolerable.

While national leaders were intolerant of resistance to law, the courts did not act simply as umpires applying the law without controversy. There may not have been any constitutional right to civil disobedience, but citizens could bring cases, and lawyers might argue them, in order to test the meaning or explore or expand the limits of laws and public policies. Early in his career Lysander Spooner, later the iconoclastic author of a case for the unconstitutionality of slavery, defied laws requiring a legal education and establishing a postal monopoly. The practice of violating a law in order to test its validity as law has become perhaps the least controversial form of civil disobedience (if indeed it is a form of civil disobedience at all).

An unusually clear instance of what everyone today would recognize as civil disobedience occurred almost simultaneously with Jackson's speeches on nullification and obedience. Jackson rose to the presidency with strong doubts about the prevailing interpretation of the Constitution that treated Indian peoples as independent nations who could not be divested of their lands except through sale or treaty in negotiations overseen by the federal government. He had long believed, as he reported to President James Monroe in 1817, that the settlement, security, and prosperity of the southern frontier depended on removal of the Indians without the "farce" of treating with them as equals.[52] As president, he advocated a law to remove the Indians to lands west of the Mississippi, with adequate funding to support the relocation and guarantees of security once they were resettled. Such a measure was debated in Congress and passed, narrowly and despite intense opposition, in May 1830. The state of Georgia was particularly impatient with the continued existence of a nation of Cherokees within its borders. It had exacted a commitment from the federal government in 1802, when it ceded to the nation its claim to western lands, that the federal government would expeditiously treat with the Cherokees to remove them from the state. If anything, Georgia's Cherokees along with those in Tennessee and North Carolina had become more deeply ensconced in what they considered their ancestral homeland. Without waiting for Congress to act, Georgia adopted its own measures to drive the Indians out. Georgia's actions raised constitutional issues, provoked emotional protests, and provided an occasion for civil disobedience. Among those who looked for a test case to strengthen the claims of Indian nationality before the Supreme Court were Cherokee leaders, prominent attorneys, religious leaders, Jackson's political opponents, and perhaps Chief Justice John Marshall. The case was *Worcester v. Georgia*, and before it was resolved two missionaries had been held for a year and a half in Georgia's penitentiary.

These disobedients were not radicals or reformers or what we would today call activists except during one exceptional, challenging period of their lives. The principal figure and spokesman, Samuel Austin Worcester, was descended from six generations of New England Puritan and Congregationalist clergy. His wife, Ann Orr, came from similar Puritan lineage, and as idealistic newlyweds the two headed south in 1825 for a life as missionaries among the Cherokees. They were sent by the American Board of Commissioners for Foreign Missions (founded in 1810), for whom the Indian nations were as foreign as India, Africa, or the Pacific Islands. The American Board was a major organization fulfilling Protestant visions of American leadership in converting and reforming the world, and this evangelical vision of service inspired the Worcesters' life work, first in Georgia and Tennessee (the boundaries of Cherokee nationality over-lapped state lines) and later, as it turned out, in what is now Oklahoma. Missionary life required many different skills. Worcester, like his father, was a printer as well as a clergyman. He served as postmaster in the mission town of New Echota, Georgia, and he would later spend his jail time studying medicine and carpentry. Because of his important role as a trans-lator, editor, and printer in Cherokee and some other Indian languages, he was given a name signifying "the messenger": A-tse-nu-sti.[53]

American Board missions were regarded by early presidential admin-istrations as important agencies for civilizing Indian peoples, and an 1819 act of Congress established subsidies for missionary efforts. Worcester was especially active in a publication program that contributed to improve-ments in Cherokee life sometimes referred to as the Cherokee renascence. The missionaries viewed changes in education, agriculture, women's roles, politics, and above all religion as an ascent from heathenism. The Christianization met opposition from Cherokee traditionalists, and some modern scholars disparage the effort as an expression of Manifest Destiny, promoting "imperial conquest" through pacifying and wiping out native cultures.[54] To Jacksonians and Georgians, the supposed renascence resulted from misguided influences on peoples whose prospects for survival and improvement were retarded by their stubborn refusal to move west.

In 1827 Cherokees adopted their own constitution modeled in part on that of the United States and declared their sovereignty over the soil within their borders. In retaliatory acts passed in 1829 and 1830 Georgia, embold-ened by Jackson's rise to the presidency, declared the supremacy of its laws, nullified Indian laws and customs, criminalized any attempt to convene a Cherokee council, assigned Indian territory to various counties, denied Indians the right to testify in court cases involving whites, and made it a crime to interfere with any Indians seeking to move west. The discovery of gold in Cherokee territory incited a land rush to which the state responded by instituting a lottery with land parcels as the prizes. No steps were taken to protect Cherokee lands from intrusion. Of particular importance in the flurry of laws, it would turn out, was one, known as the "oath law," requiring all white males residing within the limits of the Cherokee nation to have a license from the governor or his delegate and to swear an oath that "I will support and defend the constitution and laws of the state of Georgia, and uprightly demean myself as a citizen thereof." The punishment for violation was set as "confinement to the penitentiary at hard labor for a term not less than four years."[55]

The oath law, as it applied to the missionaries themselves, was something that they could challenge, and in so doing, they set a pattern for civil disobedience that is still recognizable. The decision to break laws could, as we shall see, present divisive issues for missionaries who were sworn to avoid politics and to be good visitors in foreign lands. But the oath act was unavoidable. In December 1830 a group of twelve from the Baptists, Moravians, and Methodists, as well as the American Board, met at Worcester's home in New Echota and issued a manifesto deploring the inevitable effects of removal on the remarkable progress of civilization and spread of Christianity among the Cherokees. Contrary to the assertions of Jacksonian proponents of removal, most Cherokees were "totally averse" to leaving their homes. Without exercising political influence on the Cherokees, the missionaries were impelled to speak out on a moral issue that tested "the faith of our country." If missionaries withheld their opinion as individuals when asked for it by the people they served in a time of crisis, "we could not hold up our heads as preachers of righteousness among a people who would universally regard us as abettors of iniquity." In January each of the missionaries received a copy of Georgia's oath law, to which they were bound to comply or leave the state by March 1. They did not meet again as an interdenominational group. The Baptists put up no resistance, and Methodist and Moravian missionaries withdrew from Georgia. The American Board missionaries met and unanimously decided that taking an oath of allegiance to Georgia was "out of the question." Giving up their right to preach the Gospel was unthinkable. They stood ready to risk imprisonment "for righteousness sake."[56]

Worcester and his colleagues had the advantage, if so it can be called, that the board to which they were accountable was headquartered in

Boston and was not heavily influenced by southern opinion or funding. The guiding presence on the American Board, an attorney named Jeremiah Evarts, was an expert on Indian law as well as an ardent champion of Christian benevolence. In 1829 he had published, under the pseudonym William Penn, twenty-four influential essays setting out with scholarly rigor and evangelical passion the case against Andrew Jackson's program of Indian removal, a program that must be stopped immediately both for the welfare of the Indians who would lose the standing guaranteed them in treaties and for the American people for whom the basis of law and order would be undermined.[57] The American Board did not advise the missionaries to risk imprisonment—that was an individual decision—but it gave them full permission and provided funds to hire lawyers in Georgia to defend them in the state courts after the inevitable arrests and to prepare to take their case all the way to the U.S. Supreme Court. The missionaries "cheerfully" (as Worcester put it) left the outcome to God. Evarts congratulated Worcester for choosing "the path of duty," a choice for which no one could accuse him of "violating any law of God." The historian William McLoughlin later called this "one of the finer moments in missionary history."[58] It was also a key moment in the history of civil disobedience.

In mid-March three American Board missionaries, including Worcester, were arrested, marched off to jail, and then swiftly and surprisingly released by a Georgia judge, Augustus Clayton, on the grounds that the financial support missionaries received from Congress and Worcester's status as postmaster made them agents of the federal government and thus exempt from the law. Governor George R. Gilmer swiftly got the Jackson administration to discharge Worcester as postmaster because of his "seditious conduct" and to certify that the missionaries were not federal agents. In Gilmer's view, as expressed in a letter to the postmaster general, "Those who, under the cloak of religious ministry, teach discord to our misguided Indian people and opposition to the rulers [sic], should be compelled to know that obedience to the laws is both a religious and civil duty."[59] Worcester held the position, as he wrote Gilmer, that he "could not conscientiously take the oath which the law requires." To acknowledge that he was a citizen of the state of Georgia would be perjury. He was "under no moral obligation" to leave his post in compliance with her enactment. His mission was religious—to spread the Gospel.[60] The governor's view, read in court, was that if the missionaries chose to suffer the penalty of the laws rather than depart, "Let them feel their full weight, since such is their choice." If they were released or gave bail, "arrest them again."[61]

In July, Worcester was taken in custody once more and placed in a group that was marched sixty miles to prison, treated harshly, and ordered to leave the state until their trial was scheduled in September. When he returned to comfort his wife after the death of their infant, he was arrested yet again and deported to Tennessee. In September he was tried and found guilty, along with ten others, in a trial in which the jury deliberated for only fifteen minutes. Nine of those convicted then accepted the judge's offer to let anyone go who would either swear loyalty or leave the state, but Worcester was joined by one other American Board missionary, a physician named Elizur Butler, as the four years at hard labor commenced in Milledgeville Penitentiary. Even as the prison gates clanged shut and the two men put on prison clothes, elaborate attempts were made to show them the danger and hardship they faced and thus to get them to change their minds. But they stayed in prison, did their work well, studied new skills, received visits from their wives, and were well regarded by other inmates. This was neither the harsh experience Governor Gilmer threatened nor the convenient resolution he came to desire as the two missionaries' sufferings drew nationwide attention in the press and as their legal appeal moved forward to the Supreme Court.[62]

We would do well to pause here to note some of the ways in which these events set a pattern that would recur in the history of civil disobedience. In the first place, Worcester repeatedly refers to constitutional right and civil rights. He denies to Governor Gilmer, for example, that he has attempted to "bias the judgment or influence the conduct of the Indians themselves," urges the governor not to believe otherwise without evidence, and asserts that in a court of law his accusers could not "adduce proof of any thing beyond that freedom in the expression of opinion, against which, under the Constitution of our country, there is no law."[63] In the clearest justification of his and Butler's civil disobedience, he wrote:

> We had no doubt of our *civil right* to refuse obedience to the law in question, appealing to the Supreme Court of the United States to sustain us in that refusal. We regarded the law as manifestly unconstitutional, and therefore *no law;* and we could not see to what purpose the constitution should forbid the enactment of such and such laws, if

when those laws *are* enacted, any individual, who suffers by them, may not rightfully appeal to the judicial tribunals against their operations.[64]

"Rights talk" of this kind was not unprecedented—after all, the Revolution had proceeded with many appeals to natural rights—but it was hardly commonplace in a legal setting in 1831 or at most later times. It reflects the aspirations of persons who protest against laws rather than the views of Hamilton, Jackson, and champions of law. In harmonizing Christian obedience with civil disobedience Worcester resembled Isaac Backus.

Worcester's appeals to civil rights and the Constitution were consistent, in his view, with Christian devotion and selflessness, and he stood fast against Georgia's laws for the most part as a missionary and definitely not as a citizen of Georgia. This important issue was clarified, though not resolved, in arguments with other missionaries who had second thoughts and withdrew their support from the manifesto of December 1830. With some implication that Worcester had engineered the manifesto, Daniel S. Butrick and two colleagues took the American Board up on its word that individual missionaries must decide what to do on their own, not under pressure from others. Instead of signing the oath, they retreated to a mission in Tennessee. Since both they and the American Board preferred to play down the disagreement among missionaries, Butrick's reasoning was not widely recognized at the time and awaited the analysis of William G. McLoughlin in a later period of interest in civil disobedience. Rather than acting as a "Cherokee patriot," Butrick argued from Scripture in order to follow "the example of our saviour, who refused meddling in such cases with this decisive question, 'Who made me a judge or divider over you?'" As a missionary to heathen who spoke a foreign language and were not voting citizens themselves, "I feel that I have a right to be dead to the political world." And who knew God's design? Perhaps the Cherokees' "afflictions are designed to take them to a far distant region and render them a light to all the nations west of the Rocky Mountains."[65] As McLoughlin pointed out, Butrick's position was based much more than Worcester's on theology and Scripture while Worcester's referred to general religious principles such as brotherly love. These differences were not idiosyncratic: similar positions were also prominent in dividing "old school" views on slavery from radical abolitionism.[66]

Moral considerations as well as constitutional ones figure prominently in the law-breaking missionaries' view of rights. The missionaries insisted their cause was not primarily political, but moral. For example, when Methodist missionaries denounced removal—and to be sure, Andrew Jackson—the bishops at the Tennessee Methodist Conference censured their political meddling. The editor of the *Cherokee Phoenix*, Worcester's close associate Elias Boudinot, vigorously protested that to the Cherokees removal was a moral issue as surely as temperance or observance of the Sabbath. Defining "the *Indian question* [as] merely a political question" was "exactly the way enemies to the Indians blind the people."[67] This theme mattered deeply to Boudinot—a Cherokee educated in the North, who had taken the name of a prominent beneficiary. When the Georgia missionaries issued their joint manifesto, he praised their recognition that the issue was strongly of "a moral nature" involving "the faith of our country" and admitting of no "neutral" stance or "halfway ground" to stand on. The *Missionary Herald* similarly insisted that missionaries had the right to speak out on "an important moral question" affecting the "moral welfare" as well as the political status of the people among whom they lived.[68] The distinction between political and moral issues went beyond rhetoric. Issues classified as moral were suitable for agitation by persons—including women, as we shall see, and clergy—who ought not to meddle in the sphere of politics. When the American Board sent Evarts to lobby against Indian removal, he was instructed not to emphasize the issue of treaty rights but to dwell only on the injuriousness of removal to an unfortunate people who should be objects of benevolence.[69] These distinctions may strike a modern reader as too fine, but they underlay the civil disobedient stance of the missionaries as representatives of a religious body like the American Board.

Second, Worcester was adept at dramatizing contrasts between his civility and courtesy and his antagonists' uncouth or oppressive behavior. Instead of denouncing Governor Gilmer's scolding of the missionaries for impeding Georgia's "humane policy . . . for the civilization of the Indians," Worcester in a published letter replied ironically that surely their "criminal opposition to the humane policy" of Georgia could not consist of "those efforts for the advancement of the Indians in knowledge and in the arts of civilized life" that the U.S. government has encouraged ever since the days of Washington. If the governor termed the drive to dispossess the tribes as "humane," then Worcester would "cheerfully acknowledge" a difference of opinion.[70] Throughout Worcester's published accounts of the missionaries' arrests and arraignment there is a notable contrast between his calm civility and the terrible things he describes: long forced marches, individuals chained or dragged by horses, the guards' cursing and blasphemy. With impressive fair-mindedness, he corrects false statements (e.g., that the two prisoners had been forced to work on "lottery wheels" used in distributing Cherokee lands and gold mines to white Georgians).[71] The leverage that practitioners of civil disobedience gain over their antagonists by displays of reasonableness would later stand out as a much-discussed claim for nonviolence.

Then there was the publicity (to use a modern word) generated by these events. When Worcester notified Evarts, who was a shrewd publicist, of the missionaries' intention to defy the oath law, Evarts replied, "If Georgia should carry some of you to prison, the fact would rouse this whole country in a manner unlike anything which has yet been experienced." Petitions would inundate Congress, the nation's president, and the state's governor. "You would do good to the poor and oppressed everywhere." Worcester did not shrink from public attention. Disturbed by the "apathy of the people," he encouraged the board to make use of his case to work up public understanding of the "moral aspect" of Indian rights and to condemn the sinfulness of public officials obtuse to the injustice occurring in Georgia.[72] Worcester's reports, which cast Georgia officials in a bad light, were distributed in widely read evangelical periodicals. Audiences were treated to descriptions of terrible conditions in Georgia's penitentiary of a sort that would soon become a regular feature of prison reform campaigns. Political figures in speeches printed for a national audience condemned the "inhuman and unconstitutional outrages committed ... upon the persons of several unoffending citizens heretofore residing as missionaries within the territory of the Cherokees." History recorded few instances, "even in the history of barbarous communities, in which the sacred character of a minister of religion has furnished so slight a protection against disrespect and violence to the persons invested with it." Petitions circulated by women—an important new development in public discourse—and memorials by writers in religious publications established a tone of nonpartisan moral protest that was much harder for removalist politicians to dismiss. Governor Gilmer later commented on the extraordinary "abuse" aroused by imprisoning the missionaries, the intense public interest "throughout the country," and the great "mortification" brought upon the people of Georgia."[73]

Often the key figures in episodes of civil disobedience come down to us as accidental heroes, people minding their own business until fate singled them out for important moral stands. We will have occasion to assess several such depictions in later chapters. Governor Gilmer regarded Worcester and Butler as very insignificant persons thrust into significance by northern partisans and enemies of southern progress. Perhaps the missionaries might have preferred lives of obscure dedication to the great cause they served, but Worcester does seem to have kept an eye on the public response to the stands he took.

Whatever he had in mind, others were certainly looking for a test case as a way to sway public opinion or slow down the removal forces after Jackson's election. To start with, a Cherokee delegation in Washington, frustrated in their efforts to gain the protection of the executive branch or Congress against Georgia's hostile policies, turned to the Supreme Court. It has been described by one legal scholar as "the ultimate irony" that the Cherokees "maintained their faith in the rule of law and its promise of justice" while Georgian officials depicted them "as a people 'incapable of complying with the obligations which the laws of civilized society imposed.' "[74] William Wirt, whom they hired as their advocate, was a Virginian who had served as U.S. attorney general for twelve years under James Monroe and John Quincy Adams. Wirt was assisted by John Sergeant, who had had a long career of representing Pennsylvania in Congress. In an extraordinary exchange through a third party, Chief Justice John Marshall had indicated his personal disagreement and sorrow at the course being taken in Indian affairs by the executive and legislative branches. After corresponding futilely with the governor of Georgia, Wirt composed and published a long legal opinion defending Cherokee sovereignty with so much clarity and detail and to such favorable reception that it might perhaps have encouraged Indians, as Jacksonians charged, to resist removal in the belief they could win their cause in the courts. Indeed, the Cherokees were being told by northern allies like Evarts, "You may be assured that if you get your case fairly before the Supreme Court your rights will be defended. All the great lawyers in the country are on your side."[75] As a careful historian has noted, however, Wirt's brief contained "not a single hint . . . as to how their rights might be tested in court."[76]

Wirt considered finding an individual Cherokee gold digger to sue Georgia as a foreign national who was being falsely imprisoned. Instead, he sought an injunction from the Supreme Court forbidding Georgia to execute its Indian laws on people of a long-recognized foreign state. The decision in *Cherokee Nation v. Georgia* (1831) was unfavorable. It is most famous for Marshall's conclusion that the Cherokees, though a distinct political society with rights to its property, were not fully independent or foreign but were more accurately "denominated domestic dependent nations," as peoples in "a state of pupilage" whose "relation to the United States resembles that of a ward to his guardian."[77] It was a complicated decision in its own time, one with considerable and unusually public division among the justices over Cherokee nationhood and property rights, but one in which the justices could not have assumed jurisdiction unless they found that the Cherokees were a foreign nation. Though critics of Marshall's paternalistic and gratuitous metaphor sometimes fail to notice it, Marshall's opinion hinted that a case raising issues of property rights— one of the justices singled out Georgia's seizure of the gold mines—might have been a more appropriate way of bringing the Cherokees' plight before the Supreme Court.[78] No justice mentioned the law under which Worcester and other missionaries had committed acts of civil disobedience as raising moral issues in a form in which the nation's legal system could address them.

While Cherokee leaders and their lawyers looked for a case centering on property rights, "petitions pleading for legislative redress" for the imprisoned missionaries, as one historian has noted, "poured" into Congress.[79] The fate of the white missionaries who refused pardon and labored still in the penitentiary—which the missionaries and thousands of evangelical sympathizers regarded as a moral issue—found its way to the courts as the test of Indian nationality. In correspondence with the American Board, President Jackson had taken the position that "as Georgia had extended her laws over the Cherokee country, the laws of Congress became inoperative and he had no authority to interfere." He did not want a test case.[80] To Georgia, which refused, as it had previously, even to appear before the Court, the issue was state sovereignty. A new governor, Wilson Lumpkin, in transmitting a writ from the Supreme Court to the legislature condemned it as an attempt "to infringe the evident right of a State to govern the entire population within its territorial limits, and to punish all offences committed against its laws within those limits." Such a "usurpation of power," if unchecked, would "inevitably eventuate in the annihilation of our beloved Union." In the Supreme Court the *Worcester* case (as well as *Butler*, which was attached to it)[81] was argued as a commerce clause case. Georgia could not unilaterally assume power over relations with Indians in violation of that clause of the Constitution. In effect, however, it was a case about personal liberty. Worcester, in Marshall's opinion, was seized in violation of treaties recognizing Cherokee control of the land where he resided. Troopers seized him as he was carrying out missionary labor under a "humane policy" approved by Congress. If this were a case about property, the opinion continued, no one could question the Supreme Court's jurisdiction. Worcester was not "less entitled to the protection of the constitution, laws, and treaties of his country" when what was at stake was his "personal liberty" and his subjection to "disgraceful punishment."[82] In a lengthy concurring opinion Associate Justice John McLean (recently appointed by President Jackson) also stressed the loss of liberty and subjection to "ignominious" punishment caused by state laws which, however understandable their purposes, conflicted with the constitution.[83]

The Court held, in short, that Georgia's law, under which the missionaries were imprisoned, was void, and that the sentence ought to be "reversed and annulled." More broadly, the acts of Georgia's legislature were found to be "repugnant" to the Constitution, treaties, and laws of the United States.[84] In other words, the case of two white missionaries who waited in the penitentiary enabled the Cherokees to secure a decision against the removal policies, an outcome they hailed as glorious and celebrated joyfully.[85] Or so it seemed on March 3, 1832, when the Supreme Court decision was announced. But Georgia soon showed that it would maintain its stance of disdain for the Supreme Court. The missionaries' sentence was not voided, they were not freed, and when they eventually were released, Georgia policies drove them out. They then found themselves involved in intra-Cherokee bitterness for which they had no zeal.

The Georgia Supreme Court not only declined to obey the mandate of the U.S. Supreme Court but also refused to record its decision and thus prevented formal notice of its action from reaching Marshall and his associates. To remedy this lack, the missionaries' Georgia counsel, Elisha Chester, wrote up his own affidavit of what had occurred and got Judge Clayton to certify it. Chester then sent a letter to Governor Lumpkin applying for the prisoners' discharges, but the governor replied, "You got round Clayton, but you shall not get round me."[86] In effect, everything was supposed to remain as though Marshall and his judicial colleagues had never spoken. Meanwhile, amid public protests in Georgia that were described as "insurrectionary" and stopping "just short of open rebellion," some prominent newspapers outside the state wrote critically of people

behaving as though defiance of the Constitution was only "a child's play."
An article in the *Niles Register* noted: "We are sick of such talks. If there is
not power in the Constitution to preserve itself, it's not worth the keeping."
Still, even at this critical moment, many nourished a hope that Georgia,
given time to cool off, and "content with executing her laws over the Indians
and their lands, will quietly release Messrs. Worcester and Butler, and so
remove the present cause of action—and cast future controversies on their
own precarious issue." Some Democratic papers expressed weariness with
the overblown and dangerous rhetoric. Some of the "more moderate"
Whig papers "joined in these sentiments." Was it not desirable to keep
tempers as calm as possible, perhaps to pardon Worcester and Butler (never
mind that they had never been willing to accept a pardon), and to remove
the cause of contention?[87] That is roughly what occurred. But not right
away, and not without raising a question about whether what was sometimes called "the *Missionaries Case*"[88] had proved an unfortunate test case
for the Indians.

While Georgia officials ignored all suggestions of leniency, Worcester
and Butler stayed in the penitentiary for nine more months. The situation
began to shift in November 1832 when Jackson won reelection and his
political opponents began to focus on other issues. In the same month
South Carolina announced its nullification ordinance, and a few weeks
later Jackson condemned that action. His speeches and actions, examined
earlier in this chapter, cast him as champion of the Union, enemy of dissent,
and in the crisis over Georgia's authority to nullify federal actions he
retained that persona because he recognized no legitimacy in Indians'
efforts to retain their previous status in law and society. But South Carolina's
defiance of the Supreme Court challenged the consistency of his viewpoint.
He never rescinded or retracted his view of Georgia's right to drive out the
Cherokees, but he became involved in complex negotiations seeking an
end to Worcester's and Butler's imprisonment that was also acceptable to
Georgia. To simply recognize that the U.S. Supreme Court had voided their
conviction was an option that was never considered, perhaps because that
would have meant also honoring the court's finding that Georgia's laws
were repugnant to the U.S. Constitution, treaties, and laws. The missionaries' civil disobedience had at least posed a dilemma, but the issue had
narrowed from the Cherokees' future to the missionaries' release.

Whatever resolution occurred followed months of negotiation by officers of the American Board, representatives of President Jackson and

Vice President-elect Van Buren, Supreme Court officials, Governor Lumpkin, a number of other prominent Georgians, and several ambitious senators and congressmen, in addition to Worcester, Butler, their Georgia attorney Chester, and their federal attorneys Wirt and Sargeant.[89] Though Jackson's intentions in Georgia were never certain, it was unlikely that he would ever have given up the commitment to Indian removal that he held deeply and that was central to his democratic agenda. The issue of a pardon was extremely touchy for both Georgia and the missionaries, and its implications for the Cherokees were especially disturbing. Indeed, besides the nullification conflict with South Carolina, the other public issue that most affected the negotiations was intense new pressure on the Cherokees, and bitter division among their leaders, to accept a treaty with the federal government and move west.

Before taking the case to the Supreme Court Wirt had advised Worcester that he was confident of gaining a favorable decision in the Supreme Court but less certain that Georgia would grant their release. "It is for yourself alone to consider . . . whether you choose to become the victim by whose suffering this question is to be raised."[90] Worcester had long said that he would leave jail when it did no good to remain. After the constitutional victory, for such it was, Wirt and Sargeant advised that there was probably nothing the Supreme Court would ever be able to do to free the missionaries. Evarts, the foremost intellectual foe of removal, had died in May 1831. Jackson won reelection in 1832. By the end of that year, there was also growing consensus among the Cherokees' former political supporters that their chances of remaining in Georgia and other eastern states were slim and that they would be wise to negotiate as favorable a treaty as possible from the Jackson administration for their removal. Those who reached this change of position included the Indians' congressional champion Theodore Frelinghuysen; Justice McLean, who had voted on their side in the Supreme Court; and the Prudential Committee of the American Board, which also concluded in response to an inquiry from the imprisoned missionaries that there was no longer any advantage in proceeding with their suit.[91]

There remained the issue of how to release Worcester and Butler, whom the Supreme Court had exonerated and who would never admit to guilt that deserved punishment. In December 1832 Georgia repealed the law they had violated so that they could be pardoned without leaving the state or signing an oath.[92] There was talk of skipping the step of a pardon and freeing them simply by an order to the keeper of the penitentiary.[93] But the threat of further Supreme Court intervention in Georgia's affairs had to be removed; that meant that the prisoners had to withdraw instructions requesting their attorneys to seek from the Court "further process." After the American Board's Prudential Committee, in answer to their inquiries, counseled that it would be "expedient" to curtail their suit, in early January 1833 they notified Governor Lumpkin that they had done so. They were concerned, they wrote, about the consequences of further divisiveness for "our beloved country." At this point events turned to tragicomedy. The governor found their letter "disrespectful" because it noted that they still believed that their cause was just and that the Supreme Court decision gave them a "perfect right to a legal discharge." He demanded a second letter honoring the state's rights. They wrote again, still without embracing Georgia's view of right and wrong but insisting that they meant no insult by their words but instead were simply leaving the issue of their confinement to the "magnanimity" of the state. This satisfied Lumpkin, until a newspaper article attacked him for bowing to pressure from foes of state sovereignty. He made the prisoners wait another five days before, on January 14, permitting their release.[94] Perhaps the reference to "magnanimity" was meant to be ironic, but it did not go over well with Cherokees caught in struggle with an implacable foe determined to uproot them from their homes.

What had the civil disobedients gained for their troubles? In an apologia Worcester wrote that not every effort must be successful. At least they had not lost the "privilege" of laboring among the Cherokees in the work of the gospel; they had gained a Supreme Court decision that might have "important bearing" on Cherokees' "future prosperity"; and they had the "consolation" of knowing they had not gained freedom at the cost of abandoning principle. In explaining why they had not in the end ventured to "move the Supreme Court to further process," they hinted at some pressure and acknowledged the changing political situation. "As far as our personal liberty was concerned, it were better to suffer unjustly, than to seek redress at the hazard of civil war." They still insisted that the deeds of Georgia officials amounted to "*injustice, oppression* and *robbery.*" Nevertheless, they abandoned their suit while claiming to harbor "no vindictive feelings" but only prayers that their antagonists' "transgressions" and those of their countrymen might be forgiven.[95]

Hope that their Supreme Court decision would benefit Indians in the future would be fulfilled, as it turned out, when Indian law changed in the

twentieth century, but not in any future immediately visible to the missionaries after they left jail.[96] It was inaccurate to suggest that they were able to
go back to their work. Georgia made that impossible. Butler was driven
from his station at the Haweis mission, according to the annals of the
American Board, "partly by force and partly by fraud"; and Worcester left
New Echota when the state seized the mission premises on behalf of a
lottery winner.[97] The Cherokee nation viewed the missionaries' deal with
the governor as a desertion, as a sign they thought the fight was over. In
later years other heroes of civil disobedience would be criticized for leaving
jail prematurely. But the bitterness of the missionaries' vilification by
Cherokees, who had celebrated around bonfires when they won their case,
has never been surpassed. Worcester was denied use of the printing press
on which he and Elias Boudinot had created translations of Christian
Scripture. The American Board, which had come to accept removal as
inevitable, supplied a new press after Worcester moved to the Indian
Territory, but its credibility had eroded too.[98] Worcester's move west in
spring 1835 was taken as a sign of complicity with a minority faction that
negotiated a treaty with the Jackson administration, accepted the eviction
of the Cherokees from their ancestral homes, and bore responsibility for
deaths and suffering on the tragic exodus that became known as the Trail
of Tears. Though remembered by the American Board (equally hated for
supporting the treaty) as a good missionary, Worcester became an isolated
figure in Cherokee society. In internecine conflict out west, gangs assassi-
nated pro-treaty leaders for negotiating an unauthorized surrender of the
Cherokee homeland. Boudinot, Worcester's old friend and closest associate, was tomahawked to death.[99] News of these murders and years of civil
war alienated many of the nation's remaining white evangelical sympathizers. Worcester and Butler were not physically harmed, but there was no
possibility of their being celebrated and remembered as heroic exemplars
of civil disobedience.

Obviously, their civil disobedience cannot be said to have ended
successfully if its goal was to prevent Cherokee removal. It is not clear what
alternative course of action, carried out by two men, or many people, could
have accomplished that. Interestingly, Daniel S. Butrick, the missionary
who had criticized Worcester's defiance of Georgia as unscriptural and too
political, felt free to attack the removal treaty, the unrepresentative Indian
leaders who usurped authority to negotiate it, and church leaders who
profited from supporting it. There was no stopping removal, however, and

Butrick accompanied a contingent of Cherokees, with much sickness and death, across the Ohio and Mississippi Rivers in the winter of 1838–39.[100]

Removal was a tragedy, but was it historically inevitable? Few historians have been comfortable facing that question, preferring instead to denounce Jackson's racism, but a strong argument can be made that keeping Indians on their southern lands was "infeasible."[101] In forgoing a suit against Georgia, the civilly disobedient missionaries followed the advice to that effect from their attorneys Wirt and Sargeant, both prominent anti-Jackson men, and from an American Board that never found a viable strategy in the South after the death of Jeremiah Evarts. And while Evarts's opposition to removal was unrelenting, he had doubted that the Cherokees possessed the capacity for "long continued courage or fortitude" needed to endure the trials of a long "slow process of law." If the missionaries left, "the Cherokees will make no stand whatever."[102] He was wrong on that point, according to scholars who have examined "the vigorous nonviolent resistance" of anti-treaty Cherokees who refused to leave homes except when taken by force and generally practiced noncooperation to armed resistance. Their acts have been described as "similar to traditional religious nonviolence, yet amenable to questions of efficacy as well," and praised as "a magnificent example of passive resistance to tyranny."[103] That campaign, however admirable, hardly counts as a successful alternative course of action. It might even have worsened the tragedy of forced migration to the west.

To understand and evaluate the different issues and movements that crisscrossed attempts to promote and block Indian removal would require an approach to moral choices and consequences in history like those that now motivate citizens and scholars seeking to "face" the history of the Holocaust and World War II.[104] Since the removal of the southern Indians was linked to the expansion of plantation agriculture across the South, and issues of resistance are central to the study of slavery, the project would definitely be worthwhile (though it is not clear how many Americans want to confront their historical amnesia on these subjects). One part of that kind of project—perhaps a small part—would be to recognize the creation of a precedent for an American tradition of civil disobedience. Though Worcester and Butler and Wirt and Marshall did not block Georgia's project for eviction and expropriation or Jackson's scheme for removal to the other side of the Mississippi, they did elicit an important (in the long run) Supreme Court decision, and they sparked political and publicity campaigns that kept the national outcome unclear for a while.

What can certainly be claimed for the missionaries' widely publicized civil disobedience is that it demonstrated one possible outcome of a post-revolutionary evangelical surge that combined a vision of converting the world with goals of perfecting American society and government. And it pointed to a promising tactic for use in the courts to carry out the ends of reformers. To the rights consciousness of democracy, Evarts and Worcester added a view that doing God's work legitimated civil dissent. The Baptists and other religious protesters of the late eighteenth century had defied the law in order to assert their own rights to worship in ways they believed were most truly Christian. The Georgia missionaries were not protecting their own rights of worship. As their law breaking aimed to aid Indian noncitizens, it pointed toward future practices of civil disobedience directed to the causes of others who were not fully citizens—slaves, blacks, women.

3

Slavery and Disobedience

If I Perish, I Perish

Historians have only in recent decades begun to emphasize the importance of Indian removal to Jacksonian democracy and the social and economic changes that magnified southern prosperity and led eventually to civil war. Indian removal was broadly popular among supporters of Andrew Jackson, and the dispossession of Choctaws, Chickasaws, Creeks and Cherokees (and eventually, after costly battles, Seminoles) led to the expansion of plantation agriculture across the cotton South, the repression of lingering antislavery sentiments among whites, and a flourishing internal slave trade as human property was led westward into new fields and markets. One forced migration—one "trail of tears"—prepared the way for another. Of the million slaves brought to the southwestern cotton "kingdom" in the antebellum period, two-thirds were sold twice, bought and then resold by traders.[1]

New and more radical reform movements arose in reaction. In a letter telling William Lloyd Garrison that he had subscribed his name to "an instrument similar to the Declaration of '76, renouncing all allegiance to the government of the United States, and asserting the title of Jesus Christ to the throne of the world," John Humphrey Noyes wrote: "When I wish to form a conception of the government of the United States . . . I picture to myself a bloated, swaggering libertine, trampling on the Bible—its own Constitution—its treaties with the Indians—the petitions of its citizens: with one hand whipping a negro tied to a liberty-pole, and with the other dashing an emaciated Indian to the ground."[2] Noyes's views were extreme, but other reformers turned with mounting emotion to angrier and more radical reform movements. Garrison inserted on the masthead of his newspaper, the *Liberator*, a scene of figures in a slave mart trampling Indian treaties underfoot. Virtually every prominent antislavery reformer who withdrew from the gradualist colonization movement in favor of immediate abolitionism linked this radical step to disgust at Jacksonian Indian policy.[3]

The American Board was hardly a radical organization, but it had supported a new kind of civil disobedience with new justifications for law breaking dramatized by the heroism of its missionaries. At the urging of Jeremiah Evarts, who stood behind the actions of Worcester and Butler, the removal debates became the occasion for petitioning on an unprecedented scale by American women. In Boston in 1829 Evarts told Catharine Beecher, daughter of his friend, the prominent clergyman Lyman Beecher, and founder of a school for young women in Hartford, Connecticut, of the "distressing and disastrous consequences" facing the southern Indian nations if Congress supported President Jackson's plans for removal. At the same time, he held out hope that "American women might save these poor, oppressed natives," and in effect he challenged her to "devise some method of intervention." Back in Hartford, the "greatly excited" Catharine Beecher drafted an unsigned "circular" headed "*To Benevolent Ladies of the U. States*," proposing public meetings in behalf of the Cherokees and the collection of signatures on petitions beseeching Congress to protect the endangered Indians. She shared the circular at a meeting with a group of friends who ranked among Hartford's "most judicious and influential ladies." Together, they planned for the document to be printed anonymously, with all involved pledged to secrecy, and then mailed in large quantities to prominent ladies in other cities with printed requests to send copies in turn to "the most influential and benevolent ladies" of their acquaintance. Even the stilted prose—the recurrent passive voice, for example—conveys the awkwardness of the public intervention. ("A meeting was convened ... the circular was read, ... measures were adopted.") But the excitement of the "simultaneous movement" that followed—the circular's appearance in leading evangelical periodicals, public meetings and the circulation of petitions in many towns and cities— remained unmistakable even many decades later when Catharine Beecher disclosed her agency. The results of this anonymous campaign privately delighted its initiators as they began to receive the same circular mailed to them, amid much guessing and dissembling about who wrote it and teasing from her sister Harriet and co-conspirators about the extravagant praise for its style.[4] The public consequences were thrilling, too. Congress was flooded with almost 1,500 women's signatures on petitions from many cities—and still more by men.

Women had previously appealed to local governments on issues of philanthropy and benevolence, but petitions on a politically contested and increasingly partisan national issue constituted something new. What made it acceptable was that the emphasis of the petitions was to be moral (saving an unfortunate race from calamity) and religious (continuing the progress of Christianity among Indian converts and the missions supported by evangelical faithful). Moreover, the cause could be called conservative (as it has been by the scholar Alisse Portnoy). The petitions were not calling for a change in existing laws and treaties, but for opposition to radical changes being advanced by President Jackson and his southern supporters. There was a bracing hint of disobedience, however, in going beyond previously understood conventions of gender in response to a moral emergency, indeed, in signing on to a campaign to stop the annihilation of a people by mobilizing the feelings of Christians. The biblical story of Esther furnished justification for embracing the role of rescuer rather than remaining a bystander:

> It may be that this [the activities in behalf of the Cherokees] will be *forbidden;* yet still we remember the Jewish princess who, being sent to supplicate for a nation's life, was thus reproved for hesitating even when *death* stared her in the way; "If thou altogether hold thy peace at this time, then shall deliverance arise from another place; but thou and thy father's house shall be destroyed. And who knoweth whether thou art come to the kingdom for such a cause as this?"[5]

Catharine Esther Beecher invoked biblical precedent to justify a willingness to break rules. But the act she justified was supplication. The rule broken by the Jewess Esther and the clandestine circularizers of Hartford was that women should not intermeddle in politics, but what needed to be done, in both cases, was to supplicate.

What drew Beecher to the story of Esther? Perhaps a covert reference to her own middle name enhanced the playful secrecy of her Hartford circle. But the story had a more powerful resonance. Esther hesitated before breaking a proscription on activity by a woman, even a queen, until

Mordecai, the uncle who had raised her, warned that she must speak out in order to prevent Haman's threat to annihilate all Jews. In her own time, Beecher viewed what was happening to the Cherokees and other Indian nations as an equivalent threat to destroy a people. For her as for Esther, the threat of holocaust authorized disobedience of law.

Surely, it would be an exaggeration to view women's petitioning as civil disobedience if supplication was the end of it. But women were subject to the laws even if they did not make them, and what if one woman entreated others to break laws that society honored as fundamental to social order? One of Beecher's contemporaries went that far, and perhaps unsurprisingly she was a woman whose transgressions of expected gender roles were bolder than Beecher's (and they both went further than many others). Angelina Grimké, brought up in a prominent and affluent Charleston slaveholding family, had left home, moved north, converted from Episcopalian first to Presbyterian and later to Quaker faith and practices, and experienced the intense emotions of religious revivalism in the North.[6] In this wave of religious self-discovery and public commitment, she and her older sister Sarah became prominent antislavery advocates.

In her search for a vocation Angelina once considered enrolling at Beecher's seminary and becoming a teacher; she had even visited Hartford. But her course led in a different direction. She began to write, at first privately, about the inconsistency of American slavery and modern government with principles taught by "our Lord and his Christ" and about the necessity to "overthrow" republican government in order to bring on "the universal reign of Truth & Righteousness in the earth."[7] In May 1835 she began to attend meetings of the Philadelphia Female Anti-Slavery Society and in August wrote a letter praising the radical abolitionist William Lloyd Garrison. She and Sarah, who preceded her on the trajectory away from Charleston, were the only women among the agents of the American Anti-Slavery Society who met in New York in November 1836 for training under the leadership of the charismatic Theodore Dwight Weld, whom she fell in love with and in 1838 married. Angelina had no equal as an abolitionist orator except perhaps Weld himself, whose speaking voice was deteriorating. She met at first with groups of women but by 1837 was lecturing effectively, on her own, to "promiscuous" audiences—that is, gatherings that included men and women—thereby arousing angry criticism from orthodox clergymen and conservative abolitionists. Soon enough, she began mixing advocacy of women's rights with her denunciations of slavery.

In this highly controversial departure, one of her sharpest critics was Catharine Beecher, who confronted her in sustained argument in print over the goals and methods of antislavery movements and the proper role of women in public agitation. At this point in her life Beecher was recovering from a nervous collapse and launching a new career that would make her the most influential interpreter of American womanhood, and she drew a line restricting invocation of Esther to extreme moments in which the life of a woman and her nation were at stake. In a campaign urging women to join abolition societies or to sign petitions to Congress, "the case of Queen Esther is not at all to be regarded as a suitable example for imitation." Petitions to congress, she now believed and emphasized, were "IN ALL CASES ... entirely without the sphere of female duty." "Petitions from females" would "exasperate" men in government and aggravate conflict in society when the proper role of women was to moderate and uplift.[8]

For Angelina Grimké, it was no exaggeration to speak of slavery as an unscriptural holocaust necessitating individual stands of opposition and rescue as she rejected the popular movement that accommodated itself to retaining the institution until its victims were colonized elsewhere. Her most remarkable call for civil disobedience came in the public *Appeal to the Christian Women of the South* (1836), which opened with this epigraph from the book of Esther:

> "Then Mordecai commanded to answer Esther, Think not within thyself that thou shalt escape the king's house more than all the Jews. For if thou altogether holdest thy peace at this time, then shall there enlargement and deliverance arise to the Jews from another place, but thou and thy father's house shall be destroyed: and who knoweth whether thou art come to the kingdom for such a time as this. And Esther bade them return Mordecai this answer, and so will I go in unto the king, which is not according to law, and *if I perish, I perish*."
> Esther IV.13–16

As one of the earliest scholars of abolitionism pointed out, the doctrine that "slavery was not only an evil but a sin, and ought immediately to be abandoned" was highly controversial even among abolitionists, some of whom recognized that it made the conversion of the South almost hopeless. Worst of all, it led into "the wilderness of 'the Bible argument,' " raising issues about slavery in ancient times and leading to exchanges of "proof-texts" that seemed capable of proving "nothing and everything."[9] In leaving the South, experiencing a religious conversion, and stepping forward as an agent of antislavery, Angelina Grimké had embraced the controversial doctrine unflinchingly, and in 1836 she still hoped to convert the women of the South—a task that was probably futile according to recent studies of slavery and the biblical argument[10]—or at least to demonstrate her sincere intentions. Her *Appeal* did not pretend to the dispassion of scholar or the authority of clergyman. She engaged to speak with calm reason and Christian honesty in addressing her relatives and other southern women, however deeply they disapproved her condemnation of slavery and reloca- tion in the North. Though she did not skirt the bewildering proof-texts, she did not start with Scripture but instead hailed a new moral light shining on slavery, as shown by the suppression of the slave trade and by the "good old doctrine" of the revolutionary forefathers that all men are created equal and have an inalienable right to liberty. Some might object, she recognized, that "our fathers were certainly mistaken, for the Bible sanctions Slavery, and that is the highest authority." She did not shrink from the challenge: "The Bible is my ultimate appeal in all matters of faith and practice, and it is to *this test* I am anxious to bring the subject at issue between us."

She began, as had Weld at the agents' training sessions, with the "charter of privileges" bestowed on mankind at the Creation and renewed after the Flood, establishing dominion over all creatures, except one—"man is never vested with this dominion *over his fellow man*," who is made in the image of his Creator and can never be a chattel.[11] In discussing whether "patriar- chal servitude [in the Old Testament] was like American slavery," she pointed to many differences by which an observant reader should be "undeceived." It is noteworthy that she turned to two volumes of commen- tary in reaching conclusions about the protections that restricted legiti- mate causes of enslavement and guarded servants, especially females, from "violence, injustice and wrong" (4).[12] Like some other abolitionists, she concluded that the type of slavery practiced in America "never existed" under the Jewish dispensation; it was an aspersion on God's character to say otherwise. Her portrait of Hebrew slavery gave her opportunity to specify, in contrast, the many "monstrous" inequalities in the laws of American slavery, which subjugated an entire race, denied the humanity of the slave, and demoted him or her from being a person to a thing (12). And what of the proslavery claim that Jesus Christ never condemned slavery? First of all, the ancient laws were not so monstrous as America's "Code Noir," but more important, what of the Golden Rule, and "can you for a moment imagine the meek, and lowly, and compassionate Saviour a slaveholder" (14)?

Grimké then urged women to read the Bible and Declaration of Independence (since other works on slavery might well be unavailable), to pray for the slave ("that he may be kept patient and submissive" until God opens "the door of freedom . . . without violence or bloodshed"), to pray also for the master ("that his heart may be softened") and for advocates of emancipation in England and the northern states, and to speak out to friends and relatives about slavery's sinfulness. Women should seek to influence neighbors and family members to treat slaves, so long as they were held as slaves, with kindness and understanding. It was not enough, however, to feel, pray, and exert influence. "Act on this subject," she tells women.

> Some of you own slaves yourselves. If you believe slavery is sinful, set them at liberty. . . . If they wish to remain with you, pay them wages. . . . Should they remain teach them, and have them taught the common branches of an English education; they have minds and those minds ought to be improved. . . . It is the duty of all, as far as they can, to improve their own mental faculties, because we are commanded to love God with all our minds, as well as with all our hearts, and we commit a great sin, if we forbid or prevent that culti- vation of the mind in others, which would enable them to perform this duty.

White women, therefore, should teach their servants to read and encourage them to believe that they have "a duty to learn, if it were only that they might read the Bible." Oppose all cruelty to the slaves that serve you, give comfort to them, see that they are well clothed and well fed. "Above all, try to persuade your husband, father, brothers and sons, that slavery is a sin against God and man" and that it is "a great sin" to keep human beings ignorant and illiterate" (18–19). And yes, petition your legislatures and follow the example of women in England and the northern states by forming women's antislavery societies.

Such advice amounted to a call for civil disobedience supported by Jewish and Protestant religious history. "Some of you will say, we can neither free our slaves nor teach them to read, for the laws of our state forbid it. Be not surprised when I say such wicked laws ought to be no barrier in the way of your duty." Here Grimké turned to a different use of both Testaments by urging Christian women to follow the examples of heroic rebels and brave martyrs who disobeyed the wicked decrees of their sovereigns, refusing to worship golden images, daring to preach in the name of Jesus (19). In doing so, they would take inspiration from a long list of women from the Old Testament—Miriam, Deborah, Jael, Huldah, and to be sure, Esther the Queen—and others in the new Testament who recognized Christ as the Messiah and ministered to him in his persecution, and the many thousands who endured persecution to advance the Christian faith in later centuries (21–23). Let the women of the South arise, let there be "but one Esther at the South," prepared to violate the laws of slavery and say, "if I perish, I perish," and "the horrible system of oppression and cruelty, licentiousness and wrong" might be overthrown by "irresistible" moral power (25–26).

She answered practical objections to emancipation. What will happen to my slaves if I free them? Will they be sold or starve? Will I myself be exposed to suffering?—with the radical abolitionist insistence that ethically we are obliged to do what is right and have faith that God will in time take care of the consequences. She turns this to a clear doctrine of civil disobedience, and one she applies to herself.

> I know the doctrine of obeying God, rather than man, will be considered as dangerous, and heretical by many, but I am not afraid openly to avow it, because it is the doctrine of the Bible, but I would not be understood to advocate resistance to any law however oppressive, if in obeying it, I was not obliged to commit *sin*. If for instance, there was a law, which imposed imprisonment or a fine on me *if* I manumitted a slave, I would on no account resist that law, I would set the slave free, and then go to prison or pay the fine. *If* a law commands me to *sin I will break it; if* it calls me to *suffer*, I will let it take its course *unresistingly.* The doctrine of blind obedience and unqualified submission to *any human* power, whether civil or ecclesiastical, is the doctrine of despotism, and ought to have no place among Republicans and Christians. (19–20)

Grimké's message to southern women flowed out of an era of evangelical vision, rapid conversion of the population, and confidence in the progress of great reform movements.[13] Not only did she seek to dispel southern misinformation on the goals of abolitionism, she also linked antislavery action to the work of the other great reform causes of the era

that together were fulfilling "prophetic promises of deliverance" and transformation. She named the "seven philanthropic associations"—"the Bible
and peace societies, anti-slavery and temperance, sabbath schools, moral
reform [anti-prostitution], and missions"—that pulled along "the millennial car" and provided a "vast machinery" to "regenerate mankind" (27). It
was, among other things, an impressive—perhaps the most impressive—
example of the antislavery biblical argument with its sense of radical
change's contingency on the sacred heroism of individuals. The optimism
of that outlook was to be severely tested, in large part by conflicts over
slavery that divided churches and reform movements in the era in which
she was writing. It would be harder for reformers in later decades to
think or act so confidently if they left "consequences" for God to oversee. It
would be hard to find later examples of abolitionist writings addressed so
ardently to a particular audience and set in such a dynamic context of
biblical exposition, civil disobedience, political action, and millennial
change.

In 1837 Angelina Grimké composed *An Appeal to the Women of the
Nominally Free States*, beginning with a millenarian epigraph: "The trem-
bling earth, the low-murmuring thunders, already admonish us of our
danger; and if females can exert any saving influence in this emergency, *it
is time for them to awake.*" The prominent place given those words in an
appeal issued by "an antislavery convention of American women" must
have irritated their author, Catharine Beecher, who had specifically recommended that women restrict expression of their feelings on slavery and
other political issues to the domestic sphere. Besides restating the scriptural argument against slavery and condemning colonizationism, much of
the *Appeal* was devoted to defending woman's political role historically and
in the American republic. The convention was interracial (as it could
hardly have been in the South), with a stanza on the *Appeal's* title page by
the Philadelphia poet Sarah Forten calling on white women to recognize
that God made them of one blood with their black sisters. Grimké urged
black women not to "shrink back" from prejudiced whites in this "transition state."[14]

Grimké's appeals, written in 1836–37, only a short time after her
conversion to abolitionism, deserve careful attention. At times her statements echo the American revolutionary rejection of the once-supposed
obligation to submit to sovereign power and entrenched custom. But they
show commitment to a different spirit of nonresistance even as one

disobeys the law. Her view has almost no similarity to the more practical position of Worcester and his American Board advisors and the attorneys searching for a test case and ready to recalculate costs and advantages—that is, consequences—as events transpire. We shall want to contrast it with the influential but surprisingly elusive stance of Henry David Thoreau. The radical abolitionist view that Grimké expressed would recur, in different formulations, with varying degrees of ideological commitment, and amid criticisms from those who advocated political action or armed violence, throughout ensuing decades of antislavery struggle until it was submerged in wartime.

We will return to northern antislavery women and civil disobedience, but we may ask here: Did Grimké's appeal spark a movement of southern antislavery women? That seems doubtful. Some scholars have pointed to women's benevolence as a great potential weakness of the master class. A recent study based on recollections of former slaves sharply questions the "ideology of a gentle and noble white womanhood" less committed to slavery than the men.[15] There certainly were examples of southern women teaching young slaves to read despite the illegality of doing so. Sarah Grimké is said to have rebelled against such prohibitions while teaching in a Negro Sunday school and surreptitiously instructing her personal maid until discovered and ordered to desist.[16] Frederick Douglass's famous narrative acknowledged "the kindly assistance" of an "amiable" mistress who gave him his initial boost into literacy, as he requested after hearing her read the Bible, but he also described how readily she refrained from further instruction after his master complained that it was illegal and could encourage thoughts of freedom.[17] Improving his ability to read on his own became central to the story of his progress from slavery to freedom. Harriet Jacobs, author of the other best-known narrative on the same theme, had the early good fortune to be taught to read and spell by a young mistress with whose family her own family was connected for several generations. Harriet herself complained that slaves were "whipped and imprisoned for teaching each other to read," but she still disobediently held secret sessions instructing an elderly man, "Uncle Fred," who sought to read the Bible to be "nearer to God" and "know how to live."[18] Jacobs continued to enjoy help from white women in the town where she was raised after the vicissitudes of the market subjected her to the ownership of a lecher. She had no kind memories of her new mistress, who might have guided and protected "the young and innocent" among her slaves but instead, well aware of her husband's lust, treated his prey with "constant suspicion and malevolence"—a state of affairs that Jacobs presents as endemic in such households of unchecked domination. Though both Douglass and Jacobs were menaced by threats to sell them to slave traders who would drive them westward, they grew up in Atlantic coastal cities, and their exposure to education, meager as it was, was exceptional. The slave population generally was more than 90 percent illiterate.[19] There are no indices to kindness given, protections extended, Christian education offered by white women to slave women in their charge, but if there were, the figures would probably be no higher. In short, Angelina Grimké issued an admirable call for civil disobedience and avoidance of by-standing, but evidence that it was heeded in the slaveholding South is scant.

The Roles of the Slaves

Nestled among the actions Angelina Grimké recommended to the South's Christian women, we find this sentence: "Pray also for that poor slave, that he may be kept patient and submissive under his hard lot, until God is pleased to open the door of freedom to him without violence or blood-shed" (17). And again: "Endeavour to inculcate submission on the part of the slaves, but whilst doing this be faithful in pleading the cause of the oppressed" (18). We have no reason to believe that Grimké wrote anything insincerely, though she was writing five years after Nat Turner's rebellion in Virginia in 1831, which had led to a rash of laws forbidding the teaching of slaves to read, and her intended audience would need reassurance that the acts she pleads for and the divine emancipation she foresees would not lead to a bloodbath. We cannot avoid the conclusion that at that moment, early in her conversion to abolitionism, Grimké did not imagine for the slaves an active role in winning their own freedom. What part, we may ask, did slaves have in the origins of civil disobedience in America?

That is not a question often raised in historical writing about American slavery. For many decades that subject was generally viewed (except by black writers) from a perspective denying the capacity of slaves and their descendants to behave capably as citizens. Consider the widely assigned textbook by the well-known scholars Samuel Eliot Morison and Henry Steele Commager. Both 1930 and 1950 editions of their *Growth of the American Republic* included this now-notorious sentence: "As for Sambo, whose wrongs moved the abolitionists to wrath and tears, there is some reason to believe that he suffered less than any other class in the South from its 'peculiar institution.'" Most slaves, it went on, "were adequately fed, well cared for, and apparently happy. . . . Although brought to America by force, the incurably optimistic Negro soon became attached to the country, and devoted to his 'white folks.'" A few pages later, the authors echoed the proslavery argument's description of slavery as a "transitional status between barbarism and civilization. The negro learned his master's language, and accepted in some degree his moral and religious standards. In return he contributed much besides his labor—music and humor for instance—to American civilization."[20] Defending the book against NAACP protests, Morison took a stand that since "Negroes were the most successful slave race," there must be "some essential docility in their character."[21] Similar quotations could be pulled from other well-respected books. Ralph Henry Gabriel's *The Course of American Democratic Thought*, long favored and assigned as an introduction to American ideas and values, described slaves as people who, "having no memory of African scenes or tribal ways or Negro languages, cheerfully made plantation life their own, for the most part accepting slavery as a matter of course and adopting their masters much as a child appropriates his parents or a pupil his teacher." These masters had to cope with the dependency of childlike people who not only required food, clothing, and shelter but also needed to be "sanitated at all times, nursed when ill, cheered when indolent, disciplined when unruly."[22]

That viewpoint persisted, but with mounting opposition by the 1950s. An early article in the *Journal of Negro History* had already documented "day-to-day" resistance to slavery ranging from malingering, petty theft, and destruction of tools to self-mutilation and suicide.[23] Kenneth Stampp's landmark work, *The Peculiar Institution* (1956), delineated the masters' program "to produce the perfect slave: accustom him to rigid discipline, demand from him unconditional submission, impress upon him his innate inferiority, develop in him a paralyzing fear of white men, train him to adopt the master's code of good behavior, and instill in him a sense of complete dependence." But slaves still showed discontentment in many ways, "as much as any people could have done in their circumstances," though not by organized rebellion after the crushing reaction to Nat Turner.[24] In the absence of a record of continuing violent revolution, scholarly portrayals of Sambo persisted, though with greater attention to the weapons of the weak and the slaves' sense of agency. One quotation from the work of Eugene Genovese is especially striking. After noting, as had other scholars, the recurrence of the Sambo stereotype throughout the world history of slavery, Genovese turned to its prevalence in pre-revolutionary Saint-Domingue. Before "the greatest slave revolution in history, nothing lay behind it but Sambo and a few hints." We should therefore be "aware of how suddenly a seemingly docile, or at least adjusted, people can rise in violence. It would be much safer to assume that dangerous and strong currents run beneath that docility and adjustment."[25]

In the American South, there were few great concentrations of slaves and no great slave insurrection, despite many rumors, especially after 1831, but what one historian has termed "a form of rebellion that neither the Confederates nor the Yankees had quite imagined" broke out soon after southerners declared their independence and Union forces entered the South. Thousands of self-declared freedmen and women fled farms and plantations, headed to army camps to demand protection or volunteer for service, and set themselves up on deserted or confiscated lands as free laborers cultivating their corn patches rather than working in gangs on plantation crops.[26] So much for the idea that some essential docility in the slaves' character rendered them unable to seize the opportunity for change. It would be stretching a point to look for any tight definition of civil disobedience in wartime actions that defied former masters, challenged Union occupiers, signified liberation, and ended slavery. For as long as slavery had flourished, southern slaves were noncitizens, scattered in small units across a vast space, subject to sale, preserving family as best they could. We cannot understand civil disobedience if we generalize it to include all forms of resistance, day-to-day or extraordinary. But when the moment was ripe, many who were enslaved knew what to do to act out their freedom.

Some blacks in the North had long entertained thoughts of mass insubordination on the part of the slaves—refusals to work without wages—that might be called civil disobedience sans citizenship. In a powerful 1843 address to the slaves Henry Highland Garnet ridiculed the "unreasonable and unnatural dogmas of non-resistance." It was sinful, he said, for slaves to submit voluntarily to captivity; it was their duty to use every means of resistance at their disposal. American revolutionary precedent, the divine law, the examples of slave rebels—all supported the motto "RESISTANCE! RESISTANCE! RESISTANCE!" Garnet did not counsel armed revolution, solely because it was "INEXPEDIENT." Slaves were outnumbered and lacked allies. Instead, they should approach their "lordly enslavers, and tell them plainly, that YOU ARE DETERMINED TO BE FREE." After speaking to the masters of the injustice and sinfulness of slavery, they should "forever cease to toil for heartless tyrants. . . . You had far better all die—*die immediately*, than live slaves, and entail your wretchedness upon your posterity."[27]

Garnet's passion had roots in family memory: his father had led a family of ten out of slavery in Maryland. It also reflected events elsewhere in the hemisphere. The historian of American slave revolts, Herbert Aptheker, pointed to similarities between Garnet's appeal to American slaves and Samuel Sharpe's call for "massive passive resistance" in the Jamaican uprising known as "the Baptist war."[28] The resemblance gains significance in light of recent scholarly analysis of emancipation in Britain's Caribbean colonies. Though Deacon Sharpe had imagined the uprising as an "orderly work stoppage," not unlike actions by European workingmen, the rebels, numbering up to 60,000, mostly converts of Protestant missionaries and committed to fight only in self-defense, caused immense damage to property, setting the skies ablaze with the burning of plantation estates. At the start of the uprising no whites lost their lives; in the conflict prolonged over months, 540 slaves and 14 whites were killed. The insurgents' restraint in avoiding bloody consequences like those in previous decades in Haiti and their understanding of the effects of their deeds on an antislavery coalition on the verge of victory in Britain were remarkable. While some Jamaican planters talked of secession and possible annexation to the United States, American slaveholders deepened their suspicions of missionaries, petitioning women, and unsupervised slave conversions. Slaves were well aware of Jamaica and the conclusions their masters derived from world events. No significant insurrections occurred, however, despite many rumors, after 1831 and before the Union armies entered the South.[29]

Rumors may not have been inconsequential, but they do not provide strong enough evidence of slave resistance on a scale that scholars have found crucial to the overthrow of colonial slavery elsewhere in the hemisphere.[30] That of course was the deficiency to which Garnet was reacting, against the wishes of many of his black abolitionist coworkers. But waiting for some significant new opportunity—"the blessed break"—in a loosely organized way, over vast distances, was not the worst "approach" to change in a preliterate culture and among people who felt they had much to lose from failure.

In the 1850s about one thousand slaves ran away each year, some to free communities in Canada, more to free black communities in northern cities, where some, especially those with children, lay low, while others participated in antislavery activities as speakers, authors, and audiences. Just by running away they provoked a national political crisis. Some wrote narratives of their lives in slavery, their escapes, their subsequent lives, often lived in jeopardy of recapture. It may be awkward to apply the term *civil disobedience* to running away (though not to *aiding* fugitives), but flight certainly was a form of law breaking, as the slave who "absconded" was described as stealing himself.[31] The act demonstrated the humanity of the slave and thus dramatized the contradiction of the slave owner's conversion of a person into a conveyable commodity. Other forms of property are not subject to law punishing their disobedience. It resounded in the assertion of abolitionists, including Angelina Grimké, that slavery was unscriptural and sinful because it treated human beings with souls as things. One fugitive slave who became a pastor in freedom, James W. C. Pennington, identified slavery with the principle that any human being so categorized can be given a price, removed from family and community, and sold. "The being of slavery, its soul and its body, lives and moves in the chattel principle, the property principle, the bill of sale principle: the cart-whip, starvation, and nakedness are its inevitable consequences."[32] The disobedient who fled placed his life on a different principle.

The slave's struggle to show his or her humanity was a central theme of many (and probably all) of the extraordinary narratives of escape that were published in antebellum America. That theme runs strongly through the two most widely read autobiographies of ex-slaves—both of whom in the end needed ransoms or payments to their masters in order to secure their freedom. Frederick Douglass and Harriet Jacobs both narrate in powerful terms that border on fiction their protagonists' refusal to succumb to the villainous power of their owners and the dehumanizing logic at the core of slavery.[33] The historian David Brion Davis, who has identified attempted dehumanization or bestialization as "the central contradiction at the very heart of slavery," praises Douglass's understanding not only of the reasons why masters compared slaves to animals but also of the experience of the enslaved person so treated. In a memorable account of being sent to a tyrannical supervisor, who had a reputation of "being a first rate hand at breaking young negroes," to have his independent spirit crushed, Douglass reports that his "intellect languished," his interest in reading disappeared, "and behold a man transformed into a brute!" After a long violent fight with his would-be tamer, he experienced "a glorious resurrection" as a man, never again in his own mind or in treatment by others to be a brute. "I was nothing before; I was A MAN NOW." He was sixteen years old.[34]

In *Incidents in the Life of a Slave Girl* Jacobs's protagonist, Linda Brent, also recounts the protracted contest of a slave against her owner. With no test of physical force, her story is one of "stubborn disobedience" in spite of her owner's threats, blows, and enticements as he attempts to seduce her. In recounting an early love, the assault on her chastity, a fairly calculated liaison which resulted in two children, and her confessions to her grandmother and daughter, Jacobs always raises the defense that in the South no laws protected her; only her own will preserved her from concubinage. Despite her feelings of vulnerability, she declared to her master that she would rather go to jail than succumb to his power. The problem of obedience and resistance is central to the book, where discussion of it is strongly gendered. She recounts instances of physical rebellion and flight to sea by males in her family, but she could not appeal to the principles of manly individualism that male authors of slave narratives voiced. She addresses herself explicitly and almost entirely to women—especially to respectable, reform-minded white women—and emphasizes issues of chastity and motherhood. As Elizabeth Fox-Genovese has pointed out, "A poignant account of the violation of a woman's virtue stood a much better chance of appealing to northern sensibilities than a pronunciamento for woman's individual rights."[35]

Most famously, Linda hides for seven years in a crawlspace—her "Loophole of Retreat"—above her grandmother's house. It is a way of overcoming, of winning a battle. The laws allowed her lecherous persecutor to go out in the "free air," while she, "guiltless of crime," lived in "pent up" discomfort "as the only means of avoiding the cruelties the laws allowed him to inflict upon me!" Linda's individual resistance has been called civil disobedience, though a broad definition ("the public expression of dissatisfaction with the state through violation of particular laws") is required to make it fit her status as property lacking the protection of law and any trace of citizenship.[36] If a declaration of individual rights is impossible in the narrative, there is still no mistaking the contest of wills at the center of her fight ("I would do any thing, every thing for the sake of defeating him"). In the slave South, this determination leads to secrecy and confinement. Retreat to her "dismal hole"—which she repeatedly describes as an imprisonment—is the best disobedience available to her.

Jacobs herself (and her protagonist Linda) escaped from slavery in 1842. She pointedly gave few particulars about how the flight was managed except to say that she traveled by schooner to Philadelphia, where she was met by black members of a Vigilant Committee who assisted refugees like her, and then made her way on a segregated "dirt car" of a train to Jersey City and thence by ferry to New York. She reconnected there with her daughter and son, whose legal status was ambiguous. As children of a slave mother they were slaves; though their white father had purchased them, they remained vulnerable to slave catchers, and as readers of *Incidents* will remember, Harriet Jacobs remained legally a slave and lived in fear, with at least one "hairbreadth escape" and other close calls, until a benefactress purchased her freedom and her children's in 1852. "So I was *sold* at last! A human being *sold* in the free city of New York!"[37]

Douglass, who had much less connection to family (a deprivation he blamed on slaveholders), presents himself as a natural-born rebel, conspiring to escape in 1836 in a plot that was betrayed and landed him briefly in jail. He fled successfully two years later, by means he would not disclose until many years later, so as to give no clues to those determined to prevent other slaves from escaping. In New York he met a fugitive slave who advised him on the ever-present danger of betrayal and capture.[38] Even after he rose to prominence as an antislavery orator and author—indeed, especially as he became "somewhat notorious"—the fear of being captured and transported southward remained, until finally in 1846, as he completed an extended lecture tour in the United Kingdom, antislavery admirers raised £150 to "effect my ransom from slavery," giving him papers to prove his freedom before they would allow him to return to America.[39] Those who aided Jacobs, Douglass, and other slaves to flee from their owners may perhaps be called civil disobedients (except by any definition that requires excessive openness, respect for the laws, and readiness to go to jail), but they were not so much trying to change the law or express their disagreement with it as to evade it.

Douglass, moreover, concludes later versions of his memoirs with his participation in attacks in the North on Jim Crow discrimination. According to her biographer, Harriet Jacobs after escaping slavery joined demonstrations against segregation on railroads, trolleys, and ships "for the rest of her life."[40] The history of opposition to slavery in the slave states is often elusive, but free blacks in the North, aided by fugitives whose freedom was in jeopardy, would make civil disobedience an important development in American religious and political life.

Black Abolitionists

"Remember I am a slave," the Syracuse clergyman Jermain Wesley Loguen proclaimed in 1856 to a white colleague who objected to his support for the Underground Railroad, "and hold my freedom only by setting the laws and ordinances which you respect in open defiance." Loguen had escaped from slavery in Davidson County, Tennessee, about twenty years before. He was, from the perspective of black abolitionists, "self-emancipated," but in the parlance of slave owners and catchers he remained a runaway slave who aided other fugitives, and his remark epitomized one obvious justification for disobeying laws and resisting government.[41] But many black leaders, including Loguen, sought the privileges of citizenship and protection of the laws, and in justifying acts of noncompliance and resistance, they tested and explored key issues related to moral obligation in a republican government. While some acknowledged almost no limits to the right of armed self-defense and insurrection, others identified themselves, even while violating laws, with republican civility and Christian obedience. In explorations of borderlines separating—and connecting—civil order and disobedient protest, they contributed to distinctive American traditions of civil disobedience at least as much as did some of their white contemporaries. In fact, it is impossible to understand the American tradition of civil disobedience without paying attention to the words and deeds of those whose citizenship was curtailed.[42] It is one thing to listen to a white reformer defending his actions as an individual expression of righteousness or independence of the state, quite another to listen to a voice like Loguen's, in some ways accepting the values of American republicanism but recognizing his own freedom as defined by defiance.

Black abolitionism is relatively unfamiliar, except to historians. Pre–World War II historiography, which described slaves as Sambos, had little positive to say about abolitionism in general and ignored black abolitionists almost entirely. Even when abolitionism's reputation improved, black abolitionists remained little known, and even black historians wrote of, at most, a "Negro component" or a "black abolitionist phalanx" in the broader antislavery movement.[43] In the 1960s the subject gained new importance and began to be discussed in very different terms. Jane H. Pease and William H. Pease observed that northern free blacks had "experienced the racist backlash" that followed the abolition of slavery in northern states; as a result, they formed institutions "to serve their race needs"; and as a further result, while they had "a link with the new abolitionism," they also had "a perspective on slavery which separated them from white abolitionists." A "very basic racial split" opened a "conceptual chasm [that] separated black from white and generated a distinct black abolitionism."[44] The concept of two abolitionisms was widely embraced by scholars, and among other influences, it shaped the now-indispensable *Black Abolitionist Papers*, in which it is reiterated as an organizing principle:

> By 1840 two distinct abolitionisms existed. Whites approached slavery and freedom on an abstract, ideological plane; blacks defined slavery and freedom in more concrete, experiential terms. White abolitionism drew largely upon evangelical theology and theories of universal reform; black abolitionism was grounded in political philosophy and shaped by daily experiences in a racist society. . . . Black abolitionists sought practical change, usually more concerned with results than tactics. Both wanted to end slavery, but unlike their white colleagues, blacks gave equal importance to the fight for racial equality. Black abolitionism extended, in [James McCune] Smith's words, "from the mere act of riding in public conveyances to the liberation of every slave."[45]

Those contrasts are open to dispute, and while the Peases and the *Black Abolitionist Papers* launched a project of scholarly investigation that is ongoing, it is unlikely that anyone today would draw the lines so sharply. No new account of the relations between black and white abolitionists has yet gained acceptance.[46]

Certainly the role of blacks in the American antislavery struggle, sometimes at the forefront, has long been underestimated. Without resolving all the issues raised in scholarship on northern black communities and movements, in this chapter I follow a balanced, well-informed survey by James and Lois Horton: there were over time many campaigns and organizations, some all-black, some better integrated than others, "where blacks and whites joined in a sometimes uneasy alliance."[47] Some blacks moved through progressions of stands on contested issues that the notion of two abolitionisms only obscures. Black leaders certainly debated in public whether movements for black uplift should ever exclude white participation, but they did not express forms of cultural nationalism that would be familiar to later generations. Their commitment to the ideology of the American Revolution and "the universal humanity of mankind" was steadfast despite disappointments and disagreements.[48]

In the practice of civil disobedience, black activists acted on their own, sometimes (as in giving aid to fugitives like Douglass and Jacobs) so secretly that their acts only partly fit the definitions of civil disobedience we are exploring. Sometimes they acted publicly, and in groups that included whites, as in protests against segregated conveyances. As national conflict over slavery intensified in the 1840s and 1850s, black and white abolitionists often joined in the same conflicts (though sometimes taking somewhat different actions to the same end). We look at such collaborations and differences in this chapter and the next. I will contend, in short, that black abolitionists stand among the originators of civil disobedience, perhaps not first in time but with an insistent and distinctive commitment to law breaking, if need be, in the name of justice, liberation, and reform.

Black abolitionists confronting oppressive laws sometimes placed their reliance on America's colonial religious past. It was to Quaker history that a woman named Zillah turned, for example, when the Pennsylvania legislature was considering a bill to prohibit black immigration, in particular to the story of a martyr who sang joyously while being whipped, felt "strengthened by an invisible power, and afterwards declared if she had been whipped to death, she should not have been dismayed. Earnestly have I prayed ... that a double portion of her humility and fortitude may be ours."[49] Blacks' expressions of fealty to divine law could be as uncompromising as Angelina Grimké's or that of any other white abolitionist. In an 1842 Thanksgiving Day sermon, "Covenants Involving Moral Wrong Are Not Obligatory Upon Man," J. C. W. Pennington asserted: "If my Saviour were again to be on earth, I should as soon go to Jerusalem, and there in obedience to the mandate of Jewish prejudice, betray him for thirty pieces of silver, as to be an agent in delivering on demand a poor fugitive from bondage."[50] Sometimes black leaders, stating a concern for public order matching that of moderate whites, recommended against mob action and insisted on peaceful responses to injustice.[51] But the resemblance between black and white abolitionists should not be overstated. Despite similar expressions of allegiance to higher law and respect for civil order, the Christianity of northern blacks was always to some degree segregated, and their political rights were curtailed. When they counseled peaceful compliance with legal penalties, the reason was more likely to be prudent acceptance of reality than a belief in the holiness or justice of submission.

Free blacks could not take citizenship for granted and thus had little reason to dismiss its importance with a morally superior gesture. As the example of Loguen illustrates, blacks found themselves poised at a boundary: sometimes their freedom came from defying the law, but in the longer run their protection must come from extending its reach. They stood at this boundary, moreover, at a moment when American republicanism offered very little official acceptance of law breaking, unlike later eras when styles of agitation and dissidence were open to experiment and negotiation. For any antebellum abolitionist to advocate law breaking required considerable courage and much effort of justification, for what they counseled was easily attacked as treason, conspiracy, and revolution. Jackson, remember, warned South Carolinians that they lived under a constitutional government, uniting the states, counting all inhabitants as citizens, and providing means for peaceful changing of the laws. In such a state the right of oppressed persons to break their "obligations to the Government" was "necessarily subjected to limitations." To be faithful to the memory of the "fathers" and preserve the "rich inheritance" they bequeathed in the form of a government of laws based on popular representation, the nation must put down and firmly punish open resistance to law.[52]

In equating resistance to law with treason, political leaders cautioned that citizens should operate within the political process and accept in good grace outcomes that displeased or injured them. But how did that logic apply to people who were not fully citizens? Would they be justified in taking up arms? That question arose sharply with regard to northern free blacks. Jackson, after all, had conceded that misrule, if "great and lasting,"[53] justified revolution, and sustained curtailment of the rights of citizenship might meet that standard. Although few American whites spent much time working through the limits of political obligation for blacks, the right of revolution might have appeared a plausible option for them, if they had not been so badly outnumbered and if so many of them had not sought acceptance within the political system. Faced with these limitations, they constituted a small but important group pressing American republicanism to modify the stark disjunction of obedience and revolution, to recognize a distinction between civil disobedience and treason, and to find ways of strengthening the law by extending citizenship.

It is hard to find a precise analogy to fit the condition of antebellum northern blacks. In some respects, they resembled a colonial people, except that they were a minority made to feel out of place in the land in which they found themselves. Perhaps they were more like migrants and "guest" workers in modern nations—nominally free, their condition defined by race, their rights severely impaired. But they also defined themselves in relation to slaves; some were fugitives, and many others accepted responsibility for aiding fugitives. Enduring partway between slavery and freedom, they were excluded by race from the suffrage in some states and subjected to discriminatory property qualifications in others. As the right to vote spread among white males, some states actually took it away from blacks.[54] In addition, laws and customs denied them civil rights to serve on juries or to give testimony in cases involving whites. Some states impeded black immigration or required surety bonds for black settlers. In the notorious *Dred Scott* decision (1857), Chief Justice Roger Taney built on such evidence to show that blacks were not citizens in any common understanding of the term and thus had "no rights which white men are bound to respect."

To deprivations of political rights must be added segregation in schools, churches, theaters, and public conveyances. Few blacks benefited from the economic opportunity of the Jacksonian era. Even white anti-slavery organizations, as blacks complained repeatedly, were reluctant to employ blacks in positions of responsibility. Widespread poverty only deepened as Irish and other immigrants took many of the marginal jobs for which unskilled blacks might have been eligible. Those few who acquired some wealth and achieved some respectability were detested by urban mobs as much as casual laborers competing with whites for jobs. Those who spoke out against northern prejudice and southern slavery were especially likely to encounter violence in the riots that became commonplace in Jacksonian cities.[55]

In view of the cruelties of life in a nation where even self-styled free states curtailed black citizenship, it is no surprise that some black leaders ridiculed patriotic depictions of America's mission to lead the world toward liberty. When the historian George Bancroft extolled America's world-historical role, the black educator William Watkins retorted that the world should not imitate a nation that tolerated the whipping of slaves and punished those who gave succor to fugitives.[56] In the 1820s and 1830s most black leaders opposed the program of the American Colonization Society to remove unenslaved blacks to Liberia: that was too clearly an expression of the racism that polluted American republicanism. But over time some thoughtful leaders came to regard emigration as the only possible response to slavery and racism. Watkins, for example, who in 1833 had led Baltimore blacks to declare the United States their "only *true and appropriate home*," recruited prospective settlers for the Haitian Emigration Bureau on the eve of the Civil War.[57] Others came to feel, especially in the 1850s, so discouraged by deprivations of citizenship that they debated and launched plans to resettle in Canada, the Caribbean, or West Africa. "Broad fertile Africa is the true home of the black man," was one retort to complaints about discrimination on railroads. "He can never conquer this land or the *prejudices . . .* of its inhabitants."[58]

In spite of threats and setbacks, however, many black leaders continued to insist that "we are American citizens. . . . 'Colored Americans' will do in the United States, but 'Africans' never."[59] Even in moments of severe discouragement, many expressed ardent patriotism. They praised black participation in the American Revolution; they repeatedly noted that Andrew Jackson had honored free black volunteers at the Battle of New Orleans as brave "fellow citizens."[60] When South Carolina's legislature in the 1830s demanded that northern states suppress antislavery societies, James Forten, Jr., called all Americans to "the standard of patriotism which their fathers reared," one that protected freedom of speech. "I love America; it is my native land; . . . I love the stars and stripes, emblem of our National Flag—and long to see the day when not a slave shall be found resting under its shadow."[61] In protest against the Fugitive Slave Law in 1850, leaders referred back to the Massachusetts of the Puritans as "our father land" and to England, where traditions of liberty had been nurtured, as "our mother country." How dare the Congress strike down habeas corpus and trial by jury, "those great bulwarks of human freedom, baptized by the blood, and sustained by the patriotic exertion of our English ancestors."[62] There are numerous examples of northern black leaders claiming descent from the Puritans, the revolutionaries, the founding generations of Americans. Unmistakably, they claimed more than the right of consent to the American political order; they claimed inclusion within the American people.[63] If his children were nothing more than "*little Africans*," one man asked whether "all white children in New England are any thing but a countless swarm of Englishmen, Scotchmen and Swiss."[64]

As the Peases, Hortons, and subsequent historians have noted, blacks gave crucial support to white antislavery endeavors, but they also

developed their own separate movements, which paid much greater attention to northern discrimination and the absence of true liberty even among
"free" blacks.[65] Programs to advance temperance, education, and self-
improvement went hand in hand with protests against Jim Crow and the
curtailment of civil rights. Some leaders went so far as to argue that alcohol
imposed a bondage equal to slavery.[66] There was some initial hope that
respectable blacks would combat prejudice and win their rights by the
example of their behavior. It soon became evident, however, that prejudice
against their color, rather than judgment of their character, caused blacks'
rights actually to shrink in the North while those of white males steadily
expanded. More than tactics were at stake in any case: to believe that self-
improvement must accompany full citizenship was consistent with
American republicanism, which once attempted to restrict the franchise to
respectable men and by the Jacksonian era regarded education and moral
uplift as essential to democracy's extension and survival.[67]

In accepting such beliefs, while pressing for civil rights and the suffrage,
blacks began to explore underlying tensions between political equality and
civic respectability and ventured in the direction of the paradoxical
American tradition of civil disobedience. On one hand, they repeatedly
encountered injustices in American laws, law enforcement, and social prejudice. The "hallmark of antebellum black radicalism," according to the
historian Vincent Harding, was "a careful, sober capacity to see the entire
American government, and the institutions and population which it represented, as the basic foe of any serious black struggle."[68] On the other hand,
they frequently clung to beliefs that civility and good character, even if they
could not earn fair treatment in the immediate future, might still be essential to the transformation of the republic. That was the spirit in which
Frederick Douglass concluded his second telling of his life, in 1855:
believing that "one of the best means of emancipating the slaves of the
south is to improve and elevate the character of the free colored people of
the north," he pledged to "labor in the future, as I have labored in the past,
to promote the moral, social, religious, and intellectual elevation of the free
colored people," while never ceasing to "advocate the great and primary
work of the universal and unconditional emancipation of my entire race."[69]
It was the spirit, too, of the Boston clothing merchant David Walker's fiery
anti-colonizationist *Appeal to the Coloured Citizens of the World* (1829),
hated in the South for its predictions of apocalyptic vengeance against
slaveholders and its implied incitements to the slaves. Walker, born free in

North Carolina because his mother was free, had traveled widely in the United States, and his view of citizenship, as his title showed, was universal, but what should also be noticed in the *Appeal* are clarion calls for mutual aid, education, moral improvement, and racial solidarity.[70]

Free blacks demonstrated their belief in the legitimacy of disobedience in their resistance to segregation, as a few examples may illustrate. In the 1855 version of his autobiography Frederick Douglass emphasized his own "personal rule" to refuse segregated seating on railroads despite the bruises and beatings conductors and brakemen inflicted on him. In one case where he clung tightly to particularly "luxuriant" seats, the conductor summoned a gang of men of "the baser sort" to drag him out, though with considerable damage to the seats. After many such confrontations, by his account, "the Jim Crow car" eventually was abandoned in New England.[71] Among many cases where blacks refused to be restricted to segregated sections of northern streetcars, perhaps the most notorious occurred when Elizabeth Jennings, a teacher on her way to church in lower Manhattan, defied a conductor's order to get off a streetcar. The conductor and driver dragged her off despite her insistence that she was "a respectable person" and it was wrong to "insult genteel persons." After suing the Third Avenue Railroad Company, she was awarded $225 and the right to ride.[72] When other blacks tried to translate this case into a victory against segregation on other New York lines, they met disappointment. The clergyman James Pennington, for example, was ejected from a white car of the Sixth Avenue line in 1856. He did not go easily but instead held on to the railing and was dragged beside the car with a conductor stomping on his hands. He also lost his legal complaint, which threatened, in the court's view, both the company's profits and the system of segregation in all city institutions.[73] In protests of this kind, black leaders always stressed the unfairness of discriminating against all blacks, regardless of their character. "All hope of reward for right conduct is cut off" by Jim Crow, Charles Lenox Remond in 1842 told a Massachusetts legislative committee considering a bill against segregation on public conveyances. "It is not true that we all behave alike ... and we claim a recognition of this difference."[74]

Robert Purvis, a prosperous Pennsylvania landowner, was furious when local school officials in 1853 excluded his children from public schools. He refused to pay his school tax, second largest in the town, and ridiculed a pious Quaker who directed him to a miserable shanty in a nearby town that served as a school for blacks. "To submit by voluntary payment of the demand is too great an outrage upon nature, and with spirit, thank God, unshackled by this, or any other wanton and cowardly act, I shall resist this tax, which before the unjust exclusion had always afforded me the highest gratification in paying. With no other than the best feeling towards yourself," he wrote the tax collector, "I am forced to this unpleasant position, in vindication of my rights and personal dignity, against an encroachment upon them as contemptibly mean, as it is infamously despotic." Local officials backed down, surely in part because they needed his substantial payments.[75] Purvis may be said to have blended courtesy and dignity with resistance in a manner showing how the civil disobedience tactic of tax refusal could go well beyond the church-state controversies of earlier times. Similar conclusions apply to boycotts that induced the Massachusetts legislature to mandate school integration in 1855.[76]

More ambiguous were the actions of the author-lecturer William Wells Brown, when he returned from England in 1854. Having forgotten, or so he said, how segregation worked in northern cities, Brown walked into three New York restaurants and was turned away at each. At a fourth he simply sat down, stabbed at a pickle and ate it, managed to get served, and paid for his dinner at the bar. When the bartender called him an impudent nigger and said he would have thrown him out except for fear of disturbing other customers, Brown claimed to have replied: "If you had, you would have taken the tablecloth, dishes and all with me. Now sir, look at me; whenever I come into your dining saloon, the best thing you can do is to let me have what I want to eat quietly." Brown's audiences enjoyed his swagger, but in this and similar stories, he exaggerated the ease with which Jim Crow could be overcome.[77] Douglass reported that when the captain of a steamer on the Hudson River recruited help to drive him from the dining cabin, other diners gave three cheers and applauded the steward uproariously "for having driven two ladies and one gentleman from the table, and deprived them of dinner."[78]

Calls for moral reform were usually associated with moral suasion as the preferred means of effecting reform, and that often meant, in turn, a reliance on nonviolent means of persuading or converting opponents and adversaries. Moral suasion was by no means exclusive to blacks; in fact it has sometimes been dismissed as a stance that white reformers led—or misled—blacks to adopt. More accurately, it was a view of the process of reform that developed out of evangelical Protestant and republican visions of social transformation in post-revolutionary America. In addition, black and white reformers learned much from the effectiveness of British reformers in winning an end to slavery in the British empire. In 1833 the founders of the American Anti-Slavery Society, including three blacks and four women, declared their rejection of violent means and insisted instead on ending slavery by "moral and political action"—by organizing local societies, circulating tracts and periodicals, enlisting support from clergy and journalists, favoring the products of free labor, and calling the nation to repentance. A year later, the same society praised people of color in New York who were improving their minds, educating their children, acquiring property, and behaving temperately, while noticing "with sorrow" that some others frequented dram shops, bought lottery tickets, and pursued other vices that, in effect, slowed "the moral and civil advancement of the colored people."[79]

It is important to note, however, that blacks were taking such stands prior to the formation of the American Anti-Slavery Society. As the scholar Tunde Adeleke has pointed out, a similar stand was taken at the First National Negro Convention in Philadelphia, in 1831, where black leaders "expressed faith in the redemptive power of moral suasion by pledging to work strenuously to 'encourage simplicity, neatness, temperance and economy in our habits' in order to disprove preconceived notions and prejudices." Similar discussions and resolutions in subsequent conventions led in 1835 to the formation of the American Moral Reform Society with its emphasis on "moral reform, intellectual culture, and persevering industry" as means of elevating blacks in northern society. Vigorous intellectual debate ensued over the causes of racism and the possibility of universal "brotherhood."[80]

Moral improvement was a continuing goal of black reformers, and moral suasion was a necessary tactic for those outside the political system. The issue of violence and retaliation, however, was more divisive to all abolitionists, but especially to blacks. At the center of controversy was the influence of William Lloyd Garrison and other white radical pacifists who took leading roles in the American Anti-Slavery Society. Blacks gave vital support to Garrison's newspaper the *Liberator*, and they honored him as a courageous and eloquent white ally. Few blacks followed Garrisonian pacifists to the extreme of denying the authority of human government and all other coercive institutions, but some regarded "non-resistance" as the appropriate method of protesting the violence of slavery and responding to proslavery hecklers and mobs of ruffians. The merchant William Whipper, a leader in the cause of moral reform, promoted a view like Garrison's in urging a reform society in 1837 to use methods of reason and persuasion rather than trying to beat down an enemy by superior force. "If I intimidate him I have made him a slave, while I reign a despot," and nothing is gained in the ensuing passion and resentment.[81] When Rev. Theodore Wright was insulted, kicked, and driven out of a meeting by a southern student at his alma mater, Princeton Seminary, he took pride in his own fidelity to "the comforting, but self-denying doctrine of non-resistance, so effective in curbing that vindictive spirit which naturally rises when suddenly assailed. Thankful am I that I was kept from lifting so much as a finger in self-defense, but continued my way out of the house." Though he did not retaliate, he used the experience as an illustration of the virulence of American racism.[82]

If nothing else, nonresistance helped to preserve self-control and personal dignity and thus signified the civility of its practitioners. In some versions it amounted to a personal form of passive aggression resembling the oxymoronic qualities of civil disobedience at the level of collective action. But was it effective in all instances, and could anyone really advise the slaves to be nonresistants? Only a few Garrisonians accepted the dogma that violence was inherently evil and thus unjustifiable even in pursuit of good ends. Whipper praised the examples of peace martyrs throughout history and identified their modern successors as the northern abolitionists, who had been "beaten and stoned, mobbed and persecuted from city to city, and never returned evil for evil, but submissively, as a sheep brought before the shearer, have they endured scoffings and scourges for the cause's sake, while they prayed for their persecutors."[83] William Powell, who ran a sailors' boardinghouse in New Bedford, thought the nonresistance doctrine "heaven-born" and joined the Garrisonians' radical peace organization. But he removed his family to England during the 1850s and avoided the most searching debates over violent means.[84]

Blacks expressed many doubts about nonresistance. In 1838 Augustus Hanson, an Episcopal clergyman, wrote Garrison to insist that he had done nothing wrong in ignoring Garrison's advice and defending himself with minimal force against an assailant, probably on a streetcar or railway.[85] In 1841, under the pseudonym "Sidney," a black leader, perhaps Henry

Highland Garnet, dismissed Whipper's appeals to nonresistance. Oppressors never retreat, he maintained, until they see that their victims know their rights and will fight for them.[86] A majority of black leaders probably agreed with William Wells Brown, who declared in 1848 that he had no wish to see "scenes of blood and carnage," but "if a favorable opening should occur to the slave population of this country, he could hardly subdue himself to counsel non-resistance, or to act upon its principles himself." The year was significant: the European revolutions of 1848 emboldened blacks to speak more freely of their support of armed uprisings than they had during Nat Turner's rebellion in 1831 or in subsequent years.[87]

Five years earlier, as we have previously noticed, Garnet had told slaves that it was "sinful in the extreme" to submit voluntarily and passively to enslavement. "You had far better all die—*die immediately*, than live slaves, and entail your wretchedness upon your posterity. . . . There is not much hope of Redemption without the shedding of blood. If you must bleed, let it all come at once—rather, *die freemen, than live to be slaves*." That speech was an unusual utterance of a suppressed thought. It criticized slaves—most directly, the males—for being too patient, for tamely submitting to the sexual exploitation of their daughters and wives. "In the name of God we ask, are you men?" Its call for widespread insubordination (tempered by considerations of expediency), envisioned something more like mass civil disobedience than armed rebellion. But it did not rule out violence, sanctified in a heritage of heroic slave rebels approved by providence. Still, the speech was treated as so controversial that the Colored Men's Convention suppressed it until 1848, when its publication together with Walker's *Appeal* was subsidized by John Brown.[88] The following year, Garnet's thought emerged again when Thomas Van Rennsellaer took satirical note of Louisiana's official expression of support for European revolutionaries and urged slaves to rise up with confidence in the governor's sympathy. Turning more serious, he added: "We do not tell you to murder the slaveholders, but we do advise you to refuse longer to work without pay. Make up your minds to die, rather than bequeath a state of slavery to your posterity."[89]

Without doubt, many northern blacks believed in a right of self-defense by any means, including violence. They voiced this belief most clearly in discussions of aid to fugitives. After New York police officers in 1836 arrested a "respectable free colored man," whom the city recorder swiftly "pronounced to be a SLAVE," a leader of the Vigilance Committee, David Ruggles, issued this warning: "We have no protection in law. . . . [W]e must look to our own safety and protection from kidnappers! remembering that 'self-defence is the first law of nature.' "[90] Views like these were somewhat controversial, even among blacks, before 1848 (Ruggles was removed as secretary of the New York Vigilance Committee for speaking and acting too indiscreetly). As Vincent Harding has pointed out, National Negro Conventions repeatedly sanctioned civil disobedience in aid of fugitives from 1835 onward.[91]

After the enactment of the new Fugitive Slave Law in 1850, no advantage derived from remaining cautious about asserting rights that whites took for granted. Thousands of northern blacks fled the United States. Among those who remained, Purvis declared his readiness "to kill every oppressor" chasing fugitives. Douglass pronounced "two or three dead slave holders" the best way to combat the law. The Baptist clergyman William P. Newman renounced nonresistance in favor of a "fixed and changeless purpose to kill any so-called man who attempts to enslave me or mine, . . . though it be Millard Fillmore himself. To do this, in defence of personal liberty . . . would be an act of the highest virtue, and white Americans must be real hypocrites if they say not to it—amen!"[92] Other events of the 1850s only deepened repudiation of nonviolence. Edward Scott, a Providence pastor who was self-emancipated, asked, "How can fugitives join the Peace Society, with Judge Taney at their back?"[93]

Atrocities like the Fugitive Slave Law, author and Congregationalist minister Samuel Ringgold Ward proclaimed at Faneuil Hall, left no recourse except "the right of Revolution, and if need be, that right we will, at whatever cost, most sacredly maintain." It was, especially for a fugitive slave like Ward, a short step from the right of self-defense to the right of revolution.[94] William H. Newby, a daguerreotypist and editor, told a California audience: "I would hail the advent of a foreign army upon our shores, if that army provided liberty to me and my people in bondage. This may be thought ultra, but in saying it I am influenced by the same motives and spirit which influenced [Patrick] Henry, when he said to the burgesses of Virginia, 'give me liberty, or give me death!' "[95]

Such reasoning was not at all abstract to the community of fugitives and free blacks who lived in Lancaster County, Pennsylvania, in a condition of constant jeopardy and conflict with gangs of local whites and slave-catchers from nearby states. Their self-emancipated leader, William Parker, had "formed a resolution that I would assist in liberating every one within my reach at the risk of my life, and that I would devise some plan for their entire liberation." One night in September 1851, as a Maryland slave owner, together with his son, other friends and family, a federal marshal, and a Philadelphia policeman approached in pursuit of fugitives whom Parker was sheltering, a Quaker neighbor came to Parker and urged him "not to resist the Fugitive Slave Law by force of arms, but to escape to Canada." According to a subsequent interview with Frederick Douglass, Parker

> replied that if the laws protected colored men as they did white men, he too would be non-resistant and not fight, but would appeal to the laws. "But," said he, "the laws for personal protection are not made for us, and we are not bound to obey them. If a fight occurs I want the whites [like his neighbor] to keep away. They have a country and may obey the laws. But we have no country."

The next morning, in a brief battle known as "the Christiana riot," or sometimes "the Christiana Tragedy," the slave owner was killed, his son wounded, and the posse routed. Parker and the young men he aided escaped to Canada.[96] One historian compares the event to the Boston Tea Party; another calls it a story that "goes to the heart of American slavery."[97] It was certainly a story that revealed limits to the obedience to law that could be expected, in the modern world, of those who are not fully citizens—who have no country.

Parker appeared to suggest that if the laws had protected him, he would not have turned to arms. Blacks who did not share his jeopardy usually posed the alternatives less starkly. Even as they complained angrily about lack of support and sympathy from whites, black leaders frequently acknowledged the benefits of law and imagined a day when all would be citizens enjoying equal protection.[98] This may be one implication of the case of Nelson Hackett, who had taken his master's gold watch, overcoat, horse, and saddle when he fled from Arkansas to Canada West. His indictment for grand larceny was used to justify extradition to Detroit and thence back to slavery. The case provoked an international outcry, but it is hard to believe that Hackett derived much comfort from knowing, as Detroit's Colored Vigilance Committee suggested, that his fame resounded in the House of Lords. Some abolitionists might have thought that his larceny was excused by his owner's previous expropriation of his labor and liberty, but the committee rejected that position. Since "all had been legally done," and "he was a felon," as their lawyer determined from examining the papers, they decided "it was better to let him go back to the prison house of slavery, than to bring a reproach upon the cause of emancipation by instituting a suit on his behalf." Perhaps they were simply sensitive to the way in which previous acts of violence had discredited antislavery activity and led to a curfew on Detroit's black residents. In any case, they repeatedly emphasized that they had "learned from experience, the superiority of moral and intellectual power, guided by calm, and deliberate reason, over that of ignorance and physical force, guided by heated and inflamed passion." They were determined to "secure justice for our own people" but also sought "to impress upon their minds the great necessity of observing the law and becoming good and peaceable citizens."[99]

Certainly, Garrisonian blacks in responding to the violence of the 1850s praised a future rule of law. The lecturer H. Ford Douglas, for example, praised John Brown's single-minded dedication to ending slavery, but he added: "I am not an advocate for insurrection; I believe the world must be educated into something better and higher than this before we can have perfect freedom, either for the black man or the white."[100] Perhaps the point may seem too obvious. What else could black leaders say except that the law should be changed so that it protected all Americans equally? Many were clear, especially in light of Chief Justice Taney's words on the rights of blacks and after the government began to enforce the Fugitive Slave Law of 1850, that their self-respect depended on defying, not obeying, the law. Douglas went on: "What is the object of Government? . . . It is to make men; and if it fails in this—as your government has done—it fails in everything and is no government." Blacks asked no special favors but only "the same rights, legally," as whites and the same opportunities to improve themselves.[101] Robert Purvis made the relationship of blacks to existing law very clear: "I never will stultify or disgrace myself by eulogizing a government that tramples me and all that are dear to me in the dust."[102]

Loguen's similar statement equating freedom with disobedience came during a bitter disagreement with a white minister who denied permission to collect funds for the Underground Railroad from his pulpit. Loguen's extensive comments exemplify ways in which blacks availed themselves of canonical heroes and texts to give specificity to the universal, but vague and unrealized, precepts of republican ideology and thus to justify disobedience to law. The white clergyman, antislavery by his own lights, viewed it as his "duty as a citizen and a Christian" to comply with the law of the land, and he quoted many lines of Scripture associating earthly rulers with the ordinations of God. Loguen's reply was angry and eloquent:

> What if Moses and Aaron, and Daniel and Elijah had adopted this wretched doctrine. . .! Why, your argument strikes at all righteousness, and blots out the only feature of the Bible which makes it merciful, sublime and Godlike. When commanded to teach no more in Christ's name, the apostle said, "we ought to obey God rather than men." . . . It was through disobedience to the Kings of Egypt and Babylon, and other false rulers, that the government of Jehovah was preserved in the Jewish dispensation. It is owing to such disobedience in the Christian dispensation that it has been preserved ever since, and that light and knowledge, liberty and religion, progress and civilization exist on earth. . . . Will you make me believe that the villain who raised his gory lash from my bleeding body, and who now holds it over the backs of my poor mother, brothers and sisters——that the scoundrels who made and execute the fugitive slave law, who chase my famishing countrymen through the States, are the ministers of the most High God, and that we ought to submit quietly to be tortured, and robbed, and murdered, "for the Lord's sake," and if [we] resist them we must be damned?

"Sir," he continued, "you don't understand the Scriptures. The very fact that there are 'higher powers ordained of God,' implies that there are lower powers ordained of Hell—that the former only are to be recognized as 'the Powers that be,' and the latter to be recognized as no Powers at all."[103] The contradiction between these two readings of the sacred past, one obliging the faithful to comply with earthly authority, the other liberating the righteous to stand against evil, was part and parcel of what David Brion Davis has termed "the problem of slavery" in Western culture.[104] But it would be hard to find a stronger statement than Loguen's, in all the years of the slavery controversy in the United States, of the duty of disobedience.

Loguen's remarks place his activities in aid of fugitives near the center of an American civil disobedience tradition. Yet Loguen differed from many successors in two ways: as we observed at the outset, he expressed absolutely no respect for American law in general; and though he was originally a Garrisonian, by the 1850s he had little aversion to violent resistance. He was indicted for his part in the rescue of William "Jerry" McHenry in Syracuse in 1851, and he boasted of assisting nearly fifteen hundred fugitives in the 1850s. During these rescues, he considered armed violence justifiable but went to some lengths to cooperate with authorities afterward. After the "Jerry" rescue he refused bail and thus escaped punishment because his arrest would have created an uproar. He recruited fighters for John Brown's raid on Harpers Ferry in 1859.[105] The nation did not bar him from becoming a clergyman and a lecturer, but it kept him in a limbo of noncitizenship and jeopardized the liberty of his fellows. That in the end is what differentiated him from contemporaries and successors who professed to love the law while defying it.

Few other blacks spoke exactly in Loguen's terms of traditional Christian justifications for disobedience, though many said generally that slavery violated the laws of God. For the most part, blacks appealed to the right of revolution, which even Andrew Jackson had conceded was the recourse for people convinced they had no protection from the regime in power. To this way of thinking, acts of disobedience were one set of options available to people who might legitimately resort to any means that promised victory over their oppressors. They must not even appear to be submissive; that would only deepen whites' prejudice that blacks were unfit to win their liberty. A stance of submissive nonresistance did not really exist for blacks who felt that they had suffered too many blows and that it was time to strike back. The sword, the physician John S. Rock told a Boston audience in 1860, was "no doubt the method by which the freedom of blacks will be brought about in this country. It is a severe method; but to severe ills it is necessary to apply severe remedies."[106] A few years later, Rock was recruiting for the famous Fifty-Fourth Massachusetts Regiment.

Definitions of civil disobedience frequently insist upon a commitment to nonviolence. Some may be uneasy about locating at the core of a civil disobedience tradition episodes and movements that are not purely pacifistic. The words and actions of Garrisonian nonresistants like Whipper and Wright raise no difficulties, but most black leaders, including Loguen, were less categorical in rejecting violence. Although the black abolitionists' calls for revolution may perhaps be criticized by those who define civil disobedience doctrinairely as "passive" resistance in what became one legacy of Garrisonian nonresistance, one should recall Mohandas K. Gandhi's teaching, often cited by Martin Luther King, Jr., that "if cowardice is the only alternative to violence, it is better to fight."[107] Surely not everyone would agree with Gandhi's prescription that only those who *revere* the law are entitled to disobey the law (though antebellum black leaders had praised the rule of law even when deploring American injustice).[108] Those blacks who contemplated insurrection included artisans, clergymen, physicians, educators, authors, men and women who appreciated civil order—but they were not fully citizens, and they spoke and acted in behalf of slaves. It is hard to see how any white critics could have denied the claim that if their liberty were similarly curtailed they would not be constrained by teachings of nonviolence.

The point to emphasize is that some antebellum blacks, in an era when governmental leaders offered no middle ground between revolution and submission, and when some contemporaries saw their only hope in emigration, showed remarkable creativity in finding ways of protesting against law, even violating law, without forsaking the quest for citizenship. Instances of tax refusal, school boycotts, railway sit-ins, and aid to fugitives may appear familiar enough in retrospect, but at that time they carried the risk of being defined as treason.[109] These efforts by black abolitionists, joined by some white allies, surely influenced other versions of civil disobedience, some of them more abstract or more polite and proper, that we will turn to next. Religious conviction and the wish to fulfill ideas of citizenship continued to blend in powerful and intricate ways long after the language of nonresistance and the right of revolution began to fade into disuse. Black abolitionists stand as exemplars warning against dogmatic definitions of civil disobedience and reminding us of the importance of citizenship, and curtailments of citizenship, in shaping American reform traditions.

4

Conflicts of Law in the Age of Reform

Must the citizen ever for a moment, or in the least degree, resign his conscience to the legislator? Why has every man a conscience, then? I think that we should be men first, and subjects afterward. It is not desirable to cultivate a respect for the law, as much as for the right. The only obligation which I have a right to assume is to do at any time what I think right.[1]

These words by Henry David Thoreau, from the essay often called "Civil Disobedience," is one of his many highly quotable dismissals of the notion that schools should teach and society should expect what Lincoln later called "reverence for the laws."[2] Another of the best-known quotations showing Thoreau's attitude toward law occurred, supposedly, when Ralph Waldo Emerson visited his fellow townsman during his night in jail and asked, as Howard Zinn has related the story, " 'What are you doing in there?' [and] it was reported that Thoreau replied, 'What are you doing out there?' " The awkwardly passive formulation may be a way of signifying that the quotation is probably apocryphal. Other writers, like the libertarian Wendy McElroy, preface the story by saying, "According to some accounts," which is true enough, but none of them date from Thoreau's or Emerson's lifetime. Peter Gay is on firm ground by saying, "We all know the colloquy," as in recent decades we do. Michael Walzer repeats the story as true: when Thoreau "greeted the visiting Emerson with the famous question, 'What are you doing out there?' he clearly implied the existence of a common obligation."[3] I am pretty sure that I first read about the exchange sometime in the 1960s in a column about sit-inners or war protesters by Murray Kempton in the *New York Post.* The two-act drama *The Night Thoreau Spent in Jail* was widely read in high schools and staged in colleges and other playhouses in the 1970s. In San Diego the actor playing Thoreau was out on bail for a charge of campus disruption. The play remains one of few popular works exploring the different personalities and philosophies of Thoreau and Emerson.[4] Nevertheless, the confrontation quoted in all these works, and numerous others, almost certainly never occurred. Neither man recorded it. Thoreau was not in jail long enough to converse with visitors, and he included in his famous essay a "whole history" of his night in prison with no mention of any such conversation or visitor. He defended his judgment in going to jail: "Under a government which imprisons any unjustly, the true place for a just man is also a prison." So perhaps he recognized a need to justify his act. McElroy, Gay, Walzer, and Zinn drew interesting insights from the nonevent, if that is all it is, and the play was successful in many productions across the country. It is unlikely that the story will cease to be familiar even if untrue. In this chapter we will focus on views of law and obedience in Thoreau's time, the age of reform, but we must remember that much of his historical reputation was not secured until a century later.

Thoreau never used the term *civil disobedience* in the period in which he wrote, thought, and acted, and neither did any of his contemporaries, even as they practiced or opposed or debated the rights and wrongs, dangers and necessity, of what we call by that name. The famous essay on civil disobedience started as a lecture in January and February 1848 at the Concord Lyceum on "The Rights and Duties of the Individual in Relation to Government." It was published in essay form in May 1849 as "Resistance to Civil Government." Perhaps that title sounded too much like secession; in any case, it was changed in 1866 in a posthumous collection of Thoreau's essays to "Civil Disobedience." There is no direct evidence that Thoreau authorized the change of title. So the essay has reverted to its old title in most scholarly editions since 1973, though not without a little controversy. Why would the editor of the posthumous volume have changed the title to a phrase that was apparently unknown during the author's lifetime? A few other editorial changes have been eliminated in the supposedly authoritative edition because of the lack of provable authorial intention. Why not the altered title, which became widely familiar decades later as Thoreau's work gained a readership it never had in his lifetime?[5] All three of the titles, as we understand them, place Thoreau's essay at the center of a great issue and an increasing practice of the era in which he wrote. It would only be misleading to suggest that disobedients used the phrase *civil disobedience* or had foresight into the tradition that would ensue.

In a passage on refusing allegiance to Massachusetts and incurring the penalty for violating a law, Thoreau linked his essay to a heritage of religious struggles: "Some years ago, the State met me in behalf of the church, and commanded me to pay a certain sum toward the support of a clergyman whose preaching my father attended, but never I myself." Thoreau "condescended," as he put it, to comply with the requirement of what was called a certificate bow—that is, a tacit acknowledgment of the town's authority accompanied by a signed request not to be counted a member of the Congregational church. That sufficed to secure an exemption from paying for future support, but the current charge remained in effect. "Pay it," said the state, "or be locked up in the jail." Despite his refusal, "unfortunately, another man saw fit" to pay it for him.[6] Mention of the event, which occurred in 1840, gives him occasion to wonder why "the priest" shouldn't equally be taxed to support a schoolmaster like him and to muse about constructing a list of all the organizations he declined to belong to or subsidize. But its purpose mostly is to set context for his subsequent tax refusal starting in 1842 and leading to a night in jail in 1846, partly in protest against the Mexican War but in fact a gesture with much larger implications for his view of the individual and society.

According to the historian William G. McLoughlin, Thoreau had acted in 1840 in the tradition of spiritual voluntarism championed in the mass protests of Baptist "martyrs" during the previous century. When he later went to jail, he redirected the dissent from the state's established church to society's conventional morality. It cannot be said that Thoreau expressed as much respect for law in general as Baptists, Quakers, or Universalists had shown when they resisted unfair religious taxation. Thoreau may actually have distorted his first tussle with government over taxes. As McLoughlin noted, it was not just his father's membership but also his own baptism as an infant that subjected him to church support until he withdrew in writing. But the statutes had changed enough that Thoreau might have won his case if a friend hadn't paid for him before his case came to court. Other scholars question Thoreau's account of the threat he faced: the procedures for signing out of church support were well known, and imprisonment was an improbable penalty. Why did Thoreau tell the story as he did? The most likely motive was self-dramatization. As one scholar observes: "Had he noted that he was just another one of many score who had been signing off the First Parish rolls, he would have undercut the persona he assumed in the text. The 'state' would have dwindled in its force, and he would have appeared less heroic. And that reduction of the first act of tax resistance might have affected his account of the subsequent ones."[7]

Readers may detect something slippery in Thoreau's account of his tax refusal beginning in 1842, his 1846 jailing, and arguments made in the essay published in 1849. Laurence Rosenwald (an admirer of Thoreau and a tax resister in his own right) states some of the problems clearly: if his objection was to the Mexican War and slavery, as the essay sometimes indicates, the taxes refused would need to have been collected specifically to fund the war and protect slave property. The federal government did not collect direct taxes for the war or any other purpose. The poll tax Thoreau refused to pay consisted of county and local taxes and only once in the decade of the 1840s included a portion for the state government. Massachusetts's personal liberty law forbade the use of state funds to implement federal fugitive slave laws. "Most of the time, then, Thoreau was refusing to pay tax to Middlesex County and the town of Concord, neither of which could plausibly be called the slave's government."[8] Thoreau professed willingness to pay the highway tax "because I am as desirous of being a good neighbor as I am of being a bad subject." Further, in a passage that undercuts much that precedes it, he simplifies his specific justification for tax refusal and substitutes an anarchistic state of mind:

> It is for no particular item in the tax-bill that I refuse to pay it. I simply wish to refuse allegiance to the State, to withdraw and stand aloof from it effectually. I do not care to trace the course of my dollar, if I could, till it buys a man, or a musket to shoot one with,—the dollar is innocent,—but I am concerned to trace the effects of my allegiance. In fact, I quietly declare war with the State, after my fashion, though I will still make what use and get what advantage of her I can, as is usual in such cases.[9]

Even as he traces the shifts and revisions, Rosenwald defends them as understandable: "In 1842, it seemed right to refuse taxes as a means of separating oneself from government, in response to the nature of government generally. In 1849, after the annexation of Texas and the Mexican War, i.e., after a clear demonstration of the expansive power of the slave interests, it still seemed right to refuse taxes, but now as a means of engaging with government, to combat those interests."[10] In an excellent essay Daniel Walker Howe also emphasizes that Thoreau had changed his mind and at some point realized that he could use his tax refusal and jailing (an "insignificant" or "trivial episode") as a hinge to a broad rejection of the war, a proslavery national government, and indeed any government that violated moral conscience.[11] Fair enough. But Thoreau's essay has become so familiar, so widely studied, and so often used in attempts to understand, define, and justify civil disobedience that the inconsistent and ambiguous passages at its core may still be considered unfortunate.

Despite allusions to the tithe and past church-state struggles, Thoreau's thoughts and actions were not shaped by the evangelical great awakenings. He was deeply influenced by his Harvard education, especially what he learned about classical languages and moral philosophy. That may seem surprising in light of what we know about his books of nature travel and especially his greatest work, *Walden*, which sometimes bears the subtitle *Life in the Woods* (even after the author dropped it). But throughout his journeys and his time in his cabin he worked on translations from classical authors, sometimes inserting them in his journal and transferring them to his books and essays. An important example for our purposes occurs in the "Monday" chapter of *A Week on the Concord and Merrimack Rivers*, when after discussion of the shallowness of reformers, he passes through his experiences of taxation and imprisonment and notes the officiousness of those employed by "the State." He edges toward the subject of civil disobedience by praising "Conscience" and a vital religion honoring the "absolutely right" that transcends historical and cultural distinctions. Exploring what a modern scholar has called "the fundamental assumption in the doctrine of civil disobedience," Thoreau quotes extensively from scenes in Sophocles's *Antigone:* first the heroine's dismissal of her sister who will not violate King Creon's edict forbidding, on pain of death, performance of burial rites for their brother. Ismene will "obey those who are placed in office, for to do extreme things is not wise" and "to act in opposition to [the chorus of] the citizens I am by nature unable." "Be such as seems good to you," Antigone replies. When brought before Creon, however, Antigone makes clear why she has dared to transgress his edicts.

It was not Zeus who proclaimed these to me, nor Justice who dwells with the gods below; it was not they who established these laws among men. Nor did I think that your proclamations were so strong, as being a mortal, to be able to transcend the unwritten and immovable laws of the gods. For not something now and yesterday, but forever these live, and no one knows from what time they appeared. I was not about to pay the penalty of violating these to the gods, fearing the presumption of any man. For I well knew that I should die, and why not? even if you had not proclaimed it.[12]

Unlike modern *civil* disobedients, Antigone behaves utterly on her own, in a "terrifying vacuum," as one classicist has described her isolation.[13] That apolitical role was not foreign to the Thoreau who acknowledges no obligation except to do what he believes is right.

But that is not the whole story. One of the extraordinary things about Thoreau's essay is its commitment to the cultivation and use of conscience as an instrument of moral reform.[14] Thoreau had encountered William Paley's *Principles of Moral and Political Philosophy* (1785) as a textbook at Harvard. He kept the book in his library and in his famous essay discusses it at greater length than any other work, though it figures mostly as an authority on the conventional morality that he rejects. The title of one of Paley's chapters, "Of the Duty of Civil Obedience, as stated in Christian Scriptures," provides a clue to the invention of the contrary term *civil disobedience* later on. Paley had been a useful whipping boy for previous philosophers, and Thoreau uses him more as a foil than as a source. He rejects Paley's equation of civil obligation with "expediency" in statements such as that "so long as the established government cannot be resisted or changed without public inconveniency, it is the will of God that the established government be obeyed, and no longer." Paley overlooks cases in which "a people, as well as an individual, must do justice, cost what it may. . . . This people must cease to hold slaves, and to make war with Mexico, though it cost them their existence as a people." In fact, he has less to say about Paley than about his neighbors' complacency encouraged by participation in the rituals of voting, which leave such vital issues as war and slavery to "the mercy of chance" or "the power of the majority." His strongest statements of civil disobedience have anti-democratic overtones: "Unjust laws exist: shall we be content to amend them, and obey them until we have succeeded, or shall we transgress them at once?" Or perhaps most famously: if institutionalized injustice "requires you to be an agent of injustice to another, then, I say, break the law. Let your life be a counter-friction to stop the machine." In rejecting Paley's appeal to public convenience, he proceeds from his failure to pay his poll tax and his night in jail to advising abolitionists to withdraw their support from the state instead of waiting to persuade a majority to join them. It is the writing and lecturing, rather than the now-famous episode at the essay's center, that creates an imagined act of civil disobedience and invokes an imaginary nation or at least an audience of civil disobedients.[15] Perhaps he might more persuasively have referred to his provision of shelter to fugitive slaves, as he does in passing in *Walden* (not published until 1854), or aiding their transition to Canada, as it has been shown that he did at least twice in the 1850s.[16] But the details are necessarily shadowy, and the essay has not lacked influence in later times without them.

In choosing the title "Resistance to Civil Government" Thoreau highlighted his opposition to "non-resistance." That may seem strange because the nonresistance movement has been counted as a source of Thoreau's thought. In January 1841 he had debated at the Concord Lyceum on the subject "Is it ever proper to offer forcible resistance?" He took the affirmative, while his friend Bronson Alcott took the negative; a month later, the lyceum sponsored a lecture on nonresistance by a prominent advocate, Adin Ballou, who fielded many questions and objections.[17] It was, for a time at least, a subject of high interest. Indeed, Thoreau was closely associated with Alcott, his Concord neighbor, a nonresistant who went to jail for his convictions and as an abolitionist was identified with the radical immediatist positions associated with William Lloyd Garrison. But Thoreau was never a pacifist, and in the essay on civil disobedience distinguishes himself from "those who call themselves no-government men"—a group that would surely include Garrison, Alcott, and other nonresistants—and calls instead for "*at once* a better government."

What was the meaning of Jesus's teachings, such as "Resist not evil" (Matthew 5:39) and "Recompense not evil for evil" (Romans 12:17)? Nonresistants took these precepts as binding on Christians, particularly in the modern era of accelerated conversions and the imminence of the "good time coming." The New England Non-Resistance Society (meant to have much broader application than the regional name suggested) arose from the dissatisfaction of ardent pacifists in the American Peace Society, which opposed only wars of aggression.[18] All wars, said the nonresistants, were defensive in the eyes of their perpetrators. The society also drew its original members from radical founders of the American Anti-Slavery Society whose commitment to moral suasion went beyond tactics and led them to nonviolent and antipolitical positions that others considered too controversial. Within the haven of a separate society, created in 1838, the radicals could claim the right to advance their pacifist positions without offense to other abolitionists and potential converts. Garrison, whose independently run *Liberator* made him the most prominent abolitionist, was free to print pacifist and other radical columns, though critics charged they disadvantaged abolitionism in public opinion. (Indeed, defenders of slavery pointed to the nonresistants as examples of the threat to civil order posed by antislavery.) Besides dissent in the peace and abolitionist movements, nonresistance had other sources. It appealed to enthusiasts who split off from old denominations they accused of moving too slowly for social reform at a time of escalating conversions in revivals. The protests of Transcendentalists within Unitarianism were a good example of mounting dissatisfaction with social and doctrinal conservatism in old institutions and denominations. Sometimes new movements of "come-outers" ("come ye out from among them; be ye separate" [2 Corinthians 6:17]) departed from old denominations that advanced too slowly on doctrinal issues and social reforms like temperance and abolitionism and paid insufficient heed to the quest for personal holiness. These currents could lead to the foundation of new communities with improved ways of living; several of these, especially the Hopedale Community, led by Adin Ballou, were explicitly founded as vanguards of nonresistance.

All nonresistants were free to violate laws peacefully and thus participate in nonviolent acts of civil disobedience. Hopedale gave haven to men and women escaping from slavery as well as to the slave rescuer called the Man with a Branded Hand. Since the community was expected to concentrate abolitionist commitment in one location, it may have provided a base for forays to break Jim Crow laws and practices; still, there is surprisingly little record of civil disobedience.[19] In general, however, the radical wing of abolitionism, including the nonresistants, produced fewer instances of civil disobedience than might be expected. Theoretically, nonresistants were not supposed to vote since even republican governments assumed powers to commit violent, unchristian acts. But there was no prohibition on taking interest in the outcomes of elections, especially since Garrison and his close associates maintained that their nonresistance advocacy was separate from their antislavery commitments. In the *Liberator* (but not the

Non-Resistant) they could urge citizens to vote against proslavery congressmen even while refusing to vote in their own right.[20] To critics, this trying to have it both ways ultimately weakened the abolitionist cause. To Garrisonians, it provided a way of living in and reforming the world without sacrificing their commitment to divine truth.

Of all the nonresistants the one least encumbered by ambiguity was Bronson Alcott, who entertained no shibboleths about representative government. "Vox populi, vox diaboli," he declared.[21] In January 1843 he was arrested for not paying his poll tax. An English friend, Charles Lane, described the incident in the *Liberator* under the heading "State Slavery . . . Dawn of Liberty." His action was based on long-held determination not to be "a voluntary party" to a government that threatened imprisonment in order to enforce tax payment. A tax collector had been appointed and given the authority, without appeal or judgment, to "snatch a man from his home" and lock him up for an indefinite period. In other words, Alcott's issue was not his poverty, state policies, or the amount demanded—it was the immorality of compulsory taxation. Lane drew a sorrowful picture of the tax collector (the same man who later arrested Thoreau) interrupting Alcott as he educated his little children, giving him time to pack a few personal items, carting him off, and then making his prisoner wait a couple of hours while he looked for the jailor who was not home. Finally, the "constable-collector" announced that the prisoner was free because someone else ("the very personification of the state") had paid the tax and the costs of the legal process. To this narrative Lane added several reflections. Alcott's protests were not based on indifference to purposes such as education that the state supported. They were founded instead on "the moral instinct which forbids every moral being, to be a party, either actively or permissively, to the destructive principles of power and might over peace and love." He drew an analogy to religious liberty. "Every one," he said, can see "the Church is wrong when it comes to men with the Bible in one hand and the sword in the other." Was it not "equally diabolical for the State to do so?"[22]

In December Lane himself was arrested for tax refusal and held briefly until someone paid for him. Alcott went on refusing to pay his tax and at least once, in 1846, was threatened with sale of his land to pay it. Let the state put its hand into his pocket if it insisted, but he was not going to do it himself "on its behalf." Needless to say, not everyone in Concord approved. After an "earnest talk" with Ralph Waldo Emerson on "civil powers and institutions," Alcott reported that the esteemed Emerson described Thoreau's tax refusal as "mean and skulking and in bad taste."[23] No doubt others would have questioned the civility of such disobedience, especially if, like Thoreau's, it originated in negligence and was resolved by others paying the taxes or fines.

Sometimes Joseph "Old Jew" Palmer, "the man with a beard," who resided for a while and invested in Alcott's small Fruitlands community, is counted within this circle of "civil resistants." In 1830 he used a penknife to fight off four men who attempted to shave him by force. He was charged with assault and refused to pay his fine or his upkeep (though he was by no means poor) and stayed in jail, refusing to cooperate, until he was carried out.[24] I would count this more as an instance of eccentricity than as civil disobedience. Neither Alcott, Lane, nor Thoreau behaved as Palmer had done.

Clearer examples of nonresistant disobedience are found if we turn our search away from Garrison's Boston and Transcendentalist Concord and look farther north to abolitionist come-outers in northern Massachusetts towns and in the Granite State of New Hampshire. Their activities were set down almost as they happened by Nathaniel Rogers, a journalist whose "free and uncalculating spirit" was much admired by Thoreau. "We do not know of another notable and public instance of such pure, youthful, and hearty indignation at all wrong." Often Rogers accompanied the reformers, preachers, and performers whose confrontations with authorities and people he dashed down in accounts in his *Herald of Freedom*. Many years later, they were retold, more ponderously, by a veteran abolitionist, Parker Pillsbury, who viewed them as a reenactment of the acts of Christ's original apostles after the Pentecost as recounted in the fifth book of the New Testament. It is uncertain how literally or metaphorically he regarded these as a new chapter of "Acts." In the 1840s there was considerable feeling—we have seen it in Angelina Grimké, for example—that purging the sin of slavery that infested Christian churches was an essential step in the millennial project signified by widening spheres of revival. By the 1880s the usage may have turned more metaphorical or nostalgic about holy work that had been overshadowed by the Civil War.[25]

Stephen S. Foster's confrontations with slavery in the churches of northern New England, often narrated by Rogers and accompanied by Pillsbury, are at the heart of the *Acts of the Anti-Slavery Apostles*. At twenty-two, after working as a carpenter, Foster had entered Dartmouth College with the intention of becoming a missionary in the Mississippi Valley, then a subject of mounting concern for evangelical Americans. While at Dartmouth he was called to militia duty, declined on Christian principles to appear, and was sent to a filthy prison where debtors were kept together with felons. Foster's written protest brought about a cleanup of the prison, abolition of imprisonment for debt, and a movement for prison reform in the state. From Dartmouth he went to Union Seminary in New York but left after the institution refused a meeting room for discussion of pacifism during a time of looming conflict between the United States and Britain over a boundary dispute. In 1839, having given up on the Congregational Church, and pretty much all churches, he became an agent for the American Anti-Slavery Society.[26] He was already demonstrably a civil disobedient, a come-outer, and as another reformer called himself, "*a most belligerent non-resistant.*"[27]

Foster became well known—some would have said notorious—for what a historian in modern times has called "speak-ins."[28] A characteristic scene of his agency, as reported by Rogers and amplified by Pillsbury, took place in Concord in 1842, when he stayed standing after an initial prayer and, before the minister could begin his sermon, stated that he would like to speak a few words in behalf of "two and a half millions of our kidnapped and enslaved countrymen." The minister objected angrily, an officer seized him; to silence him as he continued to talk in "a serene, gentle, orderly and respectful manner," the choir was signaled to resume singing and drown him out, while a number of men ejected him "by brute forces" and bolted the door behind him. Foster gave "no resistance ... by using his own strength or limbs." Against the advice of Rogers and other associates, he returned for an afternoon service and was immediately seized by a group of young men who dragged him down the aisle, "hurled" him down a "murderous" (Rogers's word) stone stairway, and beat and kicked him as they threw him out the door to the applause of a "violent, vociferating mob" of churchgoers proclaiming the sacredness of their meetinghouse. Abolitionist friends, who had also been driven out, took him home, called a doctor, and tended to his injuries. Thus ended, in Pillsbury's words, "the tragic portion of this wondrous spectacle," and a farce ensued when the church and clergyman brought a charge against Foster of disturbing public worship. When the sheriff came to get him, Foster refused to cooperate and had to be carried. In court he raised serious questions about the law under which he was charged and the evidence presented. He asked the witnesses whether it would be illegal for him to enter the church to inform the congregation that the roof was on fire or that one of their children had been kidnapped. In the end, the magistrate pronounced Foster guilty and fined him five dollars and costs. People in the audience (not abolitionists, reported Rogers, but nearer to the movement than they knew) rushed forward and threw down money. The sheriff, a decent man, declined payment for his services; the magistrate, with the feeling in the courtroom plainly running against his verdict, remitted the fine and waived his payment, too. When the judge asked what should be done with the pile of silver on the table, the audience by acclamation awarded it to Foster, who said he would devote it to the antislavery cause. At a meeting shortly afterward to debate a resolution condemning actions like Foster's as a gross violation of the clergy's prerogatives and the people's right, one feeble *yea* was drowned out by a chorus of *no*'s.[29]

This story may sound too good to be altogether true. To be sure, Pillsbury relates other stories with less happy outcomes—with beatings, fines, jailings, mobbings[30]—but these illustrate his contention that the northern clergy were as bad as the politicians in their determination to keep people from discovering the truth on the life-and-death issue of slavery. According to Pillsbury, abolitionist luminaries in Massachusetts like Garrison and Wendell Phillips were skeptical, but Foster had no doubts about "the great utility of his new method," as he repeated ten or twelve times, observing that "the ends sometimes justify the means" and returning to the hypothetical example of the church with its roof ablaze. Interestingly, both Foster and Amos Wood, the man who took him into his home, had been imprisoned for refusing military duty (neither was a Quaker nor from any other peace church). They provide a link between antebellum nonviolence and the antislavery struggle. Foster, whose "non-resistance principles … always put him into a perfectly passive state," is one antebellum example of the practice later called "going limp." But the context in which Pillsbury sets these church invasions had a less pacific side. Pillsbury concluded the discussion of means and ends in this way: "Nothing like it, or unlike it, before or afterward, so stirred the whole people, until John Brown, with his twenty heroes, marched on Harper's Ferry and challenged the supporters of slavery to mortal combat."[31]

The book of Acts, as Pillsbury reminded readers, mentions "honorable women, not a few," and his new version could do the same. He did not give much space to the recounting, however, and little of what he does include relates to civil disobedience. He includes a church withdrawal letter in the come-outer spirit protesting the Concord South Congregational Church's indifference to the sins, especially violations of family and morality, of slaveholders. The signers were members "denied all rights of speech or prayer, in private as well as public assemblies," and their action may be seen as prelude to other expressions of women's rights.[32] Pillsbury had witnessed Lucy Stone in "truly ferocious mobs. . . . I once saw her hit on the head by a large Swedenborgian prayer-book, hurled across the hall with a velocity and force worthy other *cannons* than the 'sacred *canons*' of the holy church."[33] He relates that Foster's colleague John Murray Spear suffered much violence in Portland before he was "finally rescued and borne off in triumph by a band of noble and heroic women," though not without physical injuries and the loss of his hat and other clothing.[34] An important study of women's service in the "Great Silent Army of Abolitionism" provides a number of examples of New England and New York women engaged in "fractious" conflict with pastors who failed to speak out on slavery. One clicked her knitting needles during a sermon, was carried out, arrested, and convicted of "contempt of worship." (Her jail keeper would not accept her as a prisoner.) Another, criticized for inviting a black member to sit with her, gave up her pew, "carried a stool into the church, placed it in the aisle next to her former pew, and occupied it during the service." A Quaker woman was "thrown out of the meetinghouse into the street 'sometimes with rough and merciless hands . . . for speaking . . . the truth.'"[35]

Some of Thoreau's antislavery and utopian contemporaries compared their struggle to those of Christian martyrs and Protestant reformers in the past. Some acted as "come-outers" seeking to destroy institutional religion; some as "no-organizationists" who were entitled to make a certificate bow and separate themselves from the authority of the state. Some, less interested in spiritual purity, undertook actions closer to stall-ins and similar acts of disobedience in later years. They were disrupting other functions of society—usually church services—in order to call attention to the evils of slavery. Few if any professed much respect for law or sought a legal niche for their actions. Precedents of religious protest must, then, be recognized in an account of the origins of the American practice of civil disobedience, but those precedents were reshaped and given new meanings in a democratic political culture in which the people's representatives ruled and obedience to law was considered essential to public order.

Civil disobedience gained new adherents in the 1840s and 1850s during crises over the issue of slavery. Those who did the most to promote it were not veteran abolitionists. More typically, they were ministers, or perhaps editors, poets and writers, even professors, who may have briefly flirted with abolitionism in the 1830s but had drifted away when the movement became stigmatized as too vituperative and disruptive. Some had never previously shown any interest; it took a special indifference to charges of dangerous radicalism to be an abolitionist. Then came war with Mexico, the Fugitive Slave Act, and other measures that undercut orderly complacency on the slavery issue and intensified anti-partyite fears. If in a sense we may view U.S.-style civil disobedience as a byproduct of political crisis in the late 1840s and 1850s, it also summed up anti-democratic feelings that had been welling up for decades.

The outset of the Mexican War gave rise to debate over what specific forms of obedience citizens owed to government. Politicians and moralists took positions on the question, as did private citizens. An anonymous writer to a Boston newspaper, for example, observed "a vast distance between submitting to unrighteous laws, and doing unrighteously in submission to law."

> Having from the beginning declared the war with Mexico unrighteous and unjust, I declare now the same; and although I submit in obedience to the laws, to the appropriation of money to the support of the war, and should even pay my portion of a direct tax, should one be laid, yet I cannot volunteer to fight, nor even serve if drafted. I submit to loss, inconvenience, suffering, in obedience to law, even if I conceive the law unjust;—but I cannot do wrong, even in order to sustain a just law. Conscience is to me supreme law; whatever law conflicts with it, is null and void.[36]

The war had many critics in Congress, from the South as well as North, and the growing feeling that the war aimed to extend slavery united reformers, even those who were not pacifists, in opposition. In the public debate prominent abolitionists signed a pledge vowing "at every sacrifice to refuse enlistment, contribution, aid and countenance to the War." For the most part, as one scholar has concluded, the abolitionists' "verbal extremism" was not substantiated by action.[37] There was no resistance to governmental policy and very little civil disobedience. The fairly empty threat not to volunteer had to suffice, since there was no draft. The war aroused patriotic feelings in many parts of the nation, and volunteers were not in short supply. Nevertheless, prominent northerners questioned whether the obligation to follow their government in iniquitous policies was absolute.

Why protests centered on that question probably deserves more extended analysis than scholars have provided.[38] What may have been crucial to rising calls to disobedience was uneasiness over the rise of political parties to power over the nation's morality and individuals' consciences. Sometimes it seemed that small majorities, acting as party representatives, made decisions of enormous moral consequence. At the news of Texas's annexation, one clergyman complained that a negative vote by either New Hampshire senator would have reversed the outcome. In his view that showed how "moral principle is divorced from politics" and how "partyism has devoured patriotism, [and] human rights & put conscience to sleep."[39] Thoreau belittled party conventions, as he dismissed the war as "the work of comparatively a few individuals using the standing government as their tool." Urging disobedience of unjust laws whether or not majorities could be mobilized to revise them, he admonished any citizen who thought he could even momentarily "resign his conscience to the legislator."[40]

Few of his countrymen imitated Thoreau's gesture of tax refusal, let alone his abstract threat to sign off from government altogether.[41] But he was not far outside a main current of moral thought that warned citizens of democratic governments, even if their party was not in the majority, that they shared guilt for unjust actions they did nothing to oppose. Consider the reaction to the Mexican War of Francis Wayland, a Baptist clergyman and president of Brown University, whose works have been called "the best statements of the common American consensus on religion, philosophy, ethics, and political economy."[42] This influential spokesman for northern evangelicalism advised Christian citizens never to obey a command to do that which is wrong. His specific counsels were only mildly disobedient: he recommended against volunteering for the army, lending money for the military effort, taking contracts from the government, or in any other way profiting from the war. In giving this counsel, Wayland described political parties as follows: "The voice of history has surely spoken in vain if it has not taught us that political parties have ever been combinations for the purposes of personal aggrandizement, advocating or denouncing whatever political principles would best subserve the selfish objects, which alone gave efficiency to their organization." To the expedient directives of political parties Wayland contrasted Christian teachings of a "power in truth and rectitude" greater than that of numbers. He concluded, "Let virtuous men then unite on the ground of *universal moral principle*, and the tyranny of party will be crushed."[43] American-style civil disobedience, as formulated by Wayland at a time of political crisis, reflected deepening anxieties about the obstacles posed by partisan politics to evangelical advance and public morality.

Wayland viewed abolitionists as moral fanatics, though he had no doubts about the "moral evil" of slavery, as he had explained in an 1838 treatise titled *The Limitations of Human Responsibility*. Like other reform associations (and somewhat like political parties in his view), antislavery societies subordinated their members to the promotion of a narrow agenda in pursuit of which they "will perpetrate acts, at which every member of the association would individually revolt."[44] As individuals, abolitionists had a right to exhort others on the evil of slavery. As citizens, abolitionist residents of northern states had no right to interfere with the constitutionally guaranteed "*free choice*" of southerners to determine the future of slavery in their states. Here his constitutional theory had a distinctively Baptist flair: "If they will not hear us, our responsibility is at an end. We have no right to force our instructions on them, either by conversation, or by lecture, or by the mail. . . . We must leave them to God, who is perfectly capable of vindicating his own laws, and executing justice among the children of men." There was no reason for abolitionist pressure on the political process in the North, no justification for "a system of societies, affiliated, not for the sake of circulating truth at the South, but for the sake of exciting and agitating the people of the North." Seeking to coerce the slaveholder by fomenting rebellion among the slaves was morally wrong (and could lead to the "annihilation of the colored population"). He conceded that a constitutional case could be made for abolishing slavery in the District of Columbia, as abolitionists proposed; in fact, he wrote with disgust and shame about the slave market in the republic's capital and appealed to southern representatives to respect feelings like his own by closing those markets "of their own accord." It troubled him that in all discussion of slavery—for example, on the right of petition—both sections' representatives "press[ed] upon the limits of the constitution to the utmost." The values he recommended to both sides in the great national debate were dispassionate decorum, patience, forbearance, "calm adherence to right." Turning to proposals to annex Texas, he praised the South's traditional warnings against resorting to "*doubtful* constitutional powers" and urged its representatives to be true to that same strict constructionism in this "*extremely doubtful*" instance. If neither section focused on the implications for slavery, "we can truly increase the practical power of the constitution," and "we shall be united, happy, and invincible."[45]

All the virtues Wayland praised in public discourse and decision making—including restraint, reasonableness, patience, mutual respect— were sorely tested in the years after 1838. Unsurprisingly, his positions changed. In *Limitations* he stood firmly against law breaking: "So long as a law exists, it must be obeyed, and no man nor any set of men, has the right to assume an authority, either distinct from the laws, or in opposition to them, as beyond them, on the ground that the laws do not come up to their notions of right, or any other ground whatever."[46] But during the Mexican War, as we have seen, he defended certain kinds of disobedience. The Christian individual must separate himself, "as far as possible," from wicked governmental policies. By 1848 he had ceased to reject sectional antislavery politics. He supported the Free Soil Party and then the Republican Party, and after John C. Frémont's electoral defeat in 1856 he expressed satisfaction that "we have at last a North." By the late 1850s he praised the Republicans, even in defeat, as a unified sectional party. He still counseled associates to restrain their passions, avoid rash measures, and await God's indication of future steps. The Fugitive Slave Law shocked him. He found this lesson in the military occupation of Boston after the seizure of Anthony Burns: "We have neglected the sighing of the captive, and said that slavery was, after all, a small matter, and God is giving us a taste of it, that we may see how we like it ourselves." He remained averse to "the extremes of denunciation to which the earlier abolitionists had been addicted."[47] His advocacy of civil disobedience was always moderate and practical. By his own account, "I have always declared that I would never aid to arrest a fugitive, or do a thing to return him to slavery. I would make no opposition to the government, but would patiently endure the penalty. This I have a right to do, on the principle that I must obey God rather than man." When one of his sons, however, took in a fugitive and sent him, bearing a letter, to Wayland, "I gave him money, clothes, mittens, and shoes. It is a clear case of humanity, and I was happy to give him shelter. . . . I am glad you sent the poor fellow."[48]

The Fugitive Slave Law provoked an opposition that lifted the rhetoric of disobedience to new levels of boldness and creativity. Respectable men and women decided that the slave power's domination of the political system justified a course of resistance. "If asked how you dared disobey the laws of this realm," advised Rev. Charles Beecher, "answer with Bunyan's Pilgrim in Vanity Fair: tell the court that you obey Christ, not Belial." In his sister Harriet's astonishingly popular novel *Uncle Tom's Cabin*, a true-hearted woman shames her estimable husband to follow his instincts and aid a fugitive mother and child in disregard of the law that he, as a senator, had voted for. By forbidding acts of kindness in the home, in fact, the law converted the supposedly private sphere into a theater of public conflict.[49] Works like Lydia Maria Child's *The Duty of Disobedience to the Fugitive Slave Law*—and there were many more—acknowledged that obedience to government was a sacred obligation. But the individual was accountable to God for moral behavior and thus was obliged to disobey when the laws contradicted widely held principles of conscience.[50] In many of these works, as in Wayland's, the Christian was not justified in undertaking forcible rebellion and must submit to the law's penalties. That kind of conservative law breaking, it was claimed, actually intensified respect for law. Such a stance might have eased the consciences of judges with antislavery convictions. At least one Ohio judge acknowledged that he might have responded charitably to a fugitive at his door, but he hoped he would then accept the law's punishment as just.[51]

The argument against cooperating with slave catchers was not new. In an 1842 sermon, as we have seen, J. C. W. Pennington asserted that he would as willingly betray his savior for thirty pieces of silver as to participate in delivering a fugitive slave to captors.[52] Why did opposition to the 1850 law reach such new heights? After all, the Constitution included a somewhat awkward reference to the rendition of fugitives, and the Congress had initiated legislation for recapture in 1793. But the new law was part of a package of measures, known as the Compromise of 1850, that in fact failed in the pacification that compromises were supposed to achieve. The standards of evidence and rigor of procedures upon which alleged fugitives would be returned were lax. Efforts to enforce the law made the conflict over slavery part of visible experience in the North. They gave vivid proof to the abolitionist charge that slavery amounted to kidnapping. Very important, the act included provisions that gave ominous new meaning to the "agency" of northern citizens. Anyone could be conscripted into a posse to assist marshals and slave catchers in the seizure and return of escaped slaves. "All good citizens" were "commanded to aid and assist in the prompt and efficient execution of this law, whenever their services may be required." Anyone who impeded a capture, even one done without a warrant, rescued a prisoner, or gave shelter to a fugitive was subject to a one-thousand-dollar fine, six months' imprisonment, and heavy civil damages.[53]

The duty to give succor to the weak and needy was a standard hypothesis in ethical theory. The heart was supposed to motivate good people to acts of sympathy and charity. The Fugitive Slave Law brought the test to reality in northern life. In a public letter to President Millard Fillmore, the prominent Transcendentalist minister Theodore Parker complained that he as pastor and his parishioners could be fined and imprisoned if they aided, fed, clothed, or sheltered fugitive slaves who belonged to his congregation— in other words, if they did "what Christianity demands." He declared this ethical choice: "I would rather lie all my life in a gaol, and starve there, than refuse to protect one of these parishioners of mine."[54] Consider also Samuel Willard, seventy-five years old, a Unitarian minister who helped coax his denomination into condemning the Fugitive Slave Act, and who declared that he would not personally deny shelter to a fugitive.

> I will perform toward the fugitive slave all the acts of kindness that I should do if there were no prohibition against it; and I will quietly endure the consequences, though enormous fines or exactions should deprive me of my last cent, and though I be thrown into prison for six months, or six years, or all the residue of my life; and I will not put the Government of my country to the expense of a single lock and key for my safe keeping.

He did not describe "all this submissiveness" as "clearly required by any Divine principle." It was a sign, rather, of the importance he personally attached to "civil order." A Congregationalist pastor, J. G. Forman, honored "the duty of submission to the civil government, but not the duty of obedience to its unjust laws." He counseled no violence but calm and firm disobedience followed by "peaceful submission" to legal penalties. Still another, Nathaniel Hall, spoke with feeling of a "sacred obligation" to obey the laws of civil government. But when government commanded sinful behavior, as it now had done, disobedience was justified—within limits: "The resistance counseled is not the forcible resistance which is rebellion, but that which consists in disobedience, with a passive submission to whatever penalty may be thereto attached."[55]

These moderate protests may be appreciated if set in the context of the prevailing conservatism on the slavery question of leading Unitarian ministers who deplored what they called abolitionism's "eloquential twaddle." Orville Dewey was criticized for proclaiming: "I would consent that my own brother, my own son should go [into slavery]; *ten times rather* would I go myself, than that this Union should be sacrificed for me or for us." Abolitionists accused him of having said "my own mother." But he was addressing the key ethical choice raised by the Fugitive Slave Law. What would he say to a fugitive who approached him, declared his right to freedom, and sought help? Dewey's reply:

> Your right to be free is not absolute, unqualified, irrespective of all consequences. If my espousal of your claim is likely to involve your race and mine together in disasters infinitely greater than your personal servitude, then you ought not to be free. In such case, personal rights ought to be sacrificed to the general good. You your-self ought to see this, and to be willing to suffer for a while—one for many. If I were in your situation I should take this ground.

One close friend and colleague, Henry W. Bellows, found the imagined response much too timid. The primary duty was to keep one's "conscience whole," not to keep the "Union whole." Faced with the same moral choice, he would adhere to the Golden Rule and help the fugitive at his door. Bellows was forced to resign his editorship of the *Christian Inquirer* after voicing criticism of the law and its advocate Daniel Webster.[56]

Some of these voices of disobedience may have been mainly rhetorical (but maybe not, as the example of Wayland showed, if a living fugitive arrived at the door). In any case, the rhetoric was not inconsequential. For one thing, these pastors spoke in a context of mounting tolerance and advocacy of armed violence as a means to block slavery's reach into the supposedly free states. Recent scholarship often approves the rejection of nonviolence, which one book calls "increasingly ludicrous" and "the beset-ting sin of reformers."[57] But the issues were complex. Resistance to the Fugitive Slave Law was seldom restricted to pacifists and armed revolution-aries; in many localities groups of blacks and whites sought some middle ground. Few questioned the slave's or fugitive's right to self-defense. They did not seek to convert or persuade the authorities, and they were not squeamish about coercion, though they might not bear arms. That was the position of Syracuse's Samuel Joseph May, who said he would not hesitate to overpower a federal marshal though he would not intentionally hurt him. It was close to the position of Theodore Parker, whose motto for resisters was "Peaceably if they can; forcibly if they must."[58] As in venerable protests against the Stamp Act, once again the people were overthrowing "a wicked law to enact Absolute Justice into their statute."[59]

Parker belonged to a group of Bostonians, calling themselves the "Anti-Man-Hunting League," who diagrammed and rehearsed a version of what in Hindi is called a *gherao*, in which protectors of an endangered fugitive would press their bodies tight around the pursuing marshals and thereby immobilize them. They were prepared, further, to "kidnap" men whom they considered "man hunters."[60] A leader of this league, Henry I. Bowditch, a prominent physician, recalled taking the escaped slave William Craft in a buggy to visit his wife Ellen, under protection in Brookline. Craft carried a large "horsepistol" in one hand and a revolver, given him by Bowditch's brother William, in the other, and he agreed to the trip only if Bowditch also held a pistol in one hand while driving with the other. Facing the unanticipated possibility of killing a human being, Bowditch "remembered the saying, which, though not intended probably to be quoted on such an occasion, I deemed most fitting in its application to me; viz., 'to do for others what you wish done for yourself;' and feeling that if I were Craft I should glory in slaying any one who attempted to make me or my wife a slave, I replied instantly, 'Yes, I accept your proposition.'" In the heightened danger Parker sheltered both Crafts for two weeks, writing his sermons with a sword and loaded pistol at hand; when they left for England he gave them a sword and a Bible.[61]

In such a milieu cautious ministers and respectable public figures who advocated a posture of unambiguous, but orderly, disobedience drew distinctions previously lacking in episodes of rebellion or nullification. The absolute nonviolence of the nonresistance society had fewer adherents, though it would prove to be enduring, with its meaning usually dependent on the threat of more unruly and even violent forms of protest.

Charles Beecher called the Fugitive Slave Law "the unexampled climax of sin" and "the vilest monument of infamy of the nineteenth century."[62] One could easily amass other quotations identifying that law as the nonpareil symbol of evil. Nothing was relative; the odium was absolute. If anything, whites whose faith in orderly progress was betrayed were more absolute in their rhetoric than black leaders, who took less for granted. Animosity toward that act of Congress was expressed, and civil disobedience therefore justified, not in terms of competing interests of sections or parties but as a conflict between human evil draped in the colors of legality and God's timeless "higher law." With kidnappers aprowl in the North that may not have seemed hyperbolic, and it took a major evil to justify disobedience to law. But there may be another point to emphasize: the concern these confrontations showed about the foundations of law and morality in a democratic society.

The name most often associated with the higher law was that of a politician who rose in 1850 to champion it and then retreated: William Henry Seward. This freshman New York senator was not speaking against the Fugitive Slave Bill in particular but against all compromise measures that aimed to perpetuate slavery by carving new slave states out of western territories. Slavery was transient, he declared; freedom was permanent and fundamental. The Constitution did not treat the western domain as spoils to be divided according to interests of residents of the original states; instead, these lands were consecrated "to union, to justice, to defence, to welfare and to liberty." But even if others differed from him on this point, he went on, "there is a higher law than the Constitution, which regulates our authority over the domain, and devotes it to the same noble purposes. The territory is a part—no inconsiderable part—of the common heritage of mankind, bestowed upon them by the Creator of the universe. We are his stewards, and must so discharge our trust as to secure, in the highest attainable degree, their happiness."[63] Like many political speeches, this one was a confusing mélange that may not repay close analysis.

Did the Constitution conflict with divine law? Did the Almighty declare immutable truths or encourage "progress" (one of Seward's favorite words) that would increase human happiness? Whatever Seward meant, proslavery listeners took him as voicing abolitionist cant that slavery was unchristian, and antislavery circles celebrated his words. Seward took delight in his standing as a leading antislavery politician, but he never again sounded quite so dogmatic about the higher law (though he did refer to "the abstractions of human rights" as society's only permanent foundations).[64] Nevertheless, the higher law rhetoric persisted, as one historian notes, "well after Seward's inglorious retreat in a fog of evasions and partial retractions."[65]

To dismiss references to "higher law" is to miss important undercurrents of feeling in the Jackson era. In the context of rising insecurity about what really was permanent and foundational, references to higher law were not merely formulaic; they often pointed to issues of deep concern. There was indeed a long history of attempts to identify the law with something fundamental—divine truth, reason, human feeling, nature, or ancient usage—and separate it from the fluctuations of politics. In America, where government rested on popular sovereignty, that long history seemed in jeopardy. It was all too easy to see the government and the laws it made as the results of partisan contests, as insecure victories or reversible losses. In addition, in the nation where political "rights" (at least voting rights) expanded beyond all precedent, it was easy to see these rights as highly vulnerable and to wish to find some more secure foundation for them than the compromises of the politicians, the obfuscations of judges, the whims of the populace.

Clearly, there was a religious dimension, too. In parallel developments, while government lost most of its sovereignty separate from the people, and nearly all white males were enfranchised (while blacks in some states actually lost the vote), churches were disestablished and all souls were encouraged to believe that redemption might be theirs. The population was Christianized as never before, not in a unified or state church but in numerous sects and congregations. There was some drive, at many levels of society, to assert that the democratization of Christianity had no implication of relativism, of agnosticism among a multiplicity of truths. Reform movements in general included religious people concerned to widen the hegemony of "moral" truth in a world too often reduced to the sphere of politics. Slavery by the 1830s became a key subject on which to explore what was absolutely true.[66]

The most radical abolitionists sometimes veered far from traditional Christian doctrine. By the late 1830s nonresistants like Wright and Garrison were contending that moral truth was absolute and unvarying, "a principle of eternal Right" or higher law that could not depend on interpretation of an uncertain text like the Bible that included ghastly scenes of slaughter and that was being interpreted to uphold slavery. Most northern anti-slavery people avoided such extreme positions (though southern polemicists charged all who called slavery a sin with infidelity to scriptural Christianity).[67] But it seemed obvious to William Hosmer, a prominent antislavery Methodist in upstate New York, in a book dedicated to Seward, that "there is an immutable distinction between right and wrong, which no human power can subvert," and slavery was unmistakably on the side of wrong.[68] Evangelicals who believed perfect "holiness" to be attainable in the current era of history and sought the Christianization of civil government could refer to a higher law, not reachable in earlier times.

That usage for the higher law has been hailed as the great contribution to abolitionism of the celebrated and controversial revivalist Charles Grandison Finney, who left a major New York pulpit for a professorship (and later the presidency) of a new college, coeducational, interracial, and committed to the work of reform, in Oberlin, Ohio. In 1839, at the inaugural meeting of the Ohio Anti-Slavery Society, he introduced resolutions defying a new state fugitive slave law as well as discriminatory "Black Laws" that had been in effect since the state's founding. These resolutions codified an important version of the higher law. According to a settled legal principle, the society resolved, "No human legislation can annul, or set aside the law or authority of God. . . . Whatever is contrary to the law of God, is not law." Further, politics and government could not be separated from religion because "no human enactments can bend the conscience, or set aside our obligation to God." The U.S. Constitution acknowledged that "rights conferred by our Creator as inalienable, can never be cancelled, or set aside by human enactments." There was no justification for temporizing on the subjects of slavery and emancipation. A few years later, in a collection of addresses to theology students, Finney went further: God would accept nothing short of complete obedience to the moral law. Christians must disobey governments that violated the moral obligations imposed by God's law.[69] Although Finney pulled back and explained that revivalism for him took priority over antislavery and other reform movements—he devoted much of his attention in the 1850s to great revivals in the United States and Britain—some Oberlin professors moved to ever-stronger calls for purifying the nation by the standards of antislavery and higher law.

It would be misleading to imply that all northern Protestants embraced the higher law, though those active in the most dynamically growing sects did so. But others were reluctant to give offense to the southern brethren, even as the largest Protestant denominations broke up over issues related to slavery. What is important to note, moreover, is that some of the more conservative/orthodox Protestant leaders in the North also upheld the existence and importance of a higher law. For example, the New Haven clergyman Leonard Bacon, famous as a champion of colonizationism and opponent of Garrison, preached on the higher law at a time when a great effort was under way to discredit the idea. Conservatives had voted at a public meeting that "we know of no higher law, as a rule of political action, than the Constitution of the United States." Bacon refuted the idea, to the surprise of some of his audience. "Conscience rules supreme, even though liable to error. We must use every effort to enlighten it; but we must follow it. The eternal law of right, which will prevail, is higher than any constitution. . . . You cannot escape it. You must obey it." There were no flights of oratory—his biographer tells us—only plain statements, and these were very effective.[70]

Theologians who stood firm against the new measures and radical expectations of evangelical reform, like the learned Moses Stuart of Andover Seminary, warned against appeals to "higher law" that really substituted contemporary passions and prejudices for inspired scriptural precedent.[71] Most formidable and most uncompromising among champions of Protestant orthodoxy was Princeton's Charles Hodge, who opposed even the modifications of Calvinism accepted by moderates like Stuart. He contributed a lengthy essay on the Fugitive Slave Law (plus another on the Bible and slavery) for the mammoth collection *Cotton Is King*, published on the eve of the Civil War. The other contributors were southern intellectuals, several of whom criticized northern rationales for violating the law. No critique was more learned than Hodge's exposition of Christian duty and abolitionist error. The Bible "never refers to the consent of the governed" as "the ground of our obligation to the higher powers." The obedience slaves owe to masters, children to parents, wives to husbands, and people to rulers "is always made to rest on the divine will as its ultimate foundation." Those who objected to orders to aid in enforcing the Fugitive Slave Law had only one recourse: "quietly submit." As for popular references to consent of the governed as underlying "the obligation to obedience," "this doctrine is so notoriously of infidel origin, and so obviously in conflict with the teachings of the Bible, that it can have no hold on the convictions of a Christian people." His conclusions were so "elemental" that he apologized for addressing them so formally.[72] His assurance of his correctness was undiminished, even years later, in his *Systematic Theology* (1872–73), where he insisted again that human government was a divine ordinance and obedience, a religious duty. He recognized a community's right of revolution in cases where governments flagrantly violate their divine purpose. But short of that, for individuals, the choice was more limited. He offered this "obvious distinction to be made between disobedience and resistance":

A man is bound to disobey a law, or a command, which requires him to sin, but it does not follow that he is at liberty to resist its execution. The Apostles refused to obey the Jewish authorities; but they submitted to the penalty inflicted. So the Christian martyrs disobeyed the laws requiring them to worship idols, but they made no resistance to the execution of the law. The Quakers disobey the law requiring military service, but quietly submit to the penalty. This is obviously right.[73]

The relevance of this orthodox view to the continuing American belief that civil disobedients must be prepared to go to jail is obvious, too.

In some very important ways contests over slavery and abolition took the form of conflicts over fundamental law. It may have been true that the positions were incommensurable (as Alasdair MacIntyre says of such debates in our time[74]); there was no authority to settle them, no consensual, traditional belief by which to decide the issues posed when southern intellectuals went from saying "we wish to maintain slavery" to "slavery is good" and their northern counterparts went from saying "we wish to contain it" to "slavery is sin." The point to notice is the overlapping and conflicting presentations of higher law. In the courts, for example, slavery was defended by one understanding of democracy: the people's laws and constitution gave positive protection to the institution. It was defended, moreover, by one version of fundamental law: the version that referred to the usages and customs of society. These defenses were often effective, especially in *Dred Scott* and other decisions of the Supreme Court. But those who wished to afford due process to alleged fugitives in communities that took personal liberty seriously could refer to versions of democracy that carried weight in northern courts. They could also appeal to the inalienable human rights by which American independence was justified in the first place and to absolute standards of natural justice by which all human institutions should be judged. Such an argument often fared poorly in the courts but proved increasingly attractive to northern public opinion.

The sensational Fugitive Slave cases of the 1850s demonstrated the incendiary symbolic value (and real effects) of a law that was presented as part of a conciliatory compromise but in fact appeared to impede neighbors and citizens from exercising their rights and duties. These cases always prompted discussions of obedience and obligation. When the U.S. Supreme Court reversed a Wisconsin Supreme Court decision discharging an

accused rescuer and finding that the Fugitive Slave Law was unconstitutional, Wisconsin (like Georgia in the case of the Cherokees) declined to
cooperate with the review. Chief Justice Taney rejected arguments about
fundamental rights and insisted on the hierarchical authority of the
Supreme Court. As for state protests, "It certainly can be no humiliation to
the citizen of a republic to yield a ready obedience to the laws as administered by the constituted authorities."[75] Some cases became treason trials—
even Daniel Webster had argued publicly that concerted resistance to this
law, no matter how peaceful, was treason. The legal response to the
Christiana "tragedy," with forty-one indictments for treason, may have
convinced more northern citizens of the nation's subservience to the "slave
power" than it awed into capitulation to a federal statute.[76] The failure to
convict on the treason charge signaled a transition from old views of
premeditated disobedience as a capital offense to recognition, however
contested, of a middle ground that might be consistent with good citizenship. The Fugitive Slave cases also reveal how misgivings about moral relativism in an age of party conflict and religious competition gave rise to
contradictory versions of the higher law, the state's—which stressed obligations of obedience—and that of antislavery reformers, with its justifications of civil disobedience. These confrontations surely had long-term
consequences for the ways in which Americans sought to reconcile moral
imperatives with obedience to civil authority.

For judges with antislavery temperaments, the Fugitive Slave cases
posed severe strains. A judge of well-recognized antislavery views who
enforced the Fugitive Slave Law as an unavoidable evil was vilified by the
Garrisonians as a Pontius Pilate.[77] Robert Cover has written of the "moral-
formal conflict" that arose for judges faithful to legal precedent, legislative
policies, Supreme Court decisions, and general belief in the benefits to
liberty and social order dependent on a rule of law, on one hand, and religious and philosophical principles condemning slavery and perhaps
suggesting that the institution itself contradicted liberty and order, on the
other hand. Some judges were able to apply the formalities of the laws in
support of slaveholders without believing that the Constitution was fundamentally proslavery. That was harder after the Fugitive Slave Law was
passed with a chorus of prominent men of the legal profession proclaiming
adherence to it as a test of fidelity to the Constitution. Much of the strain
resulted from persistent confrontation with the law on the part of men and
women, some of them equal in prominence to the worthies of the law,

speaking and acting in behalf of a never-ending flow of fugitives.[78] To the legal issues concerning slavery raised and decided in courts were added newer ones concerning the propriety and even necessity of resistance to law and civil disobedience raising moral issues in a republican society. That was a subject emerging from the speeches and writings of Thoreau, Foster, Wayland, and many others.

For good examples of the civil disobedience logic as it had taken shape by the eve of the Civil War, we can turn to the 1859 trial of residents of Oberlin, Ohio, who had converged on nearby Wellington and released a young black man held in a hotel with preparations under way to transport him to Kentucky. Thirty-seven rescuers were tried for violating the Fugitive Slave Law. In an eloquent address before the judge, the black schoolteacher Charles H. Langston stressed his vulnerability to a legal system that denied him protection and rewarded his would-be kidnappers. Though Langston believed in a slave's right to free himself, all he had done was to insist on scrutiny of the warrants proffered before the accused was rushed off to Kentucky. To demand justice under the law was his positive "duty as a citizen of Ohio"—he corrected himself, as "an *outlaw* of the United States"—and whatever his penalty, he promised to accept it. Denying characterizations of the court as biased and unmovable, the judge took note of Langston's "advice to others to pursue a legal course" and imposed what he termed a "comparatively light" sentence.[79]

The rescuers' attorney, Albert Gallatin Riddle, proved adept in showing ambiguities in the law and in the perceptions of skin color used to identify a black man for transportation into slavery. He also rejected the judge's instructions to the grand jury to eschew the higher law doctrine that elevated individual conscience and rendered government utopian, imaginary, really a nonexistent "no government." Riddle stood before the court as "a votary of that Higher Law!" Only someone with a higher morality than was found in the penal code could in fact be a good citizen.

Right, and its everlasting opposite, *Wrong*, [Riddle continued] existed anterior to the feeble enactments of men . . . and must ever remain Right and Wrong. . . . Will any mortal say that there can be no right, no wrong, outside of the U.S. Statutes at Large? Dare any man arise here and say in the face of this sun, that the gossamer threads of human enactments, can break through or bind down the everlasting pillars of justice, as set up by the Almighty himself?

Regardless of this religious posture, Riddle focused his argument on good citizenship. This version of higher law had no anti-democratic implications. All his clients, he stressed—like Langston—came "unresistingly" to court. As to condemnation of law breaking, he asked, "How do you obey the law? Why either by doing the things it enjoins, or submitting to the penalty it imposes. Both are equally obedience. Every citizen has this choice held out to him, by every penal statute, and you cannot proclaim a man a bad citizen when he acts conscientiously on his choice, nor say he disobeys your law when he submits to its requirements." If he is wrong, he still deserves respect; if he is right, his cell will become a "luminous sanctuary" in the annals of social progress.[80] Here was a more dynamic view of obligation than the familiar orthodox one.

The civil disobedience tradition is closely linked to citizenship—to ideals of good citizenship as well as to critiques of curtailed citizenship. Riddle, as we shall see, holds an interesting place in the passage from the antislavery struggle to the arena where the civil disobedience tradition would next gain prominence—the struggle for woman suffrage. Before taking that step with him, we should end this chapter with another event of 1859—the famous raid on Harpers Ferry—and with another believer in a higher law, one greatly admired by Thoreau, a man contemptuous of much public wrangling by abolitionists, lawyers, and theologians over obligation and disobedience: John Brown.

Brown, like Riddle, was born in New England and grew up in the intense religious fervor and antislavery ferment of the Western Reserve in northeastern Ohio. Riddle came west as a boy as part of a Universalist migration, and without appealing directly to a loving and all-forgiving God, he dedicated himself to the work of steady moral reform and political progress. He placed his engagement in the moral and political conflicts over slavery as participation in "one of the great epochs of human history."[81] Brown, an unwavering son of Puritanism, considered himself a nineteenth-century Oliver Cromwell, fiercely allegiant to the Calvinists' vengeful God. It is probably accurate to say that no white American exceeded him in zealous commitment to destroy slavery and racial prejudice, as shown during his brave service as a conductor on the Underground Railroad, organizer of black settlements in the Adirondacks, and later in "Bloody Kansas" as captain of a guard to protect antislavery immigrants and fight off proslavery Missourians. Some of his actions in that conflict gained him a reputation, then and now, as a terrorist. After Kansas he returned with renewed zeal to a plan to invade the Upper South and conduct raids modeled on guerilla warfare in Spain, Haiti, and elsewhere in the Caribbean. In September 1859 he led seventeen men, five of them blacks, into Harpers Ferry, Virginia, and briefly took the town before being trapped and captured, as Frederick Douglass had forewarned in declining to join in the adventure. There was some talk of finding Brown insane and thereby diminishing his martyrdom, but that option was not taken. All seven captured invaders (ten others were killed in action), after having aroused furious and fearful reactions across the South, were convicted of murder, treason, and attempting to incite a slave insurrection—and hanged.[82]

The raid aroused fear and belligerence across the South as a clear instance of what had long been feared—a northern-financed, interracial conspiracy to incite slaves to rise up against their masters. Southern states armed and mobilized as never before. The threat was not wholly imaginary. The turmoil of fugitive slave rescues in Boston, Syracuse, Wellington, and Milwaukee had already revealed the existence of coteries of antislavery northerners who had no aversion to violent confrontation. In the border states, groups of "aggressive" abolitionists planned and sometimes executed armed incursions to liberate slaves and lead them to freedom.[83] Brown's raid was especially shocking, and politicians like Lincoln and Seward who sought electoral success deplored what they regarded as a mad, irresponsible scheme. As news of the raid spread, backers who might have been implicated fled the country or disowned any connection with the deed. "I have always been more distinguished for running than fighting," wrote Frederick Douglass as he prepared to get out of the country. Those words sound strange, perhaps, in light of his dramatic accounts of fighting his cruel overseer, but even decades later he denied direct involvement and gave only qualified approval to an event that could be ranked "with the most cold-blooded and atrocious wrongs ever perpetrated."[84] In the weeks following the raid, Brown's dignity in facing death and a deeply moving last speech won the sympathy of many thousands of mourners for whom his life and death were transformed into a kind of tribute to inexorable divine purpose. In a military anthem his truth goes marching on.

Brown defended his actions as obedience to God's law, but Virginia's Governor Henry Wise attributed the raid to "the Atheism of a 'higher law'" prevailing in a section led astray by "the doctrine of absolute individual rights, independent of all relations of man to man in a conventional and social form; and that each man for himself has the prerogative to set up his conscience, his will and his judgment over and above all legal enactments and social institutions."[85] In this mini-debate on obedience to law, it remains clear that Brown had no use for nonviolence, moral suasion, respectful political discourse, or—in most definitions—civil disobedience. His most eloquent white champions, however, were writers who *had* been close to nonresistance and civil disobedience. At a memorial service in Concord, while a crowd of their neighbors outside First Parish hanged and burned an effigy of Brown, Thoreau said Brown had "a spark of divinity in him," and Alcott called him "worthy of the glories of the cross." Emerson made the most famous (or was it notorious?) prediction that Brown's execution would make "the gallows glorious like the cross." To most of the nation Brown was a fanatic; the abolitionists of Concord, still defying convention, called him a saint.[86] The line that separated him from the civil disobedience tradition is easily blurred, as shown by this paragraph in his most recent and controversial biography:

> Thoreau and his associates planted the seed that eventually grew into the North's veneration of John Brown. In *Walden*, Thoreau, describing the impact of an idea, wrote that "a tide rises and falls behind every man which can float the British empire like a chip"—a notion that would be borne out by Mahatma Gandhi and Martin Luther King, Jr., both of whom would use a Thoreauvian concept, civil disobedience, to help float away social injustice. Thoreau and his fellow Concordians did their part to rid America of slavery by introducing a radically new idea: the leader of the raid on Harpers Ferry was not a lunatic but a hero.[87]

It is not really clear how the truncated, out-of-context quotation and the surrounding assertions add up. Gandhi and King must both have respected Brown's freedom from racial prejudice and his courage and dignity while in prison facing execution. Whatever Thoreau meant to say about every man's ideas, it seems unlikely that Gandhi (who was influenced by Thoreau more than Brown) and King (who admired Thoreau and Gandhi but not especially Brown) relied on ideas in the same way. And the power of the Concordians' estimation of Brown's sanity seems exaggerated.

Still, Brown would be peripheral to this account of the career of civil disobedience if he himself hadn't rejected it, if he hadn't come to stand in the decades between the 1880s and 1940s as a deplorable example of how law breaking could escalate into terror and internecine warfare, and if he had not come to represent, for impatient militants in the civil rights era, the hopeful alternative to civil disobedience when radical advance reached an impasse. On one hand, Brown was Exhibit A in accounts of the Civil War as the tragic work of a blundering generation of uncompromising fanatics; on the other, he became the hero of armed militants and "underground" Weathermen chanting "John Brown, live like him, dare to struggle, dare to win" as they smashed store windows.[88]

A similar point could be made about Brown's attractiveness or horror as the symbolic, radical alternative to progressive political reform. In Sean Wilentz's summation, "John Brown was a violent charismatic anti-slavery terrorist" who "actually damaged the mainstream campaign against slavery, which by the late 1850s was a serious mass political movement contending for national power, and not, as Brown and some of his radical friends saw it, a fraud even more dangerous to the cause of liberty than the slaveholders."[89] It is hard, of course, even to imagine how slavery could have been abolished without violence. On that point there can be no quarrel with Reynolds's concluding statement: "John Brown was right."[90] But we may still question the rigid and false disjunctions that define alternative judgments of that terrible conflict. And we may proceed to think of civil disobedience as one via media, with reform politics as another, between terrorism and acquiescence. Riddle and Lincoln were right enough as well.

5

"Wild, Unaccountable Things"

Civil Disobedience and Woman Suffrage

JUDGE HUNT—The Court must insist the prisoner has been tried according to the established forms of law.

MISS ANTHONY—Yes, your honor, but by forms of law all made by men, interpreted by men, administered by men, in favor of men, and against women; and hence, your honor's ordered verdict of guilty, against a United States citizen for the exercise of "that citizen's right to vote," simply because that citizen was a woman and not a man. But, yesterday, the same man-made forms of law, declared it a crime punishable with $1,000 fine and six months' imprisonment, for you, or me, or any of us, to give a cup of cold water, a crust of bread, or a night's shelter to a panting fugitive as he was tracking his way to Canada. And every man or woman in whose veins coursed a drop of human sympathy violated that wicked law, reckless of consequences, and was justified in so doing. As then, the slaves who got their freedom must take it over, or under, or through the unjust forms of law, precisely so, now, must women, to get their right to a voice in this government, take it; and I have taken mine, and mean to take it at every possible opportunity.

JUDGE HUNT—The Court orders the prisoner to sit down. It will not allow another word.[1]

Unlike wars of recent times, the Civil War occasioned little civil disobedience. It did create challenges for would-be conscientious objectors, but civil wars are inherently difficult for pacifism. American peace movements

126

(largely clustered in the North) declined to find the war an unjust, aggressive war or to oppose it with any dramatic action. With very few exceptions, abolitionist nonresistants, who had once called for sweeping renunciation even of so-called defensive wars, unhesitatingly committed themselves to a war against slavery. Few in the younger generation—their children—had much interest in pacifism or avoiding military service when their parents' antiwar convictions had been on hold at least since Harpers Ferry. Quaker communities were more divided and strained, especially since the conscription act permitted paying for a substitute but allowed for no conscientious exemption. There was no southern pacifist movement, but the South was home to many Quakers, and they suffered more hardship than those in the North.[2] If Elihu Burritt's 1867 vision of a workingmen's worldwide general strike against "the whole war system" had ever come about, that would have represented a return to civil disobedience on a grand scale.[3] But such was not to be, and war resistance was invisible until at least 1898.

The Civil War, however, was only a moratorium in the development of the civil disobedience that had emerged in the 1840s and 1850s. In fact, a crucial period in the making of American traditions of civil disobedience occurred in the decades from Emancipation to 1920, between the extensive public discussion of the rights of freedmen and the constitutional amendment securing woman suffrage. This resumption is unsurprising, inasmuch as war between the states and the end of slavery led to incessant debate over national citizenship and oversight of state and local restrictions of civil rights. There were certainly advances and clarifications of rights, but advance was always contested and impeded. That was true for ex-slaves, whose civil rights, even after they were guaranteed constitutionally, were narrowed and even negated by local repression and U.S. Supreme Court decisions. It was at least as true for women, whose advocates insisted that their rights antecedent to the war against slavery were even more fortified by the Reconstruction amendments, which abolished slavery (1865), guaranteed civil rights (1868), and prohibited racial discrimination in voting rights (1870).

Civil disobedience as a tactic for advancing women's rights is an important theme of the post-emancipation decades, but it has been somewhat neglected, perhaps because scholars have been focused, understandably, on Reconstruction and the securing of rights for the former slaves (especially the men among them). The neglect is unfortunate because the early woman suffrage movement attempted to do in that era precisely what Hannah Arendt later commended as a legitimate purpose of civil disobedience—the assertion of expanded conceptions of equal rights for all citizens through agitation leading to test cases and innovative legal thinking.[4] With significant exceptions, most of them fairly recent, the efforts of women to attain the suffrage during and after Reconstruction have been ignored or dismissed as far-fetched, self-interested, and of no lasting consequence. What I will here contend is that women whose citizenship seemed anachronistically compromised in an era of expanding national rights made inventive use of precedents of civil disobedience and did so in ways of crucial significance for our understanding of American citizenship.

The groundwork for arguments in behalf of women's citizenship preceded the Civil War.[5] In the 1850s some woman's rights activists refused to pay taxes for as long as their rights as citizens were curtailed. By that time in New York, Massachusetts, and elsewhere, radical reformers had begun to assert a nonrestrictive view of citizenship that excluded no one on the basis of race, intellectual ability, or sex. In 1854 an address by Elizabeth Cady Stanton, arraigning the tyrant Custom before the bar of Common Sense, was placed on the desks of New York legislators. In 1858 Wendell Phillips, Thomas Wentworth Higginson, and Caroline Dall addressed a Massachusetts legislative committee in support of woman's right of suffrage.[6] In that year and the two following, Sarah Wall of Worcester refused to pay taxes until the word *male* was stricken from qualifications for voting in the state, and several other women made appeals to the Declaration of Independence, the Boston Tea Party, and the Revolution generally as they entered similar protests. Furthermore, the pre–Civil War campaigns of black and some white abolitionists for equal rights of citizenship continued after the war. It would be misleading, in other words, to regard black issues and tactics as *ante*-bellum and women's as *post*-bellum.[7]

Pursuit of blacks' civil rights and women's may be viewed as interwoven strands in the histories of republicanism and reform, even if, as we shall notice, they sometimes sounded antagonistic in goals and rhetoric. Sojourner Truth's defiance of horsecar segregation in Washington in 1865—she would run alongside and jump aboard whites-only cars—and Ida B. Wells's defiance of orders to leave a car in Memphis in 1882—she bit the conductor's hand and sued the company—followed a pattern from the antebellum black abolitionists and inspired women in later confrontations in the long civil rights movement.[8] In Atlanta in 1896, women organized a boycott of a streetcar company that sent a black passenger to jail for refusing to sit in Jim Crow seats. The company gave in.[9]

Protests against racial segregation on New Orleans streetcars erupted in 1867, followed by counter-protests against the protesters and the creation of a public emergency. After tense confrontations and careful negotiation by the mayor, the issue was defused, and black radicals moved on to confrontations over equality in theaters, restaurants, and public schools. Those other campaigns often had disappointing outcomes, but streetcars were not resegregated, and then only by state law, until 1902.[10] Similar confrontations erupted in Louisville, where black leaders decided to launch what an essay many decades later called "a full-scale 'ride-in.' " A young African American boy boarded a streetcar, walked past the driver, sat in the midst of white travelers, and ignored calls to move, even when jeering young whites boarded the car, taunted him, dragged him off, and began to beat him—at which point, as he started to defend himself, city police hauled him away and booked him for disturbing the peace. The local judge fined him and issued a warning against any similar violations of local law. But these warnings did not deter other blacks from sitting where they weren't supposed to and, when the drivers vacated their cars, taking over themselves, as black spectators cheered. Faced with widespread criticism and threats of federal intervention, the city and its streetcar company accepted the inevitability of mixed seating. In a strict sense these protests might not qualify as civil disobedience as they were not wholly nonviolent and they did not violate state or local ordinances enforcing segregation— these did not come until later in the century. But the policies under attack resembled those in effect in northern cities in previous decades. These events showed, according to one writer in the 1960s, that "Louisville Negroes deserve a place in the history of American efforts to validate nonresistance doctrines" because "they helped to ensure that loyalty to the value of nonviolence constituted a living, vital strand in an American subculture—a strand that neither the majority nor time could efface."[11]

A series of Supreme Court decisions cut short post–Civil War drives for civil rights and racial equality. Two were directly related to the use of civil disobedience to end segregation or racial exclusion on railroads, streetcars, restaurants, theaters, inns, amusement parks, and in other public places. A major decision that grouped together five *Civil Rights Cases*[12] held that despite the Reconstruction amendments and the Civil Rights Act of 1875, which Charles Sumner had steered through Congress, the federal government could not interfere with the acts of private individuals, such as conductors, ticket sellers, and innkeepers, in the states. Nor were discriminatory private actions a vestigial sign of enslavement. Some of those cases may have been deliberate legal tests, but there were not, as yet, state laws actually requiring segregation. By the time of the Court's *Plessy v. Ferguson* decision (1896)[13] the states of the former Confederacy had begun to impose Jim Crow through legislation. A shoemaker named Homer Plessy, seven-eighths white and not discernibly "colored" but still black under Louisiana law, was asked by a citizens' committee to violate the law, and the railroad was notified in advance of his intentions. He politely defied a Louisiana statute requiring railroad companies to provide separate accommodations for whites and blacks. His insistence on seating himself in a whites-only car until removed by force, jailed, and convicted of breaking a state law prompted the decision that separate facilities were constitutionally permissible (so long as nominally equal), a precedent that controlled race relations in the South until overturned with regard to schools and later restaurants and transportation lines in the 1950s and 1960s. One justice, the Kentuckian John Marshall Harlan, wrote vigorous, and subsequently influential, dissents to both the *Civil Rights* and *Plessy* decisions, but no Supreme Court revision came for half a century.[14] For many years any endeavor by women to secure their own constitutional rights as citizens were blocked by courts that had limited the civil rights of the ex-slaves.

Controversy lingers over the original connections between antebellum feminism and abolitionism. Some feminists developed their own "rights consciousness" after first pleading the cause of the slave; others distanced themselves from what they took to be a competitive movement.[15] During the war and afterward, as black men received the franchise and constitutional protections, mostly denied to women, the line dividing abolitionism and feminism became sharper. Some women reformers accepted these discriminations as temporarily necessary; others opposed the Fourteenth and especially the Fifteenth Amendments for embedding women's inferior status in the Constitution. Not only did some feminists speak against granting rights circumscribed by gender lines, but they sometimes argued in a racist manner—and perhaps gratuitously, since they could argue that they were advocating the rights of African-American women as much as their own.[16] In fact, some South Carolina African-American women were enabled to vote, with the aid of African-American election officials, under the Fifteenth Amendment.[17] "If intelligence, justice, and morality are to be placed in the government," said Susan B. Anthony to suffragists' applause, "then let the question of woman be brought up first and that of the negro last."[18] They offended some contemporaries by allying themselves with bigoted opponents of universal male suffrage like the copperhead George Francis Train, who spoke loosely of "niggers" and Sambos, warned of future rape cases being tried by "twelve negro jurymen," and ridiculed the prospect of Fifth Avenue white women having to "petition their boot blacks, barbers, porters, waiters and coachmen for the high-toned privilege of casting a ballot."[19] Nevertheless, despite the friction between the movements, suffragist leaders like Susan B. Anthony and Elizabeth Cady Stanton regularly referred to abolitionism's history for tactical precedents and legitimacy. After all, most of the women had antislavery backgrounds, and they were aided by men like Parker Pillsbury, Thomas Wentworth Higginson, Frederick Douglass, and Albert Gallatin Riddle, who had figured prominently in antislavery activity.

Replying to William Lloyd Garrison's denunciation of their alliance with Train, Stanton argued that Garrison had enrolled in his movement "every man and woman who believed in his idea; and a motley-minded class they were who wheeled into the anti-slavery ranks thirty years ago!" The analogy may not be altogether fitting: Garrisonians had indeed tolerated eccentrics and encouraged free speech, as Stanton said, and they had not shrunk from public denunciation, but they had taken a broad view of human rights even if doing so divided their movement. (Her husband Henry B. Stanton had been prominent among abolitionist critics of Garrison's fidelity to "extraneous" causes.)[20]

Yet the use Stanton made of her analogy is significant: the willingness to work in concert with Train (even to support his presidential aspirations!) signified an openness to any and all means that came to hand.

Placid conservatism still wonders at the wild, unaccountable things they [abolitionists] did in every part of the country—Mr. Garrison himself burning the Federal Constitution on the 4th of July, in the presence of the multitude.

Behold them stirring up mobs, dragged through the streets with ropes around their necks, breaking up Sunday meetings by rushing into the midst of congregations, and pouring out their vials of wrath on the heads of a sleeping people.

Behold them imprisoned as disturbers of the peace; shot down in the streets; arraigned at the bar of justice; hung on the gallows; a target for the civilized world; denounced, ridiculed, hissed at by the press as idiots, lunatics, fanatics: and yet Mr. Garrison affiliated with all these.[21]

A more accurate analogy might actually have been with antebellum black abolitionists, who had claimed the right to use any means available to win equality and free the enslaved and who often favored more broad-based political appeals than Garrison's purism countenanced.[22] To women's rights activists, a shared unenslaved noncitizenship imposed on them similar strategic openness to civil disobedience and means that enfranchised men might consider wild and unaccountable.[23]

Nevertheless, woman suffrage advocates did link themselves with abolitionism in a tradition of moral agitation (even as they criticized abolitionists' failure to advance civil rights for women). Stanton and Anthony proclaimed in 1868: "As the *Liberator*, in the hands of Mr. Garrison, was the pioneer, the pillar of light and of fire to the slave's emancipation, so we have endeavored to make 'THE REVOLUTION' the guiding star to the enfranchisement of woman."[24] The old abolitionist Pillsbury was for a time one of the newspaper's editors, and he frequently pointed to strong parallels. Once antislavery had been the most stirring moral revolution in the world; now that distinction belonged to woman suffrage.[25] Just as abolitionists had "harrowed up" American hearts with tales of slave mothers powerless to protect their babies, now the public must learn that white mothers, too, had no power the law must respect. Unfairness and cruelty in divorce law resulted from woman's noncitizenship.[26]

The civil disobedience tradition is closely linked to citizenship—to ideals of good citizenship as well as critiques of curtailed citizenship. The previous chapter ended with Albert Gallatin Riddle, an attorney for the Oberlin-Wellington rescuers, who holds an interesting place in the passage from the antislavery struggle to an arena where the civil disobedience tradition would next gain prominence—the struggle for woman suffrage. Riddle had been attorney in the case following the "Wellington Rescue" of a fugitive slave in 1858–59, later a Republican congressman, a consul in Civil

War–era Cuba, and a prosecutor in the trial of John Suratt as an accomplice in President Lincoln's assassination. In a major speech to an 1871 suffrage convention, as a prominent Republican politician in Washington, he championed the view that the Fourteenth Amendment had made women "full and complete citizens" when it declared, "All persons born or naturalized in the United States and subject to the jurisdiction thereof, are citizens of the United States and of the state wherein they reside," and went on: "No states shall make or enforce any law which shall abridge the privileges or immunities of citizens." On that occasion he announced his plan to bring test cases in the District of Columbia courts challenging any denial of women's right to register and vote.[27] In the years that followed, state courts and the U.S. Supreme Court would reject any suggestion that even the Fifteenth Amendment created any positive right to vote associated with national citizenship. But for a time the case for suffrage rested on the argument that Riddle made and the similar ones that Francis Minor presented for his wife Virginia in Missouri and that Susan B. Anthony, who publicly praised Riddle's efforts,[28] defended in her 1873 trial for unlawful voting in Rochester, New York. Civil disobedience was, in this account, closely linked to the nonrestrictive view of citizenship that had been ventured in Massachusetts before the war. Riddle's approach to achieving that goal— "We need only intelligent, firm, decisive, and deciding—reasonably brave courts, and to have a question brought to their adjudication"—turned out to be too optimistic. Change would not come so easily, and civil disobedience would often in the future become a pressure tactic rather than a vindication of eternal principles of justice. Nevertheless, a century later, when political philosophers and legal scholars defended civil disobedience, their views of American politics and law were much like Riddle's.

Other ties to the past were significant, too. Perhaps surprisingly, we may even draw connections between the cause of woman suffrage and the infamous *Dred Scott* decision. Certainly "the Taney settlement," as Frederick Douglass called the outcome derisively, was a major provocation in a line of events that emboldened radical stances, making the law seem less sacred and at least some governmental institutions a little less divinely ordained. In the civil disobedience tradition *Dred Scott* took its place as the classic demonstration that decided law was not necessarily to be bowed down to. "What the decision of the Supreme Court of the United States in the Dred Scott case was to the rights of negroes as citizens of the United States," the decision of the Supreme Court in *Bradwell v. Illinois* (1873) "is to the political rights of women in Illinois—annihilation." For Myra Bradwell's supporters, that word summed up her rejected plea to be admitted to practice law. "The recent decision in the United States Supreme Court" in *Minor v. Happersett* (1875) "will have as much force in suppressing the individuality and self-assertion of women as had the opinion of Judge Taney, in the Dred-Scott case, in suppressing the emancipation of slavery. The day has come when precedents are made rather than blindly followed." That is how an annual report at the National Woman Suffrage convention in 1876 reported the outcome of the test case of woman's right to vote without any further act of Congress or amendment to the Constitution.[29] These were not test cases provoked by acts of civil disobedience. The women were plaintiffs who lost these landmark cases. Virginia Minor of St. Louis did not violate any laws in order to create a test case. Her claim, in which she was joined and represented by her husband, Francis Minor, was that the registrar unlawfully refused to enroll her on the list of voters and thus deprived her of her right to vote. They pursued that claim in order to broaden discussion and galvanize public opinion as well as to seek new interpretations of the law—purposes that would eventually be recognized as a justification for civil disobedience.[30]

Susan B. Anthony, about a year later, made it to court when she was charged with illegal voting after she succeeded in intimidating (with threats of a lawsuit) registrars to enroll her and poll inspectors to deposit her ballot in the ballot box. Thirteen other Rochester women registered with her, and seven or eight of them voted, too. Hundreds of other women voted or tried to vote in this period as part of a campaign asserting that women as citizens had the right to vote.[31] In the end, Anthony's judge directed a verdict of guilty. The case stands as a memorable act of civil disobedience even though she did not go to jail. Sometimes this campaign is described as based on the argument that the Fourteenth Amendment enfranchised women. Anthony made that argument but did not stop there. She and other suffragists drew an argument from *Dred Scott*, especially from the broad assertion in Taney's opinion that "the words people of the United States, and citizens, are synonymous terms, and mean the same thing."[32] That was a key step in Taney's determination that blacks had never been included among the people and thus had no rights as citizens. But for Anthony emancipation had changed the meaning: "Thus does Judge Taney's decision, which was such a terrible ban to the black man, while he was a slave, now, that he is a person, no longer property, pronounce him a citizen possessed of an entire equality of privileges, civil and political. And not only the black man, but the black woman, and all women as well."[33]

One problem with hailing Taney as an authority, however clever it must have seemed, was that Taney had noted in passing: "Undoubtedly, a person may be a citizen, that is, a member of the community who form the sovereignty, although he exercises no share of the political power, and is incapacitated from holding particular offices. Women and minors, who form a part of the political family, cannot vote; and when a property qualification is required to vote or hold a particular office, those who have not the necessary qualification cannot vote or hold the office, yet they are citizens."[34] The suffragists never quoted those sentences. They preferred the even broader remarks about citizenship found in the concurring opinion of the most proslavery justice, Peter Daniel, who argued that "the African negro race" throughout history had been "subjects of capture and purchase" rather than being recognized as "partaking of the character of nationality, or civil or political polity; . . . and that the introduction of that race into every section of this country was not as members of civil or political society, but as slaves, as property in the strictest sense of the term." Daniel followed that observation with a sweeping summation. "There is not, it is believed, to be found in the theories of writers on government, or in any actual experiment heretofore tried, an exposition of the term citizen, which has not been considered as conferring the actual possession and enjoyment of the perfect right of acquisition and enjoyment of an entire equality of privileges, civil and political."[35] All this to show that Dred Scott did not have the status of citizen required to be a plaintiff or defendant in federal courts.

In a widely delivered speech on the question titled "Is It a Crime for a Citizen of the United States to Vote?" Anthony recognized that the justices had spoken copiously of citizenship as part of an argument about what blacks as noncitizens must lack. But times had changed; slaves were emancipated; and only after "the negroes became free men, hence citizens," had some Republican judges and lawmakers sought to curtail Taney's and Daniel's sweeping principles by asserting that "the phrase, a citizen of the United States, without addition or qualification, means neither more nor less than a member of the nation."[36] If that alteration were accepted, Anthony complained, then being a citizen of the American republic implied nothing more than being "a subject of an empire"—a "base conclusion" that "all true and patriotic citizens must repudiate."

> We all know that American citizenship, without addition or qualifi-
> cation, means the possession of equal rights, civil and political. We all
> know that the crowning glory of every citizen of the United States is,
> that he can either give or withhold his vote from every law and every
> legislator under the government.[37]

The point here is a fairly simple one: *Dred Scott* linked democratic ideas
and patriotic emotions of the antebellum era to new kinds of law breaking
pursued by champions of woman suffrage in the 1860s and 1870s.

We might note, finally, that suffragists as civil disobedients never cited
Thoreau, though some may perhaps have known him. His scorn for political rights was not harmonious with their goals, and in any case his period
of influence lay in the future. But they did place themselves in the context
of a nonrestrictive view of citizenship that in the 1850s some radical
reformers had begun to advance and some jurists, who were by no means
radical, had curiously articulated. In light of the Reconstruction amendments, it could be argued, there was no longer a doubt that women had
the legal right to vote, and the National Woman Suffrage Association no
longer appealed for legislation to gain a right that women already possessed.
"We ask the judges," Anthony wrote, in cases challenging that right,
"to render true and unprejudiced opinions of the law, and wherever
there is room for a doubt to give its benefit on the side of liberty and
equal rights to women, remembering that 'the true rule of interpretation
under our national constitution, especially since its amendments, is that
anything for human rights is constitutional, everything against human
right unconstitutional.'"[38]

One otherwise useful study of "suffrage militancy" states that Anthony's
focus on suffrage "estranged" her from Stanton; by 1872 she "stood alone"
as she cast her vote in the presidential election, and she had only one real
ally when she faced the judge. That study cites the jail narrative of a later
militant, Doris Stevens, which opened with an account of Anthony's isolation as "the only figure in the nation appealing for the rights of women
when the rights of black men were agitating the public mind."[39] Here we
have another example of a tendency in civil disobedience stories to exaggerate the singularity of the individual protester. It may tell us something
about early twentieth-century militants' wish to claim Anthony as a heroine
isolated by mild-mannered associates abandoning her on the path toward

their kind of activism. But it is simply inaccurate. Factional conflict and disagreement over ends and means abounded in the long struggle for suffrage. But Anthony was never all alone, and certainly not when she cast her ballot, as it happened, for Grant.

Post–Civil War activists developed a critique of women's legal situation that emboldened them, as Anthony explained, not to sue patiently for the franchise but to assert defiantly that by right they already had it. That assertion was called the "New Departure." The *Revolution*, the voice of the National Woman Suffrage Association (NWSA), frequently urged women to appear at polling places and insist on their right to cast a ballot. Train gave examples from Britain (where he was traveling and imprisoned in summer 1868) and urged American women to simply walk in and vote— and if cast out, to refuse to pay taxes.[40]

From this assertion they moved to action. Issue after issue of *Revolution* carried reports of women voting in localities that permitted it—114 casting their ballots for prohibition in one Michigan town, for example—in proof that respectable women had no aversion to the franchise.[41] There was encouraging news from Colorado, Wyoming, and the West. Other reports showed a building movement to demand the franchise in federal elections and wherever else it was denied. Vineland, New Jersey, a reform community, was the scene of important efforts. In November 1868, after being turned away from the official polls, over 160 women publicly cast votes in their own ballot box.[42] In Mount Vernon, New York, where a majority of taxpayers happened to be women, there was a serious challenge, ultimately unsuccessful, to women's exclusion from voting on appropriations of money. After losing out in a town meeting (attended by Anthony), three women brought ballots to the inspector of elections, who simply placed them *under* the ballot box.[43] In April 1869 a delegation of women attempted to register in Washington, D.C. A similar delegation two years later included the writers E. D. E. N. Southworth and Grace Greenwood, and "several lady physicians"—accompanied by Frederick Douglass.[44] In St. Louis, Minor was preparing to take legal action if denied the vote.[45] A ticket representing Massachusetts women who claimed the franchise under the Fourteenth Amendment was put forward in November 1869, and a young Worcester woman "outwitted the male despotism" and got her vote in.[46] It seems clear that rather than Anthony standing alone, at least 200, and maybe many more, women pressed their right to vote similarly in a concerted campaign.[47]

There may be some doubt that these activists, though they approached the edges of civil disobedience, really thought that voting was a right that could be won by such means. It was a form of agitation, at its best earnest and educational, but potentially dismissible as merely theatrical and ultimately giving way—for better or worse—to courtroom decision. At a NWSA meeting in October 1869, after Charlotte B. Wilbour read an essay on the educational effects of the ballot for women, S. F. Norton proposed a resolution calling on New York women to cast ballots at someone's house, present them to election officials, and if turned back, mount a court challenge. Wilbour, though sympathetic, thought the tactic "would cause a good deal of ridicule." Norton admitted "it might be called something of a play," but it would show, contrary to what some men claimed, that "women really wanted the ballot." Stanton brought discussion to a halt with the opinion that "this playing at voting [was] absurd."

> The laws are not very good to be sure, but still, women should do nothing illegal. We should not think of going to the polls until we have our full rights. What woman ought to do is not to Play Voter but to educate herself to understand what she wants and what the ballot would do for her.[48]

This charge of "playing voter" was made against women at Vineland and elsewhere if they went beyond advocacy to some kind of action to show their interest in the suffrage.[49] It is hard to see how educating themselves on the good policies women voters could bring into being was a sufficient substitute for some kind of symbolic demonstration. Pillsbury used theatrical metaphors to describe an effort by sixty women in a Boston suburb to vote—their action was "a rehearsal of Woman Suffrage," and the men who jeered at them were the lewd fellows of the pit—but he applauded their action, while only hoping that soon Wyoming or some jurisdiction where women could vote would send a woman to Congress.[50]

What were the alternative strategies for enfranchisement? Stanton and the NWSA executive committee recommended pressure in Washington to secure a sixteenth amendment. This was considered more feasible than working state by state trying to organize inexperienced women to petition ignorant men (defined by ethnic stereotypes) for equal rights. A third recourse, as we have seen, was appeal to the courts, since there was nothing in the Constitution to forbid woman's voting—an alternative that had "the advantage of referring the decision to the best minds of the nation." Thus she approved of Wilbour's report and Minor's contemplated action.[51] By January 1871 Anthony was advocating a Supreme Court test of what "we" now claimed: that the Fourteenth and Fifteenth Amendments granted women the vote.[52] In what was hailed as the movement's "new phase," Victoria Woodhull, a fascinating and notorious public figure, made the same argument in an address to a committee of Congress. She also launched her campaign for the U.S. presidency. The same points were presented in a memorial to the Judiciary Committee of the House of Representatives making this claim. Woodhull was supported by, among others, Albert Gallatin Riddle, who was prepared to advance her cause in the courts.[53] He also represented the plaintiff in *Sarah J. Spencer v. The Board of Registration*, who had presented herself to vote and been turned away and whose case was decided in the Supreme Court of the District of Columbia in October 1871.[54] A neglected figure in our history, Riddle clearly ranks among a handful of male lawyers who were key formulators of a new view of voting and women's citizenship.

There was some reluctance to get a judicial rejection too speedily. As the abolitionist Wendell Phillips pointed out, the claims under the two amendments amounted to "too good a handle for agitation" and shouldn't be squandered.[55] From this point of view some theatrics might actually have informed the better strategy. At the least, we should note the possibility that what Phillips warned against actually occurred: one reason for the stagnancy of suffragism by 1900 was that a promising line of argument had indeed been snuffed out in the courts.

In October, the *Spencer* case was lost. Riddle had argued, together with an attorney named Francis Miller in an associated case, essentially that nothing in the Constitution precluded women from voting, which was a natural right, that well-understood definitions of citizenship depended on the suffrage, that the Fourteenth Amendment forbade states to abridge "the privileges or immunities of citizens," and the Fifteenth specifically barred denials of the suffrage. That was essentially Woodhull's argument, too. It is not an argument that has received as much attention as it deserves. It did not carry the day; it paid no heed to prevailing prejudices against women's participation in public life; and we all know it took an amendment to secure woman suffrage. The justices did not comment on Miller's challenge that they could gain "true glory," such as Lord Mansfield had won in the *Somersett* decision ending slavery in England. In a brief opinion they found that the right to be a voter was not absolute but required legislative action, which had not occurred in the District of Columbia.[56]

Two other court cases, also unsuccessful, culminated this line of ideological and tactical experimentation: *Anthony* and *Minor*. In the first, Susan B. Anthony was convicted of violating an 1870 statute by "knowingly voting without having a lawful right to vote." Sometimes this case is presented as a dramatic show of civil disobedience: "In 1872 she tested the discriminatory effect of the 14th Amendment by barging into a Rochester polling place and casting a defiantly illegal ballot for the Presidency."[57] Perhaps she was more confrontational than Riddle's and Miller's clients. But in actuality, though only she was charged, fourteen women were defendants; they all had appeared to register as voters, and their registration had been accepted by a two-to-one vote of the election inspectors with the advice of a government supervisor. On Election Day their names were on the poll list; their votes had been received. All three inspectors, including the dissenter, were indicted, and convicted, in the same proceedings for having knowingly received illegal votes.

Anthony's defense was that her vote was legal under the Fourteenth Amendment. If it was not, she thought it was, counsel had advised her that it was; all she had done was to present her vote. The judge rejected good-faith error as a defense and directed the jury to find her guilty. Anthony was denied the opportunity to speak in her own behalf, except at sentencing, and then the judge tried quickly to cut her off. She ignored him and spoke at length. Her attorney, Henry Selden, a prominent ex-judge, had advised her, by his own account, that there was no way to test the legality of voting except by presenting herself to vote; therefore, it was unjust to find her criminal for doing what she had no way of knowing in advance would be so found. Selden argued at length that there was no equal justice in finding a woman a criminal for doing something a man can do with honor, under a law she had no voice in making; that such inequality puts a woman in a position of noncitizenship analogous to the political situation of slaves; and that the three Reconstruction amendments defined citizenship in such a way that women could not be turned away from the polls. If anyone paid attention, the trial thus served as a good forum for making an important argument, and Selden emphasized that the absurdity of the criminal charge only strengthened the case for woman suffrage. Perhaps the case did benefit the cause—it certainly got attention—but it is clear that the case was dealt with summarily and had no good legal result.[58]

At the conclusion, as the judge moved to silence her, Anthony managed to protest the particular decision and to express outrage at a legal system in which no woman's voice could be heard (even her attorney was male) on matters of fundamental consequence to women. The case raised issues concerning the meanings of slavery and what the laws had changed by abolishing it, and those issues brought Anthony directly to the precedents for civil disobedience. The "man made forms of law" applied in the Fugitive Slave Act had made it a crime punishable with imprisonment and a heavy fine "for you, or me, or any of us, to give a cup of cold water, a crust of bread, or a night's shelter to a panting fugitive as he was tracking his way to Canada."

> And every man or woman in whose veins coursed a drop of human sympathy violated that wicked law, reckless of consequences, and was justified in so doing. As then, the slaves who got their freedom must take it over, or under, or through the unjust forms of law, precisely so, now, must women, to get their right to a voice in this government, take it; and I have taken mine, and mean to take it at every possible opportunity.

From an unjust judge she asked not leniency "but rather the full rigors of the law." Given a fine of $100 and court costs, she vowed never to "pay a dollar."[59]

In a speech delivered throughout her county before the trial, Anthony had expounded on the right of revolution and the evil of taxation without representation while urging women to refuse to pay taxes. She gave many examples, including Sarah Wall of Worcester, Massachusetts, who had refused for twenty years. Eventually, the government tired of seizing Wall's possessions and simply removed her from the tax rolls.[60] Besides justifying civil disobedience, in the style of antebellum blacks, under the right of revolution, however, Anthony hoped to take her case further, in a different use of civil disobedience, as a test of the constitutional meaning of citizenship. Apparently, this intention was thwarted by the court's failure to enforce the fine, thus giving the case no standing for appeal.[61]

Supreme Court adjudication awaited the *Minor* case. The historian Norma Basch has speculated that, in the controversy aroused by *Anthony,* the justices sought a case that would settle the constitutional issues and that they decided the case on constitutional grounds rather than others that were available.[62] Minor, represented by her husband Francis Minor, sued the St. Louis registrar on grounds very similar to those raised by Riddle in *Spencer*. Both cases combined a bold reading of the recent amendments with an argument that the Constitution had for long been distorted and its fundamental compatibility with natural rights suppressed. Chief Justice Waite, for a unanimous court, denied the argument that the Fourteenth Amendment had created or recognized any new national rights pertaining to citizenship; the amendment's effects operated only through state law. The court was not impressed with Minor's strong arguments based on the republican guarantee clause. It was established by long practice, shown in many different ways, from the origins of the nation that women were in fact citizens but that citizenship did not require, and in the case of women usually did not entail, the right to vote.[63]

Once again, judged by immediate results, this line of action was a failure—worse than inconsequential since unfavorable Supreme Court decisions can cut off future action. We should note, nevertheless, that Basch in a probing article calls Francis Minor's argument "a dazzling reconstruction of law as it ought to be, and a trenchant indictment of the way it was."[64] The Minors had raised to the level of constitutional discourse fundamental questions about women's political existence and challenged lingering assumptions about women's differences from men. Such a confluence of brilliant rereadings of constitutional possibility, in a context of mounting acceptance of national definitions of rights, had a potential importance going beyond how a line of cases was decided in the short term.[65]

In her defense of "illegal voting," Anthony urged "the women of this republic, at once, [to] resolve, never again to submit of taxation, until their right to vote be recognized. Amen." She thereby pointed to another form of civil disobedience—tax resistance—that many women engaged in from the late 1850s onward and especially in the late 1870s. Petitioners insistently asked: If women were unrepresented, how could they be taxed?[66] "Let every woman property holder refuse to pay her tax to build town-house, or school house, bridge or sidewalk, until she is allowed to vote as to whether the improvements shall be made, and town officers will very soon find no by-laws to prohibit women's voting."[67] As *Revolution*'s publisher, Anthony paid the newspaper's tax under protest even though she was unrepresented in the government. "I had thought of resisting the payment of this tax on high moral grounds, ... but learning that the courts do not take cognizance of moral questions, I have decided to send you the sum ($14.10) enclosed."[68] The physician Harriot Hunt paid her taxes under protest and published her protests in the newspapers for years, it was said, "until the poetry of the act has long since expired." After Anthony's correspondence was read at a meeting of the National Woman's Suffrage Association, some claimed to have legal advice that taxation of women "could not stand the test of the courts" if women refused to pay.[69] Stanton envisioned women tax refusers prompting policemen to seize their furniture and the state to auction it off—"what a practical demonstration they would make of their faith in the good old doctrine of 'THE REVOLUTION'—[']Taxation without representation is tyranny.' Agitation! Agitation!!"[70]

When the tax collector sued Sarah Wall, however, the court found these arguments without merit.[71] Lucy Stone refused to pay her taxes in Orange, New Jersey, and had her property sold in front of her house in the cold of January 1858.[72] In the 1870s, tax refusal became much more common. In one of two widely publicized cases, Abigail Kelley and her husband Stephen S. Foster lost a cow and annually repurchased their own farm at auction so that the city of Worcester could take their tax by legal action rather than voluntary payment. The city held on to the deed to the farm until, in the face of Stephen's declining health in 1880, the couple settled their tax bill and reclaimed ownership. In a letter to an 1874 Convention on Taxation without Representation in Worcester, Thomas Wentworth Higginson wrote: "These sales of property are to the Woman Suffrage Movement what the Fugitive Slave cases were to the Anti-slavery movement."[73]

None of these cases led to a Supreme Court test of the limits on taxation of women nonvoters. There were, in fact, serious problems with any assumption that no one could be taxed unless he or she could vote, even though slogans from the *Revolution* suggested otherwise. But the issue had its day in the long pursuit of women's equality, and it did lead to examples of an important version of civil disobedience—tax resistance. One of these examples stands as an especially dramatic parable in the midst of the nineteenth-century Americanization of civil disobedience.

Julia Evelina Smith and Abigail Hadassah Smith were celebrated in the suffrage movement of the mid–1870s for refusing to pay their property taxes in Glastonbury, Connecticut. Denied the right to vote, the sisters charged that they and other unmarried women were assessed unfairly. In

1877, when she was eighty-two and her sister was seventy-seven, Julia published what she called her scrapbook, entitled it *Abby Smith and Her Cows*, and told the story of their stand against "taxation without representation," the losses they suffered, and their surprising celebrity. In contrast to the tax-resistant Thoreau's posthumous rise to fame, the sisters' fame soon faded. In a recent scholar's summation, "If their personal tax rebellion is remembered at all it is an amusing anecdote, not the heroic battle of two aged women standing against their world."[74] That may be too dismissive. Though the scrapbook format no longer suits popular reading habits, Julia's work, with the many voices it records, local and national, supportive or critical, deserves attention as a classic work in the American civil disobedience tradition.

The sisters, who ranked among their town's wealthiest residents and largest taxpayers, could not be said to be "virtually" represented by their deceased father or nonexistent husbands. Protesting that their rates were raised unfairly, they vowed "to test legal and Constitutional objections to the utmost . . . by acting according to their own views of what is lawful as well as just."[75] To justify resistance, they took up the language of the Revolution, whose centennial festivities were at a peak, and the antislavery movement, which northern states by that time treated as venerable. They stood for the same "American principle as did the citizens who ripped open the tea-chests in Boston harbor," and they upheld the great truth that the slave masters failed to grasp: "The slave wanted the control of his own earnings; and so does every human being of what rightfully belongs to him."[76]

In June 1869 the overseer of the highway entered their home to ask for an early payment of $18 because he "could get no money from the men"— this is the episode where Julia begins her chronicle—and he returned to seek the same payment again in October, explaining that part of it would go toward $600 in per diems, horse hire, meals, and other expenses needed in order to register male voters' names. Julia not only objected to being double-charged but pointed out that the town was being overcharged, "for I have no doubt one woman would write down every name in town for half that money." The sisters paid up, but the contest was on.

In 1872 their annual town tax was raised $100. Two widows also suffered increases, but (so far as the sisters knew) no men did.[77] The sisters still paid the tax. In October 1873, they refused to pay. In November they refused again. In the same month, Abby received permission to address the town assembly and delivered a stirring speech on liberty, equality, and the heritage of the Revolution. Because of their nonpayment, on January 1, 1874, the tax collector seized seven of the sisters' Alderney cows, penned them, and in a scene out of a Thomas Hardy novel, led them to the town's signpost, where a crowd marched forward, "with a dog and a drum," to bid ridiculously low prices.[78] The sisters bought back their cows, but they were offended that neighbors had bid so low in an effort to "buy an Alderney cow cheap."[79] In April 1874, denied a second chance to address the town meeting, Abby climbed up on a wagon to present her vision of a community in which neighbors and friends respected the rights of women and the contributions they made to the larger family. By this time, town leaders had seized fifteen acres of meadow land, worth about $2,000, to settle the tax bill and had auctioned the land to the only bidder, an unscrupulous neighbor, for $78.35. That sale led to three court cases, which the sisters won in the end—but on grounds narrowly related to the seizure of land rather than disposable property and emphatically not on grounds that enfranchised women property holders. After that, the town seized shares of bank stock and sold them at public auction to settle the tax bill. More cows were auctioned, all but one bought back again by the sisters, later in 1876.[80] Less ceremony (no dog or drum) accompanied these sales, but it still astonished the sisters that close neighbors would bid to take their property.

Abby Smith and Her Cows is notable for the cleverness with which it displays special domestic scenes—two elderly women and their cows, who provide rich cream, and a house brimming with memories of parents and sisters—all imperiled by inept town officers and greedy neighbors who behaved like "banditti" under cover of male-created and male-enforced laws. The sisters stand up for the sanctity of their home and claim their revolutionary heritage in a spirit of "passive resistance." They don't shriek or cause a disturbance, according to one reporter; "they are good nature itself."[81] But they also personify noncooperation; they bow to governmental injustice only "at the point of the bayonet."[82]

Julia's scrapbook bears some resemblance to Thoreau's more famous account of tax resistance. Both express a wish to go on with life without the interference of the "tax gatherer." Both express contempt for the bumbling behavior of the state's representatives. Both object stubbornly to the state's invasion of privacy. In ending his famous essay on civil disobedience, Thoreau imagines a government that could permit "a few . . . to live apart from it, not meddling with it, nor embraced by it, who fulfilled all the duties of neighbors and fellow-men."[83] The Smiths told the tax collector, "We had hoped they [the government] would let us live in peace the rest of our lives." I will not claim that the Smiths' book is stylistically equal to Thoreau's essay, though its "quaint" and "artless" simplicity and plain speaking earned praise in its day.[84] I cannot imagine Thoreau indulging in the pathos of the Alderney cows, with their pet names, imprinted on Julia and moaning mournfully when taken away.[85] Nevertheless, the sisters' book is distinctive, ironic, mischievous. It shares with Thoreau's essay some of the tactics of conflict that Richard Gregg would later describe in *The Power of Nonviolence* as "moral jiu-jitsu," carried out in the presence of onlookers.[86]

When suffragists began to celebrate Julia and Abby Smith, they often emphasized the sisters' antislavery background. Lucy Stone reported that William Lloyd Garrison had spoken in the shade of the elms of their "forever historic" home when no other place could be found for an abolitionist meeting.[87] Abby Smith and her cows, said Isabella Beecher Hooker, "were marching on like John Brown's soul."[88] The obituary of Julia Smith in the *Woman's Journal* described her, perhaps with a little exaggeration, as "an historic woman, who, after doing what she could in the anti-slavery cause, opposed all the power she had against the sin and shame which taxes and governs women without their consent."[89] It was true enough: Julia, her mother, and her sisters had been engaged in charitable work and antislavery petitioning, and after the deaths of their parents and sisters Abby and Julia came to the attention of the suffragists. What should not be ignored, however, is that both antislavery and the turn to suffragist protest were related to a complex family history.

The father, Zephaniah Hollister Smith, after a Yale education and a false start as a Standing Order clergyman, adopted Restorationist religious views (in Scotland, England, and colonial America called Sandemanian or Glasian), rejected the hireling ministry, and moved on to a new career in law and politics. His wife, Hannah Hadassah Hickok, sold family property in South Britain, Connecticut, that she, as an only child, had inherited, and in 1795 she bought the farm and splendid home in Glastonbury. In his new career Zephaniah did well. That is, he made money and held public office, though his wife's inheritance surely helped. There were five girls, all with special names, some biblical, others classical or poetical; they were unusually well educated, and some had taught in schools away from home. None of them married, though at least some had suitors. In Julia's and Abby's recollection, their father "had imbibed a prejudice against marriage laws, and a distrust of man's chivalry, while discharging his duties as a lawyer!"[90] The family developed into a community, dividing up the housework, active in charitable work, and pursuing individual talents in music, needlework, and painting.[91] Hannah and her daughters took active roles in women's antislavery activity in the 1830s and 1840s. They taught young "negresses" in Sunday school and composed and circulated antislavery petitions among female factory operatives. In petitions protesting the "gag rule" by which Congress avoided receiving petitions, they stressed unenfranchised women's lack of access to their rulers. Hannah wrote the radical abolitionist Abigail Kelley in 1838 of her daughters' frustration in visiting "almost every house in this town" and finding women unwilling to discuss slavery or express an opinion contrary to their husbands'.[92]

Julia's scholarly attainments were the boast of the family. She was apparently most devoted to her father's restorationist beliefs, though all five sisters had in the time of "the Miller excitement" (1843) prepared for the prophesied Second Coming. Competent in Greek, Latin, and Hebrew, Julia translated the Bible five times in its entirety and finally published a translation in the 1870s, during the tax controversy, to "show that one woman has done, without aid, what one man has never done." When a delegation from the town demanded tax money, Julia told them, among other things, that "she would never have published her Bible had not the town used us so ill." By using bank stock to pay for printing the Bible, the sisters reduced their estate and eliminated one-half of their tax bill.[93] If the work ever made any profit, they wished it to go to "the suffragists." A theologically well-informed study identifies Julia's initial motive as not so much feminist as restorationist and adventist. Despite errors in his predictions William Miller had awakened a desire to know "the exact meaning of every word" of the Bible. Julia rejected commentaries that guided readers to accept one favored reading.[94] But the confrontations with the town made her want to show that women's intellectual potential was at least equal to men's.[95]

In other words, the Smiths were linked to antebellum reform traditions, and though hardly leading feminists, were keenly sensitive to issues of women's inhibited and unequal participation in public life. I come back to the artfulness of Julia's account in that book. "Perhaps the public would like to learn," she begins, slightly disingenuously, how two innocent women, brought up with "no idea of going contrary to men's laws," were "driven into their present unpleasant situation."[96] Yet much of the energy of *Abby*

Smith and Her Cows derives from the extended glimpses of a cultivated and sentimental family community—like the March family with father home and without the marriages—rather than the pathetic tale of the cows and the gratification of mounting fame.[97] Abby and Julia delayed their resolution to resist unjust taxation during the months of the illness and death of their eldest sister, Hancy, in 1871.

That's the main story, initially told as a local drama but soon attracting a wider audience. Regional and, later, national newspapers reported events in Glastonbury. Inexorably, the national suffrage movement provided a context for interpreting the cause célèbre. The sisters attended the first convention of the Connecticut Woman Suffrage Association in Hartford in 1869, then a meeting of the American Woman Suffrage Association, a rival of NWSA, in New York in 1873 (*after* which they began their tax refusal). A great 1874 tax protest meeting in Worcester received them as notables. Suffrage leaders brought friendship and publicity to the sisters' home. In January 1878, Julia was invited to speak to a NWSA convention in Washington and summarize the story of how their cows were taken away "to satisfy the tax-collector." At a reception in her honor, attended by "many women, notable in art, science, and literature, and men high in political station"—as the Stanton-Anthony-Gage *History of Woman Suffrage* described it—she said she was down to two cows, Taxey and Votey. (The pet names disappeared as the cows became political symbols.) Taxey—she said—was "very obtrusive," confronting her as soon as she stepped outdoors, while Votey was "quiet and shy." But things were looking up, "and it is my opinion, that in a very short time, wherever you find Taxey there Votey will be also."[98]

In a study of women and citizenship, Linda Kerber has quoted the latter remark somewhat critically. Tax paying was an obligation, and its "reciprocal" was not representation, as suffragists contended, but the protection of government.[99] The theoretical "fallacy" of the Smiths' stand was in fact pointed out by an otherwise sympathetic writer for the *New York Tribune:* "it is the property that pays the tax and not the owner of it," and the property of non-adult boys and out-of-state residents, as well as women, was protected even though they could not vote.[100] In the practical world, however, the Smiths might have replied that elected officials favored and protected those who voted in elections.

The literalist dissenting spirit of Julia's Bible project is important to understanding the sisters' courage to resist human authority. Consider a letter she and Abby cosigned in November 1876: " 'Satan is the god of this world,' the Bible says, and nothing looks more like it than to be robbed of our property in this way, sanctioned by law."[101] One interviewer praised Abby as a theologian who relied solely on a "deep under-current of the Bible." Over time she, too, had ceased to care about a "single literal interpretation," while valuing languages as a way of getting close to "a faint idea of eternal truth."[102] The sisters did not turn the Bible to political purposes, but Abby made sure it appeared repeatedly in the drama. In fact a notice for Julia's *Literal and Exact Translation of the Holy Bible* appeared inside the cover of *Abby Smith and Her Cows*.[103]

The Smiths' tax resistance had no important legal outcome. After three trials the sisters got neither the vote nor relief from taxes.[104] No appeal decided any great constitutional issue. The family idyll came to a bitter end after Abby died in July 1878 at the age of eighty-one. The next year Julia, eighty-six, married a retired New Hampshire judge, who had come across her Bible, sought out her acquaintance, and swiftly made her, as one scholar puts it, "his third well-to-do bride."[105] This husband began to pay Glastonbury taxes, for the first time in seven years, thus ending the tax protest, and he sold off the family property, amid bitter conflict with former friends and neighbors.[106]

A final perspective: the woman's movement's adoption of taxation as a key issue for showing the injustice of women's disfranchisement has been criticized for attaching suffrage advocacy narrowly to rights of property rather than to more universal claims of human rights. On one hand, this version of tax resistance marked an impoverishment of democratic thinking about the individual's relation to society and the state. On the other, it reflected insensitivity to economic distinctions in society. Julia omitted from her scrapbook one letter to the *Woman's Journal* charging that the Smiths' complaints must "seem rather Quixotic to the hardworking farmers of Glastonbury, many of whom would, undoubtedly, gladly surrender their right to vote, for a good slice of the property of those sisters."[107] There's no doubt that the Smiths, unmarried and rich, were consistent voices for the "taxation without representation" argument. They willingly paid a drain tax, for example, because they could vote on it.[108] They did, occasionally, admit that poor women needed the vote even more than property holders, because as voters perhaps they could close the grogshops and get town officials to protect them from men's brutality.[109] At least they did not ridicule the efforts of poor, uneducated freedmen to vote, as did the *History of Woman Suffrage* in the same pages that recorded Julia's remarks to the illustrious society of Washington.

With constitutional appeals and tax refusals reaching dead ends, the rival organizations of the Reconstruction Era merged in 1890 to form a new National American Woman Suffrage Association (NAWSA), which pursued suffrage for women with a more cautious tone and on a state-by-state basis (as the *Minor* decision required). Dissatisfied with a gradual political approach (unlikely ever to extend to all forty-eight states), radicals created a new organization, called the Congressional Union and eventually the National Woman's Party (NWP), with the intention of taking more militant steps to press Congress to adopt a new constitutional amendment, often called the Susan B. Anthony Amendment, composed and submitted to Congress in 1878 by a California senator and friend of Anthony and resubmitted almost every term thereafter. Short and to the point, it made up for the deficiencies in the Fifteenth Amendment by enfranchising women across the nation.[110] Congress passed the Nineteenth Amendment in May and June 1919, and the necessary thirty-six states had ratified it by August 1920. The NAWSA was not, of course, opposed to the amendment, nor was the NWP unmoved by suffrage's victories in states, especially large ones like California in 1911 and New York, in the East, where progress was slower, in 1917. What differentiated the two organizations were the constituencies they appealed to and the tactics and rhetoric they preferred to advance their goals. To the extent that any "wild" acts of disobedience by suffragists are familiar today, they are those of NWP "militants" in the years running up to passage of the Nineteenth Amendment.

If American court decisions necessitated a state-by-state outlook, events overseas encouraged a bolder perspective. British antislavery forces, successful in establishing a policy of emancipation by 1833, had exemplified to some Americans the advantages of taking a moderate political course without confrontational rhetoric and divisive means. British suffragism, however, encountered less consensus than had antislavery; it was less immediately successful, angrier, and less conciliatory; and it was willing to alienate public opinion and sometimes even to resort to (and suffer) violence. Anne Cobden-Sanderson, for example, daughter of a prominent political leader, had declared: "I shall never obey any law in the making of which I had no hand; I will not accept the authority of the court executing those laws; if you send me to gaol, I will go there, but I shall on no account pay a fine." She did go to jail, and afterward, in 1907 on a U.S. lecture tour, she spoke at Bryn Mawr on "Why I Went to Prison."[111]

The NWP militance is one clear instance of international influence on the practice of civil disobedience in America. Such influence should not be surprising: feminist movements, as they came to be called, were active in many nations, more than had been true of antislavery, and they definitely compared notes as they sought the most effective routes to progress in their respective lands. Nor was the learning and comparing restricted to women or to Europe. As a young barrister Mohandas Gandhi, residing in England while searching for ways to motivate his countrymen in Transvaal in South Africa, reported to his weekly paper *Indian Opinion* on the courage of the remarkable English women who willingly went to jail, after trying other means to persuade the male rulers to grant them the vote. Gandhi editorialized:

> Today the whole country is laughing at them, and they have only a few people on their side. But undaunted, these women work on steadfast in their cause. They are bound to succeed and gain the franchise, for the simple reason that deeds are better than words. Even those who laughed at them would be left wondering. If even women display such courage, will the Transvaal Indians fail in their duty and be afraid of gaol? Or would they rather consider the gaol a palace and readily go there? When that time comes, India's bonds will snap of themselves.[112]

In a later chapter we will see that motivating his countrymen in Transvaal to overcome fear of incarceration was very much on Gandhi's mind in his adaptation of what he recognized as Thoreau's idea of "civil disobedience."

The NWP leaders Alice Paul, Lucy Burns, and Anne Martin all participated directly in the "guerilla militancy" of the English "suffragettes" associated with Emmeline Pankhurst (who told a crowd at Carnegie Hall in 1909, "by going to prison we will eventually win over all England") and her daughters Christabel and Sylvia. The Americans had not, apparently, thrown stones, clipped telegraph wires, slashed paintings, burned homes, or engaged in other acts of violence, but they had disrupted speakers, thrown ink bottles, and broken windows (and Burns had slapped a constable) while engaged in the British movement, which permitted acts against property that American militants would eschew. All served time in British jails. Martin was roughed up by police. Paul and Burns engaged in hunger strikes and experienced the horror of forcible feeding. The organizations with which they were associated after returning to the United States, especially the NWP, were often criticized for being tainted with English militant methods that were "un-American." When Burns was arrested in Washington for chalking up the sidewalk with notices of meetings, one woman drew the line: "We will not be like England." Paul and her American colleagues, though defending the actions of their British counterparts, accepted the same distinction: English-style militancy was uncalled for in the United States. For that matter, Emmeline Pankhurst noted that the American political system and "the unusual generosity of American men toward women" called for different tactics.[113]

In addition, Paul, raised as a Quaker and a brilliant political strategist in her own right, was critical (as was Gandhi) of the English suffragettes' perpetration of violence. She was willing to endure imprisonment and harsh treatment but kept in view her political objective—enactment of the amendment making women in all forty-eight states voting citizens. She has not always received recognition from scholars or feminists, but recent biographers have hailed her as a major figure, perhaps unexcelled, in the development of a successful civil disobedience campaign grounded in nonviolence and featuring spectacle with a clear view of political purpose.[114]

The NWP suffragists had little patience for gradual, state-by-state progress that was unlikely ever to end in national citizenship for all women. Recognizing that suffrage was a moribund issue in Washington, they adopted tactics that many, including mainstream NAWSA suffragists, found offensive: organizing parades and mass demonstrations, staging tableaux in front of government buildings, heckling candidates, stationing "silent sentinels" outside the White House when President Woodrow Wilson declined to see them, refusing to shake his hand on other occasions when he greeted them. In wartime, when police attempted to call a stop to pickets and demonstrations, and when onlookers regarded some of their provocative banners as unpatriotic, they gained dramatic opportunities to show the effectiveness of passive resistance to mobs, police, and prison officials, demanding (but not receiving) political prisoner status, carrying out hunger strikes, and enduring forcible feedings in America. The issue was not so much that the militants engaged in civil disobedience in a manner that tested objectionable laws. By enforcing laws intended to prevent the obstruction of traffic in an arbitrary way, authorities gave them opportunities to stand forth as martyrs.[115]

After a particularly horrible police rampage in the Occoquan Workhouse, the so-called Night of Terror in November 1918, some of these suffragists saw themselves as exemplars of female powerlessness in a male tyranny. The view that "civil militancy"[116] was unnecessary in republican America gave way to ever-stronger commitment to dramatic confrontations. Radical demonstrators appealed to the symbolism of fire: women burned the president in effigy, torched copies of his speeches, lit watch fires in honor of heroines of the past, brought wood from all across the Union and kept it alight in front of the White House despite official efforts to extinguish it, and on one occasion leapt into the White House grounds and lit fires that threatened the trees.[117] Such actions led to more jailings and hunger strikes. A bloody confrontation occurred when Wilson was scheduled to speak at New York's Metropolitan Opera House on his way to Versailles. Alice Paul prepared to burn each of his lies about American freedom as he uttered it, but police broke up the demonstration with clubs. "If we are breaking any law, arrest us. Don't beat us in this cowardly fashion," Doris Stevens remembered complaining. The protestors were charged with assault.[118]

Was picketing in front of the White House civil disobedience? It had never been done before 1917, and once it became clear that it would lead to arrests and jail, the answer was clearly yes. It was the kind of peaceable-assembly civil disobedience that radical and labor movements would continue to carry out in the name of free speech. But the pickets were violating no law. When the government had to charge arrested picketers, it chose to accuse them of blocking traffic (even when they restricted their numbers and stayed on the sidewalk). According to many accounts, they actually kept moving, as the police instructed, while carrying their signs and banners, with a new group taking over and continuing the movement as their predecessors were arrested. They won a court test of their right to picket the White House, and many other protesters have benefited from that decision ever since. Picketing the White House had become a legitimate means of political expression.[119] But their action broke no law that was at the heart of their campaign, and while the court victory gave some protection to their activities, it had no relevance to woman suffrage. They carried banners quoting the president's words on extending democratic rights to European men—and why not American women? Their aim was to press Wilson, during the events leading to U.S. involvement in world war, to press Congress to pass a voting rights amendment to send to the states. They even dispatched the "Prison Special," a carload of women who had been incarcerated, dressed in prison garb, touring the nation to publicize their cause.[120] But the processes for constitutional change were more cumbersome than those for mobilizing troops to go to war.

According to legend, NWP pickets, including Alice Paul, chained themselves to the White House gates, presumably so that they could not easily be ignored or removed. Assertions to that effect are all over the Internet today, and they appear elsewhere, too (even in works by excellent historians), except where they should be if true—in memoirs or contemporary works about the picketers.[121] Since the pickets kept moving, it would have been an exceptional and memorable event. It is true that later protesters have followed what even D.C. police officers came to believe had been "a favorite attention getter" of the suffragists. In 1948 James Peck, a conscientious objector (who was also prominent in anti-segregation activities), took the White House tour, removed his outer shirt to reveal a white one painted with the slogan "Veto the Draft," and chained himself to a banister near the East Room.[122] In 1977, as later feminists sought publicity to advance passage of another NWP measure, the Equal Rights Amendment, news outlets reported that an elderly suffragist anticipated entering the White House gates where she had chained herself about sixty years before.[123] The tradition goes on (most recently, when six military veterans chained themselves to the gates to demand repeal of the military's "don't ask, don't tell" policy[124]), but its origin is uncertain.

Unsurprisingly, scholars disagree, sometimes sharply, over guerilla militance's effectiveness. In spite of what is sometimes said about radicalism in academia, scholars tend to favor reformers who work through conventional political processes. The majority of suffrage advocates rejected what they considered "wayward actions" and "publicity tactics" that played into the hands of suffrage's opponents.[125] Carrie Chapman Catt, NAWSA's president, patronized the militant pickets as "lagging behind the times and trying to fit 1872 methods to 1917," as clinging to a politics of "resentments" and "belligerency" when the "stunt era" was over and victory was at hand.[126] Perhaps it is a fair summary of current knowledge, however, to say that the militants did exert significant pressure on the president and Congress in getting the Nineteenth Amendment passed at the federal level, that their existence benefited in obvious ways the access of less radical NAWSA suffragists to political leaders, and that the militants had little positive influence in the ratification process in the states.[127]

For current purposes, it is interesting to think about a different kind of influence—the formation of traditions and exploration of alternative roles for citizens. Suffrage militance in the World War I era provided significant precedent for later times of civil disobedience. The Catholic radical Dorothy Day, revered in the 1960s for her saintly nonviolent resistance to war and economic injustice, served her first time in prison at Occoquan during the "Night of Terror." In this book we might pause to consider assertions that NWP militance was exceptional and unprecedented. Linda G. Ford, who makes excellent use of analyses of civil disobedience in other times and places, states that Paul and her comrades constituted "the first organized American political protest to use—and use successfully—classic methods of nonviolent resistance" and that their use of nonviolent civil disobedience was "another first for American politics."[128] Ford recognizes, however, that the nonviolent techniques of Paul and the NWP, while influenced by English suffragettes and perhaps by Gandhi, also drew upon "earlier feminist protesters, American labor activists, and Quaker pacifists" (and we might broaden the list of civil disobedient influences). What was extraordinary about the NWP and what subsequent American nonviolent movements have seldom equaled is their direct political confrontation with the president and Congress, all the more remarkable in a time of war.

The militants of 1914–20, while their links to later understandings of civic activism are notable, had much in common with Anthony, Minor, and their allies of the 1870s. It was the "mild-mannered feminism" that came after the New Departure that they sought to supplant while recovering and building on the earlier spirit of confrontation. The earlier militants and the later ones agreed that a republic that denied women the vote was in fact not a republic: it partook of tyranny, despotism, enslavement. The irritation shown by Judge Hunt at Anthony's remarks after he ordered a verdict of guilty and the public offense at the later militants' banners about "Kaiser" Wilson were both significant reactions to a new era of disobedience in which dramatic demonstrations of legal incongruities set amid an emerging sense of national rights of citizenship could give offense to those who held fast to traditional definitions of propriety. Both authorities and protesters in the antebellum era (in the controversy over the Nullification Proclamation, for example, as well as the Fugitive Slave rescues) tended to see the right of revolution as the only legitimate grounds for resistance to law (though some steps toward recognition of a higher law embedded in national law were taken in the 1850s). The suffragists of the

1870s almost perfected (*almost*, because they lost in the courtroom) the use of civil disobedience to advance the rights and aspirations of groups of citizens; and the idea that the highest courts should adjudicate in terms of the broad principles implicit in the Constitution no longer is as unthinkable as it appeared to Chief Justice Waite in the *Minor* decision. Their successors in the era of World War I resorted, in ways that seem more familiar to us than to most of their contemporaries, to civil disobedience as a means for organized citizens to seek publicity, to apply pressure, and to achieve change, while ignoring appeals for moderation, but without quite engaging in revolution.

6

Beyond Submissiveness

From Temperance Crusade to Sit-Down Strikes

Two years of struggle in this temperance reform have shown me, as they have ten thousand other women, so clearly and impressively, my duty, that I have passed the Rubicon of Silence and am ready for any battle that shall be involved in this honest declaration of faith that is within me. "Fight behind masked batteries a little longer," whisper good friends and true. So I have been fighting hitherto; but it is a style of warfare altogether foreign to my temperament and mode of life. Reared in the prairies, I seemed predetermined to join the cavalry force in this great spiritual war, and I must tilt a free lance henceforth in the splendid battlefield of this reform.
  —*Frances Willard, "Home Protection," 1876*

I tell you this: the workers of my generation from the early days up to now had what you might call a labor insurrection in changing from a plain, humble, submissive creature into a man. . . . Before they were submissive. Today they are men.
  —*Nick DiGaetano, former Wobbly and Auto Worker unionist, 1959*

During the long decades of the struggle for women's rights and woman suffrage, other movements took the practice of civil disobedience in new directions. Some, like the crusades against intemperance, could be regarded as repressive, though they usually emphasized the release of the human spirit from collective apathy and enslavement to vice. Others sought to liberate individuals by defying laws that restricted free expression and marital and reproductive freedom. Perhaps least familiar today are labor organizations that aimed to achieve and practice the greatest degree of

157

personal liberty in mines, forests, and factories. The epigraphs to the chapter, taken from the beginning and end of the period, alert us to a crucial theme in this history: the achievement of self-confidence and assertiveness by groups not prominent in the nation's original constitutional framework.

Interest in techniques of civil disobedience with the power to effect change coursed through other movements besides woman suffrage. *Nora Wilmot*, a temperance novel of the 1850s, had included a description of a knitting party of women who occupy a saloon and pressure its owner to sell his stock and quit his business. The scene might be taken as a sign of female resentment of male-dominated political parties, contesting slavery and territorial issues yet blocking the advance of temperance reform—that is, the passing of prohibition laws that might obstruct the advance of drinking habits, which had once seemed in retreat but were now unchecked. The Civil War years that followed, with men away in the camps, further diminished any hope of control over intemperance and widened women's interest in "confrontation and extralegal force."[1]

The drama of moralistic women finding the power to confront business-minded men reemerged in the postwar years. In Clyde, Ohio, according to a report in *Revolution*, women, after failing to "uproot" the liquor traffic by "moral and legal suasion," formed an association called a Knitting Machine, which, without warning, could march into a drinking or billiard saloon, take possession of the seats, and quietly settle down to knitting, with the avowed purpose to "knit all the liquor-sellers out of town." To defend themselves, the regular customers of one saloon "began smoking in the most furious manner, and the ladies were fairly or unfairly smoked out." In Apalachin, New York, women staged an "invasion" of a gambling saloon, and after their embarrassed menfolk rapidly departed, they informed the proprietor that "his place was a nuisance, and they would give him just one week to abate it."[2] What works, what gets results, what kind of machine will halt immoral business and create a good society?

In the post–Civil War decades, as temperance movements became increasingly movements of women, they continued to use group prayer as well as axe wielding (and knitting) as weapons to combat saloons and press for votes for prohibition. During eleven months in 1873–74, a rising series of protests erupted into the so-called Woman's Crusade, which historians have called "a sort of civil and social insurrection" and "the largest mass movement of women yet seen in the United States."[3] In over nine hundred towns women carried out nonviolent mass marches, knelt on sidewalks in confrontations with tipplers and tavern keepers, circulated petitions, and organized for the future. The historian Anne Firor Scott offers an apt comparison: "Not until a group of young blacks sat down at a lunch counter in Greensboro, North Carolina, in 1960 did the country again witness such a spontaneous, unplanned, powerful uprising."[4]

In Cincinnati some were arrested. In the words of one crusader: "There was a Sidewalk Ordinance which forbade the obstruction of the streets, and under that we were arrested, though we were careful to use only the two feet in width that the law allowed us when we stood in front of a saloon and sang at it, and quoted texts of Scripture at it, and knelt down and prayed against it and for the souls of those who kept it." She continued:

> The seven policemen who were detailed to arrest us were crying like whipped children; but they had to do it, and we, like good, law-abiding citizens, submitted, and went in procession to prison—forty-three of us—singing all the way. . . .
>
> We were released after about four hours. Bail was offered us, but we refused it, on the ground that we had done nothing against the law, and those who arrested us should take the full responsibility of their outrageous act.[5]

Besides arrests, some were harassed in their homes, but as a scholar has pointed out, the indignities and atrocities benefited the insurgent women by creating sympathy and maintaining a battle mentality.[6] One result of the crusade, furthermore, was creation of the Woman's Christian Temperance Union (WCTU), with many thousands of members, a political orientation, several goals (including suffrage), and acceptance of a variety of means, but especially long marches, to employ in the name of "home protection."

An extended series of communications to the *Woman's Journal* explored the significance for suffragism of this new departure in temperance. Antagonism should not be exaggerated: temperance women came to support the suffrage; suffragists deplored the effects of alcoholism on American families and communities. But there were differences. Both sides recognized that they were challenging nonpolitical ideals of womanhood. "A woman knocking out the head of a whiskey barrel with an ax" while belting out the hymn Old Hundred "is not the ideal woman sitting on a sofa, dining on strawberries and cream. . . . She is as far from it as Susan B. Anthony was, when pushing her ballot into the box." The suffragist might claim, however, that the crusader was too single-minded in focusing on drink, that the effects of cries and songs in the streets would be "spasmodic," and that lasting reform would depend on women getting the vote and serving as lawyers, jurors, and judges.[7] There were reports, soon enough, that temperance actions were giving rise to recognition of the importance of the ballot: "And all at once they discover that Woman Suffrage is just what is needed to carry on this work to completion." Men were now heard to say, "I want these women, who suffer from the evils of intemperance more than any other class, to have the privilege of fighting it at the polls."[8]

One new subscriber to the *Woman's Journal*, writing from Worcester, Massachusetts, took offense at a poem entitled "My Vote Is My Prayer" that sneered at the power of prayer and spoke dismissively of "the women that kneel in the street, With prayers and hymns at the rumseller's feet." Although she herself had taken her stand for woman suffrage for over a year, she never expected, "for a moment," that goal to be won without God's help. In her view the new temperance crusade among women was setting the stage for suffrage "as surely and speedily as the sale of the famous Alderneys" or the forcible sales of property. One victory the crusaders had certainly achieved: "No man can ever again affirm that women will be demoralized by coming into contact with the dregs of society, by voting." That assertion was demolished by the actions of women in state after state. For her part, she would continue to fight for woman suffrage and women's equality, but she would also join with "reverent awe and unspeakable delight" in the temperance agitation.[9] In general, though some rejected the idea of women praying and singing in the saloons or in the streets, there were at least as many who expressed belief that it would benefit women's emancipation as well as temperance goals. To those outside, "the movement seems grotesque, ill-advised, ill-conceived and futile; but get once within the magic circle and all is changed. No one can attend the prayer meetings and listen to the reports of the ladies without feeling the tremendous power that is being exerted." Politicians were watching, too, seeking to discover what will be "the winning side."[10]

One sympathetic clergyman gave an interesting appraisal of what he disapproved and approved as the movement began to ebb. Among the former: "the disregard of law" was understandable but unjustifiable;

"lawlessness is a game that two parties can play at." The women had no legal right to crowd into a saloon and conduct a prayer meeting without the owner's consent. They had no more right to block the sidewalk for hours in front of a saloon than to block a store or church. He also disapproved the misuse of prayer as a noisy method of "bombarding" saloons and the excessive noise and excitement throughout the movement. On the positive side, he applauded endeavors to treat the liquor dealers "kindly and with consideration," not to curse them but to regard them as errant human beings. Most important of all, the crusade was a movement of women, the preeminent victims of intemperance, rising up, not for the first time, but on a scale never seen before, to demand protection from the scourge of drunkenness. "Let the men of this country who oppose the cause of Temperance mark well—they are unwittingly doing what lies in their power to do, to prepare, for this country, Woman Suffrage, just as truly as was the Parliament of Great Britain when it imposed the tax upon American tea, preparing independence for the colonies."[11] His vision of a lawful movement that was not mean-spirited toward its foes and carried within it, if not given a satisfactory response, a capacity for social and political transformation anticipates twentieth-century accounts of great campaigns of civil resistance or nonviolent revolution.

In fact, accommodations were made, quite apart from the long, slow progress of a Woman Suffrage Amendment to the U.S. Constitution. Municipalities, counties, and states could, and sometimes did, accord women the privilege of voting on issues of the greatest concern to them— preeminently education (as more and more became teachers) and liquor licenses (since they were the primary victims of drunken domestic violence). At the state level parties could divide over such issues. In Indiana, for example, the House of Representatives voted for woman suffrage repeatedly in the 1880s, but filibusters in the senate blocked it out of fear of what women voters would do to liquor sales.[12]

From the 1870s on, "Home Protection" became an effective identifying slogan for the WCTU's purposes. Introduced by Frances Willard in an 1876 speech, it was from the start an ingenious call to a kind of defensive aggressiveness in the crusaders' war against the rum power, including pursuit of new political initiatives to provide women a special temperance ballot when saloons were proposed in their neighborhoods. Home protection pointed to a different argument for woman suffrage besides the natural rights of a woman as an individual human being. After the Illinois

Senate refused to hear her speak on the issue, Willard became an all-out suffragist.

In a brilliant book on the rise and fall of Prohibition, Daniel Okrent criticizes the home protection argument as conducive to pathetic images: "the weeping mother, children in threadbare clothes, the banker at the door with repossession papers."[13] Those images can all be found in Willard's speech. More striking, however, is the tale she tells about herself and her sister as children, when their father and brother went off to vote.

> I said, "Don't you wish that we could go with them when we are old enough? Don't we love our country just as well as they do?" and her little frightened voice piped out: "Yes, of course we ought. Don't I know that; but you mustn't tell a soul, not mother even; we should be called strong-minded."[14]

From this memory Willard moves to her contemporary conviction, with which this chapter began, that she has crossed "the Rubicon of silence" and is ready for a leading role in combat.

At the turn of the new century, in the widely reported "hatchetations" of Carry Nation "home protection" gained an association with images of destroying the equipment and wares and intimidating the owners of saloons. Nation's more than thirty arrests and trials and the notoriety that she evidently welcomed as a means of creating support for prohibition laws brought the cause closer to triumph. By starting in Kansas, where her targets were governmental representatives who failed to enforce prohibition laws, she actually avoided some of the ambiguities of using violence to close down saloons. The *New Voice*, a Prohibition Party newspaper, without commenting on legal issues to be tested in court in Kansas, a legally dry state, defended her in these terms: "When public officials openly allow criminals to violate the law, there is much to be said in justification of the citizen who appeals to force."[15] Prohibition passed as a national constitutional amendment in 1920 for many reasons, but one was the persistent agitation of politically organized and determined women in previous decades. "You wouldn't give me the vote," Nation told the Kansas legislature, "so I had to use a rock!"[16]

Though they are not well remembered today, some prominent reformers advocated free love during the same Victorian decades when woman suffrage was slowly advancing to victory. Like suffragists, they identified their beliefs and efforts with the antebellum legacy of antislavery, together with emerging movements of communitarianism, spiritualism, and individualist anarchism.[17] Some advocated affectional freedom as a natural right of all human beings, though often with heaviest emphasis on the liberation of wives and daughters from the domination and coercion of husbands and fathers in procreation and other relations of family life. Some defended the health and well-being of wives and mothers. (Marital rape was not illegal in the United States until the late twentieth century.) Some believed that children of intentional and voluntary sexual relations would be healthier, happier, and better citizens—some spoke of this goal as eugenics. Many, but by no means all, of these public advocates were men. Angela Heywood, who edited the *Word* with her husband Ezra, wrote most frankly of male and female genitalia and most rapturously of the pleasures of sex. They adopted a policy of using plain English words and refusing to censor the language chosen by their contributors.[18] The public figure who gained the most celebrity in the cause of free love, and one of few to publicly profess her personal promiscuity, was Victoria Woodhull,[19] until she left a life of notoriety behind and moved to England in 1877, married a banker, and retired to country life.

Many of these advocates of free love went to jail. They were prime targets of a purity movement with antebellum origins that sought to extirpate temptations to lewdness and vice in the cities, a movement that broadened after the Civil War into a sustained national campaign to suppress pornography, prostitution, obscenity, birth control information and devices, and all incentives to lascivious behavior ranging from medical discussions of gynecological disorders to "obscene and immoral rubber articles" (condoms, diaphragms, dildos) along with books and photographs.[20] Though the purity campaigns had broad support from Protestant denominations and organizations like the Young Men's Christian Association, it was closely identified with state and federal laws secured by Anthony Comstock, a postal inspector and officer of the New York Society for the Suppression of Vice, who worked determinedly over a long career to put an end to indecency and vice wherever they threatened public morality in industrializing America. The British playwright George Bernard Shaw ridiculed the vice hunter who notified the New York police that his "problem" drama *Mrs. Warren's Profession* concerned prostitution. The play was not stopped, and its audiences may actually have increased,[21] but publishers of books and periodicals on contraception and other banned subjects sent through the U.S. mails were relentlessly targeted for suppression under the so-called Comstock law (1873) and similar laws in many states.

Woodhull and her sister Tennessee Claflin went to jail in 1872 after Comstock used an alias (his preferred modus operandi) to order and receive through the mails a special issue of their newspaper featuring the sensational case of the prominent minister Henry Ward Beecher's adulterous affair with a parishioner. They were eventually released on a technicality.[22] Ezra Heywood, a labor reformer and author of a pamphlet entitled *Cupid's Yokes*,[23] advocating rational—but voluntary and not state-regulated—self-control in sexual relations as a key to social advancement, was Comstock's next prey. While urging couples to develop "habits of continence," Heywood referred to, but hardly recommended, the "unnatural means" available to prevent conception. That was enough to get Comstock's attention, and Heywood's dismissive reference to the vice hunter as a "religious *mono-maniac*" at war with "free inquiry" almost guaranteed that he would receive decoy letters requesting a copy of *Cupid's Yokes* to be sent by mail.[24] Having sprung his trap, Comstock personally arrested Heywood in 1877 at a Boston convention of those whom he called "free-lusters." Heywood was convicted, fined, and sentenced to two years in prison, of which he served six months before President Rutherford B. Hayes pardoned him. He was tried again in 1882 for distributing not only *Cupid's Yokes* and an advertisement for a douching syringe but also two poems by Walt Whitman. A jury acquitted him. Comstock arrested him once more in 1887, this time for publishing a speech by his wife Angela, but the U.S. attorney declined to prosecute. Finally, in 1891, Heywood was taken to court once again, on less specific charges concerning lewdness in the *Word*. Convicted by a jury, he received a sentence of two years at hard labor (he spent those years sewing prison uniforms). There was no pardon. He died in 1893.[25]

Moses Harman's *Lucifer, the Light Bearer*, published in Valley Falls, Kansas (and later in Topeka and Chicago), fell afoul of the Comstock law by printing what became known as "the Markland letter," reporting the consequences of the marital rape of a young mother who was "severely torn" during childbirth, repaired by doctors, and beginning to recover when her husband "forced himself into her bed and the stitches were torn from her healing flesh." That was followed by a series of other "awful letters" (as Harman ironically termed them) on contraception, sexual abstinence, and marital infidelity (which the Harman circle actually opposed). In 1887 Harman and his coeditors were arrested on 270 counts of obscenity.[26] Successfully defended against the indictment, he was re-indicted on charges related to the Markland letter in 1890, found guilty, fined, sentenced to hard labor at the penitentiary, released after four months, then committed again for another year. In the meantime, he was tried anew on obscenity charges for publishing another document, the somewhat unfocused "O'Neill letter," in which a New York physician disclosed perversions and abuses he had treated, including injurious scenes like those Markland had described and matter-of-fact accounts, shocking to Victorian Kansans, of addictions to orogenital sex. For that offense, another year was added to his sentence.[27] In 1905 issues of *Lucifer* were seized, destroyed, and banned from the mails in Chicago, and the seventy-five-year-old Harman received a sentence of a year at hard labor, breaking rocks all day, during which time his health broke down. In his few remaining years (he died in 1910) he gave *Lucifer* the look of a scholarly journal and renamed it the *American Journal of Eugenics.*[28]

By that time Harman had garnered widespread support for his right to publish, recognition of the importance of discussion and knowledge of issues related to sexuality, and sympathy for the atrocious way in which he was treated by American philistines. In a front-page interview in the *New York Times*, George Bernard Shaw condemned the shameful fact "that a journal has just been confiscated and its editor imprisoned in America for urging that a married woman should be protected from domestic molesta-tion when childbearing." He told a London interviewer that the United States was "infested by moral brigands, who have turned the Post Office into a most Unholy Inquisition."[29] The free love publishers' persistence had occasioned short-run triumphs for the implacable Comstock, but they had also set a stage for eventual victories for free speech and the First Amendment. At the very least, they created precedents that courts in future decades would overturn.

Their relation to civil disobedience deserves a closer look. These men and women were of course concerned about freedom of speech. They were also concerned about turning a profit on their publications. And they were determined to change, so far as they could, the ways in which men and women in America negotiated their conjugal relations. They proceeded, moreover, with a sense of history discussed by a careful historian in explaining "a strategy of publicity" that underlay Harman's persistence in printing the "awful letters." Harman knew that publicity not only could expose the censors' repressive motives but also could turn *Lucifer* into a paying enterprise and assure Harman a hero's niche in history. "Would not Ezra Heywood compare Harman to William Lloyd Garrison and John Brown, as well as to [the free thought publisher] D. M. Bennett, whose trial and imprisonment 'boomed his books, made his paper a paying, world-wide power, and himself immortal in history!'"[30]

The free love advocates would surely have caught the eye of authorities like Comstock in any case, but they went out of their way to court suppression by the state. The intention to test marriage laws seems to lie behind the 1886 "autonomistic" marriage ceremony, unauthorized by church or state, of Harman's sixteen-year-old daughter Lillian to *Lucifer's* thirty-seven-year-old coeditor Edwin Walker, a divorcé with two children from a previous marriage.[31] That it was a "manufactured" event is the speculation, at least, of the sympathetic author Hal Sears who notes that there was ample advance warning of the event in *Lucifer* and that a family member swore the complaint a day after the event. In any event, the couple's convictions and jail sentences drew widespread attention. Lillian Harman and Walker remained in jail in adjacent cells until they were needed to keep *Lucifer* running while other Harmans were in custody.[32] Publication, dissemination, and controversial matrimony were all expressions of civil disobedience intended to test and overthrow the Comstock laws as violations of the First Amendment, natural right, and good policy.

Some advocates of unfettered liberty came to reject civil disobedience as a tactic leading to any worthwhile kind of victory. The supremely logical Benjamin R. Tucker, who gave priority to economic liberty though he certainly believed in freedom of the affections, had praised the tactic of "passive resistance," a term he preferred to "non-resistance" because it implied decisions about policy and tactics rather than inflexible commitments of principle.[33] He gave the example of withholding taxes, so long as it could be done in sufficient numbers (say, a fifth of the population) so that the government could not burden the rest of the population with the costs of enforcement. Or it might be a viable tactic for a single individual if it goaded the government into acts of torture that could contribute to "propagandism" by well-organized allies outside the prison walls and awaken substantial resistance. "There is not a tyrant in the civilized world today who would not do anything in his power to precipitate a bloody revolution rather than see himself confronted by any large fraction of his subjects determined not to obey."[34] But he concluded, from observing the government crackdown on radicalism after the 1886 bombing in Chicago's Haymarket Square as well as the debilitating jail terms of Heywood and Harman, that the costs of needless provocation outweighed any putative gains. A contemporary individualist anarchist, Wendy McElroy explains that as he grew older, Tucker "grew increasingly hostile to civil disobedience as a strategy." He preferred education to civil disobedience, especially when the outcome was likely to be repressive laws or martyrdom.[35] Other writers have agreed with free love advocates to whom Tucker's reluctance to defy Comstock was a cowardly example of acquiescence and intimidation. There was, at best, a conundrum in Tucker's position. Was free expression always worth going to jail for even if it silenced or distracted the prisoner? It was hard to advance public understanding of fundamental aspects of liberty from prison cell or even a courtroom.[36]

In a 1915 interview, Comstock boasted that since 1872 he had brought to conviction close to three thousand foes of moral purity, enough to fill a train sixty cars long, and his confiscation of obscene materials was similarly prodigious. Asked why he placed information about contraception in the same class as pornography, "He replied—with scant patience of 'theorizers' who do not know human nature: 'If you open the door to anything, the filth will all pour in and the degradation of youth will follow.'"[37] It became increasingly clear in his twentieth-century purity campaigns that his targets were those who dispensed information about birth control. After all, as he told the interviewer, virtually all of the immoral books that initially alarmed him had been suppressed; and the sex radicals who defied him in court had been effectively defeated. In a new era, public discussion of contraception focused less on Comstockian fears about the unchecked imaginations and degradation of boys and more on issues of overpopulation and poverty, on women's emancipation and fulfillment, and on couples' planning and intimacy.

This change did not occur without tests of the law and jail time. Emma Goldman, an immigrant revolutionary (eventually a deportee) and touring lecturer on many political and literary subjects, spoke widely on contraception and went to jail for doing so as did her lover Ben Reitman. She was inspired to take up the theme after the arrests and jailing of Margaret Sanger and her first husband William Sanger.[38] The free speech trials were all episodes of civil disobedience in a new secular vein and indeed, initially at least, in a context of revolutionary struggle. They still required tests of the law, often unsuccessful, and often enough leading to time in jail. But they moved away from the nineteenth-century language of passive resistance and higher law.

Both Emma Goldman and Margaret Sanger lectured, published, and gave support to organizing efforts under the auspices of the Industrial Workers of the World. A labor organization like no other in U.S. history, the IWW ignored traditional distinctions of craft and trade, organized factory workers, hoboes, and casual labor, and refused to negotiate long-term contracts. Dedicated to revolution and free speech, deplored by most politicians and editorial writers, fascinating to many artists and writers, the IWW's adherents were remembered later for expressions of exuberant nonconformity ("Hallelujah I'm a bum") as well as scenes of brutal repression. To "wholesale jailing by the authorities," who were alarmed by remarks deemed "seditious, incendiary, unpatriotic, immoral, *etc.*," they responded as a sympathetic economist put it, with "a policy of sullen non-resistance."[39] But they could be notably joyous and humorous, too. A review of a pageant in Madison Square Garden in which a thousand workers enacted scenes from a strike in Paterson, New Jersey, used words like *gayety, gusto, dash* and *enthusiasm* to convey the mood of depictions of the conflict.[40] The Wobblies, as they were known, were loosely organized, had contradictory goals and programs, were certainly not a pacifist organization and yet held a key role in some forms of protest that are critical to the civil disobedience tradition—lecturing on prohibited subjects (like birth control), holding mass meetings in forbidden places, filling the jails, refusing to cooperate with unjust legal processes, and engaging in ingenious labor actions, such as "folded arms" strikes.

There is a paradox in the IWW's relation to civil disobedience. On one hand, it would be hard to find a movement less committed to *civil* obedience or respect for the laws or for the state. On the other hand, the Wobblies exemplified some qualities that might well appear in handbooks of nonviolent action in subsequent decades. They were, like many civil disobedients, people in the middle, in a via media. As Elizabeth Gurley Flynn put it, they were criticized from every side: "For the socialists we were too radical, for the anarchists we were too conservative, for we were impossible."[41]

Wobblies did not court martyrdom, though they did not shrink from it, and they knew how to gain public advantage and group cohesion from the well-publicized celebration of a martyr like Joe Hill, a Swedish immigrant, drifter, and labor organizer shot by a Utah firing squad in 1915. Hill's guilt or innocence and the fairness of his trial may always be disputed. His stature as a gifted lyricist is undeniable. He had "a knack for setting rebel words" to familiar popular and religious music, so as to undermine "the timidity, moralism, and the whole manner and content of the standard American culture," which turned out to offer only "pie in the sky." The aptness of his telegram from jail to Big Bill Haywood as he faced death became legendary: "Don't mourn for me[,] organize."[42] A poem written in 1925, and set to music in 1936, describes him as returning to say, "What they can never kill / Went on to organize." As an anthem of labor organizing and, since the 1960s, of civil rights determination, these words, as sung by Paul Robeson, Pete Seeger, and many others, have never died. Joan Baez sang them to a huge "counterculture" audience at Woodstock in 1969 and in the 1970 film of that event. In 2005 she sang them again at the vigil of antiwar mother Cindy Sheehan on the road outside George W. Bush's summer residence at Crawford, Texas.[43]

The IWW, since it was never a trade union, was open to organizing the homeless and unemployed. In March 1914 a twenty-one-year-old Austrian immigrant named Frank Tannenbaum, "a vivid youth," as Emma Goldman remembered him, who had recently joined the IWW, alarmed some Manhattan churches, received a welcome at others, and absolutely infuriated the priests at St. Adolphus Catholic Church as he led growing numbers of unemployed men seeking food and shelter. He reportedly told the "church invaders" that "everything in this world belongs to us, and we're going to take it." The *New York Times* and other newspapers carried stories of harangues, agitators, anarchists, and dynamite, and Max Eastman in the *Masses* reported on Tannenbaum's trial as "an arbitrary assault upon a young man's liberty and his right to live." The judge found him guilty, curiously, of "unlawful assembly," lectured him on "the great opportunities" for advancement available in this country, and imposed a one-year sentence at Blackwell's Island, where he almost immediately landed in solitary confinement for organizing protests against the warden and prison conditions. "One hero-soul in this our coward State," Upton Sinclair called him in a poem. Remarkably, after his release, despite having almost no formal education, he succeeded in being admitted to Columbia University and after that to doctoral study at the Brookings Institution. He then began a brilliant scholarly career with interests in prison reform, slavery, and Mexican history.[44]

The Wobblies had no predilection to violence—but no aversion either. Their attitude, as Elizabeth Gurley Flynn wrote during the great textile strike in Paterson, was "utilitarian": "Only where violence is necessary should violence be used. . . . Where there is no call for it there is no reason why we should resort to it." It was in practice often a sign of desperation and weakness and actually "an old-fashioned method of conducting a strike. And mass action, paralyzing all industry, is a new-fashioned and much more feared method."[45] Their attitude toward pageantry and spectacle may have borrowed from labor traditions, suffrage demonstrations, and the woman's crusade. They added a belief in the need for constant activity, keeping people busy and committed in planned activities—"great mass meetings, women's meetings, children's meetings, . . . mass picketing and mass funerals," all concentrated on the strike, building and maintaining feelings of mutual concern "to the point where they will go to jail and refuse fines, and go hundreds of them together."[46] That also sounds like the remarkable cohesion achieved decades later in civil rights movements of the South.

The importance of the IWW to the civil disobedience tradition becomes clearer if we look at the free speech confrontations of the decade from 1906 to 1916. All told, there were about thirty of these battles, most of them in the West. In some years a new one seemed to burst out every month. Two were savage experiences: in San Diego vigilantes seized demonstrators; took them out of town; clubbed, tarred, and tortured them. Despite public criticism, there were no prosecutions. In Everett, Washington, where IWW organizers worked with striking sawmill workers, police deputies forced one group of protesters to run a gauntlet while striking them with spiked bats. A second group of Wobblies were attacked by gunfire from armed vigilantes as they arrived by boat. Roger Baldwin, a World War I conscientious objector and later director of the American Civil Liberties Union, recalled that these free speech fights "wrote a chapter in the history of American liberties like that of the struggle of the Quakers for freedom to meet and worship, of the militant suffragists to carry their propaganda to the seats of government, and of the Abolitionists to be heard."[47] For his role in support of striking workers' right to hold meetings in their own hall in Paterson, New Jersey, in 1924, Baldwin himself and four strikers were convicted of unlawful assembly—he had been reading aloud the Bill of Rights on the city hall plaza when the police "swarmed in," swinging their nightsticks. He received a six-month jail sentence. The state's highest court reversed the conviction four years later.[48] These battles, along with some of Joe Hill's songs, are largely responsible for whatever favorable public impression the IWW retains after decades of repression, governmental denunciation, and expatriation.

Two indispensable books on the IWW start chapters on the free speech campaigns with romantic-sounding calls, sent out in 1909, to Missoula, Montana. "Foot loose rebels . . . come at once to defend the Bill of Rights," called one. "Quit your job. Go to Missoula. Fight with the Lumber Jacks for Free Speech," urged the other.[49] Sometimes these actions are recalled as victorious. Indeed, for Baldwin they could not be anything but victorious: they "demonstrated the powerlessness of all the forces of law and order in the face of men determined to fill the jails if necessary to win their right to talk. No power on earth can beat men with the courage to go to jail, willingly and cheerfully for a principle." (He added, "Not if there are enough of them.") He had learned about the free speech fights from IWW "boys" who had just won their fight in Kansas City and then mounted a campaign for shelter and food for homeless men on the streets of St. Louis. They won there, too, by going to jail, making speeches in court, threatening that thousands of men were about to descend on the city, until the city passed an emergency bill. They won, in short, with "the same tactics, the same dramatic and moral appeal that won free speech."[50]

A basic Wobbly pamphlet states simply: "The I.W.W. stirred the west with free speech fights bitterly fought to wrest the right to talk unionism to the migratory workers of the lumber, agricultural and construction industries."[51] Nevertheless, many diehard Wobblies regarded these campaigns for the Bill of Rights as a diversion of resources to conflicts that did little to undermine exploitative capitalism. Pacific Coast IWW representatives actually tried to keep them from proliferating.[52] These campaigns arose without much planning and developed their own dramatic structure with marches or crowded rides to urban centers where casual laborers were hired for jobs in western forests, mines, ports, or fields. The fights were over the right to speak from soapboxes without being jailed and, too often, beaten or even tortured. To some Wobbly critics, these were side issues in campaigns to organize workers at their worksites and eliminate the labor "sharks" who dominated the hiring processes and kept transient, unorganized labor poorly paid and readily victimized.

Yet soapbox orators did make some converts to the larger cause while in the short run communicating with those gathered to seek work. Police forces, detective agencies, and even political leaders and courts—especially as more "foot loose" vagrants made their way to town—showed no interest in civil liberties while seeking to intimidate and destroy the enemies of a labor system in which would-be workers had little voice. Baldwin conceded that winning the right to speak did not usually organize workers, but he answered revolutionary Wobbly critics of the free speech campaigns by pointing to "exhibitions of solidarity, of the sacrifice of the individual to the interests of his class, of uncompromising purpose. . . . Certainly no fight for free speech before or since has approached it in determination, dramatic tactics or success in its immediate purposes."[53] In no case did the IWW wish to give up its presence on the streets where it competed with another great source of urban music and street oratory, the Salvation Army, which dispensed "pie in the sky."

In one of its core pamphlets the IWW explained the "direct action" on the job "for which the I.W.W. is famous." This was not only an approach to improving or protecting working conditions; it was a model for the way in which workers would control those conditions in a future reorganization of industry. The pamphlet gave the example of the method by which the IWW "modernized" the lumber industry on the Pacific Coast.

> Its members established the eight-hour day by blowing their own whistle at the end of eight hours and quitting. Some crews were fired, but the next crew blew its whistle too, and the eight-hour day became established practice. . . . The old practice had been to sleep in double-deck, muzzle-loading bunks and to carry one's own bedding to the job. Organized lumberjacks made bonfires of the bunks and the bedding and told the companies that thereafter if they wanted men they would have to provide decent cots, mattresses and clean sheets and blankets.

As a general policy, the IWW sought to avoid long strikes. They could accomplish more, with less cost to the workers, through short strikes or direct confrontations:

> Why walk out because the company refuses to get rid of an unsafe foreman? Why not have the men under him elect the man whose judgement they trust best to direct the work, and then carry out his instructions instead of the instructions of the company-appointed

foreman? With the backing of their fellow workers this sort of thing can usually be done. Why walk out because your fellow worker is fired for union activity? It will cost you nothing and cost the company far more if you go to work and express your sorrow by the way in which you work—and if the man fired for union activity helps the union spread more union ideas, it ought to make the companies careful about providing these additional organizers.

The IWW expected to "build a decent world" by applying one simple "secret of direct action": "If workers quit doing what they are told to do, and do instead what they have collectively decided to do, there isn't anything much that can be done to stop them." Out of many struggles members of the IWW had developed a fund of trustworthy principles that assured success in the familiar conflicts over wages and working conditions as well as in the longer-term endeavor to build "a sane social order."[54]

Because of the Wobblies' reputation and their persecution by the government, their policy of avoiding unnecessary conflict and, above all, not abandoning the scene of contention may seem surprising. But it is a key to understanding practices of considerable later influence, especially the "folded arms" strike, in which there is no walkout, no violence. That policy was present in the IWW from the start. At the founding convention in 1905, Lucy Parsons, widow of the Haymarket martyr Albert Parsons, declared: "My conception of the strike of the future is not to strike and go out and starve, but to strike and remain in and take possession of the necessary property of production." It has been pointed out that these words "presage" the sit-down strikes of the 1930s and the sit-ins for civil rights in the 1960s, but of more direct relevance was the staging of a three-day occupation of a General Electric plant in Schenectady, New York, in 1906, which was known as a "folded arms" strike.[55] At scenes of industrial conflict in early twentieth-century America that term connoted an alternative to violence and political action. "Your power is in your folded arms," as "Big Bill" Haywood told strikers in Paterson. "You have killed the mills; you have stopped production; you have broken off the profits. Any other violence you may commit is less than this, and it will only react upon yourselves."[56]

The image of a strike with folded arms was not exclusively American. European syndicalists believed that such a strike in one branch of industry could lead to similar actions in all branches. That vision of a general strike recurred in Europe in arguments among socialists, anarchists, syndicalists, and unionists about class struggle, direct action, and the replacement of capitalism with a more just arrangement of work and society.[57] Some in Europe regarded the folded-arms general strikes as a means of overthrowing the old order. Others rejected that view. In the 1880s Errico Malatesta, the leading Italian anarchist, dismissed the notion that "the revolution will come by itself, like manna from heaven, and that we have only to fold our arms to assist impassively in the collapse of the old society."[58] English Trotskyists contended the "'folded arms' illusion" had been discredited in Chartist actions in the 1840s and "killed" in a failed general strike in 1926.[59] Russian communists and anarchists argued heatedly about whose preferred methods had succeeded in overthrowing the old order. In the United States some "new Socialists"—prominently including Haywood and the Wobblies—viewed barricades and street fighting as utterly obsolete as long as the capitalist class possessed "all the machinery of war." The only reliable weapon was "the power of the workers peacefully to fold their arms in such numbers as to paralyze industry and force the unconditional surrender of the capitalist class." In this scenario the victorious workers would be able to keep "the world's work" under way without much disruption or chaos.[60] To others, this solution fell apart over the difficulties of waging a folded-arms general strike against a powerful state with no blood spilt, when most who joined unions were not seeking revolution. Italian syndicalists, for example, were skeptical (to put it mildly) of the viability of war against the state with folded arms.

The IWW's fascination with the folded-arms strike has not been well remembered. An exception is Howard Zinn's widely read *People's History*, where it is related to European anarcho-syndicalism. Zinn quotes the IWW organizer Joseph Ettor: if the workers of the world want to win, "they have nothing to do but fold their arms and the world will stop."[61] Zinn certainly gives more attention to the IWW (let alone anarcho-syndicalism) than most surveys of U.S. history, before moving on to further accounts of labor struggles in a corporation-dominated society. For our purposes, it is useful to pause for a closer look at the idea and practice of folded arms as they rose to prominence in the sit-down strikes during the era of the Great Depression. Zinn describes the sit-downs as "a new kind of tactic" in which angry workers remained in their factory instead of walking out.[62] These strikes were unprecedented in the size of some of the mass-production, assembly-line plants in

Akron, Ohio, Flint, Michigan, and elsewhere where they occurred, but they were staged with the same recognition that the Wobblies had voiced—that workers had more to lose than to gain by leaving their workplaces. And they sometimes wrested from employers some control over work rules on the assembly lines that made auto bodies, tires, and other products of a new era. It should also be noted (as Zinn did not) that considerable public revulsion at the sit-downs arose from recognition that they were violations of the corporations' premises and from disapproval of strikes seeking contracts that would compel some workers into unions against their will. Their legacy was ambiguous to the extent that they created fears of public disorder and of unions of a size and power previously unfamiliar in the United States. A lingering influence would sometimes be evident in later struggles against racial discrimination and inequality.

Industrial conflict had become disturbingly frequent—on the West Coast docks, in southern textile mills, in trucking centers like Minneapolis—from 1919 through the 1920s. After the election of Franklin D. Roosevelt the right of workers to organize became recognized federal policy. In 1935 Congress enacted and President Roosevelt signed the National Labor Relations Act (NLRA), which restricted unfair practices by employers in response to workers seeking union representation and encouraged the development of collective bargaining in setting terms of employment. But it took more than federal policy and legislation to establish large unionized workforces in industrial centers. "Sit-down" or "stay-in" strikes gained national attention in February 1936 when rubber workers in Akron stayed inside and idled their plants to protest violations of customary labor conditions. Similar strikes, on a larger scale, followed at automobile plants in Flint and other Michigan cities, where workers particularly resented a management-imposed speedup that had fundamentally changed their lives. All told, forty-eight sit-down strikes had seized attention by the end of the year, many of them associated with organizing campaigns in industries where workers were previously represented, if at all, by company unions.[63] At least five hundred more took place in the next two years. Vitally important to new unions seeking to organize workers in large industries like autos, tires, and steel, the NLRA and the sit-down strikes alarmed other Americans for whom they symbolized a momentous threat to private enterprise and the American way of life.

Though ubiquitous for a while, sit-downs did not become a normal part of industrial relations, especially after a second world war made stoppages of production intolerable even to a government that welcomed growth of union membership as an alternative to industrial strife. Short-lived as they were in practice, sit-downs were crucial to union organizing in mass-production industries, and they have been remembered as dramatic episodes of courage in transforming American labor relations. They were, however, extremely controversial in their own time, and government officials did not regard sustained trespass as acceptable practice. Commentators began to ask how extraordinary they were and rediscovered precedents for staying in instead of walking out. Michigan's governor Frank Murphy, a politician at the center of the storm, found precedents in work stoppages by construction workers in ancient Egypt and early modern France.[64] Historians added to the list American instances going back to the occupation of a Cincinnati brewery in 1884 and, in greater numbers, "quickie" sit-downs in the early 1930s at various industrial plants. Detroit's Catholic bishop traced the "illegal sit-downs" to "the Communists of France," and indeed massive factory occupations in France's auto industry, greeted enthusiastically by Catholic unionists as well as reds, earlier in 1936, had been preceded by sit-downs, usually not extending overnight, at Citroën, Fiat, and Renault factories in previous years. Like the American events that followed, they did not seek to nationalize the factories or deny the private property rights of the existing order.[65] Most aptly, the radical Slovenian writer Louis Adamic, who had come to America in 1913, disputed a *New York Times* reporter's suggestion that the sit-downs resembled "the old Oriental practice of passive resistance" and explained to readers of the *Nation* that they were more likely "a development of the old I.W.W. 'folded arm' strike and of 'striking on the job'; only it is better, manlier than the latter, which required men to pretend they were working, and to accomplish as little as possible without being discharged," which was unnatural for good workers.[66]

Overcoming its previous resistance to the New Deal response to industrial change and economic depression, the Supreme Court eventually recognized that Congress could reasonably view collective bargaining as essential to the nation's "industrial peace." It validated the constitutionality of the NLRA in a case involving a steel company's dismissal of employees who sought to form a union.[67] But two years later in *NLRB v. Fansteel Metallurgical Corp.*, the court withdrew all constitutional protection for a sit-down strike, which it viewed simply as "an illegal seizure of the buildings in order to prevent their use by the employer in a lawful manner."

There was something contradictory here, since company use of its ownership of buildings and equipment to suppress workers' organizing efforts and their pursuit of collective bargaining had been found to be unlawful by Congress and the Supreme Court itself. To many contemporaries, the sit-downs were indeed illegal trespasses, analogous to invading someone's home but on a much more serious scale. Attorneys and justices did not delve further into the strikers' views of their rights vis-à-vis machines where they had invested time and labor. Contradictory or not, *Fansteel* had erected a legal boundary, and employee sit-downs after *Fansteel* became brief and infrequent.[68]

In the longer run, the case for occupations as expressions of civil disobedience, squelched by the *Fansteel* decision, might merit another look. Defenders of the sit-downs scoffed at any analogy with home ownership, where property rights were undeniably enshrined in the common law. The corporation's control of its factory was not so absolute; it had to be balanced against workers' "property right" or, more properly, "community rights" in jobs where they produced wealth and advanced society's prosperity.[69] Human rights had expanded over time. "Every right, every liberty, every privilege"—union activists pointed out—had been won "by men who dared to defy some law," by men who dared to be "illegal." People just like modern unionists had taken stands "in defiance of old traditions, of legal restraints and a hostile judiciary" and won labor's right to organize, picket, strike, and boycott; and now would come victories for the right "to sit down, stand up, or roll over, as suits their fancy, in the plants which the brain and brawn and genius of the working class have brought into being." The goal of this view of history was, as the United Auto Workers (UAW) informed its organizers, to instill courage and determination. "Destroy fear of jail . . . by recalling the prison terms of William Penn, John Brown and other famous Americans." These may not have been the best possible examples but the law could not be changed unless someone was ready to break it, and "disobedience of the law as it existed at any particular moment," as the legal scholar Jim Pope sums up the sit-downers' understanding, "carried no necessary connotation of disrespect for law." It simply recognized that official understandings of law were subject to change in keeping with the changing practice of workers, management, and government.[70] It is worth noting how different this approach to civil disobedience is (even though it hails some of the same heroes) from those of an earlier era that appealed to timeless, higher, unvarying law.

We should take care not to exaggerate the sit-down strikes' resemblance to civil disobedience campaigns in later decades. It was significant that they did not escalate into larger scale political insurrections, and they helped some participants overcome the dehumanization of the assembly line. In general, they were remarkably orderly takeovers, even if they were not strictly nonviolent. Though the occupiers declined suggestions that they needed firearms, they accumulated metal objects that could be hurled in self-defense. "Everything hinges on the hinges," joked the UAW leader Victor Reuther after strikers at the Fisher Body No. 2 used two-pound automobile hinges to drive off police attacking them with firearms and tear gas.[71] In an early sit-down Akron rubber workers imprisoned Goodyear officials and nonunion workers for twelve hours in what they called a "Bullpen"—and got away with it when a jury failed to agree on a verdict.[72] Strikers set up rules for behavior, held trials, and imposed penalties on themselves that ranged from confinement, to KP duty, to in a few cases lashing with a belt.[73] What deserves emphasis in the enforcement of regulations, however, is less the occasional infliction of pain than the remarkable concern about good order. They created an example of communal reform and left memories of the achievement of significant goals by generally well-behaved law breaking that would influence religious leaders and civil rights reformers in later years. They created a link between labor struggles and the subject of our next chapter—systems of nonviolent social change.[74]

Sit-downs were not legitimated by the Supreme Court, but the New Deal support of labor organizing, collective bargaining, and NLRB review of the fairness of labor and management practices stayed in place. That did not please everyone, of course. In an act of civil disobedience protesting the violation of his rights and owners' loss of control over their businesses, especially in wartime, when the government preferred to compel union recognition rather than suffer work disruptions, one corporation head, Seward Avery of Montgomery Ward, gained wide publicity as the subject of a photograph mocking the tradition of civil disobedience by requiring national guardsmen to carry him from his office.[75]

A final perspective on the sit-downs was provided by a clergyman greatly admired in the tradition of civil disobedience in the postwar years: A. J. Muste. After training to be a Dutch Reformed minister, Muste had abandoned Calvinism and spent two decades as a labor educator and radical organizer, for a time as leader of a Trotskyist workers' movement known as the Musteites. He observed violent conflict at auto parts factories in Toledo and sit-downs by workers at Goodyear in Akron and at automobile factories in Detroit and Flint. On the eve of World War II he returned to the Christian ministry, with an unwavering pacifist commitment that had caused him to lose one pulpit during World War I. There will be occasion to mention him in relation to civil rights and antiwar protests in the postwar era. His labor background was important; his life in fact demonstrated a linkage between labor struggles and Christian ministry.

It is interesting here to consider his 1937 essay "Sit-Downs and Lie-Downs," which reflected on the actions of young women at the Berkshire Mills in Reading, Pennsylvania, who followed the pacifist teachings of Richard Gregg (more to come on him) by staging a "lie-down strike" instead of a sit-down. They lay flat in front of the Berkie's main gate, sometimes in slush and snow, forcing strikebreakers to step over their prostrate bodies to get inside. "They could not be dislodged by tear or vomit gas," according to one police report, until they finally were arrested for "blocking the sidewalk."[76] The strikers' CIO-affiliated union had not instigated the nonviolent action, but Muste took note that the union had proceeded to encourage study of the use of nonviolent methods in labor disputes. While the sit-downs had not been terribly violent, Muste noted, some coercion was insidious, on the part of sit-downers who might actually be only a minority of workers, or less courageous workers "who secretly hope the sit-down may succeed" but in the meantime sign up with both a company union and a "bona fide" one, or the corporations that stockpile weapons and pay huge sums for labor spies. It was clear that "the concept of property rights was in flux," and perhaps sit-down strikes would eventually be regarded as no more an invasion than more familiar forms of strikes and picketing. (He was writing before *Fansteel.*) But Muste emphasized that, from a nonviolent viewpoint, "lie-down picketing" as exemplified at Reading was superior because it was more clearly motivated by "the spirit of love, even toward their enemies," and it "openly depended upon the appeal to the higher sentiments and feelings of others rather than upon physical means for success."[77]

The women striking at the "Berkie," even as they lay in the snow, exemplified the transition from submissiveness to "insurrection" noted early in this chapter. Their courageous nonviolence also indicated a new direction in which the civil-disobedience tradition would proceed. Muste's own career would be widely admired; he was both principled and adaptable.

The sincerity of his wish to ground power in love, or in truth, rather than physical force would attract other adherents in other causes in decades to come. But it was a hard wish to realize, in a depression and, soon enough, during a world war with fearsome and hateful enemies. Muste's saintly version of pacifism would have critics who sought, and believed they found, more realistic and more demonstrably effective routes to peace and social change. Still, his influence as a link to socialist and Christian traditions and ardent champion of peace and social justice would be long-lasting.

7

Adapting a Philosophy of Nonviolence

At the 1963 March on Washington, A. Philip Randolph introduced Martin Luther King, Jr., as "the moral leader of our nation, a great dedicated man, a philosopher of a nonviolent system of behavior, in seeking to bring about social change for the advancement of justice and freedom and human dignity."[1] That reference to a philosophy or nonviolent system of behavior points us toward what might be called America's Gandhian moment, beginning with the Montgomery bus boycott (1955–56), reaching its high-water mark in the sit-ins and freedom rides, and receiving continued expression in peace movements and agricultural workers' marches and boycotts. In the longer history of civil disobedience in America, that moment was extraordinary, though of course not entirely unprecedented. How different Randolph's words sound from traditional defenses of law breaking as loyalty to a higher law, as vindication of democratic rights, or in more recent times as a tactic designed to pressure a sluggish government or resist its immoral policies.

How did that change come about? King's success in voicing a philosophy of human behavior intended to advance the causes of freedom, justice, and human dignity flowed from his ascent to leadership of a great social movement. "While the nature of this account causes me to make frequent use of the pronoun 'I,'" he wrote in his autobiographical *Stride Toward Freedom*, "in every important part of the story it should be 'we.'" He also made it clear that he made his own "pilgrimage" to nonviolence by engaging with lectures and books by predecessors who had thought deeply about the relevance to American society of Mahatma Gandhi's leadership of the independence struggle in India.[2]

Except for a few brief statements, Gandhi, who was killed in January 1948, did not address Americans directly. Americans learned of his teachings and practices primarily through the writings of journalists and biographers.[3] Frequently Gandhi was presented in heroic terms but usually with no suggestion that American social movements should take him and his followers as models. In this chapter I focus on two interpreters of Gandhi for Americans—Richard Bartlett Gregg and Krishnalal Shridharani—and two books published in the 1930s—Gregg's *The Power of Non-Violence* and Shridharani's *War without Violence*—that should be counted as key transmitters of influence. The two men never met, though their projects of showing how Gandhi's techniques could be used outside India shared many similarities.

Shridharani, who returned to India in 1946 and died there in 1960, wrote little about the American civil rights movement. But Gregg's papers give us touching instances of what it was like, not to be young, but to be in your mid-seventies at that hour. In September 1960, as the sit-ins were spreading across the American South, Gregg, seventy-five years old, exulted to an old pacifist friend, Rev. John Nevin Sayre of the Fellowship of Reconciliation (FOR), that the two of them and A. J. Muste "and a few others of us greyheads (are we grey eggheads?)" had lived to see "the full extent of the growth of the idea of loving nonviolence and the acceptance by increasing numbers of people of a belief in its power and effectiveness."

> The two times that I have spoken to Southern Negro audiences were most satisfying to me. They didn't listen as if it were an interesting but starry-eyed idea. They wanted it; they had felt the increase in self-respect from its use; they wanted to put it to work promptly more and more. What they have done[,] and their discipline, thrill me. Young high school girls and boys full of courage and deep belief in the power and religious content of the thing. It is a wonderful time to be alive and see dreams come true.[4]

A few months later he wrote Sayre: "What especially thrills me these days is the wonderful courage, understanding, discipline, enthusiasm and tenacity of the Negroes in our South, especially the students." It reminded him of a theory presented in a book of popular mathematics. Ideas are not adopted for practical use until "a social need" arises. The "seed idea" of logarithms, discovered by one of the ancient Greeks, went unnoticed until navigators needed it to calculate tables of latitude and longitude. "In like fashion, maybe, the idea of nonviolent resistance has not been put to work on a mass scale in America until the Negroes, having a strong social need for it, have picked it up and put it to work. The developments are going to be exciting, I think."[5]

Cross-cultural intellectual influence can be a tricky matter to discuss even when the supposed influence is that of one thinker on another, but it is much more so when the ideas in question are linked to broad social movements and political conflict. The strength of both Gregg's and Shridharani's books is that they take clear stands, and for the most part similar stands, on basic questions: was Gandhi's nonviolent program distinctively Indian and thus hard to translate into American terms? Shridharani is particularly lively in rejecting depictions of satyagraha as an "Oriental mystic doctrine baffling the Occidental mind."[6] Both insisted that Gandhi had identified methods that could be applied in any modern nation. Was Gandhi's program derived from a universal religious impulse? Nonviolence almost inevitably appears to transcend questions of nationality. In a preface to the first edition of Gregg's *Power of Nonviolence*, the Quaker scholar Rufus Jones placed Gandhi's teachings in a spiritual tradition that included Jesus, St. Francis, George Fox, and Leo Tolstoy as well as Hindu, Mohammedan, Buddhist, and Jewish prophets and seers. Gandhi often pointed to similar religious justification that transcended Hinduism. He did not limit his inspiration to religious prophets, however, but urged Indians to emulate such exemplars of courageous defiance of social convention as Luther, Galileo, Columbus, and Thoreau. Washington, Lincoln, Mazzini, and Lord Nelson were also presented as paragons of civil selflessness.[7] Both Gregg and Shridharani found this view better than thinking of Gandhi's teachings and actions as restrictively Indian. Shridharani was more secular than Gregg, who noted the value of *some* religious faith to provide a source of courage and steadfastness outside conventional morality, but both downplayed the religious content and emphasized the problem-solving effectiveness of nonviolent action. Both placed their ideas in a context that was social scientific and progressive. Unlike some of the movements we have been discussing, they sought to reconcile a drive for social justice and a tolerance for civic conflict with an abhorrence of social disruption. The ambiguities in their positions bear a strong resemblance to

Gandhi's own uncompromising adherence to justice joined to a belief in courtesy, negotiation, and compromise.

Was there an American tradition on which Gandhi drew? Gregg and Shridharani followed Gandhi's example in emphasizing the importance of Thoreau. In 1907 Gandhi published several articles praising Thoreau for going to jail rather than complying with legalized injustice and for writing about and publicizing his imprisonment. He summarized Thoreau's essay on civil disobedience, published lengthy excerpts in his newspaper, and reissued these excerpts in pamphlet form. "Historians say," Gandhi reported, "that the chief cause of the abolition of slavery in America was Thoreau's imprisonment and the publication by him of the above-mentioned book after his release." Thoreau was "a great writer, philosopher, poet and withal a most practical man"; his essay was "sanctified by suffering," its logic was "unanswerable" and valid for "all time." Gandhi urged Indians in the Transvaal to eradicate their "deep-rooted superstition that a law cannot be disobeyed." By defying a racist regime and refusing to carry Asiatic registration cards as required by the so-called Black Act, they could become "Thoreaus in miniature."[8]

Obviously, Gandhi was misinformed about Thoreau's importance in the American antislavery struggle, and he exaggerated the suffering Thoreau experienced in one night in jail. It is clear, however, that he attributed an international, even American, origin to civil disobedience and sought to inspire his Indian readers to take moral stands and actions raised to a new level of historical significance. One scholar notes as a "striking feature" of Gandhi's thinking before 1906, when he was radicalized by South Africa's racist laws, "not merely his reliance upon Western examples and values but his dependence on them to the exclusion of anything Indian."[9] We may take his references to Thoreau as a lingering trace of the same trait, even though Thoreau served as an inspiration for resistance.

Before long, however, Gandhi urged his comrades to "use as few foreign words as possible," to place their actions within Indian traditions, and to give new names to *civil disobedience, passive resistance,* and other terms that had no exact Gujarati equivalent. At the end of a newspaper contest he chose the new word *satyagraha,* coined from Sanskrit roots connoting "truth force" or "firmness in truth" to signify nonviolent resistance (though the English "civil disobedience" continued in use). In his *Autobiography* (1927) and *Satyagraha in South Africa* (1924), the principal account of events that led to his first world fame, Thoreau went curiously unmentioned, and in a 1935 letter Gandhi denied having derived his understanding of civil disobedience from reading Thoreau. At other times he suggested that he read Thoreau's essay for the first time while imprisoned in Pretoria in 1909. Despite these inconsistencies, he usually emphasized how deeply he cherished Thoreau's insight that his soul remained free despite incarceration.[10]

As Gandhi rose to international fame, the doctrine of satyagraha sounded strange, oriental, to Americans. They had their own traditions, and it might be asked why they needed Gandhi. Oswald Garrison Villard, editor of the *Nation* (and grandson of William Lloyd Garrison), gave one answer in a preface to Shridharani's *War without Violence:* "The progress of non-resistance and non-violent resistance was almost nil until Gandhi appeared." That was especially disappointing because a nonresistance society had emerged in the United States a century before, categorically rejecting all forms of violence while pledging, in "words that Gandhi might have written," that "they would 'in no case resist the operation of the law, except by meekly submitting to the penalty of disobedience.'"[11] Villard knew his Garrisonian ancestry, but we may question the depth of his understanding of Gandhi or the book he was introducing. There are too many false notes in his emphasis on meekness and submission. Villard's remarks may typify sentiments of the U.S. peace movement after the Civil War, but they overlook the practical, militant goals and tactics that both Gregg and Shridharani located in Gandhi and the message of civil disobedience that both raised in criticizing traditional American religious pacifism. Both hated cowardice, as did Gandhi, and admired such military virtues as discipline and courage. Gregg wrote of resisters' "semi-military" discipline, and his most famous chapter portrayed nonviolent resistance as analogous to a martial art, as "a form of moral jiu-jitsu." Shridharani, who put "war" in his title, emphasized Gandhi's departure from the familiar passivity that rendered most nonresistance a weapon of the weak. Both turned to Gandhi to justify a call to break from tradition.

The break was not total. These were pacifists; they rejected violence. They expressed respect for law. There were continuities with previous exponents of civil disobedience (though not necessarily Thoreau) in America. I will argue that they have even more to do with traditions of progressive reform and labor protest. They strive to make what they advocate psychologically plausible. Although honoring Gandhi's admonitions about means and ends (which were reminiscent of what antebellum pacifists might have claimed), they scorned stands on principle that were not aimed at practical results. Shridharani was especially devoted to this kind of pragmatic reasoning.

It may be surprising that neither had much to say, notably in the first editions of their books, about American race relations. They were more directly concerned with issues salient in the 1930s—labor disputes, class struggle, the rights of colonial populations, and renewed threats of world war—and in revised editions, with the lessons of World War II and the dangers of nuclear warfare. Though Martin Luther King, Jr., wrote the foreword to Gregg's second edition, it should be clear that we are trying to reconstruct the prehistory of the civil rights era in America. King's world differed substantially from that of Gandhi's interpreters.[12]

To readers coming to Gregg's *Power of Non-Violence* from the nineteenth-century American tradition, one striking feature is the lack of emphasis on obedience to an absolute higher law and, in its place, a focus on the conversion or persuasion of an antagonist. "The aim of the non-violent resister," Gregg wrote, "is to convert the opponent, to change his understanding and his sense of values so that he will join wholeheartedly with the resister in seeking a settlement truly amicable and truly satisfying to both sides."[13] It will come as little surprise to learn that Gregg had begun his career as a labor lawyer, and we can detect in his adaptation of Gandhi traces of the long search by some Americans in the Progressive Era for methods to secure industrial peace on the basis of a just settlement to which two sides, "both parties to a conflict," consent.[14]

People who knew Gregg invariably described him as humble, gentle, caring, almost too painstaking to write or speak with brilliance or power. A writer in the *Friends Journal* called him "one of the quietest radicals in history." She described a conference of the Fellowship of Reconciliation (FOR) in 1932 at which questions about Gandhian nonviolent resistance were being bandied about, and "there rose up a slight man who spoke with a hesitancy that verged on a stutter, and we instantly recognized the voice of one speaking with authority. All his life . . . Richard Gregg would say the most positive things in the most diffident manner." In her view, he was "the real father of the movement toward nonviolent resistance in this country."[15] His *Power of Nonviolence*, according to the historian Charles Chatfield, "became virtually a manual of style for pacifist action." John M. Swomley, Jr., of the FOR observed that this "pacifist best seller" served as "a kind of second Bible to those who did nonviolent battle against white supremacy during and immediately following the Montgomery bus boycott."[16]

The son of a Congregationalist minister,[17] Gregg was born in 1885 in Colorado Springs, where he grew up and lived until he went off to Harvard in 1903. After his graduation in 1907, he taught mathematics and chemistry for a year at a private school in Massachusetts. That kind of teaching was one of the several identities he would hold on to for the rest of his life. He received a law degree from Harvard in 1911 and then practiced in a corporate law office in Boston for three years. Knowledge of legal approaches to dispute settlement was always a strong element in Gregg's later life, especially after he came in contact with another old lawyer, Mohandas K. Gandhi. He worked for seven years in the rising field of industrial relations, first in a partnership with prominent progressives Robert G. Valentine and Ordway Tead overseeing protocol standards in the Ladies Dress and Waist industry in New York (which both sides charged went "too far"), then for three years in Chicago as statistician and economic counsel for the Federation of Railway Shop Employees before, during, and after a nationwide strike in 1921–22. He referred to those experiences when he felt challenged as to his knowledge and sympathies.[18]

During these years the ever-restless Gregg took time to work on a farm and to take courses on agriculture at the University of Wisconsin. These steps defined an interest that would grow stronger in the years ahead. Later he would study and practice biodynamic farming—the intensive use of the soil in raised beds, enriched by compost, with careful attention to which plants grow well in close "companionship"—under one of its most noted exponents, Ehrenfried Pfeiffer. For a long period (1943–56) Gregg combined farming with teaching at a progressive school in Putney, Vermont, that was a center for pacifist thought and belief in integrated lives of work and study. The farming was much more than a hobby. Gregg's work on companionate plants is still in print and in use by organic gardeners who may know nothing of his works on nonviolence.[19]

He married only in 1929, after returning from four years in India. Information about his wife is elusive, except that much of her life was tormented by mental illness. Some of Gregg's friends praised his strength in holding up under marital tragedy, an undercurrent to the quiet gentleness they admired. Gandhi responded to the news of the illness of Radha (as he called Mrs. Gregg) in 1947: "I see that for you there is no bed of roses. It is all thorns." Two years later, he was heartened by Gregg's report that Radha was "'slowly but steadily' improving through vegetarian dietetics." Perhaps that might be the subject of an article in *Harijan* (Child of God), one of several newspapers published by Gandhi, who rejected the term "untouchable" and the notion of untouchability. But there was no cure, as Gregg recorded in a grim autobiographical statement: "After a long mental illness, his wife died in May 1954."[20] In 1956, at seventy-one, he married Evelyn Speiden, a veteran of many years of teaching in China and a dedicated advocate of organic farming. They had met while studying farming with Dr. Pfeiffer. They announced that immediately after a biodynamic conference, they were heading off to India, where Richard had agreed to teach at a Gandhian training center for village workers and Evelyn would "probably teach composting."[21]

This trip would be Richard Gregg's fifth and final one to India.[22] His second visit, 1925–1929, demands special attention because it brought together all the parts of his identity as he found his voice as an author. As Gregg told the story, published later in an Indian journal, during the nationwide railway strike of 1921 he had happened upon Gandhi's writings and was so struck by the contrast between Gandhi's approach to conflict resolution and events surrounding him in America that he was driven to visit India and learn as much as he could about the nonviolent philosophy.[23] After arriving in India, he spent seven months (until his digestive system rebelled) at Gandhi's Satyagraha Ashram at Sabarmati. For several months he traveled to various villages and absorbed Indian culture.[24] He also spent three years teaching mathematics and physics in Kotgarh in the Simla Hills in view of the Himalayas. Gandhi encouraged Gregg's endeavor to improve the "education of the children of [the] backward classes" and took great interest in a textbook Gregg wrote to adapt math and science instruction to Indian experience.[25]

Gregg's immersion in India came during a long period that came after rioting had prompted Gandhi to call off the early campaign of noncooperation with British rule and to promote a "constructive program" aiming at economic autonomy, local improvement, and individual self-control. The next stage of confrontation with the Raj, which would popularize the notion of "civil disobedience" worldwide, occurred after Gregg's important sojourn in India. In the constructive interval, Gandhi found Gregg's knowledge of labor economics and agricultural science very useful. He converted Gregg to the values of *charka* (the spinning wheel) and *khaddar* (homespun cloth). Gregg wrote a book defending the efficiency of decentralized handiwork for poor colonial peoples. He also condemned large-scale industrial capitalism as "contrary to the fundamental spiritual and moral unity of mankind."[26] Gandhi and Gregg corresponded extensively on the proper uses of "nightsoil" as fertilizer as well as on proper diets to control flatulence and constipation and alternative treatments for other health problems. These two old lawyers had a lot in common.[27] The timing of Gregg's sojourn meant that his vision of the power of nonviolence would reflect no direct observation of civil disobedience but would show great appreciation of the importance of training, morale, and community living.

Despite his many other interests, Gregg's links to the Progressive tradition and its long search for industrial peace and social order remained keen. In the midst of the labor conflicts of the 1930s he enlisted with three others, and was given staff support, to write a pamphlet for mass distribution on nonviolent solutions to labor disputes. Gregg and the Emergency Peace Campaign that recruited him thought of the pamphlet as an important offset to books like Louis Adamic's *Dynamite*, which fostered the widely held belief that labor struggle was inevitably violent. The committee sent out inquiries and dispatched staff to conduct interviews, but the pamphlet does not seem to have been completed. It was hard to write a book by committee. Some of the unionists surveyed turned out, almost comically, not to be fully committed to nonviolence. One union armed its goons with staves, for example, but instructed them not to hit people on the head. Gregg left the project abruptly, giving the reason that *The Power of Non-Violence* was being adopted "as a sort of text book" by a Peace Pledge Union in England with more than 100,000 members alarmed by the imminence of war and determined to move beyond endless "talky-talky" and "get down to action." He accepted an invitation to hurry over at their expense, with the idea, he explained, that if war could not be stopped in England, the United States would be dragged in.[28] He was not the first or last peace activist to feel overwhelmed by the prospect of war and urgent calls to action.

Let us return to Gregg's famous image of "moral jiu-jitsu," which has been adopted, with or without acknowledgment, by many other writers on civil disobedience. The fearless nonviolent resister throws his assailant, who expects either cowardice or equivalent belief in violence, off balance. The resister captures the favor of onlookers with his willingness to endure pain, and his evident good will—even love—creates in the attacker, first, confusion and fear, followed by an awareness of human unity and openness to new ideas, and leading, soon enough, to a kind of conversion, a change of values, a new outlook. "The function of the nonviolent type of resistance is not to harm the opponent nor impose a solution against his will, but to help both parties into a more secure, creative, happy, and truthful relationship."[29] The image is almost unforgettable, but it may focus too much attention on individuals' conflict in a book that aims at proposing disciplined mass action.[30] Further, Gregg himself acknowledges that the reference to "love" may be unconvincing ("too sentimental")[31] in this martial arts context. We may add that it is harder to see the combat as a display of human unity than it is to see it in terms Gregg borrowed from one of the many psychologists he quotes, as a form of "manipulative activity."[32]

Any reader of *The Power of Nonviolence* will be struck by Gregg's wide reading, especially by the ranks of psychologists of divergent views from whom he extracts quotations to draw a plausible analysis of "what happens" during struggle.[33] He enlists both behaviorists and Freudians, for example, to support the likelihood that people's fundamental views may be transformed in a confrontational moment. We might characterize Gregg (who was very interested in popularization) as himself a popularizer, with considerable confidence in his own knowledge, who stood prepared to cite any works at hand and who believed that all problems had solutions that were "natural" even if some parts of civilization had gone astray. Even capitalists, he said in reply to Marxists, "because they are living creatures and subject to the laws of stimulus and response, cannot help being changeable, and because they are persons, cannot help being educable and capable of conversion."[34] The same might be said, presumably, of imperialist police forces or fascist soldiers. In some respects, this eclectic work bears the stamp of the interwar years, and it echoes the assumptions about human nature of rising new fields like advertising, public relations, influence management, and personnel psychology. Gregg invokes the spirit of science against fixed ways of doing things. We would not have engines or electric lights without the bold inquiries of persecuted scientists in the past and the adventurous experiments of inventors in more recent times. In view of the failure of familiar approaches to conflict resolution and "social truth," he asks, "Why not experiment with something new and scientific?"[35]

The jiu-jitsu metaphor portrayed nonviolent resistance in highly abstract terms. The conflict does not take place in India, South Africa, or in any other real place, though lots of actual events are alluded to. Today it might be played out in a video game. The scenario was grounded in eclectic reading in psychology and military theory—with surprisingly little reference to religion. The portrait certainly invited an orthodox critique that its 1920s-style optimism about human nature overlooks both the reality of sin and necessity of grace. But it equally certainly wrested nonviolence from Christian definitions that emphasized turning the other cheek rather than concerted action to achieve social justice. Gregg focuses attention on "power," but in a sense closer to the usages of motivational speakers than of social critics or theologians. Whatever criticisms may be justified, Gregg's book deserves recognition as a major transitional work, one that offered new thinking even if presented in now-unfashionable language of popular psychology from a different era. As pacifists proceeded to study Gandhi in search of universal values and methods, the "definitive works," in Charles Chatfield's phrase, were "the analyses of Richard Gregg."[36]

There are still readers who find *The Power of Nonviolence* definitive. But we may read it today as illustrating issues in dispute as civil disobedience has been adapted to new eras of struggle for civil rights in America. Consider these five brief examples. First, take the standard of cleanliness it sets as essential to the appearance and behavior of protesters seeking to convert their antagonists.[37] That standard would be first adopted and later contested in the American civil rights movement. Second, consider the goal of compromise, of negotiated settlement, the recognition that both sides held parts of the truth, which Gregg drew from Gandhi, American labor history, and his understanding of jiu-jitsu. That goal could conflict in practice with earlier understandings of higher law and with newer aspirations for "Freedom Now."[38] Third, consider hair-splitting distinctions between different types of coercion and pressure that Gregg explored in order to keep satyagraha safe in a pure realm of compelling truth and moral choice.[39] He might mollify those who worried that pressure group politics diluted high moral principles, but it is doubtful that he could have persuaded Alice Paul or A. Philip Randolph, for example, that governments did not need to be pressured, even coerced. Fourth, remember the importance of onlookers at the jiu-jitsu battleground. Does the play to spectators point forward to later accusations that civil disobedients staged events to win media attention rather than opponent's hearts? Fifth, Gregg deflects criticism that law-breaking campaigns undermine respect for public order by pointing out that injustice also promotes violence and disorder. But he suspends final judgment on whether satyagraha in India in 1921 and 1930 had provoked excessive violence.[40] He may be criticized for omitting that question in the 1960 edition of *The Power of Nonviolence*, revised after spending eighteen more months in an independent India. The question whether civil disobedience undermines respect for law would be inescapable by the mid–1960s in American appraisals of "nonviolent" direct action.

Shridharani's *War without Violence* is a very different book. I confess that I was unfamiliar with it until Homer Jack, whom I met on a research trip, informed me that *this* was the book, rather than Gregg's, that he and other founders of the Congress of Racial Equality (CORE) studied systematically in the early 1940s as they worked out a nonviolent strategy for confronting segregation. That recollection is confirmed in August Meier's and Elliott Rudwick's study of CORE: in weekly sessions the founding cell "studied and debated" the book, "chapter by chapter," with the aim to translate what they learned into "real action." According to the civil rights historian Taylor Branch, Bayard Rustin and James Farmer, who both worked for CORE as well as FOR, "sat at the feet" of Shridharani, whose book became "the semi-official bible of CORE." Farmer recalled that he and his comrades, all eager to "change the world," adopted the book, "at least in the beginning, to the letter."[41] Noting how widely it was used in other organizations, including the Harlem Ashram, Richard G. Fox calls *War without Violence* "the most widely read primer on Gandhian nonviolent resistance until after World War II." An FOR abbreviation of the text in pamphlet form sold for fifteen cents.[42] Mary King reports that "dog-eared copies" of Shridharani's book "had to be passed from hand to hand before reaching Martin Luther King, Jr., and others in the mid-twentieth-century American South who absorbed his riveting descriptions of Gandhi's campaigns."[43]

"Riveting" (a word she repeats) is not one I would choose to describe the book. Too often, especially in early chapters, it blends a kind of elevated dissertationese with left-sectarian persiflage. Readers are addressed as "vociferants of the twentieth century," as "suppositional victims of hypothetical powers," and "we" are swiftly dragged into a kind of "shadow-boxing" with the fuzzy thinking of pacifists who attack social conflict without correctly identifying the true causes of war.[44] Obviously, it takes imagination to read this book as it might have been read in 1939 or 1942. It may take an effort to understand why Glenn Smiley, a leading civil rights advocate who worked for FOR, called it in 1989 "a tiny pebble . . . thrown into the pond" whose "resulting ripples and waves" were still working their way toward "the distant shores of the planet."[45] Perhaps what made Shridharani's accounts of the Salt March or Civil Disobedience campaign so influential was the main contention that Satyagraha was not exclusively foreign, or oriental, but was instead a universally valid means that could be used in solving problems of justice in any modern nation and one that was especially valuable in democracies.

Shridharani would be an excellent subject for a biography in this era of global citizenship and Asian American intellectual history. Born in 1911, he was a caste Hindu (in fact of the same caste, the Vaishyas, and of the same regional descent, Gujarati, as Gandhi). His religious training was not dogmatic (one trait he admired in Gandhi was his openness to truth received from many sources). His father, a successful lawyer, died when he was eight. His mother made sure her talented son had a nationalist education at boarding school, then at a university Gandhi founded at Ahmedabad, and later at Visva-Bharati, a famous center of learning overseen by Rabindranath Tagore in Bengal, which he remembered as a poet's paradise. Shridharani himself won fame as a dramatist and poet at an early age (by American standards anyway). He left India in 1934, with a scholarship from the Maharajah of Bhavnagar, to study in the United States, where he chose Columbia University because it was "at the top" in his two fields of interest—journalism and sociology.[46] He completed his dissertation in the latter field in 1939, and when it was immediately published by a commercial press, he thanked prominent social scientists for their help.[47] He must have been a pleasure to teach: fluent in two cultures, intellectually ambitious, but by no means a grind. His enjoyment of his status at the margins of two societies became plain in a long memoir published in 1941. He published two additional full-length books in English before returning to India in 1946.[48] He moved to Delhi where he held a position for a time in the foreign affairs ministry of the new Indian government, and he was well acquainted with the nation's political leaders. But he preferred to make his career as an author of poems and dramas and as a journalist and was described as a pipe-smoking, nattily dressed, Indian nationalist. He died at forty-nine in 1960.[49]

His life stands in contrast to Gregg's in important respects. He was an Indian who spent twelve years in the United States. He had direct experience of civil disobedience. He exhibited a kind of bravado in public that was foreign to Gregg. When he was "what American collegians call a sophomore" at Ahmedabad, without telling his family, he answered Gandhi's call and marched to the sea among the heroic "first batch" of sixty who defied the imperial Salt Law. He was assigned to the group of speakers who visited villages along the way and spoke to farmer-labor rallies. Eventually he was arrested—"Give me all you can," he told the sentencing judge, "because if you don't, I'll be here again and for the same reason"—and jailed for three months. After his release he wrote a novel, *I Shall Kill the Human in You!* (in Gujarati), based on interviews with his imprisoned companions. British authorities proscribed it, he reported, thereby adding to its sales and his reputation. Such flamboyance must have been attractive to the "scores of on-campus clubs" that he addressed as an international student in America.[50]

Taylor Branch reports, in fact, that "the hard-drinking, cigar-smoking, woman-chasing Shridharani taught the wide-eyed young Americans [of CORE] that Gandhian politics did not require a life of dull asceticism." His taste for Cuban cigars has been confirmed, but it is hard to know what to make of the other characterizations.[51] We may at least wonder how CORE's founders would have reconciled such behavior with Shridharani's description of Gandhi's "exacting attitude" toward the people he counted on. For example, one morning when he showed Gandhi a sonnet he had composed the night before, praising his beloved Bapuji as the "Good Son" of Mother India, Gandhi whirled on him and asked, "Why should you spin poetry when you can well use your time spinning cotton?"[52]

What, besides the experienced and flamboyant voice of the narrator, drew civil rights protesters to Shridharani's work? What held their attention? Certainly not the author's interest in American racial injustice. The first edition of *War without Violence* made no reference to American race relations. A revised posthumous edition (1962) added only two perfunctory sentences on Martin Luther King, Jr., and Montgomery.[53] There was potential excitement in his contention, based on his "contact with the Western world[,] ... that, contrary to popular belief, Satyagraha, once consciously and deliberately adopted, has more fertile fields in which to grow and flourish in the West than in the Orient."[54] Perhaps what most engaged the CORE founders was the first long chapter of the book, which provided guidelines for that adoption. "How Is It Done?," as this chapter is called, defines satyagraha in terms of a sequence of events to be carried out in pursuit of a "Cause."

Shridharani's first sentence on the first stage of organized mass action reads: "No avenue leading toward the peaceful settlement of a given conflict

should be left unexplored before embarking upon a program of Satyagraha."
Gandhi had set this rule and others that called for openness and negotiation before agitation or the issuing of an ultimatum. Each stage includes
further steps: agitation, for example, may take the form of speeches, rallies,
catchy songs and slogans, the dissemination of newspapers and
pamphlets—all to build up "cause consciousness." Next comes a stage of
demonstrations, followed by a stage of "self-purification" in which the
satyagrahis strive to reform their own habits and beliefs that may have
contributed to the injustice they protest. And so on, through further picketing, sit-down strikes, boycotts, tax refusal, migration, noncooperation,
ostracism, civil disobedience, and the setting up of alternative institutions
parallel to the government. Some of these stages may be omitted or may
occur in different orders, but the sequence is nevertheless important
enough that Shridharani presents it in a diagram.[55] Today it may be hard to
see why this chapter would have seemed extraordinary in 1942. Many of
the steps will now seem utterly familiar to left- and right-wing groups, few
of which worry about the idea of earning the right to break the law by a
pattern of explaining positions and seeking accommodation peacefully.
We may be able to understand, however, why the Gandhian (and in
Shridharani's terms, Rousseauian) political theory—holding that the
people are justified in setting up their own institutions as government
refuses to negotiate over their just demands—might have excited foes of
Jim Crow during and after World War II.

Another chapter that must have seemed highly relevant to American
racial injustice is the ninth, "Direct Action in Democracy." In the American
context, Shridharani did not imagine satyagraha becoming as revolutionary as in imperial India. His critique of American pacifism and liberalism found them too reluctant to address social problems that might
erupt into violent conflict. Modern democracies urgently needed "techniques for the peaceful, intelligent, and constructive resolution of conflicts."
Satyagraha, employed when—*and only when*—all else fails and no alternative exists except violence, may actually preserve constitutional order.[56]
Though he never mentions racial segregation in this discussion, it is easy
to relate this analysis to the prehistory of the civil rights movement.

Shridharani's emphasis on conflict resolution reminds us of what he shared
with Gregg and how they were joined in common work. Though of different
ages and nationalities, they were linked by traditions of late-Progressive

social thought. Gregg, for example, built an important chapter entitled "An Effective Substitute for War" around a quotation from an article by Walter Lippmann, "The Political Equivalent of War." Lippmann's point was not merely that a peaceful society requires outlets for belligerent attitudes and martial posturing. War was not simply outmoded and irrational; it was also an institution through which decisions were made and conflicts resolved. Since it would be utopian to imagine a society without causes of dispute, in the real world politics must include methods for resolving them that fall short of war.[57] Lippmann was himself building on William James's great essay "A Moral Equivalent for War," which Gregg attempts to improve by arguing that nonviolent resistance is "much superior" to the environmental and social-service corps that James suggested. Why superior? Because "it does not require State organization, direction or assistance; it is not used against the exterior forces and conditions of Nature but against human wrongs and evils." It was more dramatic and alluring, to women as well as men; and it enabled displays of daring and "truly fine and noble romance" more than equal to "the chivalrous violent fighting of by-gone ages."[58]

James's essay was central to a Progressive tradition that both these interpreters of Gandhi kept alive. The spirit of James hovers at almost every turn in Shridharani's argument. James is there, for example, in descriptions of the organization and discipline of the forces of satyagraha as well as in analysis of how satyagraha can repair democracy. It is there, moreover, when Shridharani claims that the social technique he advocates is pragmatic, whereas liberalism and pacifism cling to doctrines that have no social use.[59] Following Louis Menand's *The Metaphysical Club*, we could also call that dimension of Gregg's and Shridharani's works "unionist." James's generation had learned from the horrors of the Civil War to be suspicious of "the violence they saw hidden in abstractions,"[60] but they were interested in techniques ("how it is done") and alternatives for improving society. As they interpreted Gandhi in a "unionist" context, however, Gregg and Shridharani prescribed techniques of dispute resolution that would reveal greater power to divide and transform society than a previous generation of Progressives would have been comfortable with.[61] Consider, for example, Shridharani's adoption of Gregg's idea of moral jiu-jitsu, in which the attacker loses his equilibrium because of his victim's refusal to retaliate physically as expected and quits his assigned role. Shridharani authenticates that scenario from personal observations on the

Salt March. Sometimes men who started out as hirelings of the government switched sides and became nonviolent soldiers. He also quotes news accounts of soldiers and policemen, even the best trained "crack troops," throwing away their guns and ignoring orders to fire on satyagrahis who would not fight back.[62]

The best-known example of attackers feeling ashamed and unnerved when their victims declined to defend themselves appeared in widely syndicated reports by Negley Farson of the *Chicago Sun-Times*, who observed policemen led by English sergeants charging into Hindu marchers on the Maidan in Bombay and beating them with lathis, "Whack! Whack! Whack!" Then came a band of fifty "splendid-looking" Sikhs, fierce and armed, who had pledged not to protect themselves or their women, one holding a baby, who marched with them. And they did not resist, even when beaten bloody by mounted policemen. One lying next to Farson gave him "a bloody smile—and stood up for more." The police could not continue: "You can't go on hitting a blighter," one said, "when he stands up to you like that." Rain came, the police left, and the Sikhs led a "triumphant procession of Gandhi's nonviolent congress followers down the streets." That was, said Farson, "the most amazing scene I ever encountered." A widely syndicated report by Webb Miller used similar terms to describe the "amazing" sight, if one could bear to look, of 2,500 or more dedicated volunteers proceeding toward the salt works at Dharsana, where policemen beat them while their own leaders stood "in front of the ranks imploring them to remember that Gandhi's soul was with them." He had never before "witnessed such harrowing scenes." Imperial attempts to censor Miller's dispatches only increased American support for Indian home rule. Reports like these made a favorable impression on American "on-lookers" who had been expressing concern that Gandhi was provoking violence. "Never in the history of the world," according to Villard's *Nation*, "has there been such amazing self-control by great masses of people."[63]

Farson's story provided an example of an attacker feeling ashamed and unnerved when his victim declined to defend himself, and Shridharani made use of it as an illustration supporting Gregg's contention that attackers are thrown off balance by nonresistance. That may be true when the nonresistants are known to be men of great valor like the Sikhs. But there may be questions and parallels to ponder that were not so evident in the 1930s. Soon enough in the American South there would be televised examples of black young people (and some white activists) submitting courageously to being beaten, tortured with lit cigarettes; these scenes would have great effect on American viewers and exert a political influence even stronger and more immediate than the news stories from India had done. There were, however, few if any stories of the brutes and bullies being shamed or tamed. And there would be strong reactions from black populations that there must be defense, that submission to atrocity is wrong. Some would say that the lessons of nonviolence had been imperfectly understood. But the need and rightfulness of self-protection is a topic that once seemed inconvenient but over time has become an unavoidable part of the story.

These two influential and very different books were milestones in the terminology and thinking of radical protest as it transitioned from "passive resistance" (or "nonresistance") to active nonviolence or "nonviolent direct action." The term "nonresistance," which was associated with radical abolitionists of the 1830s, carried echoes of even earlier theological and political discussions of the obligations of citizenship. It also converted Christ's injunction to "resist not evil" into a method of resistance to ill-doing authority. The term was still used in the 1930s, but in the interwar years "passive resistance" was usually prevalent, perhaps because the operative noun plainly referred to forceful opposition, though to be sure carried out in a passive manner. It was associated with Leo Tolstoy, who gained an international following that included Gandhi and some prominent Americans for a time between the 1890s and World War I. It was used, as we have noticed, in many movements—among them, woman suffrage, temperance, individualist anarchism, and, yes, the IWW—to define their approaches to contests and confrontations over privileges, powers, and rights. But the vocabulary of "direct action," which the IWW preferred, and satyagraha, or eventually, "nonviolent direct action," had the appeal of not being passive.[64] That was a promise Gregg and Shridharani popularized— nonviolence as a source of power.

Power peacefully exerted to socially good ends. But is it also exerted coercively, even undemocratically? Both Gregg and Shridharani took pains to show the consideration of opponents that must accompany satyagraha, but these presentations may not convince skeptics or scholars.[65] The intersection of coercion with nonviolence had been explored by a major work in the relatively new field of sociology in 1923, Clarence Marsh Case's *Non-Violent Coercion*.[66] After reflecting on the relatively large numbers of conscientious objectors to World War I and examining the persistence of "pacifist" sects and individuals throughout the history of Christianity and other great religions, Case turned to a subject on which believers in passive resistance were divided—strikes and boycotts. To some "leading non-resistants," a strike was "incompatible with passive resistance" because it was not a method of peaceful persuasion or agitation but "a method of coercion." Others were finding it impossible to maintain their wartime absolute pacifism in the postwar world. Case took his stand with those who recognized "the inability of absolutist theories of conduct to solve the concrete problems of daily life in the actual, striving, rough-and-tumble world." Strikes, then, were permissible if we "define passive resistance as the exercise of social constraint by non-violent means." Boycotts were acceptable as a form of passive resistance so long as they do not turn to violence.[67] Case concluded with high praise for Gandhi. Writing shortly after Gandhi had suspended a campaign of mass civil disobedience that let loose too much undisciplined violence and had begun a six-year jail sentence, Case judged that he had "presented the most extraordinary manifestation of passive resistance and non-violent coercion in the history of the world." Gandhi, according to Case, had shown the uses of "a form of social pressure," not to be confused with physical force, that might help society to realize "social purposes and ideals" without resort to violence.[68]

Case's book not only defines useful terms for understanding Gregg's and Shridharani's militant (aggressive) pacifism, it also evokes the milieu in which Gregg as an employee of a railway employees union during their 1922 strike came across an article about Gandhi and decided to go to India.[69] In *The Power of Nonviolence* Gregg would cite Case only in passing as a source of useful and inspiring stories for nonresistants-in-training to study.[70] He gave no indication of disagreement with Case's remarks on coercion except perhaps his preference, even in analyzing scenes of combat, for the language of conversion. But in the first edition he did confront potential critics of group nonviolent resistance who claimed that it could be hurtful and thus "was not generically different from other forms of coercion." Coercion was, "at best," he said, an ambiguous and misleading word, inapplicable to "true" nonviolent resistance, which "results ultimately in changing the purposes and desires (values) of the opponent so that he and the resister finally agree without any remaining sense of frustration."[71] (He was probably wise to drop that passage in later editions.) To a reader coming to Gregg's *Power of Nonviolence* from the nineteenth-century American tradition, which includes Thoreau, one striking feature is its lack of emphasis on obedience to an absolute higher law and its focus instead on the conversion or persuasion of an antagonist. The nonviolent resister, Gregg writes, strives for conversion of a formerly violent opponent: "The function of the nonviolent type of resistance is not to harm the opponent nor impose a solution against his will, but to help both parties into a more secure, creative, happy, and truthful relationship."[72]

Shridharani must have studied Case's book in graduate school. In the published version of his dissertation he dissented from Case's description of satyagraha as coercion, a term that goes too far by implying a demand for "revenge and punishment," but he also faulted Gandhi and some of his followers for calling satyagraha purely a process of conversion when in the face of the worst atrocities Gandhi's goal was, in his own words, to "*compel repentance.*" Shridharani himself prefers the term *compulsion,* which does not imply physical injury to opponents.[73] In fact, then, he settled roughly where Case did and dissented from the language of conversion that Gregg appeared to prefer. What matters, in any case, is that in applications of satyagraha by American civil rights activists in following years, the goals of conversion and reconciliation were fervently expressed, and occasionally attained, but appeals to government for armed, coercive intervention were also made and sometimes granted.

Gregg and Shridharani presented their accounts of nonviolent direct action during a decade when earlier versions of pacifism seemed irrelevant to the challenges of labor radicalism on the home front and the menace of nationalistic dictatorships overseas. Both books had new introductions in second editions. In 1962 Shridharani's publishers removed to an appendix a few excerpts from Villard's introduction, which had recalled the traditions of the New Testament and Garrisonian nonresistance. In its place appeared a brief endorsement by Sarvepalli Radhakrishnan, a philosopher who served as president of an independent (but partitioned) India, and a new, longer introduction by the author himself on satyagraha as a pragmatic substitute for war. In Gregg's second edition (1960), the introduction by the Quaker scholar Rufus M. Jones, emphasizing the sacred texts of the world's great religions, disappeared. In its place appeared a brief foreword by Martin Luther King, Jr., stressing the horrors of modern war as revealed during World War II and giving some examples of nonviolent resistance that pointed toward new techniques for winning freedom and achieving social change in the American South. By the time these revised editions appeared, what may be called America's Gandhian moment was under way,[74] and events like the Montgomery bus boycott in 1954 and the sit-ins in Nashville and Greensboro in 1960 were being hailed for launching an exciting nonviolent era of social change.

Those events will be discussed in chapter 8. What must be stressed here is that American experiments with Gandhi's teachings—the events of civil disobedience, such as bus boycotts and sit-ins—did not "begin" in 1954 or 1960. If anything, they began in the late 1930s and 1940s. They began with networks of small organizations affiliated with socialism and organized labor, slightly larger remnants of an antiwar movement that had originated in World War I and assumed new urgency as conscription and world war returned (the nonsectarian War Resisters League and the religiously defined Fellowship of Reconciliation), and newer organizations pressing for elimination of the structures of racial segregation on a grand or small scale (the March on Washington Movement and Congress for Racial Equality). Besides desegregation, all these movements held strong interests in labor and were increasingly antiwar. As we have seen, Gregg, always keenly interested in industrial conflict, had encouraged the factory women who in 1936 staged a "lie-in" in the ice and snow outside the gate of the Berkshire hosiery factory. These hosiery workers were more directly supported by two ex-Methodist missionaries, Jay Holmes Smith and Ralph Templin, whom British authorities had expelled from India for associating with nationalists and refusing to pledge loyalty to the empire. The two men set up a "Kristagraha" community, merging Gandhian methods and Christian faith, among the hosiery workers before moving on to establish a well-known ashram in Harlem. Shridharani, who knew them both and had visited the ashram, commented that Kristagraha "can well be used for the good of all concerned when legal procedures fail and leave direct action as the only alternative—in the problem of race relations, for instance, and in that of the sharecroppers."[75]

Gregg also gave encouragement, at a distance, to organizing efforts among southern tenant farmers, who refused to resort to violence even in the heart of "one of the most volcanic and violent areas of America." The black farmer-preacher Owen Whitfield, who led an "exodus" of nearly two thousand, mostly black, sharecroppers from their farms, like the children of Israel escaping "old Boss Pharoh," carrying all their possessions with them, encamping along Missouri bootheel highways in 1939, based his commitment to nonviolence on the Bible—and prudence. "We must obey the law, . . . don't let anyone say we're trying to make trouble. It seems to be almost a criminal offense to wake people up so they take peaceful group action." There were more accusations of communist influences and few if any references to Gandhi. Removed from the roadsides and living under threats of violence, many of the croppers eventually received new quarters built by the Farm Security Administration and took ownership of new homes, at least for a while, with financial help from St. Louis philanthropies.[76] These scenes occurred in regions of the South where Gandhi's and Gregg's ideas about village agriculture and handcraft labor might not have seemed inapt. The South would begin to change rapidly during the next decade, the 1940s, as more than two million blacks migrated to growing industrial areas outside the South, another million moved into southern cities, and according to some historians, the civil rights era commenced.[77]

In American renderings of Gandhian struggle, it was never the case that the individual was all important, like Thoreau moving from his cabin to the town jail for an overnight stay or even the jiu-jitsu gladiator in Gregg's cockpit. Consider, for example, the flamboyant, charismatic African American activist Bayard Rustin, who in his travels as a peace organizer for FOR in 1942 decided to move forward from the rear of a bus in Tennessee. That impulsive act (spurred by an overheard comment from a white mother to her child) took him off message. His insistence that his conscience prevented him from complying with an unjust law got him a fierce beating, despite the sympathetic protests of some white passengers. But he kept a Gandhian stance of refusal to fight back as the beating continued in the station and the police captain said in amazement, "Nigger, you're supposed to be scared when you come in here." It was not the last time that Rustin would act in a scene that might have been scripted by Richard Gregg. A couple of years later, as a prisoner in a penitentiary for refusing to cooperate with the war effort and with segregation in prison, he earned the applause of other prisoners and his warden for his courage in accepting the blows of a white supremacist wielding a mop handle.[78] Few others could equal Ruskin's charisma and courage, but a point to stress is that he belonged to a movement that sustained him before and after moments of spontaneous courage.

Another example of incipient change is young Pauli Murray's unplanned confrontation with Jim Crow laws on buses in Virginia in 1940, when she traveled to spend Easter holidays with family in Durham and took along a West Indian friend who wanted to see the South. Trouble began when they had to board a broken-down bus for one leg of the journey, and her friend began to feel ill from sitting above one of the rear wheels. Murray's request to move forward, contrary to state segregation laws, led to an increasingly ugly confrontation with the driver, then arrest, a weekend in the Petersburg City Prison, ending with a conviction and a fine for violating the segregation law. That charge was revised, when an NAACP team prepared to defend the two women, to "creating a distur- bance." Murray and her friend refused to pay the fine and instead returned for several more days in the prison, where they received much better treat- ment. Murray devoted an entire chapter of her autobiography to this misadventure, recounting the experience in dramatic detail and making it clear that though "inexperienced in Gandhi's method," and with no initial interest in confrontation, the two friends had improvised a kind of satya- graha, displaying courtesy toward their jailers while voicing clear demands for justice.[79]

She was not a humble, uninformed victim. She had recently read Shridharani's *War without Violence*. She was living in Harlem, in close touch with other strong-minded people (including founders of the ashram, where she would reside shortly afterward).[80] In the midst of experiences that led her from seeking a career in creative writing to one in the law, she had met Eleanor Roosevelt, with whom she corresponded about National Sharecroppers Week and racial segregation in Washington, among other subjects. In the process of her arrest she arranged for word to be sent to the first lady, who replied sympathetically but somewhat patronizingly, "As long as these laws exist, it does no one much good to violate them." Though an admirer of Mrs. Roosevelt, and destined to closer association in the future, Murray concluded that "she had little understanding of what it meant to be a Negro in the United States at that time."[81] A few years later, as a law student at Howard, Murray joined with others in well-organized, nonviolent combat against Jim Crow at Washington lunch counters and cafeterias. Decades later, a *Washington Post* reporter noted with some surprise that long before the famous marches and rallies of the 1960s, and even before World War II, civil rights protests had begun one neighbor- hood and one institution at a time.[82]

What deserves emphasis is the collective efforts of the young profes- sionals in these protests years before the Montgomery bus boycott or

Greensboro sit-in. "Ideas about the use of nonviolent resistance to racial injustice, modeled on Gandhi's movement in India, were in the air," Murray recalled in her autobiography. In 1942 A. Philip Randolph announced that the March on Washington Movement (MOWM) was considering "a campaign of civil disobedience and non-cooperation." "Although Mr. Randolph stood virtually alone among established Negro leaders in advocating this form of protest," Murray continued, "several young Negroes were eager to adapt Gandhi's techniques to our own struggle, and I was among them." Others included Rustin and James Farmer, staff members of the pacifist FOR, who were already experimenting with the technique in small groups, and both were active in founding the Congress of Racial Equality (CORE) in the spring of 1942. As a contributing member of FOR, Murray had studied its literature and had shown, in the Petersburg jail, her grasp of the "philosophical and religious principles" of nonviolent action derived from Gandhi. "I also felt," she added, "that the most effective way to use nonviolence in our racial struggle was to combine it with American techniques of showmanship."[83]

In 1942, her second year at Howard, Murray participated in an MOWM planning conference and, together with others, formulated a plan for nonviolent direct action and maximum publicity in demonstrations demanding fairness in employment and public accommodations, a plan that has been credited with setting out "the strategy for the modern civil rights movement." The plan required intensive knowledge of the targeted locality's legal environment—were there civil rights laws under which justice could be claimed? In states with segregation statutes well-trained leaders and students would need to pursue "carefully planned" and relentless nonviolent programs of refusal to accept discrimination in any part of public life.[84]

A succession of influential black intellectuals showed keen interest in Gandhi and believed that his leadership in India held lessons for African Americans. Among others, Benjamin Mays, the president of Morehouse, King's undergraduate college, who urged young ministers to preach on real-life issues, traveled to India in 1936. The president of Howard, Mordecai Johnson, had been urging blacks to study the Indian leader's theories and methods since 1930. After visiting India in 1950 Johnson gave an "electrifying" lecture on Gandhi that King credited with inspiring his own "pilgrimage" to nonviolence.[85] But no one's interest in Gandhi's methods of revolution had more consequence than that of Randolph, who evaluated them practically and strategically, asking how a large, racially defined underclass could rebel successfully against a dominant power in the United States as it had in South Asia. Committed to overcoming the legacies of slavery and Jim Crow in the American South and the feelings of dislocation and insinuations of inferiority imposed by societies outside the South, which blacks were entering in large numbers during the great migration, he promoted and led campaigns of disobedience through conflicts and controversies over several decades.

Previous chapters have noted Randolph's and MOWM's references to the black abolitionists and the Underground Railroad as examples of a heritage of black militance to be reclaimed in order to seize opportunities to advance the civil rights of African Americans while their services were needed during wartime. Randolph brought to this project his leadership of a national union, the Brotherhood of Sleeping Car Porters, that had fought intense employer opposition in order to achieve representation for workers in an occupation reserved for blacks and had then won for them wages and working conditions that made them proud and financially secure members of a network of communities across the nation. Randolph was a remarkable man. Born in Florida, the son of a preacher, he had migrated northward to seek a career as an actor in New York and built a reputation in Harlem as a labor organizer, socialist street orator, and editor of an influential magazine, the *Messenger*. He was an atheist and a realist with no illusions about government's sacredness, but as a man of principle, he appealed to a "higher law of righteousness." He had no doubt about the potential usefulness of political action to achieve important goals. Through a progression of organizations Randolph pursued the creation of a black voting bloc and a national third party representing blacks and labor (one goal he never fully attained).

He expressed no interest in Gandhi as an ascetic, a religious guru, a holy pacifist, but he came to appreciate Gandhi's tactics of nonviolent direct action, the marches and civil disobedience, but not the self-punishing fasts, for the force they exerted on British rule—and for the model they set for American blacks striving to overcome discrimination and subjugation. He viewed the Indian people's struggle for independence in racial terms. Why should American blacks, he asked, be conscripted in a war to support British rulers' denial of the national aspirations of colored people in South Asia?[86]

He called off his first threatened march on Washington (which he envisioned as ten thousand black protesters converging on the White

House) in 1941 after President Franklin Roosevelt, with important interventions by Eleanor, proclaimed a wartime Fair Employment Practices policy in defense industries.[87] But MOWM continued to meet, and related acts of disobedience and major urban rallies proceeded on the home front. Later in the decade, as a new war approached, the temporary policy had expired and the armed forces were still segregated, as were many other institutions in the United States. By that time peace organizations, reacting to the many atrocities of war, and especially to the horror of atomic warfare on Japanese cities, were moving toward ever-stronger rejection of the militarization of U.S. society.[88]

In 1948, as the federal government moved toward a new cold war draft, the secretary of the army advised President Harry Truman that segregation was "in the interest of national defense." But a meeting between Truman and black spokesmen turned frosty when Randolph reported "the mood among Negroes . . . that they will never bear arms again until all forms of bias and discrimination are abolished." A few days later he told the Senate Armed Services Committee, "I personally will advise Negroes to refuse to fight as slaves for a democracy they cannot possess and cannot enjoy." He promised a Harlem crowd that he would "oppose a Jim Crow army" until "I rot in jail." Not long after, he marched in front of the White House, giving out buttons that said "Don't join a Jim Crow ARMY" and carrying a sign declaring "If we must die for our country let us die as free men—not as Jim Crow slaves."[89] Through organizations called the League for Non-Violent Civil Disobedience and the Emergency Committee against Military Jim Crow, he and many other blacks joined forces with pacifist groups like FOR and young radicals who called themselves Peacemakers, to conduct an interracial campaign of draft refusal. When President Harry Truman issued a proclamation ending Jim Crow in the armed services in 1948, he was careful to avoid the appearance of a capitulation. But the accusation was unavoidable. One prominent southern senator, Georgia's Richard B. Russell, who had sought a clause in the draft act giving any man the right to serve only with members of his own race, denounced Truman's order as "unconditional surrender . . . to the treasonable civil disobedience campaign organized by the Negroes." No doubt Truman's order took account of many crosscurrents in a turbulent political moment, but it would be hard not to see it as the unprecedented result of what was to that point the widest and longest civil disobedience campaign in U.S. history.[90]

After Truman's proclamation, Randolph called off his opposition to a new draft law. This time, cessation of threats of civil disobedience caused great bitterness among pacifists with whom he had joined forces. James Peck called it "a tragic sellout." Bayard Rustin called it "a grave and tragic mistake." Randolph defended the importance of compromise and "above board dealings" with black youth who supported an anti–Jim Crow campaign, not opposition to all war whatsoever. To the pacifists, he had not been aboveboard in betraying them by calling off a campaign for a second time.[91] His relations were eventually repaired with Muste and Rustin (who became Randolph's key aide), but the breach did illuminate differences between a "religious pacifist nucleus" (as Randolph referred to it) and those with a more pragmatic disposition. We might attribute his willingness to find an agreement and stick with it to his labor union orientation. Both Gregg and Shridharani describe the goal of a "just settlement," which may be found prior to "direct action," as integral to satyagraha. As one of Gandhi's best expositors writes, "Compromise, like non-cooperation and civil disobedience, is one of the tools which may be used in the promotion of a satyagraha campaign." Resistance to compromise may lead to "self-righteousness" and "stiff-necked opposition." "There is a time and place for compromise and to know that time and place is one of the skills which every leader of satyagraha should master."[92] The questions of when is the right time and what is a just accommodation are not easily answered. But the two different understandings of radicalism and direct action, apparent in this episode—one set on ending segregation, the other on ending war—would recur in decades to come.

Was it treason for Randolph to promote draft resistance at a moment of danger to the republic? By taking his stand against conscription with such overt defiance, this well-known public man raised that question almost unavoidably—and not just in the minds of segregationists. Wayne Morse, a well-known liberal U.S. senator and a board member of the NAACP, went to the floor of the Senate to rehash his "cross-examination" of Randolph over the stand he had taken before the Armed Services Committee. Addressing Randolph with great personal respect and emphasizing his personal wish to see Jim Crow eradicated and his willingness to work to that end, Morse nevertheless classified Randolph's action as treason. No "legal principle of the Constitution" would tolerate Randolph's program of civil disobedience during a "national emergency" (that is, the cold war, soon to be followed by armed conflict in Korea). The only constitutional ground for refusing military service was conscientious objection to war based on religious training and conviction. Counseling others to disobey a call was even more treasonable. Randolph replied that he and other "Negroes who refused to participate in the armed forces" were prepared to face terrorism, concentration camps, and adverse legal decisions. As non-resistants who considered themselves more faithful to American democracy than segregationists, they would "participate in no overt acts against the government." Morse questioned whether Randolph's program could really be "passive." Events would get out of control, and the civil disobedients would be the "proximate cause" and be held legally responsible. Randolph disputed that view of causation by offering a comparison with a union calling a strike and antiunion forces creating violence. If Morse was correct about the legal doctrine of treason as currently understood, he was willing to "face the music." But he denied that legal precedents were as clear as Morse asserted.

> I do not believe the law up to the present time has been faced with such conditions as to enable it to envisage these principles. In other words, American jurisprudence has never been faced with this kind of condition and consequently its definition of treason could not possibl[y] take in the type and nature of action which we propose in civil disobedience. But however the law may be construed we would be willing to face it on the grounds that our actions would be in obedience and in conformity with the higher law of righteousness than that set forth in the so-called law of treason.[93]

The historical drama in this respectful exchange arose ironically from Morse's assurance that he was right, while Randolph's prediction of expanding legal respect for conscientious expression would be tested in later U.S. draft card cases.

Similar irony was evident when Morse, in remarks to his Senate colleagues, denied the validity of Randolph's resort to justifications of civil disobedience in "the philosophy of Gandhi." That philosophy could not be "applied" in the United States. "Gandhi had no responsibility to a written constitution" and was not subject to the same legal obligations as Americans like Randolph and his "followers." In Morse's judgment (he was no longer just predicting what courts would say), if anyone took Randolph's "bad advice in regard to a program of civil disobedience . . . the law of treason

should be applied." The "very passiveness" of their program would "constitute an overt act," and they would be guilty of conspiring to aid and abet an
enemy. The call to civil disobedience, Morse added, was not helping the
"cause of civil rights legislation" in Congress, and Randolph's supporters
"must assume a great deal of responsibility for setting back a legislative
program of civil rights."[94] If we remember that Morse was one of the
friendliest senators toward civil rights, his brandishing of the law of treason
will show the real courage required of those who considered a program of
Gandhian civil disobedience as a way to combat segregation.

Conscription was a major issue in the emergence of modern American
civil disobedience. Morse was right: the conscientious exemption recognized in World War I applied only to members of the historic peace
churches (Friends, Anabaptists, and Mennonites). That war and its draft
had aroused many radical opponents. In 1918 Randolph and his socialist
coeditor, Chandler Owen, spent two nights in jail in Cleveland, Ohio,
where they were threatened with indictment for treason for distributing
the *Messenger* and urging blacks to resist conscription.[95] Many others,
socialists and Wobblies, were jailed for longer periods for opposing that
war, and in the "Red Scare" after the armistice many were rounded up and
deported.

The Selective Service Act of 1940, enacted after several years of public
and legislative controversy over "preparedness," was America's first peacetime draft. Under its terms sixteen million American males between the
ages of twenty-one and thirty-six were swiftly registered with local draft
boards; the number tripled as the ages were expanded to eighteen and
forty-five. The law allowed for a wider range of exemptions from military
service based on religious principles and more opportunities for alternative duties. Pacifists denounced it, initially and unsurprisingly, as an abandonment of neutrality and a step toward war; to more radical pacifists, it
was something worse—a step toward transforming American democracy
into a totalitarian state. The "Union Eight," seminary students at Union
Theological School in New York City, who refused to register (even though
they would have been exempt from service), declared: "It is a totalitarian
move when our government insists that the manpower of the nation take
a year of military service." Along with other measures mobilizing industry
to serve national defense, it amounted to "American Hitlerism."[96] Their
much-admired professor Reinhold Niebuhr agreed with their jail sentence,

observing that in a time of national danger they had gone beyond "contending for the right of the Christian to abstain from war"; their contention that conscription itself is totalitarian was "anarchistic" and insupportable.[97]

In highly publicized proceedings the eight were tried together, found guilty, handcuffed, and transported to serve sentences of a year and a day at the federal penitentiary in Danbury, Connecticut. They were not the most obedient prisoners. Most of them were soon confined to their cells for participating in a prison strike over denial of permission for antiwar activities. They defied racial segregation and joined with draft resisters in other prisons in seeking to expand the rights accorded all inmates. Gandhian techniques, including hunger strikes, became common practice in many penitentiaries holding draft protesters. Some ended up in solitary confinement, an experience the best known, David Dellinger, wrote about at length.[98]

To my knowledge, neither the Union Eight nor other draft resisters who fought segregation and the suspension of civil liberties in prison have been mentioned in the recent years of celebration of the "greatest generation."[99] But they, along with some of the other radical pacifists of the 1940s (including Dorothy Day, Ammon Hennacy, and the Catholic Worker Movement) might well be remembered as peace heroes of the World War II era. The subsequent importance of the most radical draft resisters will be evident at many points in the pages to follow.[100] One point deserves emphasis: their essential suspicion and rejection of a militarist proto-totalitarian America, both in the "preparedness" ideology that underlay the peacetime draft of 1940 and the postwar militarization during cold and hot wars and amid threats of nuclear annihilation. Some devoted efforts to creating small, meaningful "intentional" communities, but that did not mean that they dropped out entirely or that they ignored the great issues of the postwar decades. They helped to define and call attention to those issues. When a new draft law was proposed in 1947, over four hundred men burned their draft cards—a "first" in U.S. history—or mailed them to President Truman. Though draft resistance most directly affected young men, the cause was supported by radical women who connected the movement to new feminist directions.

World War II draft objectors later took part in acts of protest against nuclear testing. Some participated in an early freedom ride (or "Journey of Reconciliation") sponsored by CORE in 1947 and in the Freedom Ride that drew worldwide attention in 1961. Some advised Martin Luther King, Jr., on the philosophy and tactics of nonviolence during the Montgomery bus boycott in 1954. Influenced by A. J. Muste in his journey to nonviolence, James Lawson carried on in the tradition and went to prison as a draft resister in 1950; a decade later in Nashville, he held training sessions with college students who conducted the dramatically successful sit-ins in that city and played a key role in founding the Student Non-Violent Coordinating Committee.[101] The civil rights and peace movements of the 1940s were often unfamiliar to the radical youth culture arising in the 1960s. But there were legacies, too, and chief among them were adaptations of Gandhi, examples of courage, and commitments to social change and, initially at least, to "a strict discipline of avoiding violence."[102]

8

The Civil Rights Revolution

"What we know as 'the Movement' had its beginnings in the late 1950s," wrote Julius Lester in a 1969 essay in *Liberation* magazine. Lester, a 1960 Fisk University graduate who went on to a distinguished career as an activist, artist, and scholar in several fields, continued: "In Afroamerica the beginning was the 1956 bus boycott in Montgomery, Alabama in which a twenty-six-year-old minister, Martin Luther King, Jr. introduced non-violent direct action as a means of attacking the problem of racial discrim-ination." Perhaps it was the use of nonviolent action for that purpose that seemed unprecedented, or at least new, because, as Lester recalled, in "the same period, similar tactics" were adopted by pacifists protesting against nuclear testing, air raid drills, and fallout shelters. "None of us who were a part of those beginnings in the Fifties could have then predicted the Sixties."

I do not quote Lester's essay in order to find fault with it. When read today, it usefully reminds readers of "the most fantastic compressions of political ideas and action" during the nine years after 1960. Early in the decade, the "movement" referred to the NAACP, CORE, SCLC, SNCC, several peace groups, and SDS (some of these were recent creations); by the end of the decade, the "movement" had ceased to be identifiable with orga-nizations to which one must belong. "Instead, there are loose groupings of people around the country who share a common outlook, common life-styles, and common aspirations." At the same time, "the media" had show-ered attention on the movement, and some agents of the movement exploited the media deftly. By decade's end, however, sharp divisions had developed over racial issues and attitudes toward violence, and those conflicts too often made movement people forgetful of the revolutionary dream that had given so much inspiration.[1]

It may be surprising to see how easily the actions of the post–World War II generation were forgotten, soon to be even more lost as the idea spread that Martin Luther King, Jr., was the herald of the new. And it is a little hard to explain. It was not as though everyone from previous generations was dead. A. Philip Randolph remained a significant champion of civil rights. He was a principal organizer of the 1963 March on Washington rally at the Lincoln Memorial, where he presided and Martin Luther King, Jr., gave his best-remembered speech. A. J. Muste cofounded, with Dave Dellinger, *Liberation* magazine, where Lester's essay appeared. But it is possible that the "fantastic" crush of events of the 1960s, the unprecedented media focus, the proliferation of new "tendencies" in a movement culture, the clashes between violent and nonviolent approaches to revolution made it hard to view the events of the 1960s as, in important respects, linked to previous tradition. It is definitely true that when King moved with his family to Montgomery in 1954, he had little awareness of what one SDS veteran and movement scholar calls the "powerful antecedents" of nonviolent direct action in the Revolutionary War, abolitionism, the women's and labor movements.[2] To the extent that he had to learn that prehistory in medias res, it is less surprising that his followers could later forget much of the legacy they shared.

This is not to suggest that there was nothing really sensational about the Montgomery bus boycott. (No one who was a college freshman when it became national news could forget its extraordinarily exciting quality.) As events proceeded from a relatively modest challenge to discrimination to all-out rejection of segregation on the city bus lines, news of the boycott was exciting at a distance and inspirational to black college students and residents of southern towns on the cusp of change. The boycott in Montgomery occurred at a time of mounting public defense of segregated institutions whose foundations federal law had begun to undercut. It followed closely after the U.S. Supreme Court's 1954 *Brown* decision on cases from four states and the District of Columbia had declared segregation in the public schools to be unconstitutional. *Brown* incited vows of "massive resistance" in Virginia and across the white South, and a "Southern Manifesto," signed by most representatives and senators from states of the old Confederacy, denounced the abuse of judicial power and pledged every effort to overcome it. The boycott shortly preceded the epic confrontations in 1957–58 between hostile mobs and national guardsmen over the integration of a first cohort of black schoolchildren in Little Rock, Arkansas.[3] In part, the national appeal of the Montgomery story was the contrast it presented between peaceful, determined action and the violent, irrational quality of other scenes of conflict.

Proponents of civil rights disagreed about the best methods to pursue equal rights—through the courts or with direct action. The NAACP favored an emphasis on legal action, with *Brown* standing as its great triumph. As early as 1946 NAACP attorney Thurgood Marshall was critical of "well-meaning radical groups" who had spoken with him about using "Gandhian tactics" and warned that "a disobedience movement on the part of Negroes" in some parts of the South would produce "wholesale slaughter with no good achieved."[4] What did Montgomery's boycott show about the methods of reform? Participants demonstrated that large numbers of people could carry out a policy of economic noncooperation for a long period of time with a good outcome. The boycott played a major role in spreading faith in nonviolent direct action; its leaders' efforts at political negotiation with white leaders were persistent but proved mostly futile; and at its end the protesters' victory depended on a court decision—and perhaps a favorable press. The political process, however, was irrelevant to any good outcome. A few years earlier that might have been different. Montgomery's city commission had in fact integrated the police force in 1954, though a backlash election and the generally incensed reactions of whites to *Brown* had made politicians wary of going further.

In some ways Montgomery was well suited to a challenge to segregation. Though it had been, for a few years, the capital of the Confederacy, it had been Alabama's capital since 1846. It was home to Alabama State College, which nourished a vision of growing civic improvement, and Maxwell Air Force Base, which was vital to Montgomery's prosperity (and where a young Rosa Parks had worked briefly as a secretary and her husband Raymond was a barber), and it was racially integrated in compliance with President Truman's orders. In the segregated South crowded buses, which both races shared, often were sites of tension. During World War II two blacks in uniform had been shot, one killed, for refusing to get up from seats reserved for whites. In years closer to the boycott, black and white airmen sometimes caused a stir by ignoring the seating rules on city buses.[5] Themes of progress intersected with themes of justice throughout the campaign against segregation laws that had been enacted at the end of Reconstruction and that had been eyed restlessly, though not yet over-thrown, since the end of World War II. In March 1945 two black citizens of Montgomery, E. D. Nixon and Rosa Parks, attended an NAACP-sponsored leadership conference in Atlanta, where they heard lectures and partici-pated in workshops led by skilled organizer Ella Baker as well as Thurgood Marshall.[6] A prominent member of the Brotherhood of Sleeping Car Porters, Nixon in the mid–1950s brought organizing skills to the presi-dency of the local NAACP, and Parks was active in the same organization. Jo Ann Robinson, a college English teacher, was a leader in the Women's Political Council, centered in the black population in the neighborhood surrounding the college, which had warned city officials that it would launch a bus boycott unless discriminatory rules were changed. Fred Gray, one of the city's two black attorneys, kept his eyes open for a legal challenge to Alabama's segregation laws.

Besides blacks impatient for reform, some whites, especially among the business leaders known as the Men of Montgomery, were ready to modify segregation. Montgomery was home to other whites who exempli-fied what the writer John Egerton has called "the heralds and antecedents," in the years before the civil rights movement, of the fight for social justice that would soon seize national attention as it rolled across the South.[7] Robert Graetz, a Lutheran, lived with his family and served as a pastor in the black community. Other opponents of segregation included Clifford Durr, a former Rhodes scholar and New Deal lawyer with a commitment to civil liberties cases, and his wife, a leading civil rights activist, Virginia Foster Durr, who supported Rosa Parks's participation in a summer work-shop on school integration at the Highlander Folk School in Middle Tennessee. That interracial school, modeled on European folk schools, with goals of training leadership for labor and civil rights movements, would become an important meeting place and refuge even after the state of Tennessee closed it down and forced it to relocate in 1961.

What makes the boycott exciting, even in memory, is its character as a disciplined community-wide campaign. This was not an uprising of the young but an expression of professional people with specific goals under the Jim Crow system. At the initial meeting that led to the boycott, Martin Luther King, Jr., recalled seeing representatives of "virtually every organi-zation of the Negro community": "I saw physicians, schoolteachers, lawyers, businessmen, postal workers, union leaders, and clergymen."[8]

They held meetings every week thereafter. In some ways it resembled a realization of Shridharani's account of "How It Is Done" (though probably few if any participants knew of that book). It was well organized, clear in its objectives, and it endured and prevailed despite violence against the movement and its leaders.

The Durrs, Gray, and Robinson had all been looking for a good case to test the treatment of black riders on the city's segregated bus system. When Parks refused a bus driver's order to give up her seat to a white rider, she seemed to fit the bill—mature, respectable, trustworthy, committed to the cause—though she always explained that there was nothing premeditated about her refusal. Her account of that refusal made it clear that she was objecting to the law: one of the arresting officers asked if the driver had asked her to stand.

> I said yes. He asked, "Why didn't you stand up?" I said I didn't think I should have to. I asked him, "Why do you push us around?" He said, "I don't know, but the law is the law, and you are under arrest." So the moment he said I was under arrest, I stood up.[9]

After double-checking that the driver wanted to press charges, the officers took her to police headquarters and then to jail. Gray was out of town that evening, but Nixon and Clifford Durr posted her bond and asked whether she would be willing to challenge the segregation law in court. After late-night consultations with her mother and husband, both terrified by the prospect of Rosa escalating her resistance—"the white folks will kill you, Rosa," said her husband—she made the decision that changed her life. That was late on a Thursday.

Over the weekend leaders in the black community made plans and distributed leaflets—aided immeasurably by an article in the city's main newspaper reporting that Negroes were organizing a boycott on Monday. On Monday morning Parks was tried, found guilty of breaking Alabama's segregation law, and fined $10 plus $4 for court costs. Several hundred blacks were present in the courtroom. The buses had almost no passengers that day.[10] In the afternoon, a meeting of black leaders decided (after some debate) to continue the boycott, named themselves the Montgomery Improvement Association (MIA), and elected a young and inexperienced minister, Martin Luther King, Jr., as their spokesman-president. That evening, he spoke to a mass meeting, with several thousand standing outside and television cameras shooting from different angles, on the injustice done to one of the city's finest citizens, Rosa Parks. The speech voiced anger and determination. The city's blacks were tired of humiliation, and they would exercise "the weapon of protest" they held as citizens. They would not imitate the violent methods of the Ku Klux Klan and White Citizens Councils. There would be no crosses burned, no murders, no defiance of the Constitution. To his emphasis on citizenship was added a vision of a God of love who was also a God of justice. "Standing beside love is always justice." "Not only are we using the tools of persuasion—but we've got to use the tools of coercion." Without much time to prepare, speaking from notes, and without, as yet, much acquaintance with the teachings of Gandhi, he remarkably voiced themes of nonviolent uprising, divine justice, and communal love that would resonate throughout his leadership during the years that lay ahead.[11]

A reporter for the *New York Times*, Wayne Phillips, caught one side of the boycott in these terms: "By emphasizing the Christian virtue of 'love thine enemy,' the boycott was made a mass movement of passive resistance—though it took months for the Gandhi similarity to be recognized. And by preaching the protests in their churches and mass meetings they gave it the dynamism of a religious crusade, bringing to bear the strongest emotional force in the Negro community."[12] But Phillips may have overlooked the theme of coercion that interacted with love to effect change. And although King's increasingly Gandhian leadership would have its day in the civil rights movement of the 1960s, on the ground in Montgomery a white political backlash had slowed the pace of integration after the police force was integrated in 1954, so that a plan for bus seating that preserved some segregation (known as the Mobile plan because it was successfully followed in that city) was no longer acceptable.[13]

The commitment of King and the MIA to nonviolence may not have been deeply ingrained, but from the start of the boycott King spoke out against violent responses to provocation. When his parsonage was bombed he reminded people who gathered, "We cannot solve this problem through retaliatory violence. . . . We must meet hate with love." Still, the Kings, like many other southerners, kept a pistol in their home, and after the home of his closest colleague, Ralph Abernathy, was bombed, the two men went to city hall to apply for permits to carry pistols. When Nixon's house was also bombed, King asked the governor for a permit to carry a pistol in his car. A network of sentries, bodyguards, and floodlights was set up, and King denied any inconsistency between his and the movement's nonviolence and the efforts to protect its leaders.[14] By that time northern pacifist organizations had recognized the potential importance of the Montgomery conflict and began to send advisors who could instruct King in the Gandhian philosophy of nonviolence. First came Bayard Rustin, who brought a vision of a successful nonviolent campaign leading to revolutionary change across the South. There is some disagreement about who sent him, but his most recent biographer argues that his mission probably arose from a meeting of northern activists (including, besides Rustin, Randolph, Farmer, journalist William Worthy, and labor leader Jerry Wurf) who decided that "somebody should be sent," somebody knowledgeable about nonviolent philosophy and techniques. A wealthy contributor to the War Resisters League (WRL) subsidized the mission.[15] Worries that Rustin's youthful activity in a communist youth group, his jail time as a war resister, and arrests for homosexual activity would undermine his usefulness were unrealized during his relatively short stint, and he was very careful about not seeming to take over the local movement. His successor, Glenn Smiley, also a former draft resister, made an agreement to teach everything he knew about nonviolence, thereby broadening the instruction, which King welcomed and blended with his Baptist upbringing, in Gandhian philosophy and methods. Near the end of the boycott, King was introduced to an attorney, Harris Wofford, who had been to India and written about civil disobedience and the law. Wofford, too, became a welcome resource for King. Surely this was a momentous passage in the transmission of the tradition of civil disobedience to the South. Some scholars have been critical of King's adoptions of the views of others, but they can be recognized instead as showing a strength of character; caught up in a struggle not initially of his choosing, King was able to learn from well-chosen mentors while exercising good judgment in the movement that he had come to lead.[16]

A boycott is not necessarily nonviolent (think of the "Boston Tea Party"), and it is not usually a form of civil disobedience. In current scholarship on resistance movements a boycott is more properly called "economic noncooperation."[17] In Montgomery, however, the city's inflexible response to the shunning of the buses meant a long succession of conflicts between the boycott's supporters and the city's use of the law. Taxi drivers, who initially aided the boycott with reduced fares, were threatened with legal action and forced to charge at scheduled rates. Police harassed drivers picking up passengers with warnings and citations and threatened boycotters waiting for rides with arrests for vagrancy and hitchhiking. King was booked for supposedly driving thirty miles an hour in a twenty-five-mile zone and kept for hours in the city jail. In late February a grand jury indicted King and about eighty-nine other protesters under a state antilabor law outlawing boycotts of legitimate businesses. The response of the grand jury made the bus boycott more clearly a campaign of civil disobedience, though the law itself and state labor policies were not central to the MIA's protest. In late March King was tried, convicted, and sentenced to pay a $500 fine or serve a 386-day sentence. (He chose jail but remained free on appeal until months later, after the triumph of the boycott, when the city's one face-saving requirement was to exact payment of his fine.) In the final weeks the city sought to close down the remarkable carpool system that was vital to the boycott by seeking and securing an injunction against running an unlicensed public business. It came too late to preserve segregation.

Of the many conflicts with the law associated with the boycott, the most famous is Rosa Parks's refusal to give up her seat to a white man and her resulting arrest on a charge of disorderly conduct. But hers was nowhere near the first act of resistance on the buses, nor was it even her first. "My resisting being mistreated on the bus did not begin with that particular arrest," she said. "I did a lot of walking in Montgomery." She had previously been ejected from a bus at least once (and by the same driver).[18] Still, the 1956 act was the one that counted, and it stands as the most famous American instance of civil disobedience. Rosa Parks was not "planted" on the bus to create a test case, said King, responding to what was invariably the first question asked about the boycott. As events unfolded, "the *Zeitgeist*—the spirit of the time"—had tracked her down.[19] Like many authentic acts, it may elude exact definition. The episode was not staged; every researched account concludes that Parks's action was "spontaneous"[20] (whatever that means), and it was always an exaggeration to say that "the Negro revolt is properly dated from the moment Mrs. Rosa Parks said 'No' to the bus driver's demand that she get up and let a White man have her seat."[21] But she certainly knew she was acting defiantly and that the driver personified the law since the rules were ambiguous. She had sat in that seat before on her way home while whites were standing.[22] She always resented depictions of her as a simple person who just got tired:

> I didn't tell anyone my feet were hurting. It was just popular [to say so] I suppose because they wanted to give some excuse other than the

fact that I didn't want to be pushed around. ... And I had been working for a long time ... a number of years in fact—to be treated as a human being with dignity not only for myself, but all those who were being mistreated.[23]

She and her husband had, in fact, been active in efforts to defend black victims of injustice—women raped with impunity; men, including the Scottsboro boys, falsely charged with rape—for many years. She had worked as an organizer in voter registration efforts and succeeded in registering herself, after several tries, in 1945. It was inaccurate to call her, as the *New York Times* later remembered her, "the accidental matriarch of the civil rights movement."[24]

She was well aware that when black women got in trouble with the bus drivers, as they easily did, there were lawyers and activists who weighed their suitability for a test case against segregation. It still took a hard night of soul searching, with her mother and husband, before she agreed to let Nixon and the Durrs use her arrest to test the law. In the end, her case was not used, as is usually assumed (and as King and the boycotters' negotiating committee initially expected). As lawyers, Durr and Gray concluded that an appeal of her conviction for disorderly conduct under state law would be subject to delays and might be decided without addressing issues of segregation. Under advice from NAACP lawyers in New York, including Thurgood Marshall, Gray grouped together other cases in order to argue directly that state and local segregated transportation laws like Montgomery's were unconstitutional.[25] Thus, the legal victory at the boycott's conclusion focused on the grievances of five other women, including some whom the lawyers had previously passed over.[26] Ultimately, the 2–1 decision in the federal district court in Montgomery rejected the lasting applicability of *Plessy v. Ferguson*'s tolerance of "separate but equal" accommodations in light of a series of more recent decisions holding segregation unconstitutional in public schools, residential choice, and interstate commerce. The U.S. Supreme Court, without much ado, accepted that understanding of the law and its previous history.[27] Many other southern cities besides Montgomery had to rethink the seating plans on their bus lines.

News of the Supreme Court decision ended the city's attempt to suppress the boycott as illegal interference with the bus company, though there was still another round of bombings, threats, and terrorism as well as proposals to do away with the bus system altogether before integrated buses became a reality. City leaders had underestimated the black population's unity and determination and overestimated their own power to intimidate, divide, and prevail. Their stalling and intransigence had led to more complete desegregation of the buses than anyone had initially proposed. In the days before integration became a reality, the MIA held mass meetings and training sessions to prepare black riders on what to expect and how to behave. They set up chairs in the pattern of a bus and conducted playacting sessions with some acting the roles of white drivers and riders while others performed as blacks behaving in new ways. They gave wide distribution to a mimeographed page of suggestions and instructions, prepared by Glenn Smiley, for calm and courteous behavior in a time of "historic" change.[28] Smiley sat next to King on the first integrated ride.

Parks's defiance ignited the boycott and inspired protesters for years to come. The more that we learn about her action—her courage, her commitment before and after to civil rights—the more clearly it deserves its high place in the history of civil disobedience. It made her and her husband targets of hostility in Montgomery. They lost their jobs; they received hate mail and threatening phone calls; and she experienced resentment of her celebrity from men inside the movement.[29] They did not stay long after the boycotters' victory. In August 1957 she and her husband and mother moved to Detroit, where her brother had preceded her in 1946, thus belatedly joining the great migration and continuing her advocacy of civil rights in a city she called "the promised land that wasn't."[30] She remained to the end an admirer of King and recognized the "tactical" usefulness of nonviolence during the boycott and in many other confrontations, but she also retained, without thinking it contradictory, a belief in self-defense that, by her account, her grandfather had instilled in her. She also acknowledged that she had become an inspiring symbol of the spirit in which she and King and many others had persevered and had finally prevailed.

In January 1957, even before the desegregation of Montgomery's buses was secured, King and other Christian ministers founded a new organization, the Southern Christian Leadership Conference (SCLC), which would initiate and coordinate bus boycotts and campaigns of civil disobedience across the urban South. Sixty community leaders launched the new program with a Gandhian pledge: "Not one hair of one head of one white person shall be harmed in the campaign for integration."[31] This was a step in keeping with Rustin's vision of massive campaigns of protest throughout the South building on the momentum of Montgomery.[32] It was also a consequence of visits to King in Montgomery by clergymen from Tallahassee, Mobile, Tuskegee, Birmingham, and other cities with plans under way for boycotts of their own. With the formation of SCLC, leadership of a civil rights revolution in the South was provided by a network of southerners, for whom nonviolent direct action was a key to social transformation at least as long as the black population remained largely disfranchised. One of SCLC's first programs, however, was the Crusade for Citizenship, a campaign for voting rights, which were not easily secured through civil disobedience, even less than in the struggle for woman suffrage since the problem was seldom explicit racial qualifications for the suffrage but a network of intimidation that made race an unwritten, but nearly invariable, qualification.[33] In all likelihood, the emphasis on nonviolent direct action was always for some, even Rustin, based on the denial of voting power.[34]

In the end the most compelling voice to emerge from the boycott, one that would resound in memory, was King's own. Rustin remembered that he became "a perfect speaker" and because he "was evolving new and exciting ideas constantly, . . . a fresh speaker."[35] A year after the boycott, Harper and Row published *Stride Toward Freedom*, a short, first-person telling of the Montgomery struggle, in which King carefully noted the contributions of others to the community's victory. Set within the community epic was a narrative of personal struggle. He had come through college without high ideals of service and then found himself late one night in terror of bomb threats to his family and himself and fearful, too, of the demoralization of the people who looked to him for leadership. All alone, he spoke directly to God:

> I am here taking a stand for what I believe is right. But now I am afraid. The people are looking to me for leadership, and if I stand before them without strength and courage, they too will falter. I am at the end of my powers. I have nothing left. I've come to the point where I can't face it alone.

Immediately, he reports, he felt "the presence of the Divine as I had never experienced Him before." He felt "the quiet assurance of an inner voice saying: 'Stand up for righteousness, stand up for truth; and God will be at your side forever.'" His fears subsided, and he was prepared to face danger and lead the people who trusted his leadership. When his house was bombed three nights later, he was able to calm a throng of angry supporters, many of them armed, gathering in his yard.[36]

There was, in short, a strong southern Protestant component in the triumph of nonviolence in Montgomery. Reporters would describe King's experience of the boycott as dynamic and Hegelian—he and the people of Montgomery were visibly discovering themselves in the test of conflict—and in doing so they used terms that King had learned in seminary and would sometimes favor in *Stride Toward Freedom*.[37] He was tapped by the Zeitgeist as strongly as Rosa Parks had been, or as Rustin put it: "There was a sense in which Martin was just picked up by the times. The times propelled him." In Ella Baker's words, "The movement made Martin rather than Martin making the movement."[38] They all were picked up by the times, and the burden of anointment would go on. But it was important that the new era of civil rights began with King's nighttime stride, that victory over fear, that recommitment to nonviolence, out of deeply personal religious experience.

Alongside the dramatic account of the prophetic inner voice, *Stride Toward Freedom* included a well-constructed account of the author's own "pilgrimage" to nonviolence, making it perhaps the single most indispensable book in the tradition-in-the-making of American civil disobedience. I have taught it as a text for exploring how intellectual currents wind their way into, and shape, lives of action and conflict. It became a classic account of a movement winning unambiguous victory, read by who knows how many students and citizens even after other books joined it on a list of civil rights standards. Because the author is scrupulous in crediting other leaders and participants in the boycott, the Montgomery story can be appreciated as the story of a community prevailing in an epic victory.

King's biographers say surprisingly little about *Stride Toward Freedom*. The actual events of the boycott are more engaging, perhaps, though it is hard to recount them outside the narrative King set down.[39] In any case, writing such a book while engaged in struggle was a significant challenge, and it is clear that King had trouble with the task, constantly missed deadlines, and worst of all, because it adds to a recurrently unattractive theme in King's life, relied on ghostwriters and sometimes on work written by others. At one point he borrowed heavily from an early essay by Wofford and elsewhere from drafts and comments given him by Rustin and his New York advisor Stanley Levison.[40] Instances of unattributed absorption of passages provided by friends and advisors would not be found shocking in other works—political speeches and sermons, for example—intended to influence public opinion, and King's narrative of a community victory succeeded as a demonstration of the promise of direct action campaigns against segregation. It certainly raised the visibility of Gandhi to a new high. Instances of plagiarism are harder to justify. Scholars have found, for example, passages absorbed without citation from the Swedish Lutheran theologian Anders Nygren's *Agape and Eros*, a work on his seminary reading lists and one still discussed in theological circles (though not by the reading public—the borrowing went unnoticed for many years). He concluded his chapter on his pilgrimage to nonviolence with seven paragraphs on *agape*, disinterested love, love of neighbors and community, love that must be put into action. I was fortunate to hear King twice in my student days, at Oberlin in 1957 and at Cornell in the early 1960s. I kept no notes, but I believe that on both occasions, certainly at Oberlin, he riffed unforgettably on the force of a type of uncompetitive love called *agape*, which overcame hatred and made nonviolent action possible and successful. Those talks would have been very different if he had cited intellectual derivations.

In *Stride Toward Freedom* King did refer credibly to reading (and rereading) Thoreau's essay on civil disobedience in his student days, then returning to it early in the boycott, with renewed appreciation of an inspiring theme that would resound throughout the decade in other movements as well as civil rights: the obligation of disconnection from evil. "To accept passively an unjust system is to cooperate with that system: thereby the oppressed becomes as evil as the oppressor. Noncooperation with evil is as much a moral obligation as is cooperation with good."[41] Similar thoughts would be expressed by war protesters and student critics of college bureaucracies, but not always with King's hopeful approach to change, as "dropping out" took its place as a theme of the age.

In addition, some of his passages on Gandhi, by his own account, take positions that "many Negroes" and other people might find it hard to accept. It may be useful to look closely at just one:

> American Negroes must come to the point where they can say to their white brothers, paraphrasing the words of Gandhi: "We will match your capacity to inflict suffering with our capacity to endure suffering. We will meet your physical force with soul force. We will not hate you, but we cannot in all good conscience obey your unjust

laws. Do to us what you will and we will still love you. Bomb our homes and threaten our children; send your hooded perpetrators of violence into our communities and drag us out on some wayside road, beating us and leaving us half dead, and we will still love you. But we will soon wear you down by our capacity to suffer. And in winning our freedom we will so appeal to your heart and conscience that we will win you in the process."[42]

Winning through the capacity to suffer was antithetical to the pursuit of respect that most civil rights protesters associated with citizenship before and certainly after Montgomery. The line about still loving lynchers after being left half dead rings false. Practically speaking, King was persuasive in stating that a commitment to "humility and self-restraint" would help allay the fears of whites that blacks, if freed, would take revenge on their former oppressors.[43] But the vision of victory was certainly more attractive than images of submission to brutality and suffering. Among King's associates in 1956, Baker, Parks, and many others believed in self-defense, though retaining the tactical self-respect of refraining from useless violence. Before long, however, King's teachings would be disputed by some whose belief in the right and efficacy of self-defense was unreserved.

It would take a while for defenses of retaliation and self-defense to arise in the fight for civil rights, but it was almost inevitable. That is to look ahead. In the aftermath of Montgomery hope spread rapidly that people—and the emphasis turned to youth—could unite in peaceful protest and win victories over inequality and injustice.[44]

It did not require even a brief book to present King's life as an inspiration to engage in civil disobedience. In 1957 the Fellowship of Reconciliation released a fourteen-page comic book entitled "Martin Luther King and the Montgomery Story," which the greatly admired civil rights veteran John Lewis has described as "wildly successful." Others have called it "a primer for the students who launched the sit-in movement." It sold for ten cents (though many copies were given out for free), and according to FOR nearly 250,000 copies were distributed in the 1950s. It stressed King's upbringing as a faithful Christian, beginning a marriage and family, becoming a clergyman and finding himself drawn into conflict over the bus system, surviving bomb attempts, and eventually achieving a communal victory, with a decision from the Supreme Court. The key to victory was the adoption of Gandhian methods, as deployed in the liberation of India and as practiced in what is called "the Montgomery Method." The concluding panels celebrate Ralph Abernathy's ability to overcome fear of jail once he discovered that God would await him there. FOR also sponsored a film entitled "Walk to Freedom" that was shown widely to young black men and women in the South as an inspiration to combat Jim Crow by nonviolent direct action. Lewis, who began his collegiate studies in 1957, has called the Montgomery boycott a life-transforming event, and he remembered the slogan heard everywhere on campus as "Free by 63."[45]

Stride Toward Freedom, for all of the credit it gives to others, and "Martin Luther King and the Montgomery Story" both depict a community victory, but with one man very much at the forefront. King became the voice of the community as the bus boycott appeared in national news coverage, although there were definitely Montgomery people who found this depiction of King somewhat idealized and inaccurate. The Southern Christian Leadership Conference, founded after Montgomery, extended the model of male, clergyman leadership in pursuit of civil rights through nonviolent methods and court decisions across the South. It had an undeniably important role in gaining victories for civil rights over the years ahead. Almost immediately, however, it was challenged by other visions of achieving civil rights by the agency of young people, women, and some northerners who were not southern Protestants and who differed in their understanding of self-protection and nonviolence. The tradition of civil disobedience became more contested and diffuse.

In mid-afternoon, on Monday, February 1, 1960, after their classes, four black freshmen at North Carolina Agricultural and Technical College bought some toothpaste and other articles at the F. W. Woolworth store in downtown Greensboro. Next they took seats at a "whites only" lunch counter and ordered sodas, coffee, and doughnuts. A waitress explained, as they already knew, that Negroes were not served at the lunch counter; a black dishwasher denounced them as ignorant troublemakers; and an elderly white customer told them she was proud of them and wished they had done this "10 or 15 years ago." The store manager, after meeting with the police chief, who said that he couldn't do anything as long as the students were well-behaved, came back and announced he was closing the store early. The four young men, their confidence soaring, promised they would return on Tuesday. "I felt as though I had gained my manhood," one recalled. The local newspaper called the event a "'sit-down' demand for service"; in a UPI syndicated story it was "a sit-down strike." Other reports would use the term "sit-down demonstrations." The students spoke of it as "a passive demand for service." Before long it would become known, somewhat inaccurately but excitingly to participants and readers of newspapers, as the first "sit-in."[46]

The action has been characterized as "impulsive."[47] Students were returning from a recess, and one of the four had been denied service the night before in a lunch counter at the train station. He was especially hurt at being told, "We don't serve Negroes here." How long are we going to endure this? he asked his friends. This was not a new question for them. Some of them were ready to act after reading the comic book about "the Montgomery story." Another had watched a TV program about Gandhi. Martin Luther King had spoken in Greensboro in 1958. Legal efforts to desegregate North Carolina schools had stalled, but the success of the Montgomery protests strengthened faith in the prospects for successful confrontations with segregation. Though it would be a distortion to make the students' action seem calculated—What is next, what are we going to do?—those questions were in the air in Greensboro at the moment.[48] What happened after that first afternoon's protest marked a turning point. On Tuesday, twenty-seven other students, including four women from Bennett College, which took particular pride in its support of King's visit to Greensboro, joined the protest; on Wednesday, more than sixty students showed up. On Thursday, white students from the University of North Carolina Woman's College and Guilford College joined scores of others, and a second sit-in commenced at S. H. Kress's lunch counter down the street. White hecklers gathered, too, often waving Confederate flags, but despite bomb threats there was little violence. By Saturday there were hundreds of protesters at the counters and even more picketers outside, including A & T football team members there to protect their fellow students. (Challenged on their right to be there, the football players replied, "We the Union Army.") The protesters agreed to a two-week halt in order to give business leaders time to find a solution, a period that was extended until April 1. Lunch counters usually closed when integrated student groups arrived. After city authorities arrested forty-five students for trespass, Greensboro blacks boycotted downtown merchants. Greensboro's sit-in went on for months. In July Woolworth's, Kress, and other stores negotiated a settlement and began to serve black customers at their lunch counters.[49]

In the week after the Greensboro sit-ins began, black college students launched similar protests in Durham, Winston-Salem, Charlotte, Raleigh, and five other North Carolina communities. Hampton, Virginia, joined the list on February 10, followed shortly after by Portsmouth, Norfolk, and Richmond and by the end of the month about thirty other cities from Tallahassee to San Antonio. The historian William H. Chafe sums up the widely spreading perception: "America would never be the same once students discovered the power of direct-action protest."[50] Though observers readily pointed to the use of "methods employed by Gandhi's non-violent resistance in India and the Rev. Martin Luther King's Montgomery, Ala., bus strike of several years ago,"[51] and some participants may well have seen films or the comic book or heard King, it is not clear that there had been intensive study of the writings of those men or practice in the methods of nonviolence. That swiftly changed, as two experienced CORE instructors came south and began holding nonviolence workshops as the sit-ins spread. Many more sit-ins and demonstrations followed in late February and March, often ending, as with Claflin College students in Orangeburg, South Carolina, and back in Montgomery itself, where Alabama State students attempted to integrate a cafeteria in the state capitol, with scenes of brutal repression.[52] All told, about seventy thousand students participated in the sit-in demonstrations, and about three thousand were arrested.

Twelve days after the Greensboro sit-ins began, sit-ins commenced in Nashville, Tennessee. "In an orderly and logical world," writes Wesley C. Hogan in her study of SNCC's vision for America, "the great wave of student sit-ins that washed across the South early in 1960 should have flowed outward from Nashville."[53] In that city students at Fisk University, Tennessee Agricultural and Industrial College, Meharry Medical College, and American Baptist Seminary had been preparing for nonviolent action for more than a year under the direction of James Lawson, a Methodist clergyman and Vanderbilt divinity student, who had been to prison as a conscientious objector, served as a missionary in India, and teamed with Glenn Smiley to lead FOR-sponsored workshops on nonviolence in preparation for what he envisioned would be "many Montgomerys." Their meetings included intergenerational study groups on race relations and what we might now call the long civil rights movement.[54] The focus moved to world religions, traditions of nonviolence, the psychology of oppression and resentment, and as they moved closer to action, to surveying Nashville institutions and training themselves through role-playing and group analysis as a nonviolent squadron to confront segregation in their city. They went home from their various colleges for winter recess and returned without the impetuousness of their four Greensboro counterparts. In Lawson's terms they "lolly-lagged" away their chance until February 13.[55] When they did launch their sit-ins at the lunch counters of Nashville department stores, they conducted themselves in keeping with their training even when doused with soda, punched (a white Fisk student most savagely), burned with cigarettes—without protection from the police— and jailed in large numbers for "disorderly conduct." Television cameras showed the story across the nation. As David Halberstam, at that time a reporter for the *Nashville Tennessean*, later reflected, no one then under- stood the increasing power of the media, particularly television, "which would amplify the moral issues at stake and thereby give ordinary Americans a chance to understand the cruelty of racial injustice in their own country."[56]

Nashville's black community boycotted stores that would not serve them food. In April, in response to a huge dynamite blast of the home of a prominent black civil rights attorney, Z. Alexander Looby, who represented the arrested sit-inners (an explosion that damaged several nearby build- ings, including at Meharry), thousands of Nashvillians marched ten miles to city hall where the politically moderate mayor responded by appealing to "all citizens to end discrimination, to have no bigotry, no bias, no hatred." Seizing the moment, an eighteen-year-old Fisk student from Chicago, Diane Nash, pressed the question: "Then, Mayor, do you recommend that the lunch counters be desegregated?" "Yes," he answered, though he had no power over the store owners. The next morning's headline in the *Tennessean* simplified the message: "INTEGRATE COUNTERS—MAYOR." The face-to-face confrontation, too, was seen on television and subsequently provided an uplifting conclusion in an NBC hour-long special report, "The Nashville Sit-In Story."

Three weeks later, on May 10, when the six downtown Nashville stores integrated their lunch counters, there was, by prior arrangement, little press coverage. The occasion was not marked by gloating. "A fundamental principle of nonviolence," remembered John Lewis, "is that there is no such thing as defeat once a conflict is justly resolved, because there are no losers when justice is achieved."[57]

One significant defeat was never really repaired. On March 3 Vanderbilt's board of trustees expelled Lawson from the university. That was a loss, too, for Vanderbilt's chancellor, Harvie Branscomb, an accomplished theologian under whose leadership the university made progress toward national scholarly recognition. By most definitions Branscomb could consider himself a moderate or even a cautiously liberal southerner. No Vanderbilt undergraduates participated in the sit-in movement (as was generally true at the most prestigious southern private institutions). There were a few black students in the professional and graduate schools, but none who engaged as cordially as Lawson in extracurricular student life. Branscomb and the board had requested the dean of the Divinity School to press Lawson not to play intramural sports with white students. During the sit-ins, when the board discovered that Lawson was training students to break the law, Branscomb directed the dean to force Lawson to retract any encouragement of civil disobedience, as Lawson conscientiously refused to do, and then to dismiss Lawson, as the dean would not do—and so the board had to act on its own. The expulsion was hurtful to Lawson, who was well along in his graduate work (later finished at Boston University) and, as some faculty members left for other positions, a blow to the university's reputation. The dispute deserves mention here because it highlighted conflicting and shifting attitudes toward the law that were challenged by the civil disobedience of the sit-ins.

Those who have examined Branscomb's behavior emphasize the difficulty of his relationship with the dominant, lifetime member of the board who was editor of the *Nashville Banner* and who hated the sit-inners as violators of a social order in which owners of businesses were free to respect the prejudices of white people and set whatever rules they liked. But Branscomb's view, as a Rhodes scholar and Guggenheim holder who had studied overseas and taught in the North, was more complex. In lectures given at the University of Wisconsin in the early 1950s Branscomb the scholar had defended the right to challenge unjust laws. This right derived from an important "contribution" of religion to American life:

> the insistence upon a law of God which is supreme above all human institutions and man-made legislation. To this divine law man owes final obedience. If the laws of states or governments deviate from this standard they have no more authority, in fact should be disregarded or rejected. This was a fundamental Christian teaching from the beginning.[58]

That understanding was not far, of course, from what Lawson had been teaching his shock troops for nonviolent change. When Lawson declined

Branscomb's demand that he resign, the board expelled him. Divinity faculty described him as practicing what they taught and what was one of the lessons of World War II; many of them left, too. It was a traumatic division not soon overcome at Vanderbilt.[59]

Though not widely noticed at the time, the Nashville sit-in brought to the surface conflict between youth and age in the broader civil rights movement. It was disappointing enough that two black leaders, both presidents of black universities, had signed on to a proposal for "partial" integration— serving the races separately in different sections of the lunch counters. It was worse when Thurgood Marshall, lecturing at Fisk at the height of the protest, praised the sit-inners but questioned their decision to stay in jail and refuse bail instead of pursuing the issue in the courts. It was increasingly clear to Lewis that Marshall and his generation of black leaders "did not understand" what younger blacks were doing. He admired Marshall, of course, but the lack of support for the endeavor to create a mass movement, in which people put their bodies on the line, prompted the reflection that "our revolt was as much against this nation's traditional black leadership structure as it was against racial segregation and discrimination."[60]

The sit-ins were early, uncoordinated steps toward achieving social change through a mass movement largely of the young. On Easter weekend—in Nashville that was the weekend just before the bombing of the Looby residence and the great march to Nashville's city hall—a new organization emerged to coordinate whatever actions were still to come. Nearly 150 students from nine states met at Shaw University in Raleigh, North Carolina, and founded the Student Non-Violent Coordinating Committee (SNCC). Ella Baker, a Shaw alumna and an experienced organizer with the NAACP and SCLC, set up the conference as a way of bringing together young people who had independently already done much to combat segregation but now needed an organizational structure, though a fairly loose one, to facilitate communication without giving up the creativity and energy of their movement. Martin Luther King hailed the attendees as youthful rebels, not only against segregation but also "against Negroes in the middle class who indulge in buying cars and homes instead of taking on the great cause that will really solve their problems; against those who have become so afraid they have yielded to the system."[61] James Lawson also indicted middle-class complacency as he influenced the group to affirm their embrace of the philosophy of nonviolence in their pursuit of a just social order.[62] In the months ahead SNCC would establish itself as a new presence in rural southern society. It would always be the case that some "SNICKers" like John Lewis would believe deeply in the religious basis for nonviolence while others were learning from experience the tactical potency of nonviolence in combat against segregation and injustice. But the radicalism in which they united was unflinching. At a fall organizational meeting in Atlanta, King and Lawson spoke again, and delegates took a further step that would distinguish SNCC's response to jail sentences for civil disobedience. Chastised by Lawson for letting adults "scurry around" raising their bail—"we should have insisted that they scurry about to end the system which had put us in jail"—SNCC adopted a "jail, no bail," policy that became a distinctive tenet of their approach to what Lawson called "social revolution."[63]

Four civil rights organizations (not counting a Southern Student Organizing Committee, founded in the early 1960s, smaller in numbers and closely cooperative with SNCC, which included but was not limited to white students following up on desegregation efforts after the Nashville sit-ins) were now active in the South. Three of them—CORE, SCLC, and SNCC—were committed to nonviolent civil disobedience as a methodology for social change. SNCC had even put "nonviolence" in its name. The national NAACP emphasized court cases, but many of these, as in Montgomery, arose from deliberately violating laws; in the South local NAACP chapters, again as in Montgomery, often stood behind those transgressions. The enthusiasm and dedication of a younger generation of southern black college students infused new energy in the civil rights network. Acutely conscious of independence movements in Africa, these students also knew that theirs was the first generation to come to maturity after the *Brown* decision and the Montgomery bus boycott. Their determination to attain full citizenship inspired others, not only in southern black communities but among northern white and black students.

In 1944 a woman named Irene Morgan, returning to her home in Baltimore, Maryland, from her mother's house in Virginia, took a seat in the "colored" section of a crowded Greyhound bus. She did this without protest, but when whites boarded and the driver demanded that she move farther back, she not only refused but got into a fracas with a sheriff's deputy summoned by the driver. She was not nonviolent. When her case came to trial, she pleaded guilty to a charge of resisting arrest and paid a $100 fine but contested a $10 fine on a charge of violating Virginia's state segregation law. With Thurgood Marshall of the NAACP as her principal attorney, the case went all the way to the U.S. Supreme Court, which ruled in 1946, somewhat remarkably, that segregation in interstate transportation constituted an "undue burden on commerce" and was therefore unconstitutional. No argument was made about the justice or constitutionality of segregation itself, only about the burdens on the carriers of arranging for seating changes when carriers crossed state lines.[64] Nothing was said, furthermore, prohibiting racial segregation in interstate bus terminals or about Jim Crow drinking fountains, seating areas, luncheonettes, and restrooms.

In 1947 CORE, impatient with NAACP caution about testing or extending the implications of *Morgan*, sent eight black and eight white men on a "Journey of Reconciliation" through Virginia, North Carolina, Tennessee, and Kentucky. They tested only the integration of the buses' front rows of seats and tried nothing provocative in station facilities. They went no farther south in order to avoid extreme violence, but they still were met with fisticuffs and bomb threats just outside Chapel Hill, and after arrests in Asheville, Bayard Rustin and two other riders wound up serving twenty-two days at hard labor on a North Carolina chain gang. The historian Raymond Arsenault has described this "nonviolent foray into the world of Jim Crow" as "an important turning point in the modern American freedom struggle," one in which a "small but determined group of radical activists seized the opportunity to take the desegregation struggle out of the courts and into the streets."[65] If it was a turning point, rather than a step along the way, it was one that reflected the radicalism of the MOWM and the courage of World War II draft resisters. In a pioneering study of CORE two scholars offered a more subdued conclusion: "The faith that nonviolent direct action would succeed where legalism had failed was misplaced." Nevertheless, the journey had garnered "publicity" and stimulated interest in nonviolence and thus "functioned as one of the many events that gradually were to make this type of protest respectable, even fashionable."[66]

The 1947 journey was not well remembered fourteen years later when CORE returned to the issue of segregation in interstate commerce, this time armed with a 1960 Supreme Court decision (*Boynton v. Virginia*) explicitly forbidding "colored only" dining facilities in interstate bus terminals.[67] A campaign to integrate buses and terminals was inspired by the anniversary of the Greensboro sit-in and by the bravery of the "Rock Hill

Nine," students who had chosen thirty days on a work gang rather than paying a fine for their sit-in at a Rock Hill, South Carolina, lunch counter. They were joined by CORE staffer Tom Gaither and soon by Diane Nash and others in what was now called a "jail-in." Working closely, SNCC and CORE mobilized more than a thousand marchers on a "pilgrimage" to Rock Hill on Lincoln's birthday, and CORE began making plans for a project Gaither strongly advocated—the Freedom Ride.[68]

The expectation was to provoke arrests, refuse bail, and "prod" the Justice Department, which was informed in advance of the plan, into enforcing "the law of the land" as defined by the *Boynton* decision. Six whites, including veteran war resisters Albert Bigelow and Jim Peck (who had traveled on the Journey of Reconciliation), joined seven blacks, including CORE's new national director Jim Farmer and young veterans of the sit-ins like John Lewis, in two teams assigned to Greyhound and Trailways buses.[69] Early stops in Virginia and North Carolina were uneventful, but in Rock Hill, where racial tension smoldered, Bigelow, Lewis, and CORE field secretary Genevieve Hughes were beaten to the ground before police intervened. In Alabama hostility and violence grew even more intense, and the story of civil disobedience in America entered a new, bloody chapter.

At the Anniston station a mob smashed windows and slashed tires of the Greyhound bus. They followed it out of town, threw a bomb inside, and beat the freedom riders savagely as they emerged. The mob then forced the local hospital to deny care to the victims, who had to be conveyed to Birmingham by car caravan. When the second bus reached Anniston, a Ku Klux Klan gang that had boarded in Atlanta ordered the black freedom riders to move to the rear of the bus, and when they refused, beat and kicked them until they were unconscious and piled them across the back seats. They then beat Peck and another white rider, who tried to shield them, until they too were bloody and unconscious, leaving a sixty-one-year-old retired professor named Walter Bergman with permanent brain damage. That bus went on to Birmingham in a grisly mock victory for Alabama's sense of order, and at the Trailways station the police commissioner "Bull" Connor allowed Ku Klux Klansmen, armed with baseball bats, iron pipes, and chains, to beat the freedom riders again for fifteen minutes. As the violence raged out of control, reporters and uninvolved bystanders were also attacked. To reporters who somehow got into his hospital room that evening, Peck vowed, "I'll be on that bus tomorrow headed for Montgomery." At a mass meeting in his church that evening, Rev. Fred Shuttlesworth, one of the stalwarts of the civil rights movement, spoke of "the greatest thing that has ever happened in Alabama. . . . When white and black men are willing to be beaten up together, it is a sure sign they will soon walk together as brothers."[70] Howard K. Smith, a CBS reporter who had been an eyewitness in the station, told nationwide audiences by radio and on television that the atrocious events were "not spontaneous," could easily have been prevented by authorities, and revealed dangerous attitudes toward law in the South. In his view, the "laws of the land and purposes of the nation need a basic restatement, perhaps by the one American assured of an intent mass hearing at any time, the President."[71]

A group of freedom riders made it back to the Birmingham bus station the next morning, but no driver would take them. Despite pressure from the U.S. attorney general, Alabama's Governor Patterson insisted that citizens were so enraged at these "rabble rousers" that he could not guarantee their safe passage. An alternative plan to take the next step of their journey by air was stopped by a bomb threat. After many hours, encircled by a mob, the freedom riders called off their journey, and after a still longer wait most of them departed by air, with a federal escort, for New Orleans. They had already succeeded, in their view, in focusing attention on racial hatred. Photographs of the burned-out bus, with black smoke pouring from its windows, and of freedom riders, blood running down their faces, had appeared on television and in newspapers around the world. But dissenters in the group warned that aborting the rides would be taken as victory by Bull Connor and the Klan. The civil rights organizations' commitment to more aggressive confrontations had collided, it seemed, with angry and unrestrained defenders of segregation and had lost.

Determined not to "let violence overcome" and ignoring dire warnings of a "massacre," the Nashville student movement decided on their own to dispatch an integrated group of ten to continue the journey. Birmingham police intercepted their bus, detained them in jail, and carried them back over the Tennessee line. But they found their way right back to Birmingham, where others joined them. The freedom riders, now numbering about twenty, made it to Montgomery under heavy police protection, but once they reached the city, the police disappeared. The ensuing scene of violence, directed at reporters and cameramen as well as incoming riders, was more ghastly than anything previous. Lewis suffered a concussion. Attackers broke one man's leg. They doused another man with kerosene and set him afire. Several pinned down a white Fisk student on exchange from Beloit College, James Zwerg, while others kicked his teeth out. Onlookers held children up to gawk. The mob seized John Siegenthaler, a federal official sent by Attorney General Robert Kennedy who had followed the bus by car, and beat him unconscious for trying to rescue two women from assault. Hours later, from a hospital bed, Zwerg told a television reporter that they would "keep coming until we can ride anywhere in the South to anyplace in the South, as Americans, without anyone making any comment."[72] The next night, a menacing mob surrounded Martin Luther King, who had come home to Montgomery, and besieged a church filled with supporters of the Freedom Ride and kept them virtually trapped until morning. Marshals struggled to prevent an attack while federal officials bargained with the governor to ensure safety. Attorney General Kennedy suggested a cooling-off period after the barely averted catastrophe in First Baptist, and some voices in the North concurred, but the riders, especially the Nashville group, would have no part of it. Undeterred, SCLC, CORE, and SNCC made plans for the rides to resume.

City and state officials in the South continually complained that integrationist intruders were violating *their* laws and *their* social order. The Kennedy administration, embarrassed by mounting worldwide criticism of the United States, made a deal, negotiated with Senator James Eastland, permitting Mississippi to enforce its Jim Crow laws in return for preventing mob violence. The hope was to get the freedom riders to their destination in New Orleans without further spectacle. The freedom riders refused to go along. When twenty-seven of them, several heavily bandaged, entered a "whites only" cafeteria in Jackson and were arrested, they declined to pay the fines and were jailed. Meanwhile, students and teachers from Berkeley, Cornell, Wisconsin, and other campuses met in New Orleans for accelerated training in nonviolence. In the months ahead, more than a thousand freedom riders, black and white, carried out a "jail-in" that strained the capacity of the Mississippi prison system.

The Freedom Ride represented the high-water mark of Gandhian nonviolent resistance in the United States. There is no evidence that it softened many hearts or converted many antagonists through moral jiu-jitsu. Instead of shaming the aggressors before spectators, the nonviolent riders' goals shifted toward revealing the atrocities of their vicious antagonists and shaming their nation before the world, thereby pressuring the federal government to take responsibility for protecting civil rights. In the fall, under petition from the attorney general, the Interstate Commerce Commission required interstate carriers and terminals to take down Jim Crow signs and end segregated practices. The Ride also punctured any optimism that equality could be achieved without brutal resistance. The Ku Klux Klan grew in strength. Segregationist leaders gained popularity in their states. Public opinion polls showed that white citizens outside the South, though horrified by segregationist violence, disapproved of "trouble making" over civil rights.

It is unknown how many critics of nonviolence and advocates of armed self-defense drew lessons from the ferocious violence and the jail terms in Mississippi's infamous prisons. Guns were a familiar part of southern culture, for blacks as well as whites (the caravan taking the injured riders from the Anniston hospital to Birmingham carried shotguns contrary to Shuttlesworth's instructions, and many in the audience trapped overnight by a hostile mob at First Baptist carried guns and knives).[73] Organized black criticism of King's and the young sit-inners' commitment to Gandhism would grow more vocal in the years ahead, but already a maverick NAACP official in Monroe, North Carolina, Robert F. Williams, was spiritedly advocating armed self-defense against white attackers, and the brutal responses to the freedom riders made this position attractive to some young SNCCers.[74]

There were also generational tensions. After the violence in Alabama had seized the attention of the national press and the Kennedy administration, some of the young people were critical of the proprietary tone of James Farmer (who had missed the Alabama mobs) concerning what he called "CORE's ride" or even "my show."[75] At the same time, some of SNCC's younger generation expected that King would at some point join in the rides. There were valid objections, but Diane Nash and others were visibly disappointed when King decided he could not go. Seeing a chance to damage King's credibility, Williams, who himself believed in meeting violence with violence, sent a telegram taunting him as a "phony" if he failed to join the ride into Mississippi. "Gandhi was always in the forefront, suffering with his people. If you are the leader of this nonviolent movement, lead the way by example."[76] That has been called "a cheap shot," as it surely was, and King will never be thought of as a man who avoided risk (though he never posed as fearless). But the episode revealed, only fifteen months after the Greensboro sit-in and at the moment of the Nashville

SNCCers' commitment to freedom ride into Mississippi, fracture lines in the nonviolent coalition.

The greatest threat to the coalition was not internal philosophical or personality conflict. It was the ghastly police and mob violence it had to overcome. That had not been so evident in Montgomery in 1956 or Greensboro in 1960 as it became in Anniston, Birmingham, and Montgomery in 1961. That reality would be demonstrated repeatedly in sniper bullets, jailhouse beatings, bombings, assaults on the sidewalks, and in car chases threatening those who came south to aid freedom's cause by teaching people to read or going with them to register to vote. One sheriff, Laurie Pritchett in Albany, Georgia, recognized that brutality, when it was too public, hurt the segregationist cause. Having read *Stride Toward Freedom*, he boasted a plan of "meeting nonviolence with nonviolence"— in public—while jailing hundreds of protesters, including Martin Luther King, Jr., on charges of disturbing the peace or parading without a permit, in prisons across the hinterlands. His strategy was not benign: students were expelled from Albany State College; four nearby black churches were bombed; a black lawyer and a pregnant woman were clubbed; treatment in remote jailhouses deteriorated. Albany's officials also exploited the disadvantages for even a well-organized local movement when it relied on outside assistance and direction. King was called to Albany to gain publicity. He came to town and went to jail, the town offered to make concessions; King left town, and what was promised never happened. SNCC, excluded from King's press conferences, questioned why he was there in the first place. Pritchett gained a reputation as a brilliant tactician; he was certainly a more skilled gamesman in his use of jails than were King and SCLC, for whom Albany was a disappointment and a failure.[77]

In the wake of that failure, civil rights leaders launched a concerted struggle in Birmingham, Alabama. In a campaign denounced in the national press as "untimely," hundreds of protesters were arrested, and King was locked up for a week in solitary confinement. White moderate clergymen published a statement criticizing him and all other "outside agitators" who "incite violence and hatred." In April 1963, writing on smuggled scraps of newspaper, King answered them in a "Letter from the Birmingham Jail" that appeared widely in national magazines and newspapers. After describing his own children's brushes with Jim Crow, King wrote, "I guess it is easy for those who have never felt the stinging darts of segregation to say, 'Wait.' " In his experience, "white moderates," who were "more devoted to 'order' than justice," were becoming "the Negro's great stumbling block," even worse than the Ku Klux Klan. The brave young protesters who went to jail with him were not stirring up disorder. "They were in reality standing up for the best in the American dream and the most sacred values in our Judeo-Christian heritage, and thus carrying our whole nation back to great wells of democracy which were dug deep by the founding fathers in the formulation of the Constitution and Declaration of Independence." If decent, moderate people stood in their way, millions of blacks would despair and perhaps turn to violent, separatist ideologies, "a development that will lead inevitably to a frightening racial nightmare."[78] The letter has become one of the best-known works in the civil disobedience tradition.

Birmingham civil rights leaders counted on Bull Connor to react so ferociously that national opinion would change about who was responsible for disorder. Connor did not disappoint. In early May, as wholesale arrests had nearly broken the spirit of most protesters, King led a thousand children, some as young as six years old, out to march in the streets in defiance of laws against demonstrations. This "children's crusade" was widely denounced, especially after Connor jailed nine hundred praying, singing boys and girls. The next day, a thousand more went out, and police beat them with nightsticks and attacked them with dogs. Firemen knocked them unconscious with high-pressure hoses. As similar brutality recurred in subsequent days, some demonstrators and onlookers broke the nonviolent discipline by throwing rocks and bottles and setting fires, and the police responded with random beatings. In general, however, with participation by clergy from other cities and from volunteers like the entertainer (and former track star) Dick Gregory, and in the presence of scores of reporters from the United States and abroad, the movement was more in control of the situation than the police or representatives of the Justice Department. One scene indicating the spirit of the confrontation occurred on a Monday morning, May 6, after Connor, trying to be more like Pritchett, had promised to end the use of water cannons. At a signal Gregory led the morning's first contingent of children out of church, and after they received the requisite warning, the paddy wagons rolled up, and they danced and sang, "I ain't scared of your jail 'cause I want my freedom want my freedom want my freedom." Gregory got five days in jail with a severe beating (permissible in the Pritchett rules when out of sight). He was able to joke about it in his comedy routine for years.[79] The pageantry and horror distinguish the Birmingham campaign from the dignified "Montgomery method." It was well organized but led to disorder. Its primary goal often appeared to be the mobilization of national emotion.

Reports and pictures of unrestrained police violence disturbed national audiences and put pressure on Birmingham business leaders and the Kennedy administration to restore social order. Chamber of Commerce leaders negotiated an agreement to hire African Americans in better jobs and to desegregate public facilities. Civil rights leaders ended their demonstrations, and King proclaimed a "magnificent victory." Some Birmingham blacks, however, protested that too little had been gained. Alabama's new governor denounced the agreement. When a bomb killed four young girls in the Sixteenth Street Baptist Church in September, the news aroused national grief and outrage. The Kennedy administration sent federal troops into the city, thus taking matters out of the governor's hands. Administration officials also began work on new civil rights legislation.

On August 28, 1963, in the midst of the Birmingham struggle, the movement experienced its well-remembered (and sometimes envied and imitated) March on Washington. That it occurred at all was a sort of triumph for unity, but there were also, though less well remembered, signs of division and crisis. A. Philip Randolph, who had laid plans for a nonviolent "March on Washington" as early as 1941, revived the idea. His assistant Bayard Rustin became its chief organizer. Initial plans called for a "mass descent" and sit-in at the Capitol pressuring Congress to pass a civil rights bill. King imagined a nationwide work stoppage and a presidential proclamation ending all forms of racial segregation by executive order.[80] To gain the approval of President Kennedy and participation of the NAACP, planners had to disavow radical goals and tactics. Though national and city authorities made preparations for vandalism and disorder, the event proved remarkably peaceful, the demonstrators in the journalist Russell Baker's words, "a vast army of quiet, middle-class Americans who had come in the spirit of the church outing."[81] About one-fifth of the throng of 250,000 that marched from the Washington Monument to the Lincoln Memorial were white. All were well dressed, as organizers insisted and reporters unfailingly noted. Many celebrities sat on stage, and singers performed folk songs, new and old, at the Lincoln Memorial. Few speeches in American history are as familiar as King's concluding oration, with its depiction of reconciliation rather than unending antagonism. "I have a dream," he prophesied, of a coming day when Americans would fulfill their commitment to equality, when the descendants of slaves and slave owners would live together in peace and justice, when his own children would "not be judged by the color of their skin but by the content of their character."[82]

Between reflections on the unfulfilled promises of the Emancipation Proclamation, the Declaration of Independence, and the Constitution, on the one hand, and reiteration of his dream for the future, on the other, this great speech made plentiful reference to the recent dramatic struggles and recognition of what lay ahead: "We will be able to work together, to pray together, to struggle together, to go to jail together, to stand up for freedom together, knowing that we will be free one day." Going to jail had become very much part of citizenship in King's beloved community. A call to continued nonviolence and interracial cooperation implicitly recognized that King's vision was already contested even among civil rights champions: "There is something that I must say to my people who stand on the warm threshold which leads into the palace of justice. In the process of gaining our rightful place we must not be guilty of wrongful deeds. Let us not seek to satisfy our thirst for freedom by drinking from the cup of bitterness and hatred."

> We must forever conduct our struggle on the high plane of dignity and discipline. We must not allow our creative protest to degenerate into physical violence. Again and again we must rise to the majestic heights of meeting physical force with soul force. The marvelous new militancy which has engulfed the Negro community must not lead us to distrust of all white people, for many of our white brothers, as evidenced by their presence here today, have come to realize that their destiny is tied up with our destiny and their freedom is inextricably bound to our freedom. We cannot walk alone.

The speech that most clearly exposed crosscurrents in the civil rights movement at the time of the march was one composed by John Lewis, as the chairman of SNCC, who sought to write a strong, militant speech that felt like "an act of protest" rather than an expression of satisfaction with what government and the more cautious civil rights organizations were doing. He was angry about beatings and arrests, some carried out by federal marshals, in southwest Georgia and about the lack of federal protection for voter registration projects in the Deep South, where SNCC had become increasingly engaged. As a draft of his speech circulated, he came under pressure—from Washington's Catholic archbishop, from leaders of NAACP and the National Urban League, from labor leaders—to tone it down by omitting denunciation of cautious politicians, for example, and dropping the word *revolution*. (Randolph defended that word choice—he hailed the audience at the event, at which he presided, as "the advance guard of a massive moral revolution.") Lewis did remove the image of marching, not just in Washington but across Dixie as General Sherman had done, but he still vowed to march across the South. "For we cannot stop, and we will not be patient." Though he did temper criticism of the federal government, he still pointed out that both major parties had racist components. "Where is our party?" he asked the crowd. "Where is the political party that will make it unnecessary to have Marches on Washington?"[83]

In an important study of SNCC and the "Black Awakening of the 1960s," Clayborne Carson observes that Lewis's criticism of American politics "reflected the moralistic orientation of many nonviolent activists in SNCC," but despite its militancy, the speech's "religious imagery and emphasis on nonviolent protest were out of step with SNCC's dominant orientation by the summer of 1963." Though some like Lewis continued to believe in nonviolent direct action and appeals to the nation's conscience, Carson continues, SNCC was becoming "a cadre of organizers seeking to mobilize blacks to coerce the federal government into using its power to achieve civil rights goals."[84] The contrast may make Lewis seem too naive, and it may undervalue the religiosity of southern blacks with whom Lewis (and King) worked. But such a contrast is crucial to understanding the complex arrest of the Gandhian moment that was taking place almost before some Americans had even thought about Gandhi.

The transition, if complex, was also rapid, almost abrupt. It was seen first at SNCC, whose leaderless governance presented little resistance to change. At its second anniversary conference, in April 1962, James Lawson, who had been highly involved in its charter and formation, was uninvited. Over the next few years SNCC removed Lewis from its chairmanship and discarded its commitment to nonviolence. He left SNCC a few months later. Calls for whites to get out of SNCC escalated. Long-term white staff members were restricted to working in white communities. The last of these were expelled in December 1966. Under Lewis's successor Stokely Carmichael, SNCC placed less stress on rural southern campaigns for voter education and more on strengthening black identity and building pride in urban areas, particularly around Atlanta and outside the South. CORE also changed course, dropping its pacifist commitment and the term "multi-racial" from its constitution. Floyd McKissick, the new director appointed in January 1966, called nonviolence a "dying philosophy" that had "outlived its usefulness."[85] Many white CORE staffers, including former freedom rider James Peck, were purged and others resigned. "The spirit, commitment, attitudes, and sacrifices that made CORE had long [since] died," said one.[86]

The break, almost as sudden as the transition from Montgomery to Greensboro and Nashville, and perhaps just as astonishing, may illustrate the kind of fantastic progression of thought and action that Julius Lester associated with the 1960s. It may seem even more dizzying if we note that SNCC leaders for the most part continued to respect nonviolence as a useful tactic and to refer to civil disobedience as a right. For the sake of clarification, it should be noted that the violence being justified was defensive; there was, at least as yet, no proposal for aggressive acts of seizure, domination, or revenge. Even the phrase "black power," as heard at this time, often referred to voting rights enabling black majorities to improve the conditions in which they lived—a goal that might be pursued without violence (except perhaps in self-defense).

It had always been easy for debate over nonviolence to become caricatured. King in *Stride Toward Freedom* and SCLC in the "Montgomery Story" comic book had rendered his understanding of nonviolence in deeper and more absolute terms than had been true in the midst of the boycott. He had gotten rid of his pistol and urged his supporters to leave their weapons at home with the recognition he had gained from Rustin and other Gandhian tutors of the probable practical consequences of their actions. Robert F. Williams, the strongest public critic of King's espousal of nonviolence, led his own nonviolent sit-ins in Monroe, North Carolina, in the exciting spring of 1960—and went to jail for doing so. He maintained that people in his movement were spared the spitting and brutality meted out elsewhere because of their expressed willingness to defend themselves. In an extensive debate with Williams published in 1959, King advocated nonviolence as an organized means of achieving social change preferable to taking up arms, but he conceded the validity of the right to defend home and family.[87]

By the mid–1960s the lines of division became more hard and fast in repeated confrontations over nonviolent direct action. One occurred during remarkable training sessions held in June 1964 on the campus of the Western College for Women in Oxford, Ohio, organized for 650 college-age volunteers from the North and the West Coast who were preparing to work in the program aimed at teaching literacy, achieving voting rights, and organizing rural Mississippi voters known as Freedom Summer. As on many previous occasions—including at the birth of SNCC—James Lawson spoke about nonviolence and directed role-playing exercises simulating situations that the volunteers were likely to encounter in Mississippi. This time, Stokely Carmichael spoke in opposition. Nonviolence had been effective, he said, when it was novel, elicited media enthusiasm, and made narrow demands for seats at lunch counters or on buses. It is not clear what the trainees got out of this debate, which grew heated, between two impressive civil rights leaders, except for awareness of disagreement over tactics. The summer volunteers would not, in any case, try to talk their host families into getting rid of their guns, any more than King had done in Montgomery or than SNCC did in the Deep South. The attempt would have been futile, and the firearms might have afforded some protection. Most of the staff and volunteers, according to one participant's report home, were "agnostic nonviolent technicians" who recognized that different personalities would handle challenging situations in different ways. Whatever their predilections, once they got south, they would be nonviolent. After a realistic simulation of a hostile mob another volunteer expressed hope that this "terrible training . . . may well save lives."[88]

Carmichael demonstrated his understanding of publicity and the news media. By June 1966 in what was proclaimed a "March against Fear" the disagreement within the movement had become more public, more dramatic, and intense. That march was launched, without much time for planning, after James Meredith, who in 1962 had been the first black student admitted (by court order) to the University of Mississippi, was shot and seriously wounded on a solo walk from Memphis, Tennessee, to Jackson, Mississippi, in support of the voting rights of African Americans. Volunteers from CORE, SNCC, SCLC, and the NAACP joined in resuming his walk, which proceeded despite harassment by Mississippi state troopers, assaults by local mobs, and the discomfort of tear gas. In one dramatic meeting in the county where three civil rights workers had been kidnapped, whipped, tortured, and killed with apparent impunity at the outset of Freedom Summer, King said he believed in his heart that the murderers were present in the crowd. Reporters heard taunts and chuckles. Carmichael took the opportunity of this march, covered by many representatives of the media, to popularize the battle cry "Black Power," usually defined as a call for electoral power but also in the excitement of the march in these terms: "The only way we gonna stop them white men from whuppin' us is to take over." His SNCC associate Willie Ricks led the young black marchers in a call-and-response that would soon ring out in many cities and college towns: "What do you want? Black power."

The march brought forth some of King's gloomiest statements about the poverty of southern black people and the pervasive violence of America. His responses to Carmichael, however, were almost playful. After holding tight to Carmichael's elbow when he lunged toward a trooper, King joked, "I restrained Stokely, *nonviolently.*"[89] To Carmichael's admission that he "deliberately decided to raise the issue on the march in order to give it a national forum and force you to take a stand for Black Power," King shrugged. "I have been used before. One more time won't matter."[90]

Was the rising debate within the civil rights movement over nonviolence? or violence? or militancy? or voting rights? To complicate the question, while black activists proclaimed the superior effectiveness of "militancy" over nonviolence, Thurgood Marshall of the NAACP was hammering on his old criticism of civil disobedience. Outside a 1966 White House conference on civil rights, radical activists marched with placards denouncing King and other "Negro Leaders" as "Uncle Toms." Inside, King, whose opposition to the Vietnam War was unappreciated, was studiously ignored, while his longtime critic Marshall held forth on the history of "Negro demonstrations" and the importance of replacing "hostile" laws with "new, friendly" ones.[91] The issue, of course, was not the importance of kindly laws but Marshall's dismissive view of what he termed King's "missionary" methods—in other words, his reliance on nonviolent direct action as methodology to combat laws that were indeed bad.

It was true that civil disobedience did get good people beaten up, put in jail, or killed. But the same could be said of concentrating on literacy and voter registration rather than lunch counters or seating in buses. The jailings and beatings could also, as in Montgomery, provide the test cases to advance legal change and do so in a collective way rather than by individual inadvertence, stubbornness, or just being tired. As in most of the great reform campaigns in which civil disobedience had a part—Indian removal, slavery, women's rights, labor organization, marriage, conscription—the issue went beyond a specific law to include a systematic inequality of power. The "law" contested in the civil rights movement was the rule of segregation and codified black inequality.

The contest was not limited to the 1960s, of course, nor to the states of the old Confederacy. CORE and the MOWM had picketed and sat-in in various places before that decade. The struggle always took courage. Since I have previously stressed the role of the World War II generation, perhaps I might conclude here with a well-known symbol of breaking the American color line: Jackie Robinson, born to a family of sharecroppers in Georgia, part of the great migration to California, a college student at UCLA, a semi-professional football player in Hawaii, drafted during World War II but court-martialed in 1944 for refusing to sit in the rear of a segregated bus, a shortstop in the segregated Negro Baseball League before breaking the color barrier and "turning the other cheek" to abuse from southern white players in a brilliant career in "Major League" baseball. Eventually he played himself in the movies, became a successful businessman, and participated in civil rights marches in Washington and Birmingham.[92]

9

The Sixties and the Great Tradition of

Social Protest

Two themes deserve attention as we broaden our look at civil disobedience in the 1960s. First, the example of the southern protesters and the northerners who joined them was contagious, especially on college campuses and among the clergy, in a culture increasingly criticized for rampant complacency. Second, intellectual concern about conformity and apathy was overshadowed soon enough by burgeoning fear of social disorder, and many public figures tried to set limits to permissible disobedience. These discordant views of civil resistance go to the heart of intellectual debate in that decade.

Like many other student radicals, Tom Hayden, founder of the VOICE party at the University of Michigan and editor of the *Michigan Daily*, admired Jack Kerouac's *On the Road* (1957). In June 1960 he hitchhiked to California, but what most fascinated him out there was not the beatnik scene but the intense radicalism stirred up by police suppression of student demonstrations against the House Un-American Activities Committee (HUAC). He also heard about a looming controversy over student political expression on campus. His experience in Berkeley, he said, helped "define my politics, and turn me on to the idea of student power." On the same trip, at the Democratic National Convention in Los Angeles, Hayden took part in picket lines supporting a strong civil rights plank in the party platform, and he interviewed Martin Luther King, Jr. "Stop writing, start acting," he told himself; that was "the implicit message" of King's life.[1]

In August he gave a talk at a student conference on how a "fervent minority" can provide models of "existential commitment" and show the uncommitted majority a path leading beyond their selfish perspectives as bystanders.[2] Some of his language carried echoes of his Catholic upbringing; it may also have shown the influence of a course on existentialism taught by Walter Kaufmann. In the fall he assumed an active role in what soon became the most important American student radical organization, Students for a Democratic Society (SDS). A call went out for students to make a "comprehensive" attack on U.S. "institutional forces." SDS's first "congress" drew only a couple of dozen students, mostly from Michigan, but one was Sandra "Casey" Cason, a white Texan and SNCC activist with a deep religious commitment to nonviolence. By fall 1961 she and Tom Hayden were newlyweds working on voter registration in McComb, Mississippi. As an informal SDS liaison to SNCC, Tom circulated reports on the violence that SNCCers faced (a photo of a Klan member socking him made national news) and on squalid jail conditions in Albany, Georgia. Like King's Birmingham "Letter," some of Hayden's meditations had to be smuggled out of jail. They explored themes that would define SDS as a radical organization in the years ahead—commitment, sacrifice, community, and active citizenship.

By the time of SDS's "inspirational" 1962 congress at a labor resort on Lake Huron, its leaders had adopted "participatory democracy" as the motto that best described their revolutionary goal. Tom Hayden drafted a manifesto that came to be known as the "Port Huron Statement," committing the organization to a programmatic vision that is sometimes described as existentialist.[3] Tentative in expressed goals and always subject to revision, the pamphlet faulted American democracy for tolerating and perpetuating injustice while leaving young citizens drifting, without clear commitments to worthwhile shared values. As a call to revolution, it was in some ways strange. It was a cry of middle-class youth, "bred in at least modest comfort, housed now in universities," living estranged and isolated lives. Too many of their classmates were caught in a depressing "apathy toward apathy" devoid of commitments as citizens. The threat of "the Bomb" unsettled them. The manifesto did not denounce capitalism or the democratic system of government, but it opposed "the Military-Industrial Complex," "the depersonalization that reduces human beings to the status of things," and the consumerism that through advertising reduced the individual to "part of the system."

Though interviewing King was a major experience for Hayden and the spring 1960 sit-ins excited many college students, SDS's founding statements were heavily shaped by a different set of literary enthusiasms, personal experiences, and political goals from those, say, of their contemporaries in Greensboro, Nashville, or Atlanta. In its sixty-three pages the *Port Huron Statement* had curiously little to say about civil rights. In a fairly stilted formulation, it credited "the permeating and victimizing fact of human degradation, symbolized by the Southern struggle against racial bigotry," with compelling "most of us from silence to activism." It counted the discrepancy between the Declaration of Independence and "the facts of Negro life" in the South and in northern cities as one of several shortcomings they had come to see in America. It complained briefly about the Kennedy administration's "cool" attitude toward "mass nonviolent movements" and toward civil rights enforcement measures that might "infuriate" southerners in Congress. It applauded students who had recently broken through "the crust of apathy" and alienation by protesting against "racial injustices." Deploring the effects of persistent segregationist politics in a region where blacks were effectively disfranchised, it hailed the current voter registration campaigns as offering hope of a breakthrough. All told, these references took up less than two or three pages.[4]

There was also a wordy, though vague, two-sentence paragraph abhorring the depersonalizing consequences of violence in social interchange and calling for abolition of "the means of violence" and support of institutions that encourage nonviolence locally, nationally, and internationally. Readers might accurately conclude that SDS approved of nuclear disarmament and disapproved of strategies of deterrence. But its intended relations with peace movements were uncertain, and there was no indication of close reading of pacifist works like Gregg's or Shridharani's or of influential communication with Muste, Randolph, or other leading activists of the preceding era. Except for a passing reference to "mass nonviolent movements," there were no explicit indications of tactical preferences.

The remedies proposed by SDS were initially vague. It called for extending New Deal–like institutions ("a proliferation of 'TVA's'") to end poverty. It called for authentic individual freedom. It envisioned universities less bureaucratic and less tied to dominant social institutions. Most of all, but still vaguely, it sought the invigoration of public institutions so that people would feel less helpless. It imagined "genuine cooperation . . .

between a new left of young people and an awakening community of allies."

By mid–1963 some of the meanings of "participatory democracy" were becoming clearer. Following the example of Swarthmore College's SDS, some chapters sought to build coalitions with inner-city communities. Tom Hayden began to advise living among the powerless who needed to be organized. But SDS activists always dissociated their intentions from "paternalistic" programs of social uplift. They talked of "democratic decision-making" and of organizing institutions "in which those who are affected by decisions make those decisions."[5] And almost from the start, beyond the sometimes stilted language of the statement, they expressed a sense of an emerging counterculture of young people who could trust each other and get beyond racism, inequality, and warfare.[6]

Links between the student movement and its predecessors—the sit-ins, freedom rides, and Freedom Summer—emerge more clearly when we turn to California and consider the role of Mario Savio, another intense lapsed Catholic, not a fluent journalist like Hayden, but an extraordinarily effective and deeply admired speaker in his own way. A philosophy student, Savio was "not a political person" but someone who practiced "a secularized liberation theology." In his later life he thought back to the black freedom struggle as being "sort of like God acting in history."[7] Brought up in the New York borough of Queens, Savio arrived at Berkeley in fall 1963, and in March 1964 he joined in an off-campus campaign, including students from San Francisco State and other colleges, against job discrimination at a San Francisco hotel. CORE and the local NAACP were sponsors; prominent performers like the humorist Dick Gregory and songwriter Malvina Reynolds entertained the protestors, who were shown how to link arms and legs during a sit-in and to "go limp" if they were arrested in order to draw out the process. Except for watching events in the South on television, this was Savio's debut in nonviolent civil disobedience, which he defined as disrupting the operation of a business without "going around breaking things." In the event, Savio was arrested but given no jail sentence. The experience gave him a sense of belonging comparable to a Native American brave's "being initiated into manhood in his tribe."[8]

He noted the Sheraton protest and arrest on his application to Freedom Summer, to which he was accepted. After reports that three civil rights workers had probably been killed, he and the other volunteers at the

Western College training sessions were informed of their own risk and offered an opportunity to bow out without disgrace. Savio stayed the course, teaching in a freedom school in Mississippi, and accompanying men and women who were subjected to humiliation as they registered to vote, with only one violent incident, when ruffians attacked him and a coworker with billy clubs. Returning to college from another profound initiation, he assumed a new stature as a student leader passionately committed to an ideal of unrestricted speech on an open campus.

In autumn 1964 University of California officials prohibited students from setting up tables, passing out information, collecting signatures, raising money, and giving speeches, as they had done for years, on a sidewalk at the gateway to the campus. Groups ranging from CORE and SNCC to libertarians, Goldwaterites, and young communists viewed the ban as an attempt to stifle students' political expression. In the protests that erupted Savio spoke at an all-night vigil outside the administration building, then joined students defying the ban by setting up their tables at the center of campus. When a dean arbitrarily singled out five students for suspension from school, Savio along with hundreds of others signed a petition of complicity, surrounded the dean's office in an "unauthorized rally," and staged a sit-in that lasted deep into the night. At midnight Savio stood on a chair, rejected a message from the administration, then argued against still another dean who criticized the sit-in. He defended free speech and civil rights as vital to college education and to feelings of solidarity that students should hold toward others who might need their aid. For their rule breaking Savio and two others were added to the suspension list.[9]

The confrontation resumed at the plaza near the administration building. University police seized Jack Weinberg, a CORE representative (and until recently a graduate student), who "went limp" as they carried him to a squad car. "Sit down," someone shouted. Hundreds, and eventually thousands, of students formed a nonviolent, sedentary blockade around the car. As Margot Adler, a freshman from New York (and later a reporter for National Public Radio) recalled, "The police car, usually such a powerful symbol of authority, seemed tiny and helpless in the face of our growing numbers." Most of the participants were inexperienced demonstrators, but their fears gave way to exhilarating feelings of "instant community and internal power."[10] Savio climbed up on the car and spoke of his recent experience as a volunteer in Mississippi. "This fall I am engaged in another phase of the same struggle, this time in Berkeley. . . . The same rights are at stake in both places—the right to participate as citizens in a democratic society."[11] The car top became a podium for free speech. A law student (later a prominent human rights attorney) named Michael Tigar pointed out that the university's president, Clark Kerr, was a leading expert on management. The university was becoming a corporate institution seeking to squelch individual personality and introduce a new brand of fascism. "We thought the only place this kind of thinking was left in the world after the 1920's was in Mussolini's Italy."[12] Savio also denounced the "depersonalized, unresponsive bureaucracy" of universities that were shaping students to become interchangeable parts in a "chrome-plated consumers paradise." And the students, almost spontaneously, were standing in the way. "We had turned the world upside down," in Adler's words, and "stopped the machinery of the state."[13] She was not the only one with that feeling. For Savio, there was such a strong sense of solidarity, of being fully alive and belonging together, in the space around the car that civil disobedience became more than a tactic; it was a ritual of community or, in his biographer's words, "an end in itself."[14]

The world was not so easily overturned. The demonstration went on. While some protestors maintained control of the car, Savio and the student government president met with the university chancellor. The meeting went nowhere. The protestors then initiated a second front by sending a delegation to the administration building, Sproul Hall. After one of their number was refused an appointment, they blocked the doors with what they called a "pack in," which they maintained until 9:00 PM. Finally, after a thirty-two-hour standoff, the university negotiated with demonstration leaders: Students paid to repair dents on the roof of the car. Weinberg would not face charges. The cases of suspended students would be resolved fairly. The gateway sidewalk would be deeded to the city so that the tables would be off-campus. But the truce included no acknowledgment of the key tenet of what would soon become an organized Free Speech Movement (FSM) at Berkeley: namely, that students did not give up their citizenship when they entered the walls, real or symbolic, of a university.

The armistice was short-lived. The university reinstated political restrictions, and on-campus demonstrations resumed. Outdoors on the plaza before a mass sit-in inside Sproul Hall on December 2 Savio made a fiery speech that defined the new militant mood: "There is a time when the operation of the machine becomes so odious . . . that you can't take part; and you've got to put your bodies upon the gears and upon the wheels, upon the levers, upon all the apparatus and you've got to make it stop."[15] The folksinger Joan Baez joined Savio in leading students into the building and stayed with them all night long. Seven hundred and seventy-three protesters, some treated brutally by Oakland police, were carried off to jail for their epic defiance. Adler justified the event to her mother by referring to the conversation between Emerson and the jailed Thoreau that, though apocryphal, had entered American tradition: "Emerson: 'What are you doing in there?' Thoreau: 'What are you doing out there?' "[16] A few days later, at a large assembly supposedly intended to cool passions, campus police grabbed Savio by the throat and dragged him off stage as he approached the microphone—or "seized" it, as President Kerr worded his offense.[17] Appalled professors voted support for free speech, with no more restrictions than was constitutional in the nation. The FSM held a victory rally. The contest over control of student political expression was not over—for one thing, hundreds of arrested students still had to face trial.[18] It was by no means clear that civil disobedience would be recognized as a protected form of political expression. Nevertheless, many of these events, appearing nationwide in the news media, were understood to represent a new era on the nation's predominantly white campuses.[19]

Amid the excitement of sit-ins, pack-ins, be-ins, and jam-ins, it was not always noticed that there were competing definitions of the freedoms that civil disobedience protected. For some, protesters principally resisted the university administration's attempts to rein in student activism. They were "driven" to civil disobedience "after a period of six years of having our liberties chopped away one by one." The administration had cut off campus ties with the student political organization SLATE, that had organized against HUAC, and with the CORE organizers who had recruited anti-Jim Crow demonstrators at Sheratons and other businesses. In an almost manic effort to record the antecedents of the cop-car siege, veteran radical Michael Rossman recruited, in October 1964, over two hundred volunteers working strenuously for about three weeks to document and publish (by typing and collating ditto sheets) "the massive, historical substance of our grievance" reaching back to the 1950s. The labor was so passionate that thirty years later, even admitting that its consequence was at most "symbolic," Rossman created a dramatic narrative of the saga of the "Rossman report."[20] In Savio's eloquent speeches freedom referred more broadly to the liberating potential of education. Besides attending lectures and passing exams, students might enter into an active citizenship, with precedents in ancient

history and the writings of the great philosophers. Savio praised an exper-
imental college, the "Tussman program," in which students and faculty
looked intensely at major works, recurring issues, and periods of intellectual crisis and change, and he urged the student movement to support this
venture in reform. In his much-praised speeches Savio sought to express
and test political positions with philosophical clarity. He exemplified a
belief, praised by those who remember his speeches, in "real discussion"
and "honest and fair dialogue."[21]

Perhaps the contrast should not be overdrawn. No one hated the
imposition of new regulations on political activity more than Savio, especially when administrators proved incapable of clear argument to justify
them, and Rossman throughout his life pursued educational purposes that
came out of the student movement—probing, as one astute reader put it,
"the theory and practice of joining life and education into a single flow of
experiences."[22] Rossman understood the cop-car episode as an educational
moment, and he embraced his own vision of "the first Free University"
acted out "in miniature" in the fifteen hours of the great December 2 sit-in
before police dragged participants off to jail. In this community of learning
there were study halls and a dozen classes, along with folk dancers and
singers, a Chanukah service, a Chaplin film, grass smoking "in the corners,"
and the initiation of at least two women into "full sexual experiences under
blankets on the roof." Adler also described most of these activities (though
not the sex) and added that television and newspaper reporters were abun-
dantly present: one observed her reading Thucydides "and wrote it down."[23]

In its final chapter FSM had to respond to what was called the "filthy
speech" movement. On March 3, in an episode that might justify some of
the administration's concerns about the activities of nonstudents on
campus, John Thomson, by his own account an "emotionally numbed-out
and badly confused street poet," political radical, and "would-be author"
who had hitchhiked from New York, got the idea that if he went to jail, he
could write a story and attract some attention. Sitting near the famous
tables, he "borrowed" a sheet of lined notebook paper and a magic marker,
wrote the word FUCK, and sat there holding it while awaiting a response. A
"fraternity-looking guy" grabbed it, balled it up, and threw it at him while
threatening to break his neck: "There are all kinds of chicks walking by
here." Eventually, a plainclothes policeman fulfilled Thomson's wish to be
busted, and in a subsequent demonstration the editors of a student literary
magazine actively tested the limits. One of them, a senior in engineering,

read in public a passage on copulation from D. H. Lawrence's *Lady Chatterley's Lover*, a novel recently found in the courts not to be obscene. At a rally on the steps of the student union, English Department chair Mark Schorer, author of an introduction to that novel, insisted on a difference between reading obscene language in a book and having it "thrust upon one's attention in a public place." To the applause of people at the rally, he warned that the controversy was detracting from the faculty's ability to protect students' "serious interests." In fact, faculty support for FSM fractured over the issue.[24]

Leaders of FSM debated the obscenity issue at length, out of respect to a few movement veterans who regarded it as an important extension of civil disobedience, but very few gave it much support until the university administration began to expel or suspend students for indecent speech. To Savio, the way in which they did so flew in the face of hard-won victories for equal "procedural justice," and thus deserved to be met with civil disobedience, except that there was little campus support for the obscene speakers' cause.[25] The FSM disbanded in late April 1965. It would be inaccurate to say with Jerry Rubin, ex-student leader of a movement in Berkeley and the Bay Area that dismissed most inhibitions and social prohibitions, that FSM activists "ostracized the FUCK-heads——they said FUCK wasn't serious." It may be more accurate to say that divisions in FSM over " 'filthy speech" were premonitions of a future "split between political radicals and the hippie/yippies."[26] The same split was implicit in the bitter reflection of philosophy professor John Searle, an admirer of his student Savio, that televised coverage of FSM "attracted to Berkeley the worst collection of kooks and nuts you've ever seen," all of them in search of "one big political, sexual drug fest."[27] This is not of course the civil disobedience tradition we are tracing, with its belief in advancing civil rights through orderly violation of unjust laws.

Michael Rossman's life defied any stereotype of radicals turning conventional or growing disillusioned with age. Until his death in 2008, he wrote poetry, played his flute and guitar, got high, lived communally, married, became a father, and taught science to schoolchildren. He called himself "an action sociologist, a specialist in learning and student of change," as he racked up four hundred days in the post-FSM years on the road, visiting seventy campuses, supported sometimes by foundations and the media, more often by audiences of radical students. He usually traveled to join in symposia, present papers, or read his poetry, while striving personally "to sort things out, to adjust my perspective from Berkeley-provincial to a national scope." In spring 1967, while working on an article about "what the War was doing to what we called the Student Movement," he stopped briefly in Kent, Ohio, choosing the university there to exemplify "some unknown dreary large public campus" to contrast with Antioch and Oberlin, small colleges further advanced in political consciousness where students had recently blocked military recruiters. A few months earlier in Kent, "a first hiccup of antiwar protest had turned out a hundred for a lonely march." He met about a dozen young people who were trying to build on that—"isolated, embattled, lonely, embittered, taking refuge in an overtight group whose talk was laced with hurtful humor and flashes of longing." They invited him to an old house, on its way to becoming a commune, where they shared thoughts about organizing, guerilla theater, and a recent antiwar protest in Berkeley in which "freaks" and "politicos" acted together for the first time.

He remembered that visit three years later, after the U.S. invasion of Cambodia, when Kent became headline news: protesters "trashed" the town and burned down the army ROTC building. The next day's reports said two thousand turned out to march, and Ohio national guardsmen shot and killed four of them. Ten days later, Mississippi police killed two Jackson State demonstrators. Rossman's thoughts drifted back to the FSM, "the first campus explosion," and the tense wait for police to drag the protesters from Sproul Hall: "Five years from now," he said he had predicted, "they'll be killing kids on campuses, all over Amerika."[28] And the prediction had been coming true: at South Carolina State in 1968, People's Park at Berkeley in 1969, then Kent State and Jackson State, and now, as he wrote, two thousand national guardsmen sent into Urbana, Illinois, where he had been a frequent visitor—and there was more to come.

What had changed? One much-quoted answer appeared in the report of the Commission on Campus Unrest, better known as the Scranton Commission, appointed (reluctantly) by President Nixon in 1970 amid public concern about the violent confrontations on campuses. The report traced the uprisings to the "Berkeley invention," in which "the high spirits and defiance of authority that had characterized the traditional school riot were now joined to youthful idealism, local concerns about fairness and respect, and to social objectives of the highest importance." The rapid growth of student bodies, the inspiration of the civil rights movement, conflicts with university administrators, police intervention—all contrib-uted to the "invention," enabling core groups of militants to lead student majorities that continued to be moderate and nonviolent.[29] Some public officials were impatient, to say the least, with a report that sought to under-stand law breaking. Vice President Spiro Agnew condemned it as "more pablum for the permissivists."[30] The report certainly did not delegitimize civil disobedience; neither did it praise it as a peaceful alternative to campus "disturbances." It is not clear whether the report was helpful to anyone. The notion of a Berkeley invention avoided discussion of the escalation of the increasingly unpopular, and seemingly unending, war in Vietnam, the draft looming over the lives of college-age male students, or the links between defense industries and university researchers that furnished new targets for campus unrest. In addition, the notion ignored the increase of urban black militancy, the eruption of "civil disorders" in many cities not far from large universities, and a system of selecting presidential candidates that was not democratized or responsive to cries for change. The assassina-tions of public figures, Martin Luther King and Robert F. Kennedy, cannot be accounted for by a model of "invention."

We can follow Rossman as a carrier of news and tracer of the lines connecting free speech, personal liberation, and expressions of civil disobe-dience carried to the edge of revolution. What made him unusual was that he reflected on his experiences so constantly and perceptively. He began 1967, for example, "as a stranger and alone, in a bare cockroachy room" in Manhattan, acquainting himself with city living and unfamiliar experi-ences of fear. Back on the West Coast, he rested for three months in Haight-Asbury (and was arrested again) just before the psychedelic culture was deluged by students and tourists; with violence imminent, everyone in public life was armed. He strongly supported the newly organized antiwar Resistance, which had "gathered its goal: 3,000 young men committed to jail, and to developing and acting out in their own lives a changed relation-ship to authority and government which would form a basis later for community and a new Way of living." During the summer he served a deferred three-month sentence for his FSM transgressions. Having served his time, he took part in the Days of Protest campaign, seeking to shut down the Oakland Induction Center—at its height, "8,000 of us paralyzed forty downtown blocks," a campaign of civil disobedience topping most others in that era.[31] Soon came a week at the Center for the Study of Democratic Institutions in Santa Barbara "rapping with the resident intellectuals about youth culture," and later a presentation to the center's New York branch, "freaking the customers with dawning apocalyptic projections and masques." In between, at a National Student Association conference in Minneapolis, the subjects were student rights and "student power." Meanwhile, Columbia SDS kids, whom he had previously met, were planning for their own spring 1968 action, which promised to be "*spectacular.*"[32]

The idea of promoting massive civil disobedience in order to change government policy—and thus in some measure to change or "take back" government itself—had diverse origins. Staughton Lynd, as a historian, connected the antiwar movement to past eras in which he was expert—the American Revolution and the antislavery struggle. Viewing the war in Vietnam as the unpopular project of a governing elite, he proposed a "new Continental Congress" that might create a new and more responsive politics. Answering those who opposed the war but were tired of demonstrations and hoped to achieve their goals through politics, he asked, "as did Wendell Phillips to the antislavery politicians in the early 1850's":

> Do you really think that you don't need our help? Do you really imagine that you can resist the inertial drift of all politics toward compromise without some of us . . . who stand outside politics and say things politicians cannot say, and so make it possible for politicians to say them? You couldn't get civil-rights legislation without marches, imprisonments and deaths in Washington and Selma; do you really think you can stop the war without marches, imprisonments and maybe deaths in, say, Chicago?

A revolution would take time. It was useful to remember that abolitionism, like the civil rights movement, "began with a decade of direct action and emphasis on morality, then went into politics." In the longer run, there might come a time for political action, but in 1966 was it clear that "the relatively superficial, ritualistic actions required of persons by an electoral campaign [could] really be expected to build a movement more effectively than the more serious commitments required by, say, a rent strike?"[33]

On the West Coast, a new era of revolutionary direct action began when Jerry Rubin and his girlfriend Barbara Gullahorn approached a prominent mathematician, Steven Smale, about organizing a "Vietnam Day" town meeting or teach-in on May 21, 1965, similar to well-publicized events at the University of Michigan and other campuses. Thus began the improbable friendship of Rubin and Smale, who recruited a few other colleagues and joined discussions in Jerry's tiny apartment in a spirit of equality that amazed Jerry and Barbara. Clara Smale, who was active in an organization called "Women Strike for Peace," helped with publicity. Other local activists took part (Smale remembered a chef who was active in the Socialist Workers Party), but the teach-in was endorsed by the faculty union and remained very much a university event. Working with Jerry was a "lot of fun" for Smale, who admired his media experience and his "do it" philosophy. Their goals were to create a spectacular event, drawing big crowds, with broadly inclusive participation and extensive media coverage. The allotted twenty-four hours were expanded to more than thirty-three. The speakers came from the arts, politics, and scholarship, perhaps not the all-star list the planners had imagined (no Castro, no Sartre, no Dean Rusk), and definitely with an antiwar tilt. It was here that Staughton Lynd proposed a new Continental Congress. The Johnson administration, having encountered hostility on other campuses, made a questionable decision no longer to send representatives (vacant chairs on stage signified their absence), and two faculty critics of the event also declined invitations to speak. Crowds reached 10,000 at peak moments. The media paid lots of attention. No one tried to close Vietnam Day down, so there was no talk of free speech or civil disobedience. The Vietnam Day Committee (VDC) began to plan for days of protest on an international scale in October.[34]

Lynd had proposed stronger action, mentioning the Oakland Army Terminal as a target. On August 4 the VDC learned that a train transporting soldiers to Oakland would pass through Berkeley the next day. With help from Women Strike for Peace, a crowd estimated at 150 blocked the tracks as the train approached at ten miles per hour; there were tense moments when protesters dodged out of the way. What most pleased Smale (who led the effort while Jerry was away): the press coverage of "the great train ambush" was excellent. The next day there were two trains with well-organized police escorts. Both sides were better organized when the next trains came through on August 12. Protesters dodged through police lines and stood along the tracks or on them, sometimes grabbing onto the sides of the railroad cars, for miles. After that, the army found ways to take soldiers to Oakland on their way to Vietnam without passing through Berkeley. It should be noted, moreover, that the troop train protests were controversial within the local antiwar movement. They were both a turning point and a dividing line for a movement that would begin to talk about taking protest to new levels of resistance. Plans for massive civil disobedience and provoking arrests in the fall at the Oakland terminal after a march from Berkeley struck some in the movement as too inflammatory, a far step from the relatively passive action of the teach-in; for others, including Smale and Rubin, it was responding with escalation to the government's escalation of the war in Vietnam.[35]

The Berkeley progression from speeches and protests to confrontation at the city line and posturings of near revolution was important in the compressed history of civil disobedience. If these events really did help, even remotely, to stop the sending of more troops to Southeast Asia, if they helped end the war, they fulfilled the purposes that Smale and Lynd had in mind. We might note at this point that even some participants in Vietnam Day recognized that its effect on the large majorities of Americans who supported the war was negligible. The troop train protests were viewed favorably by only a minority of Berkeleyites and Californians who already opposed the war. We will return to intellectual debates about civil disobedience provoked or resumed in this era, but we may say here that the VDC events pushing, as Lynd recommended, for a new examination of the Constitution were advances in clarity and commitment for those with the deepest antiwar feelings. But their practicality in ending the war, long before the costs in American personnel had discouraged the majority of Americans, has been disputed in postmortems and reexaminations.[36]

Antiwar activities nationwide preceded the electrifying campus protests in Greensboro and Berkeley, and they were by no means the exclusive province of the young. In the late 1950s, protesters against the danger of nuclear armament showed a determination to "go beyond words" that did not always feature law breaking—there were silent vigils, for example, and a well-publicized San Francisco to Moscow "Walk for Peace"—but they also experimented with dramatic new activities—sailing into the prohibited waters in the Pacific where nuclear tests were carried out, protests against research on germ warfare at Fort Detrick, Maryland, and attempts to board nuclear-missile-bearing submarines at Groton, Connecticut. To protest and publicize the construction of a base for ICBMs (intercontinental ballistic missiles) near Omaha, Nebraska, in 1959, A. J. Muste and dozens of other "peacemakers" repeatedly crossed barbed-wire barriers and accepted jail sentences.[37]

Campaigns to defy compulsory civil defense drills took the form of noncompliance with laws requiring everyone to take shelter as if their city was under nuclear attack—a provision that peace activists viewed as delusional and provocative. Many people who were children at the time would later remember their own early refusal to cooperate with what seemed like silly drills (holding a book over your head as if it would give real protection) in school.[38] In New York, as "Operation Alert" became an annual event enforced by law, Dorothy Day, Ammon Hennacy, and other Catholic Workers (who believed in greater attention to the needs of the poor and hungry) stayed out in parks and sidewalks, carrying signs and distributing literature, until they were arrested and then went to jail rather than pay fines. Jailed for the fifth straight year in 1959, Day received a scolding letter from Eleanor Roosevelt, a prominent champion of civil defense: "Such measures are, after all, meant for your own safety, so I cannot see why you go to such extremes to avoid complying with the rules."[39] After the May 1960 protests enlisted a broader coalition of participants than ever before, Jim Peck (shortly to be beaten bloody on the Freedom Ride) called the civil defense protests "as phenomenal as the southern sit-ins." In 1961 well-dressed young mothers with children were joined by 2,500 others, and college students held demonstrations on several campuses. Operation Alert came to a halt in 1962.[40]

Most antiwar actions of the 1950s were led by pacifists from the eras of World War II or even, as in the case of Muste, the 1930s. A significant new movement founded during the 1961 Berlin crisis was Women Strike for Peace (WSP). Its founders initially described themselves as housewives, though in response to criticism of the failure to emphasize their citizenship, they soon added "teachers, writers, social workers, artists, secretaries, executives, saleswomen." They all rejected the "male 'logic'" that both the USSR and United States followed in resuming nuclear testing. It was time to let husbands and bosses take over women's routines for a day while "worried mothers" protested atmospheric danger. Four thousand women rallied and heard speeches in Los Angeles. In New York thousands more marched in protest. Picketers in other cities carried signs reading "Ban All Atomic Weapons" and "Let's Not Imitate the Russians." These events gained considerable attention, in part because of the style in which they were carried out. Instead of forming an organization, strikers used personal phone and address lists to spread the word. Like SNCC and SDS, WSP took pride in its grassroots methods and "structurelessness."[41] And we have seen how valuable the WSP style of organizing would prove to Smale and Rubin.

Initially, WSPers did not strike or break laws, but such reluctance diminished. Two WSP leaders briefly obstructed a shipment of napalm bombs headed for Vietnam. Their aim was "to invoke the law, not to disobey it," they explained, and they received the lightest of sentences. Others banged their shoes on the locked doors of the Pentagon and demanded to speak with the generals who were burning Vietnamese children.[42] Eventually, on missions raising some risk of prosecution, delegations of WSP women met with Vietnamese women in Djakarta, Hanoi, and Paris. Support of acts of civil disobedience, such as draft card burning (females were exempt from the draft), led to confrontation with police, including sit-ins and a lie-in, at the entry to the White House in 1967. These tactics remained controversial, however, and some WSPers valued their movement's avoidance of extremes as vital to toning down conflict and rebuilding unity in society.[43] In October when the antiwar movement converged on the Pentagon women were, by Norman Mailer's account, more likely to be arrested and to be beaten more brutally than men like himself.[44]

Interest in pacifism surged among college students. One 1962 survey showed that over 20 percent considered war immoral and about 45 percent took pacifism seriously. "What has suddenly happened" to the "silent generation?" an editorial in the pacifist magazine *Fellowship* asked in May 1960.[45] News from the South certainly inspired widespread discussions of nonviolence, and the military buildup and foreign-policy crises of the New Frontier focused intense interest on the Selective Service system. There was no new draft law to protest; under 1948 and 1951 laws registration was still required for all men over eighteen. Proposals to require twelve months of military service of all males never passed. Deferments for higher education were available, but only until age twenty-four. Exemptions for married men were added by President Kennedy in 1961 and limited (but not retroactively) by President Johnson in 1965 to those with children. A 1967 act expanded the upper age limit for conscription from twenty-six to thirty-five.[46] Conscientious objector status, with obligations to alternative service, was not available to those whose antiwar convictions arose from opposition to U.S. foreign policy or nuclear armament. The symbol of these policies, which affected vital decisions of virtually all U.S. male college students, was the draft card each was expected to keep in his possession "at all times."

It recorded the holder's draft status and the location of his draft board, but the value of the cards for identification purposes was slight compared to their value to movements opposed to conscription. Draft card burnings would join sit-ins (now relocated to college presidents' offices to demand action on military training and recruitment on campus) as the decade's signature forms of civil disobedience.

These events were not unprecedented. There had been draft card burn-ings in 1947 during controversy over imminent reintroduction of a draft. A young Catholic pacifist, Tom Cornell, was aware of tradition when he burned his first card in 1960, and he burned every one he received there-after. In November 1962 he led twenty-five other men in burning their cards. Increasing draft calls brought attention to this form of private or public disobedience. By May 1964 protesters had begun to burn them in "corporate" protest against continuation of the draft in an age of nuclear threat. In the following years many more cards (an estimated 25,000) were destroyed in acts of public resistance that blended protests against viola-tions of individual conscience and the atrocities of American military intervention in Vietnam.[47] In a ceremony of resistance at Boston's Arlington Street Church, some appealed to tradition by standing at the candlestick of the antebellum Unitarian reformer William Ellery Channing to set their cards aflame. Congress voted overwhelmingly to set stiff penalties—up to $10,000 and five years in prison for actions that were made tantamount to treason. On April 15, 1967, 158 young men, mostly students, but including one Marine Reserve Green Beret in uniform, gathered in Sheep Meadow in New York's Central Park, where they were sheltered by sympathetic onlookers as they set fire to their cards. One held up a sign declaring himself "20 YEARS UNREGISTERED." The Green Beret may have been the only one tracked down and punished.

Never mind that the young men were risking arrest and jeopardizing their deferments. Critics complained, as was often true of civil disobedi-ence, that the actions were too radical or too moderate. When Paul Goodman, a well-known writer and father of one of the Cornell students who had issued the call, praised their action in the New York Review of Books, he received dismissive criticism in a subsequent issue—from a man who spoke in favor of moderate or liberal political action and against the radicalism of an unrepresentative minority, and from a University of Wisconsin graduate student who dismissed such action as a "pathetic" and "hopeless" pursuit of "individual and momentary purgation" instead of an

effective deployment of "power" matching "organization with organization." Goodman's essay provoked such reactions with its explicit expression of hope for "open populist revolt" and for "public non-violent"
conspiracy against the state.[48]

Not all protesters burned their cards. Some cards were mutilated, so
that their holders remained publicly identifiable, and turned over to
authorities. In October 1967 on the steps of the Justice Department the
famous pediatrician and author Benjamin Spock, Yale's chaplain William
Sloane Coffin, and eight other prominent intellectuals collected close to a
thousand draft cards from student protestors, adding their own if they
were young enough to have them, and departed to deposit them inside,
while emphasizing that they were deliberately violating the law by aiding
and abetting the young lawbreakers. The demonstration fizzled. The
attorney general was absent. No one would receive the bag of cards on
behalf of the government. (At the news, President Johnson was furious,
complaining about "the dumb sonofabitch . . . who would let somebody
leave a bunch of draft cards in front of the Justice Department and then let
them walk away.") A few days later the Selective Service director instructed
local draft boards to draft anyone who violated draft laws or interfered
with recruiters.[49] Having failed as intermediaries, the intellectuals knew
they had to get arrested the next day in order to make it plain that it was
not just the young who were disaffected from the war.[50]

Throughout the October 1967 confrontation at the Pentagon, as Mailer
reconstructed it in the best book on civil disobedience at the height of the
1960s, the government recognized that it had to tolerate some defiant and
illegal activity but sought to keep it under control. Protesters choosing the
option of civil disobedience exhibited a radical moderation, a frustrating
recognition of the impossibility of launching a protest that was more than
symbolic, that truly matched strength for strength and thereby altered
government policy through provocative action, democratic organization,
acts of violence or absurdity or even subversion. Mailer presented conun-
drums of history in the form of a novel as he analyzed the gestures and
decisions of a range of antiwar radicals with two contrasting leaders,
Dellinger and Rubin, trying to chart a passage "from Dissent to Resistance"
or even to "incalculable acts of revolution." Marijuana smoking was
confused with increasing militance; peaceful gestures led to scenes of
clawing at soldiers and getting clubbed; and as the authorities prevailed,
protesters were driven "from their new resistance down to the passive

disobedience of the helpless" that the movement supposedly had outgrown. Amid the "absurd" changes of posture and compromises, Mailer himself and the others he calls the "Notables" succeeded in getting themselves arrested by overstepping an arbitrarily imposed boundary. He expected to be jailed overnight but instead was held for five days for being a bad influence on young people.[51]

Rubin's sidekick Abby Hoffman never really expected to "levitate" the Pentagon (though some of those who chanted with him may not have understood the effort as purely theatrical). High on LSD, he was free to urinate on the building. Watching intently from an office window, Secretary of Defense Robert McNamara was no longer convinced of the administration's war strategy. Later he would speculate that if the demonstrators had "been more disciplined—more Gandhi-like—they could have achieved their objective of shutting us down. All they had to do was to lie on the pavement around the building. We would have found it impossible to remove enough of them to keep the Pentagon open."[52]

McNamara's view sometimes receives more respect than it deserves. Its speculation is implausible. As one skeptic has asked, where would the protesters have gotten the training? How long could they have lain there, and can one really imagine President Johnson announcing, "Well boys, they're still out there lying on the pavement after a full week; I guess we'll have to call off the war."[53] That is not to say, however, that more discipline, better behavior, and unified leadership would not have made a more favorable effect on the American public. Some of the "Notables" and to some extent Dellinger may have been trying to establish an impression of decent, sensible, but resolute, opposition to the war. But that had become a hard role to sustain.

Draft resistance included refusal to serve and support for those who refused, either before or after entering the armed forces. Comparisons with the Underground Railroad were inevitable, especially in the Pacific Northwest, where there existed a long-standing radical and antiwar movement, but also along the Great Lakes and New England frontiers, where the original Underground Railroad had flourished. Sometimes by stealth—but sometimes in open defiance of the laws—churches, families, and citizens' groups provided shelter and transportation. By 1969 over 250 college student body presidents, together with thousands of other students, signed statements to the White House declaring their personal intention to refuse induction.[54] More young men resisted the draft than cities could prosecute, and so many fled the country to "dodge" induction or desert the armed services that in 1977 President Carter proclaimed a general amnesty in an attempt to calm bitter memories and bring them home. Not all returned. Disobedience had occurred to an unprecedented and even astonishing extent, in the army and in the draft pool as well as in broad segments of the population who for reasons of sex or age were free of personal risk. In Charles DeBenedetti's summation, as civil disobedience was extended into draft resistance:

> The evolution from individual refusal of military service to the burning and turning in of draft cards had taken conscientious objection to organized resistance, and from universal pacifism to selective objection [to specific wars]. Prominent intellectuals had courted complicity in resistance to allegedly illegitimate authority, and several church bodies had endorsed selective objection to war.[55]

Yet the "movement" was as divided and disunified as it was evolving and adaptive. There was not much choice but to move and adapt, but these were not steps toward unity.

Draft boards presented another target. Barry Bondhus of Big Lake, Minnesota, reported to the Elk River draft board in February 1966 and dumped two buckets of human excrement into the drawers of draft files. His father, Tom Bondhus, accompanied him, insisting that the military would take none of his ten sons, and perhaps participated in the defilement. Barry was arrested a few days later and eventually served fourteen months for destroying government property and impeding the work of the Selective Service Administration. The father, who had founded a religious sect of his own, opposed most killing, though he was not fully nonviolent and threatened to shoot anyone who entered his property to take his sons. He was not charged with an offense, and none of his nine other sons was drafted. The episode received some publicity at the time and continues to have a kind of notoriety in popular culture. It was the start of a long line of assaults on draft files, many of them by Catholic radicals.[56] According to a September 1969 report by Francine du Plessix Gray in the *New York Review of Books*, over sixty protesters had come to constitute an "Ultra-Resistance" by destroying draft records with blood, paint, fire and napalm.[57]

The rise of ultra-resistance caused divisions and required adjustments among Catholic radicals. These included converts with backgrounds in an earlier era's socialist and anarchist movements. Ammon Hennacy had spent nineteen months in a federal penitentiary for draft refusal during World War I, and Dorothy Day had gone on hunger strike with the suffragists at Occoquan in 1917. "Thanks to Hennacy," writes Garry Wills, "Day would still be going to jail in her seventies with the striking farmworkers of Cesar Chavez." Hennacy, the one-man revolution, fasted and picketed at nuclear missile sites, paid no federal taxes, and pioneered techniques of ultra-resistance (even if he later criticized them).[58] Also included were Trappist monk and widely read author Thomas Merton, another convert, and many priests and laity in Catholic Worker communities offering food and shelter in American cities. These houses of hospitality also became, as they remain, centers for pacifist response to public issues, and some of their residents held prominent roles in the Fellowship of Reconciliation and other groups of peacemakers during and after the Vietnam War.

Merton, as we have seen, set a stringent standard for nonviolence—not highly political, not too self-righteous or dogmatic, but still concerned about effectiveness. That standard was easier to hold in silence in a monastery than out on the streets. Events could lead him to egotistical overreactions, jumping to conclusions, drawing lines about what he could countenance. Three immolations occurred in 1965: an eighty-two-year-old Quaker woman, Alice Herz, in Detroit in March; Norman Morrison, father of three, carrying his one-year-old daughter, in front of the Pentagon and before the eyes of Secretary of Defense Robert McNamara in November (bystanders grabbed the child out of his arms); then a week later, a young man, Roger LaPorte, across the street from the United Nations. Because LaPorte had recently become involved with the Catholic Workers, the press blamed the movement, and Dorothy Day in particular, for oversimplifying complex issues and doing great harm. New York's Cardinal Spellman disciplined priests in the movement for apparently encouraging the sin of suicide. And Merton, attributing blame to the peace movement generally for encouraging defiant actions rather than offering "patient, constructive and pastoral work," from his silence in Kentucky resigned by telegram from the Catholic Peace Fellowship. A barrage of letters from New York assured Merton that the writers barely knew LaPorte and argued that it was the war that had frustrated calm, rational discussion and action. Merton withdrew his resignation and remained a much-respected, if remote, presence in the peace movement.[59]

But the issue of sane, civil, temperate response had been raised. LaPorte had been present at a large rally of support for a draft card burning in Union Square where Day and A. J. Muste, standing beside her, voiced their "solidarity of purpose" with the courageous young men and pointed out that "we, too, are breaking the law." Jeering counter-demonstrators had yelled, "Burn yourselves, not your cards."[60] There is no evidence that LaPorte's suicide was a response to that challenge. His act eluded understanding. He had not planned it in consultation with others. One person who knew him insisted that he was not responding to any pathological compulsion.[61] The immolation could be taken as a response to American society by a young man of heightened religious feeling rather than as a tragedy caused by irresponsibility in the peace movement. Were immolations personal acts of civil disobedience even though other American antiwar protesters disowned them? Did they challenge onlookers, asking what are you willing to do? Staughton Lynd reported that people in Hanoi celebrated Norman Morrison's heroic action and asked why so few American young men were ready to refuse to serve in the army.[62] The question made less sense in a couple of years as draft resistance increased.

The fissure within Catholic radicalism threatened to widen in 1968 when the brothers Daniel and Philip Berrigan, a Jesuit and a Josephite priest, launched an antiwar campaign of attacks on draft boards. First, Philip, who was a World War II combat veteran, with three other men, entered a Selective Service office in Baltimore in the middle of the day and poured blood (their own mixed with calf's and duck's blood purchased at a market) on files of draft-eligible males. The "Baltimore four" had alerted the press, who took photographs, and waited outside to be arrested. In May, Daniel, who had traveled to Hanoi with Howard Zinn and brought back three imprisoned U.S. pilots (as far as Laos, at any rate), returned home to join Philip. Together with seven others, including two women, they entered the Catonsville, Maryland, draft board offices carrying ten pounds of homemade napalm (gasoline mixed with Ivory flakes), seized records of those most eligible for immediate induction, carried them in a big wire trash basket out to a parking lot, and set them aflame. The group recited the Lord's Prayer and sang hymns while photographers took pictures. A poet and well versed in American radical tradition, Daniel wrote a widely produced play, "The Trial of the Catonsville Nine," based on the trial transcript.[63] Both brothers served time for breaking the law, though Philip disappeared for ten days and Daniel eluded government agents for four months. Another of the nine dyed her red hair black and turned herself in only ten years later. Escapades underground would lead to predictions like William Sloane Coffin's that "there is no doubt that thirty years from now the Berrigan brothers will be genuine folk heroes, widely celebrated in song and story and celluloid."[64]

Heroic or not, taking flight violated traditional definitions of civil disobedience in which willingness to accept punishment signifies respect for the civil order. Of course, by 1968 respect for the state was in short supply in the antiwar movement. It was not clear that all, or even most, antiwar activists approved of the violence of destroying property, frightening staff workers, lighting fires, splashing blood (this would become even more controversial later on during the AIDS epidemic). Among Catholic Workers, Tom Cornell was particularly uneasy with the violation of Gandhian precepts of openness and nonviolence. Both Merton and Day recognized that hit-and-run strikes at draft boards—and more were to come—conflicted with their own religious and pacifist views. Actions like these might lead (as perhaps they did) to further violence by more secular "underground" radicals. Though disagreeing with the Berrigans' "methods of action," Merton considered them friends and did not disown them. Day said repeatedly, "These actions are not ours." She and Hennacy were old-timers who never accepted the new direction of the Berrigans: symbolic property destruction, flight from punishment, intense courtroom defenses. But no one wrote more insightfully about the inspirational effect of her life than did Daniel Berrigan. Without her example, "the resistance we have offered would have been simply unthinkable." Hers was a voice from an era that seemed to be passing away. Her favored mode of protest was picketing. She once told a young Worker: "We plead guilty. And we don't take bail." She reserved most of her public criticism, however, for the government that waged war, the populace that accepted it, and American bishops who condoned "mass murder in Vietnam."[65]

Property destruction was a dividing-line issue for opponents of the war. In *Liberation* Staughton Lynd, in jail for picketing in support of a sit-in by black students in a local high school, justified the record burnings by analogy with the Boston Tea Party. No innocent person was endangered because "the property which could not be permitted to exist was carefully moved to a nonflammable surrounding" to be destroyed. But unlike the famous tea partiers, they were not disguised and did not disappear after their action. Unlike some contemporaries, they avoided threats and name-calling (no denunciation of "pigs") and did not threaten repression against repression. They stayed (at least initially) to accept arrest and punishment if it came, to let a political process continue, thus performing a type of civil disobedience that might enliven democratic—and in Lynd's view, religious—discourse.[66]

As the Vietnam War dragged on, civil disobedience flourished. Unity was less easily maintained (or dissembled) in the broader antiwar movement as it came into contact with national politics. The movement had many advantages: older leaders with experience extending over decades (Muste, Day, and Randolph) and middle-aged leaders of "the greatest generation," with experience rooted in the 1940s (Peck, Rustin, Dellinger); support from eloquent African American leaders of two generations with impressive recent experience in sit-ins and boycotts; a rapidly expanding college population with antiwar cultural heroes of its own (John Lennon, Joan Baez); a popular culture that valorized rejection of old shibboleths and openness to change. *Time* magazine's Man of the Year in 1966 was the entire generation under twenty-five. The movement also faced a population of voters increasingly disturbed by the suddenness of change, the ubiquity of disloyalty and disorder, urban riots, and a series of assassinations, successful and attempted. The peace movement sometimes appeared to be an agency of disorderly youth rather than of social harmony. For some young people, like Terry Sullivan, who had served time in Parchman as a freedom rider and in Danbury as a draft resister (even though he was 4-F he mutilated his card), the "movement" was an ideal that had begun to lose its sharp definition.[67]

The most dramatic of many crises, the perfect storm, came at the 1968 Democratic Convention, set up to nominate Vice President Hubert Humphrey, who had not campaigned in a primary or won a single delegate. Chicago's Mayor Richard Daley, determined to project a semblance of order no matter how much ugly violence it took, gave no permits for demonstration or parades. Three recognizable groups of protesters had come to Chicago with very different purposes: a small core, led by Dellinger, believed in nonviolence. Some SDSers, led by Tom Hayden, were pledged to nonviolence but when Daley's police, shouting "Kill Kill Kill" began to attack, swiftly reneged. "Nonviolence is dead," Hayden announced. Jerry Rubin and his legion, now called Yippie!, came to mock the entire process, and they attracted many students fascinated by their irreverence and theatricality. Rossman had warned his friend Jerry against bringing so many young people there without planning or amenities, and many of them were beaten brutally in what was officially determined to be a "police riot." Only sporadically under Dellinger's leadership was there anything resembling peaceful civil disobedience—and when it occurred it was smashed. Police recognized no distinctions between orderly demonstrations and quite different methods. In March 1969 the Nixon administration entered charges of conspiracy to riot, using incendiary devices, against Dellinger, Hayden, Rubin, and five others, not all of whom knew each other, and kept the travesty of the Chicago convention in the news for many months, especially after the judge had ordered the binding and gagging of a leading Black Panther, Bobby Seale, who had nothing to do with events in Chicago.

In the aftermath of smashed heads, unpopular candidates, and judicial suppression of dissent, one faction of SDS carried out what they called "days of rage," fighting with police and smashing windows in Chicago's Loop. Some then went underground to create what came to be known as the Weathermen or the Weather Underground Organization (WUO), giving up all contact with family and friends and carrying out bombings at police stations, court buildings, prison offices, and corporate headquarters across the United States. To the urban disorders and riots of the preceding years were added attempted robberies and shootouts, explosions in the U.S. Capitol, occupation and "trashing" of university administration buildings and laboratories, and lives taken in actions that defied the ordinary ground rules of civil society.

These actions received historical and theoretical justification in an extended statement, "Prairie Fire," printed at first underground and then slightly more publicly in 1974.[68] Though writing from underground and dedicated to anti-imperial revolution, the authors refrained from denunciation of "the struggles of the sixties." Those struggles had "changed everything," and to disown them would be to do "the enemy's work." They had contributed to the heroic communist opposition to U.S. imperialism in Vietnam; advanced the fight against racism in the United States and throughout the world; overthrown the "rotten values" of male supremacy and consumerism; and given birth to new insurgent cultures. After breaking from "the powerless past" with methods that were initially peaceful, they had learned that change is blocked by violence "every step of the way." They had come to see the necessity of worldwide guerrilla action and armed resistance. The voices they most celebrated were those of Che Guevara, Fidel Castro, and Ho Chi Minh as well as U.S. black liberation leaders. Though maintaining their connection to the spirit of the sixties, they had developed a critique of its ideological weaknesses: primarily its belief in American exceptionalism and a commitment to "reformism." The American radical movement, in their view, was too wedded to belief in the "essential goodness of American society," too attached to "pacifist and conciliatory ideas," and too attracted to a strategy of "peaceful transition" to socialism. With its "exaggerated emphasis on legality and electoral struggle," the movement failed to understand that "revolution is a dialectical process of destruction and creation."[69] What must be added—it was easily forgotten—is the long perseverance of the core members of the WUO who lived under cover from winter 1969–70 well into the 1980s (with the last surrender in 1994).[70]

Civil disobedience did not subside on campuses or on the streets. Even the disappointments of the presidential elections of 1968 (when no major antiwar candidate made it past the debacle of Daley's convention) and 1972 (which brought the electoral trouncing of a peace candidate, George McGovern, and reelection of Richard Nixon, who courted southern segregationist votes, called student protesters "bums," and escalated bombing in Southeast Asia) failed to stifle hope of ending the war through organized demonstrations and defiance, now often calling itself "the Resistance." While civil disobedience was not invented in 1960—surely we have shown that much—its familiarity greatly increased with the bus boycott and sit-ins and freedom rides, with the teaching of Martin Luther King, Jr., and James Lawson, who had their own teachers and inspirations—and critics. It reached deeply across the rural South and changed American cities. After Berkeley, where Mario Savio mounted a car to explain what it was and urge large crowds to embrace it, civil disobedience had become an increasingly familiar concept and sometimes explosive occurrence on many campuses— at coed liberal arts colleges (Oberlin, Antioch, Swarthmore), women's colleges (Wellesley, Spelman), Ivy League universities (Princeton, Cornell), state universities (San Francisco, Buffalo, Kent), huge state universities (Wisconsin, Minnesota), and with stirrings even at small sectarian colleges that received little attention in the national press.[71] Some of the on-campus conflicts became so intense and destructive that they became national news. At many, if not most, American universities, stories about the protests of the 1960s (really the "long" 1960s) would live on in the telling of old-timers, including faculty, while they grew tiresome to new generations of students.

Less well remembered is the conflict in the streets in the early 1970s during the Nixon administration's efforts to beat down an opposition that was determined to stop the war. After observing what he called a riot in Cambridge, the student chairman of the *Harvard Crimson*, Frank Rich, quoted another student saying sarcastically, "*This* will do a lot to end the war." Taking the riot more seriously and comparing it to other confrontations after Chicago, Rich wrote: "The wholesale window-breaking and looting ... made the night successful [for the protesters]. . . . Where have the years of marching gotten us? . . . The smashing and looting . . . are desperate measures, but what is left but desperation after every other kind of protest has failed to stop the killing in Asia and at home?"[72] The volatility and frustration of the time are evident from a *Time* magazine interview with Rich seven months later concerning the popularity of a book on the "greening" of America that predicted the decline of militant antagonism and its replacement by a more mellow, spiritual "hippie" revolution: "Students are still concerned about the war, racism and poverty; some are very active with ecology groups. But most are just waiting, with their pot and their Dylan records, for the grass to grow through the concrete. Last year they would have laughed [the author Charles] Reich right off the campus."[73]

Events in the days surrounding May Day, 1971, cast much doubt on the predictions of America's "greening" and "cooling," as the internationally famous linguist and antiwar activist Noam Chomsky summed up the evidence: several hundred thousand demonstrators at the Capitol, veterans testifying before Congress, others engaged in lobbying or "passive" civil disobedience in government buildings, with many arrests and some "atrocious treatment," and additional demonstrations in other cities and at military bases. No doubt, as Chomsky noted, the Nixon administration and some members of Congress would have been pleased to see more cooling, and some argued that civil disobedience has no place in a democracy. There seemed to be rising recognition that pursuing the war through conscription had been a mistake. Still, from Chomsky's observation, the brutality of the police toward demonstrators, though "far from that of, say, Chicago, 1968, . . . was surely well beyond the bounds of law."[74]

Recurrent on campuses and in the streets, civil disobedience became a recognized topic of extensive discussion in public life. The term remained a little strange: library subject catalogs still had cards for civil disobedience that read, "see Government, resistance to." But there was some temptation to see the phenomenon it referred to as nothing new. Hannah Arendt contended in the *New Yorker*, for example, that "civil disobedients are nothing but the latest form of voluntary association, and that they are thus quite in tune with the oldest traditions of the country."[75] New or old, there appeared to be increasing consensus that civil disobedience was "here to stay," that it was likely to enjoy "a progressively expanding role," and that it was not a sign of weakness but rather a source of strength in America's democratic system.[76] Both critics and advocates of disobedience agreed that matters of the greatest urgency were at issue. Arendt's adoption of the image of a "smoldering volcano"[77] did not seem overwrought.

So long as civil disobedients had presented themselves as men and women of moral principle, ready to submit to the penalty of the law, strong claims for respect and tolerance could be presented. By the turn of the decade the charge that civil disobedience was merely a tactical position adopted by revolutionaries who behaved like outlaws and conspired with criminals no longer seemed so far-fetched. The columnist Stewart Alsop in *Newsweek* in 1971 defined civil disobedience as "a euphemism for breaking those laws in which the law breaker does not believe." It had, he commented, "become both respectable and relatively safe. The civil rights movement of the early sixties began to make it respectable, and the increasing unpopularity of the Vietnam war has helped to make it safe as well as respectable."[78] To the well-known author Father Andrew Greeley, the "New Left of the 1970s" was comparable to the Nazi Party in Germany of the 1930s, rejecting reason and rationality, disrupting universities and other institutions, spreading impatience with liberal reformers, moving steadily toward violence.[79] "Disobedience abounds," growled the University of Chicago constitutional scholar Herbert J. Storing, "but it has thrust civility aside." Like some other critics, Storing professed support of the civil disobedients' goals while faulting the weakness of their political strategy. There had been too little consideration of the question "whether the encouragement of disobedience endangers law and civil society, and the answer seems clear enough today, if it was ever in doubt, that it does."[80]

Some writers on civil disobedience were prominent political figures like Justices Abe Fortas and William O. Douglas; as a sign of the extent of the audience for the topic, some of their works were mass-market paper-backs.[81] Mailer's book on the siege of the Pentagon won a Pulitzer Prize. Writers on civil disobedience included moral philosophers, law professors, and political theorists who discovered a sizeable audience for discussions of obligation and conscience. As Mulford Q. Sibley rejoiced in 1965, "Dry questions that a few years ago seemed to be appropriate only for desiccated professors of philosophy have suddenly taken on new life."[82] Surveying this voluminous recent literature on civil disobedience in 1983, I was much impressed by "the most sustained discussion of political obligation at any time since the 1850s, perhaps in all of American history."[83] The trade books and scholarly investigations may still stand today on library shelves (if they have not been relegated to storage repositories or used book bins) next to calls to "direct action" and justifications of "nonviolent resistance" written by admirers of Martin Luther King, Jr., or A. J. Muste or by veterans of SDS or SNCC. Although there has been excellent scholarship on the civil rights movement and university conflicts, the intellectual focus has shifted from nonviolence and civil disobedience. Because of the persistence of civil disobedience in American life, however, it is important to take note of the serious debates surrounding that subject in the heyday of the 1960s and 1970s.

With the familiarity of civil disobedience came recurrent debate over when, if it all, it was legitimate. Martin Luther King, Jr., always had critics who championed law and order and appealed to the virtues of moderation and restraint. That was the case with the Birmingham ministers whose published appeal for moderation King singled out in his strong words from their city's jail. Many years later, afforded another chance to be heard, they still defended their cautious temporizing without showing much sign of recognizing King's logic in the revolution through which they all were passing.[84] With no pretense of moderation, the intellectuals gathered by the *National Review* during its ascent as the voice of a new conservative intellectual movement rejected the doctrines of racial equality, majority rule, and cultural integration so long as the South did "not exploit the fact of Negro backwardness to preserve the Negro as a servile class." (Its founder William F. Buckley later regretted that stance.) Specifically on civil disobedience, the theologian Will Herberg contended in the *National Review* that the only laws that a Christian or Jew was entitled to violate were those commanding idolatry. In a moment of national panic he charged that King and the "apostles of 'non-violence' " were "the guilty ones" to blame for the looting and rioting of the 1965 Watts riots. For years the civil rights advocates had been "deliberately undermining the foundations of internal order in this country," with the result that they had subverted the "secure internal order based on custom and respect for constituted authority" that previous generations had achieved despite the challenges of immigration and the frontier.[85]

More surprising than *NR*'s expressly conservative views may be the observation of Herbert Storing, in an essay completed a few days before the murder of Martin Luther King, Jr., that civil disobedience was widely recognized as obsolete or irrelevant to "the problems of today." Storing professed great respect for King, and he recognized that nonviolent direct action had forced public attention on long-neglected issues of racial subjugation and won some important victories in public accommodations. But it was at most a tactic, and its lack of a political capacity meant that it could not achieve revolutionary goals and thus made it vulnerable to the criticisms of Malcolm X and other black radicals. Storing offered, in contrast, the example of Frederick Douglass, a "sitter-in" who moved from nonviolent abolitionism to utopian political action and then to the Republican Party and "patient reform" once it had accepted black people as American citizens. Storing did not answer the likely objection that a patient political stance had not empowered Douglass and the freedmen's allies to prevent the political repression that King and SNCC combated with nonviolent action. Storing did not refer to the war or its opponents, but his case against civil disobedience and for political action had relevance for issues besides civil rights.

The issue of political effectiveness was central to a 1968 symposium in the independent socialist magazine *Dissent*. Michael Walzer, an editor and at that time a professor at Harvard, addressed civil disobedience as a course of action tempting to many of his friends and readers in response to the "sheer ghastliness" of the war, but one that still required clear moral and political justification in what he termed "a partially democratic society" like the United States. Walzer, one of many writers who stressed the function of the word *civil* in discussions of civil disobedience, noted a requirement that "disobedience, when it is thought necessary, be of a carefully limited character, that it aim at specific changes (not necessarily minor ones) in law, policy, or social structure, but not at a total transformation of state or society." The "self-limitation" showed itself especially by a commitment to nonviolence during the law breaking and arrest. In this approach to civil disobedience it was important to consider the political consequences of any action—what effect might be expected on those whose opposition to the war was more moderate or timorous? Nothing should be done that prevented the buildup of the largest possible, politically significant, antiwar movement. In the months ahead Walzer in fact worked actively in the Eugene McCarthy campaign.[86]

Walzer sent his short position paper to four other writers, who did not generally share his caution about the tactical usefulness of civil disobedience to the antiwar movement. The philosopher Hilary Putnam thought it would be more "hurtful if electoral politics and resistance" came to be viewed as alternatives or antitheses rather than as complementary tactics. It was highly unlikely that either electoral politics or civil disobedience could end the war in 1968; both could possibly contribute to movement building and that was the important objective in the longer run. In the near term, as Walzer had neglected to say, there were obligations that arose from considerations that were moral rather than tactical. When young men refused induction, at the risk of heavy fines and sentences, and their supporters protested at induction centers, was there not some obligation to show support for those who acted, "not as a tactic at all, but as a moral duty?"[87] Robert Pickus, a Quaker and pacifist leader, also rejected the idea that civil disobedience, which was really a form of persuasion, might be antithetical to "more moderate forms of political action" in building an effective antiwar movement. He emphasized, however, that he referred to "*genuine* civil disobedience," whose practitioners eschewed violence and accepted the law's penalties, not to crazies and insurrectionists who boasted of "accepting all means necessary, including sabotage and armed resistance, to make it difficult if not impossible for the U.S. to continue to slaughter people in other countries as well as in the ghettos at home."[88]

Arnold S. Kaufman, a political scientist experienced in the teach-ins, stressed the potential weakness of radical responses to the war that exaggerated reliance on individual civil disobedience and left political action unexplored. "Thoreau's position," he wrote, "is morally, hence politically, irresponsible." It was encouraging, therefore, to witness "the present resurgence of conventional political activity," especially as shown in the McCarthy campaign. "Only *mindless radicals* equate radicalism with the most extreme tactics and refuse to try to make existing political institutions function in behalf of radical goals."[89]

Henry Pachter, a German émigré and New York intellectual who taught at City College, showed even less respect for civil disobedience, which he described in terms similar to those of Greggian jiu-jitsu. "Let's be frank: civil disobedience and nonviolent resistance are neither civil nor nonviolent in intention: they always are designed to reveal the opponent's inability to maintain civility and nonviolence." His remarks seemed to be colored by encounters with "naive" New Left students and contempt for "the antics of the flower children." In support of his rejection of civil disobedience, Pachter, like many other critics, cited Socrates's acceptance of the judges' authority to sentence him to death. It was not clear how much hope Pachter placed in political action in pursuit of antiwar aims.[90]

"Disobedience" in the *Dissent* symposium never focused on violating specific laws in order to challenge their constitutionality. The focus instead was on militant opposition to the war. Thus at a time when, as Walzer put it, "some of us" were thinking of engaging in "kinds of civil disobedience far more serious than those in which we were enthusiastically involved during the early years of the civil rights struggle," no thought was being given to the kind of law breaking most often considered justifiable by scholars, politicians, and judges. The institution of judicial review provides for what Storing called "a kind of tamed or civilized 'civil disobedience,'" as it diverts "civil disobedience and even revolution into the channel of law" while it also "mediates" between the claims of legislators and governors and "the universal claims of justice" as discovered in "the higher positive law of the Constitution."[91] Skill in making use of that kind of process is what Thurgood Marshall and the NAACP brought to the civil rights revolution, but it is doubtful that many opponents of the U.S. wars by 1968 were especially concerned about changing interpretations of their rights under the law. They wanted the wars to stop.

And yet many accommodations and justifications of civil disobedience went about as far as Storing's "mediating" position (perhaps with references to Socrates or Gandhi or Rosa Parks) and no further. Some ventured not so far. In presenting his stand that in a society like ours there is no "right" of civil disobedience, Eugene V. Rostow, formerly dean of Yale Law School and a State Department official in the Lyndon Johnson administration, created an "imaginary dialogue" between Socrates and Thoreau in which the former, submitting to the decision of "a reasonable legal system," has the last word and drinks his poison.[92]

Socrates, Gandhi, and Rosa Parks were all featured in the short book that was a best seller among mass-market paperbacks: *Concerning Dissent and Civil Disobedience* by Abe Fortas, a Supreme Court justice and close advisor to President Johnson. "We have an alternative to violence," the book quoted itself on its cover, not to the violence in Vietnam but to violent confrontations in the United States. Sometimes law breaking was necessary, as events in the segregated South had shown, but the law breakers still must be ready to "acquiesce in the ultimate judgment of the courts." Protesters must serve their penalties if the Supreme Court or another deciding authority finds their actions unlawful or the end they sought unconstitutional. Fortas emphasized this point by referring to two decisions in which he participated where the outcome was decided by a five-to-four majority and exploring a series of considerations that might have changed the outcomes. A reader might therefore have concluded that "the law" is a highly uncertain business. But Fortas emphasized that protesters cannot expect to get away with violating "valid" laws no matter how admirable their cause or adamant their feelings (he alluded to a case under review on draft card burning). He praised Martin Luther King, Jr., for accepting, "without complaint or histrionics," the penalty incurred by his "misjudgment." Without mentioning the famous letter from the Birmingham jail, Fortas acclaimed King's imprisonment, about which he had no choice, as "action in the great tradition of social protest in a democratic society where all citizens, including protesters, are subject to the rule of law."[93]

This emphasis on submission to court-defined law as the hallmark of a "great tradition" may seem less puzzling if we remember that from the 1950s onward much of the dramatic advance in civil rights had depended on enforcement of federal decisions against local opposition. The crisis in Little Rock centered on compelling obedience to a legal decision. In his radio address to the nation on the admission of James Meredith to the University of Mississippi, as ordered by an appeals court and enforced by federal marshals, President Kennedy said: "Our nation is founded on the principle that observance of the law is the eternal safeguard of liberty and defiance of the law is the surest road to tyranny. . . . Americans are free, in short, to disagree with the law, but not to disobey it."[94] Writing in the Birmingham jail, King had noted that his clergymen critics expressed "a great deal of anxiety over our willingness to break laws," and he acknowledged that the concern was "legitimate."

> Since we so diligently urge people to obey the Supreme Court's deci-
> sion of 1954 outlawing segregation in the public schools, it is rather
> strange and paradoxical to find us consciously breaking laws. One
> may well ask: "How can you advocate breaking some laws and obeying
> others?" The answer is found in the fact that there are two types of
> laws: There are just laws and there are unjust laws. I would be the first
> to advocate obeying just laws. One has not only a legal but moral
> responsibility to obey just laws. Conversely, one has a moral respon-
> sibility to disobey unjust laws. I would agree with Saint Augustine
> that "An unjust law is no law at all."

On this important distinction he also cited St. Thomas Aquinas and the
modern theologians Martin Buber and Paul Tillich.

The image of a person sitting in jail in dramatic protest against an
unjust law was central to civil disobedience in the American tradition. Still,
Fortas's emphasis on precarious five-to-four decisions, with "liberal"
judges sometimes voting on the "wrong" side and with hypothetical factors
that might have reversed the outcome, may seem odd in a paean to anything
called a "great tradition" upholding "the rule of law."[95] King, after all, was
working to change the way in which "the law" was enforced in the Deep
South, and he acted not as a solitary Thoreauvian individual but as one
leader of a rising popular movement. Well before Fortas wrote, CORE,
SNCC, and other organizations were guiding groups through workshops
on nonviolent action, and a manual of advice and information from organizing and demonstrating to behavior under arrest and in jail was available
in paperback.[96]

One champion of civil disobedience, for whom Fortas's "great tradition" amounted to "the sanctification of the law," was Howard Zinn, a
historian from an immigrant, working-class background, a World War II
veteran who had served as a bombardier in Germany and went to college
on the G.I. Bill, a Columbia Ph.D. who became head of the history department at Spelman College in Atlanta, where he marched with his students,
became an advisor to SNCC, angered his administration, and got fired,
with a settlement that gave him a year to write two more books on SNCC
and southern race relations. After securing a position at Boston University,
he had an extremely successful writing career, almost always focusing on
American traditions of popular protest and the defense of civil disobedience. His *Disobedience and Democracy* was a sharply negative response to

Fortas's public identification with the legal repression of draft resistance. Fortas voted with the 7–1 Supreme Court majority affirming the conviction of David O'Brien under the 1965 law against draft card burning and rejecting the argument that the law violated his First Amendment right to free expression. A Boston judge presiding at the U.S. district court conviction of Dr. Spock, Coffin, and two other men (a fifth was found not guilty) invoked Fortas's best-selling booklet—"Lawlessness cannot be tolerated"—and added his own warning: "Where law and order stops, obviously anarchy begins."[97]

An additional sign of the times for Zinn was the legislation, now nearly forgotten, called the Civil Obedience Act of 1968, enacted as one title in an omnibus Civil Rights Act passed during riots after Dr. King's assassination and expected to outlaw most housing discrimination. The Civil Obedience Act established fines and imprisonment for anyone demonstrating the use of Molotov cocktails, transporting weapons, or obstructing firemen or police officers during a civil disorder. The only arrest under the act came in 1970 when Howard Mechanic, a student at Washington University in St. Louis, was convicted of tossing a cherry bomb toward police and firefighters trying to put out a fire at an Air Force ROTC building, amid a large crowd of protesters, on the night of the Kent State shootings. (Sentenced to five years in prison, he went underground for twenty-eight years. Eventually discovered, he served almost a year before receiving a pardon from President Clinton in 2001.)[98] One other use of the act turned up years later in FBI files, released by court order, revealing the Nixon administration's 1971–72 attempt to deport John Lennon and thereby prevent concerts and rallies across the country leading up to the Republican National Convention. Such rallies, it was claimed, would violate the Civil Obedience Act.[99]

Identifying a series of "fallacies" in Fortas's booklet and other official attempts to suppress resistance, Zinn rejected the extreme concern about dissent and protest, the excessive nervousness about disorder, the insistence that all disobedients had to be willing to serve jail time, or that even a little violence was always intolerable, anarchic, or un-American. So much for the great tradition! Zinn also had occasion to testify repeatedly in courtrooms and in the media as an expert witness for civil disobedients on trial.[100] The civil disobedience he defended might not be purely nonviolent in the spirit of Gandhi or his American interpreters, though he advised its practitioners to "choose tactics which are as nonviolent as possible, consistent with the effectiveness of their protest and the importance of the issue."[101]

In retrospect, though with a few conspicuous exceptions like Rostow, it is striking how little effort there was in the United States in the 1960s and 1970s to curtail the respectability of civil disobedience, how extensive agreement there was on its strengthening influence on our institutions. The successes of the civil rights movement in violating unjust local statutes while appealing to neglected amendments to the Constitution and important Supreme Court decisions and dramatizing the need for better federal legislation obviously help to explain this pattern. The criminal acts that cost Agnew and Nixon their offices may also have discredited their hatred of civil disobedients. Martin Luther King, Jr., and Thurgood Marshall, one a martyr, the other a Supreme Court justice, protected civic activism and civil rights. The philosophical exploration of civil disobedience that began to flourish in the 1960s showed no sign of diminishing as a shared international concern, inspired by conflict in the United States but referring as well to Britain, South Africa, and around the world.[102]

In the works of many American writers of the 1960s and 1970s we can see a shared goal of setting limits for disobedience that could confer legitimacy on some illegal acts while rejecting others. A pattern of legitimizing and delimiting civil disobedience is evident in views as different as Abe Fortas's and Hannah Arendt's, though they disagreed considerably on what was its proper scope. Fortas, Storing, and especially Rostow would have limited it to the testing of the "constitutionality" of allegedly unjust laws while upholding the "rule of law" as the basis of civic obligation. Arendt imagined a "niche" for disobedience comparable to those enjoyed by lobbies and pressure groups—a view she linked to Tocqueville's nineteenth-century observations on the vitality of nongovernmental citizens' groups in American life. In looking beyond individuals facing the law, her views had at least something in common with Zinn's and Lynd's focus on popular activism and with the rejection by Patricia Roberts Harris of Rostow's "'drink the hemlock' theory" of minority acquiescence in all decisions of the majority. Harris, a Howard University law professor who had been a sit-inner in her student days at Howard in the 1940s and later served as secretary of housing and urban development and then of health, education, and welfare in the Carter administration, insisted that civil disobedience was a "rational and often essential extension" of democracy.[103] The pattern is evident in the monographs of philosophers and political theorists asking under what conditions the obligation to obey the law is suspended—an ancient issue in philosophy, to be sure, but now raised in response to urgent public controversy. The etiquette of legitimacy was well illustrated by the National Council of Churches of Christ, which formulated ground rules for peaceful and orderly civil disobedience, kept within the bounds of "Christian tradition and the American political and legal heritage."[104]

10

The Day of the Demonstrations Isn't Over

Perhaps the most inaccurate generalization about civil disobedience in the late 1960s, and asserted by one of its most intelligent observers, was the political scientist Herbert J. Storing's prediction that because of its irrelevance to contemporary problems, "the fashion in civil disobedience seems likely to die out as quickly as it burst into flame with the actions of the Montgomery bus boycotters and the words of Martin Luther King."[1] Most observers today would call that prediction mistaken, though there exists a tendency to forget the bitter and violent conflicts of the era and regard the sit-ins, be-ins, teach-ins, bed-ins, and other "-ins" as bygone fads like ukelele playing and goldfish swallowing in the 1920s.[2] But some at the time thought civil disobedience had reached its limits, though resorting to democratic politics also had frustrations. In the months before his assassination King and his associates debated the future of nonviolence and civil disobedience. "The day of the demonstrations isn't over," said King as he proposed a "camp-in," evoking memories of previous marches on Washington and confronting the nation's politicians with issues of poverty.[3] After his death, the camp-in would be realized as a "poor people's campaign," with few results to offset skeptics' doubts about the political effectiveness of nonviolent demonstrations.

Rumors of civil disobedience's death were exaggerated, but there were signs of burn-out, misfires, and contracted aims and by the end of the 1970s a detectable lull or doldrums. Leaders had died or aged; important publications like *Liberation* had closed down; college generations (as always) turned over rapidly; and with a disgraced Nixon driven from office,

America defeated in Vietnam, changes in the nominating processes to prevent a recurrence of Chicago 1968, and two presidents (Ford and Carter) trying in different ways to cool the antagonisms of the recent past, civility became a watchword and disobedience seized fewer headlines. There were claims of subdued symbolic triumph for the preceding era's idealism. Carter captured a national wish when he declared, mangling a Bob Dylan lyric, after many months of campaigning, "We have an America that . . . is busy being born, not busy dying."[4] Neither Ford nor Carter had especially successful presidencies, but the streets were quieter.

As the heyday of Gandhian militancy subsided, some commentators remembered the nonviolent protests of a few years before as preferable to the disorder they competed with. There was in many quarters an effort to redefine civil disobedience as part of the American constitutional and political system, to give it legitimacy, to set rules for conduct, to repudiate or isolate unruly versions, to see it as essential to moral progress and order, and to downplay the idea that it ought to entail penalties—except perhaps reduced ones if played out within the rules. That endeavor is a principal subject of this chapter. We have already glimpsed it in Arendt's appeal to give civil disobedience a constitutional niche, and it had appeared in hand-books and guidelines published by lawyers and judges, by clergy and religious organizations, and by scholars and pundits. Legitimized and to some degree circumscribed—that was the new status of civil disobedience. Well, perhaps not altogether new. Shridharani, in particular, had emphasized Gandhi's guidelines for courteous behavior and appearance, and King and southern ministers had tried to establish a kind of civility that SNCC and other student movements sometimes rejected as bourgeois. But the many discussions of guidelines, objectives, and penalties could be read as a significant adjustment in public policy.

By the mid-seventies the new legitimacy scarcely mattered as civil disobedience subsided on most campuses and in many cities. The voluminous recent literature on resistance looked almost quaint. Instances of civil disobedience in the early eighties were few and far between. Students didn't have the vaguest idea (at least in my informal sample) what the term meant. Nor were they concerned. Perhaps civil disobedience had become at most a historical subject of interest to scholars in philosophy and religious ethics. The volcano described by Hannah Arendt seemed dormant.

But perhaps it only seemed so, and not for long. In 1974 Sam Lovejoy, a veteran of antiwar protests at Amherst College and resident of an organic farm in western Massachusetts, decided on his own to foil the government's scheme to sneak "nukes" into the sparsely populated area. In the middle of the night, using a crowbar, he unbuckled the supports and toppled a five-hundred-foot-tall weather tower collecting information preparatory to installation of a twin nuclear power plant. He hitched a ride in a passing police car to the police station where he informed the sergeant on duty that the tower was missing and handed him a prepared statement explaining his action. Accepting only minimal legal representation so that he could speak for himself at his "unbelievable" two-week trial, he enlisted a "nuclear expert" to testify on the dangers of radiation and Howard Zinn to testify on civil disobedience (notably, he explained that damage to property did not qualify as violence). The judge threw out the indictment on a technicality, dismissed the jury, and Lovejoy did not have to spend several months in jail as he had anticipated. The twin nuclear plants were never built. As an antinuclear organizer traveling "all over the country" in the next two years, he was a founder of the Clamshell Alliance in New Hampshire, with its "model of attacking a nuclear plant by occupying the building site," active in organizing the Abalone Alliance in California, and engaged, as he put it, in "civil disobedience training for like 15 or 20 organizations." Few new plants were proposed, and some old ones were closed down. Lovejoy's reflection on his initial, individual deed: "When you do a radical act, you give instant credibility to all the more moderate people who looked like they were radicals before." But some residents of the region considered his deed an act of terrorism resembling actions of the Weather Underground and warned that radical acts like Lovejoy's could be adopted by movements on the political right as well as the left.[5]

In spite of factional disagreements over tactics of confrontation and the limitations of nonviolence, Barbara Epstein has described "the intoxicating, almost addictive nature of civil disobedience" in campaigns to close down nuclear power installations and nuclear weapons laboratories in New Hampshire and California.[6] In the early 1980s, women's marches sought to encircle the Pentagon and weave its doors shut with colored yarn, and at Seneca Army Depot, New York, and the Nevada Test Site, women held vigils, climbed over fences, painted messages, and wove webs. Thousands were arrested, some repeatedly. Despite the often colorful and theatrical protests, these actions eschewed conventional politics while professing revolutionary and countercultural goals. They remained, except in the localities where they occurred, marginal.

Public attention to civil disobedience might be sporadic, but predictions that it would die out were contradicted by protests against South African apartheid. In autumn 1984 civil disobedience at the South African Embassy in Washington became daily news. Beginning on November 21, with arrests of District of Columbia delegate to Congress Walter Fauntroy, attorney Randall Robinson, and U.S. Commission on Civil Rights member Mary Berry, this anti-apartheid activity soon was joined by Senator Lowell Weicker, nineteen congressmen, Coretta Scott King, Amy Carter, and other well-known Americans. "We had no idea that what we did last Thanksgiving eve ... would amount to anything more than a personal statement," said Robinson according to the *New York Times*, which noted "a tinge of life revisited" at this new inception of civil disobedience. "My God," said civil rights veteran and Georgetown University professor Eleanor Holmes Norton, "middle-aged professionals talking about sitting in again after all these years." By August 1985 the *Times* reported: "The protest has become a velvet-rope success in Washington and other cities as Kennedy children have called up along with entertainers, scrambling politicians and an ever enlarging spectrum of Establishment leaders to book 'arrest opportunity' time outside the embassy."[7] From Kansas, Columbia, Wesleyan, and other campuses came further news of civil disobedience and hundreds of arrests. At Cornell over one thousand anti-apartheid arrests were reported, many of them in connection with building and rebuilding a shantytown on the arts quadrangle in protest against the university's continuing investments in companies making profits in South Africa. Todd Gitlin, an SDS veteran, surveying events at Berkeley and other campuses, noticed that students disliked comparisons with their predecessors twenty years before. Nonetheless, they were "reinventing," as he put it, "the history of the 1960s."[8]

Apartheid had few defenders and existed far away: thus it could provide a "velvet rope attraction." There were other indications of civil disobedience recapturing the aura of urgency that surrounded it a decade before. One day, members of the Young Conservative Foundation were holding a sit-in in the office of California Assemblyman Tom Hayden (of SDS fame) because he declined to sign a petition protesting the University of California's investments in companies doing business in the USSR.[9] Then, members of Earth First! masqueraded as bears and demanded rooms and meals at a Yellowstone hotel. For their protests against humanity's incursion into the bears' habitat, they were arrested and fined.[10] Then sit-inners at the University of Pennsylvania's Head Injury Research Laboratory stole videotapes of experiments on primates.[11] After that, anti-abortion movements received the most publicity for acts of civil disobedience; they also were most explicit in connecting their actions to a tradition dating back to antislavery movements. I will return to them. But there seemed to be no political issue that could not generate instances, super-serious or irreverent: "Civil disobedience is the only thing politicians listen to," asserted a Guardian Angel as he jumped a turnstile at the start of the new year 1992 to protest a fare increase on the New York subways.[12] At the news that Mayor Edward Koch was openly defying New York's law against taking wine into restaurants that lacked liquor licenses, the columnist William Safire gibed: "This example of civil disobedience is worthy of Henry David Thoreau, and we all look forward to that picture of the Mayor brandishing a brown bag behind bars, his acceptance of incarceration giving meaning to his beliefs."[13]

In a serious and recurrent effort, news stories on civil disobedience sought to differentiate between rowdiness and order, peacefulness and violence, illegality and legitimacy. The *Nation* reported sadly that besides "decorous" disobedients who were arrested, Berkeley had a problem with slobs, vandals, and "hotheads" looking for "ways to escalate the protest." Reporters noted splits in the anti-abortion movement between "mainstreamers" and "confrontationists." Similar disputes surfaced in the contest for the presidency of the National Organization of Women.[14] "Bombing is not civil disobedience" and "Moralism's Limits" were the boldface captions on an op-ed piece by Tom Wicker. It was "intellectually fallacious to equate bombing an abortion clinic with civil rights sit-ins," he wrote; the "true" civil disobedient broke the law publicly and accepted an unjust legal penalty while the bomber operated stealthily and destructively.[15]

Comments like these were reminders that civil disobedience has sometimes gained acceptance in the United States as an alternative to actions more threatening to public order. Without minimizing the importance of the issues on which reformers of the left and right disagreed with each other and among themselves, we can detect some consensus on available strategic choices. If we think in terms of three categories of action—*mainstreaming, civil disobedience,* and *terrorism*—the first was clearly more orderly than the second, though opinions may differ over which would be more effective. But the world had also entered the age of the terrorist, guerrilla, militia man, who might be imagined to be a kind of voluntary convert from more peaceful strategies. After a bomb exploded at Frankfurt airport in 1985, a group made up, apparently, of environmental activists and calling itself the Peace Conquerors, took credit for the damage and threatened more. "They have *chosen* violence, they said, 'because it is our final and only solution.' " "It doesn't bother us if women and children are killed," their statement continued, omitting men as perhaps too obvious. "There is no innocence."[16] The threat of this third category made the civil disobedient, the person in the middle, appear orderly, law-abiding, decorous, responsible.

Discussions of civil disobedience often emphasize the law. For Gandhi, respect for law and a willingness to accept its penalties were prerequisites to civil disobedience. Americans have sometimes made the same point— only the morally righteous, those who respect civil law and accept its binding force, can violate specific laws.[17] Gandhi criticized his own "Himalayan" mistakes in inciting undisciplined people. Newspaper editorials sometimes threw that example at Martin Luther King, Jr. On the eve of his assassination the *New York Times* urged King not to make a similar " 'Himalayan miscalculation' by asking his people to adopt civil disobedience before they understood or were ready for it."[18] Yet it is obvious that civil disobedience—or "CD"—is sometimes no more than a tactic adopted to stimulate the democratic system, a way of exerting pressure and attracting publicity. And the democratic system may be challenged more severely by the morally righteous, united in substantial numbers in defiance of laws that others uphold.

In the late 1970s several Christian groups had begun to mobilize activity against the Supreme Court's decision in *Roe v. Wade* (1973) that a woman had a right to choose to terminate a pregnancy during the period before the fetus became "viable" (determined to be about twenty-eight weeks) and in some circumstances even later. One of the most controversial decisions in the history of the court, it voided prohibitions on most abortions in every state and strengthened the right for couples, and especially women, to determine family size without state interference. It led, almost immediately, to new state laws and federal lawsuits intended to overturn or limit the reach of *Roe*. Supporters of women's rights mobilized in defense of "choice," and other citizens' groups, often motivated by religious convictions, campaigned to reverse the *Roe* decision and protect the lives of the defenseless unborn. Of course no one conceived or terminated a fetus in order to uphold the law, and many supporters and opponents of *Roe* expressed themselves through conventional political action. Nevertheless, the decision unleashed waves of angry protest by groups seeking to close down family planning clinics, to "persuade" pregnant women not to use them, or to influence state officials to raise issues that might get the Supreme Court to narrow its ruling. The result was a torrent of words and actions concerning the morality of abortion, the uses of civil disobedience, and the limits on dissent.

In 1978 a federal judge in Alexandria, Virginia, enjoined eleven "right to life" demonstrators from invading a clinic or harassing others who were going in and out. In Maryland protesters were convicted of trespassing when they refused to leave a clinic at the request of police, though other judges had given acquittals in similar cases. In a letter to the *Washington Post*, Robert J. Henle, a philosophy professor at Saint Louis University (and former president of Georgetown), explained that "if one is convinced that abortion is a violation of the primary and most sacred civil and human right," then of course one would try to "reduce the number of abortions and thereby save as many human lives as possible." In time, he predicted, *Roe* will be "classed with *Dred Scott*" for its denial of human rights. However it is regarded in the future, the *Post* editorialized, "that decision is now law," and those who avail themselves of it should not be intimidated or attacked, and its opponents must stay within "legal bounds," as Father Henle had done in writing his letter, or "choose the course of civil disobedience and accept the penalties." It was essential for judges to establish "firm, reasonable ground rules."[19] That was a lesson that many thought the 1960s had taught.

Ten years later, a portrait in the *Post* of a zealous activist, Christy Anne Collins, on trial in Richmond, showed how unresolved the boundaries of legitimate protest remained. Collins had at least nine previous arrests, usually going free with little or no penalty, for sitting in at clinics, blocking elevators, harassing patients with a bullhorn; in Richmond she told the judge that she had trespassed in order to prevent "a greater evil—the killing of the unborn." The judge admitted that he was "very much impressed" with Collins and her philosophy, but he had to apply the law—guilty and a $50 fine. She and her associates rejoiced that she could rejoin their activities.[20]

In the decades after the Supreme Court's 1973 decision, the boundaries and ground rules of legitimate protest were tested repeatedly, and often dramatically, without getting significantly clearer. Most abortions were no longer illegal and had become less dangerous; besides hospitals, hundreds of clinics made them routine (and some critics would say, turned atrocity into banality). A large percentage of the population accepted them, if done early, or if the pregnancy resulted from rape or incest or threatened the life of the mother. Dismayed by the slow pace at which political action during the Reagan administration or in the states succeeded in limiting abortions, opponents turned increasingly to direct action. Civil disobedience now became as commonplace at clinics as it had been at colleges and draft boards in fairly recent memory. Anti-abortion activism ensured that civil disobedience would not fade away, but it also raised questions rooted in uncompromisable convictions outside the religious and political mainstream, more similar to the Plowshares, Earth First!, or even the IWW or the Weather Underground than to sit-ins, boycotts, or campus vigils.

Much of the opposition was deeply religious. Collins was a lapsed Catholic, a former drug user, a McGovern worker, converted to a holy mission after hearing the word of God in an Episcopal service and going on to found Sanctity of Life Ministries, through which she received donations from various churches and individuals. To the *Post* reporter she was "a classic specimen of what Eric Hoffer called the True Believer—'the man of fanatical faith who is ready to sacrifice his life for a holy cause.'" That description would only partially fit the Catholic movement, Lambs for Christ, founded in 1989 by Rev. Norman Weslin, who aspired to imitate the serious commitment of Gandhi, Martin Luther King, Jr., and Mother Teresa (though with a tolerance of violent confrontation unequaled by those three). Their several thousand members included a tier of about one hundred zealots ready to leave home for months at a time, and some intended to spend the rest of their lives traveling together, doing good works, and offering up Hail Marys in the anti-abortion cause. They held vigils at the homes of clinic directors and pleaded with patients not to terminate their pregnancies, offering them food, shelter, medical care, even money, and crying out as ventriloquists for the unborn, "Mommy, please don't kill me." After practicing what they called "passive disobedience" to block clinic entrances and doctors' cars, they refused to cooperate with the authorities by giving their real names and instead took baby names when they went to jail. Martin Marty, a Lutheran religious scholar and University of Chicago professor, praised their revival of old traditions of sacrifice. Defenders of abortion rights found some of their tactics, especially offering money to pregnant women under stress, "outrageous." In the longer run, their association with at least one murderer and fugitive would tarnish their saintly image.[21]

"Hundreds of Christians plan to fan out across the capital," the *New York Times* reported in May 1985, "kneel down in Government offices and keep praying until they are arrested." Calling themselves Sojourners, these evangelicals saw themselves as "an emerging 'peace church,'" opposed to many Reagan administration policies and also seeking to end abortions. Critics red-baited the movement, calling them undeviatingly pro-Soviet, a charge that in the post–cold war era had lost some of its force. (They were in fact picketing the Soviet Embassy over the violence in Afghanistan.) Besides praying at the White House in opposition to the arms race, in support of aid to the poor, who were "the primary victims" of budget priorities, and for an end to violence in Central America, Sojourners also planned demonstrations at the South African Embassy for an end to apartheid and at the Supreme Court for an end to the death penalty. Central to these protests was the Department of Health and Human Services, where they would appeal for the unborn and for alternatives to abortion. With more than fifty thousand Protestant and Catholic subscribers to their journal *Sojourners*, and with support from the prominent revivalist Billy Graham, they portrayed themselves as a Christian alternative to right-wing televangelists who claimed to speak for a conservative "moral majority." Prior to the demonstrations, they held a three-day conference at Catholic University, publicized as "the first national gathering on Christian nonviolence and civil disobedience" and as a "signal to our Government and to the governments of other nations that there is serious and substantial resistance to their policies in the churches."[22]

Bombings and fires at clinics, frequently at night, followed by notes claiming responsibility for the "Army of God," signified changing tactics of anti-abortion movements in the early 1980s. A threatening letter to Justice Harry Blackmun, author of the *Roe* opinion, also referred to the Army of God. There were kidnappings, vandalism, slashed tires, splashed paint, threatening phone calls, and other menacing acts, though information about an organized Army of God was scarce. Other anti-abortion forces, out in the open and publicly persistent, laid claim to the nonviolent legacy of the civil rights movement. Joseph Scheidler, founder and leader of the Pro-Life Action League in Chicago and a key spokesman in national anti-abortion endeavors, had marched in Selma in his student days. He opposed "anything that would cause physical damage to property or person" but still favored strongly confrontational tactics. Author of a book subtitled *Closed: 99 Ways to Close the Abortion Clinics,* he described sit-ins as "obedience to a higher law. I'll stay after I'm told to leave as an act of desperation because I'm trying to save a life."[23] By emphasizing his right to engage in "sidewalk counseling," even in gangs or with a bullhorn, as pregnant women made their way to a clinic, he associated pro-life action with a highly controversial interpretation of free speech.[24]

Controversy heightened during anti-abortion campaigns in Atlanta during the 1988 Democratic National Convention, then in Hartford (1989), Wichita (1991), Buffalo (1991), and other cities. Scheidler was often prominent, but by far the most highly publicized movement was Operation Rescue (OR) and its attention-seizing founder Randall Terry, a charismatic Binghamton, New York, used car salesman and Pentecostal preacher who boasted that the movement had almost disappeared until he began to dominate the scene as "Mr. Anti-Abortion." The credo he imparted to the cause was simple: "If you believe abortion is murder, act like it is murder"— mass sit-ins blocking clinic doors were his favorite tactic—and "do everything possible to rescue babies and their mothers from the nightmare of abortion on the very doorstep of local abortion clinics" (which he called "abortuaries") was his strategy. "Everything possible" came to include making fake appointments and then chaining themselves inside clinics, pouring raw eggs and maple syrup on surgical equipment, shoving a dead fetus at presidential candidate Bill Clinton, and crossing the street, when ordered to do so, in "the Wichita baby walk," which might take forty-five minutes or more. As arrests and jail sentences mounted in besieged cities—almost 29,000 arrests by OR's count between May 1988 and June 1989, with Terry himself serving four months in a Georgia prison during a great radicalizing experience for pro-life leadership—he preached that the nation was in decline because of the persecution of altruistic Christians and the treachery of godless judges who were "in the hip pocket" of the multimillion-dollar abortion industry. Contrasting the fines and jail sentences he and his forces received to those imposed on the gay rights group Act Up for disrupting mass at St. Patrick's Cathedral, he said, "I'll tell you, if we were homosexual, we'd be treated a lot better in the courts." He also pointed to Gay Pride Week, AIDS, the banning of prayer in public schools, pornography, and no-fault divorce as signs of the nation's moral ruin. In time, he had to face further controversy over his own divorce and remarriage to a younger woman who had worked for him in a congressional campaign. He went on to careers in talk radio, religious songwriting, and political candidacy, and OR moved on under new leadership as Operation Save America.[25]

Terry led the anti-abortion cause to new heights of zeal, membership, and arrests, but a cause mobilized as a crusade in collision with the law, the courts, and American morality often looked like a force of lawless outsiders laying siege to a community. Majorities turned against them in cities like Buffalo, where they had expected a victorious welcome. When new controversy surrounded the movement because of threats and murders of doctors in Pensacola, Buffalo, Wichita, and other cities, Terry denied any involvement ("I hope he didn't do it," he said of one assassin whom he had met in jail in Atlanta). But he refused to reduce the tension: "If my little girl was about to be murdered," he was widely quoted as saying, "I certainly would not write a letter to the editor. If a child you love was about to have his arms and legs ripped off, what would you do? Would you write your congressman? No! You would do whatever you could to physically intervene and save the life of that child! That is the appropriate response to murder."[26] That logic undercut the traditional moderation of civil disobedience.

Anti-abortion protesters routinely compared themselves to Martin Luther King, Jr., and the civil rights protesters of a few decades before. In Atlanta in 1988 the Southern Baptist clergyman Jerry Falwell praised picketers for exhibiting the same spirit of "sacrifice" as civil rights demonstrators in the 1960s as he urged a national campaign of nonviolent civil disobedience in support of an anti-abortion amendment to the Constitution. Opponents retorted that there was nothing nonviolent about blocking clinics and harassing pregnant women. Civil rights veterans, like Julian Bond, were offended by the appropriation of King and the freedom riders by "yesterday's opponents of black rights" like Falwell. One dismissed the Operation Rescue demonstrators as people who "don't know anything about civil disobedience except that they were against it when blacks did it."[27] In Buffalo, too, these appropriations elicited "bewilderment and contempt" and were dismissed as "perverse" by city residents with actual experience in the civil rights movement. A *New York Times* reporter identified the out-of-towners' repeated equations of abortions in Buffalo with slavery and the Holocaust as an offensive flaw in Operation Rescue's strategy.[28]

Appropriation of the mantle of Martin Luther King, Jr., by people who gave him no support in his lifetime may have seemed disingenuous and infuriating. But not all "pro-life" activists in the 1980s and 1990s had been social conservatives in preceding decades. Daniel Berrigan and some Plowshares activists opposed abortions, though usually without seeking to criminalize them.[29] More important, some defenses of clinic blockades presented well-thought-out appreciation of the importance of civil disobedience in American history. In articulating the tradition, they helped to clarify and deepen understanding of it. Consider, for example, the argument prepared in 1991 for his attorney by an Oregon clergyman, Randy Alcorn, defending himself and thirty other pro-lifers sued for punitive damages by a Portland abortion clinic: "Peaceful civil disobedience has had a strategic role in defending human rights in our country." It is not "ordinary law breaking"; it is not "revolution"; and "the history of such disobedience is long and varied, and is woven into the very heart of our society." Its practitioners are "model citizens" who do not flee or defy the courts, acting in the tradition of the Underground Railroad and the civil rights movement.[30]

Memories of the 1960s and divergent views of the consequences of militant social protest in that decade were once again evident in 1992 congressional hearings on proposed federal legislation to protect access to clinics. Some witnesses reported on anti-abortion mobs that brought back memories of organized attacks on civil rights activists, with inadequate police protection, in Little Rock or Montgomery.[31] Other witnesses, however, placed the "pro-life" demonstrations in the context of a long history reaching back to the Boston Tea Party and including abolitionists, suffragists, and more recently, civil rights and antiwar activists. In the words of Jay Sekulow, OR's legal counsel, "Federalizing and criminalizing non-violent civil disobedience is an ominous development, jeopardizing a method of inducing societal change that is as American as Rev. Martin Luther King, Jr. . . . If Congress can criminalize obstruction of abortion facilities by anti-abortion protesters it can criminalize lunch counter sit-ins by blacks seeking equality under law, or the underground railroads run by sympathetic abolitionists."[32] Scheidler protested that "civil disobedience has been the recourse of citizens bent on redress of injustice from the beginning of our Nation's history." Some anti-abortion witnesses carefully distanced their actions from Terry's no-holds-barred tactics. "I've never once asked somebody to go and sit down in front of a door," said OR's director Keith Tucci, who had himself been imprisoned twice behind the "iron curtain" for aiding political prisoners. "I've told them to do what their conscience dictated to them as long as it was passive, nonviolent and to not injure or hurt a person's being or property."[33] Only one Army of God witness spoke in favor of destroying abortion facilities or "terminating" abortionists.[34] All anti-abortion witnesses protested that their activities were already punished by law more harshly than those of others and therefore there was no need for new legislation. Nevertheless, Congress in 1994 enacted the Freedom of Access to Clinic Entrances Act, which set ground rules in the continuing confrontations in many cities.

It might be misleading to imply that the abortion controversy really caused widespread reevaluation of radical abolitionists (or any other radicals). But to prominent political opponents of abortion slavery had the rhetorical advantage that it could be depicted as an evil institution to which immoderate disobedience had been justified, as was the case with abortions, too. When organizers of Missouri Citizens for Life staged their first big rally, drawing an estimated thirty thousand demonstrators ten months after the *Roe* decision, they chose a location in front of St. Louis's Old Courthouse, where the slave Dred Scott and his wife Harriet had launched the ultimately unsuccessful legal appeals for their liberty.[35] In the years that followed, as *Dred Scott* was equated with *Roe* (both were said to deny the value of a class of human lives), the Underground Railroad was celebrated as a precursor to the rescue of "babies" from "abortuaries." In a brief book titled *Abortion and the Conscience of the Nation*, published during his presidency, Ronald Reagan emphasized that equation and expressed a belief that if the Supreme Court took "another look" at *Roe* it might "change its mind once again," just as its *Brown* decision had reversed previous holdings on "separate but equal" education.[36]

The president said nothing about civil disobedience, but other earnest pro-lifers sought inspiration in antislavery history for their modern-day tactical choices. Jack C. Willke, a Cincinnati physician who lectured and published extensively on "the right to life," examined the slavery-abortion analogy, which the pro-choice side disputed, and reported that he became more and more convinced of its truth. Willke's analysis gets a little strained. For example, the tightening "noose of total control by pro-slavery forces" in pre–Civil War decades was comparable to "the mother's (the owner's) total control of her unborn baby (her property)," and as it drew "tighter and tighter," fathers, parents, and the state were powerless to interfere. On antislavery strategy and tactics, Willke criticized William Lloyd Garrison for his harsh language, his nonvoting pacifism, and for "excessively campaigning for women's rights"; he was pleased to report, however, that like their mainstream abolitionist counterparts, right-to-life leaders also "respect the law and continue to work under the law and through the law to again re-establish protection for an entire class of citizens, this time the unborn." He cited Charles Beecher's call to disobey the law, go to jail, and be rewarded by God on the "last day."[37]

It is unlikely that anti-abortion activists knew very much about "the underground railroads run by sympathetic abolitionists" (as Sekulow had called them). With their self-image as child-savers protecting the lives of helpless fetuses, they understandably showed no curiosity about a line of scholarship, already under way in the 1980s, that debunked the "myth" of the Underground Railroad and explored the actions and decisions of slaves, fugitives, and free blacks.[38] It is still significant that awareness, even if slightly distorted, of a tradition that sanctioned law breaking in good causes formed part of the political backdrop of the pro-life movement. For some, like Willke, there remained too much radicalism in the Garrisonian precedent, but others were engaged by debate over the place of "extremism" in American political and social life. In the nation's leading evangelical magazine, *Christianity Today*, one thoughtful writer came to "reluctant praise" of extremism after serious comparison of the abolitionists and OR, whereas a Buffalo pro-life clergyman rejected OR's insistence that "rescuing" was the most effective way to stop abortions.[39]

"Extremism" may not have been the most useful category to aid in understanding the anti-abortion protests, at least those which could be called "sit-ins." In an illuminating article, the legal scholar Bruce Ledewitz expressed dismay at the threat to a long-standing "practice of substantial toleration for sit-ins as a form of political practice," sometimes even spoken of as a right, frequently with no sanctions, increasingly familiar since the 1950s.[40] But were "rescues" really sit-ins? Toleration of some purposeful law breaking as part of the political process was severely challenged when protesters engaged in violence and damaged property, when arson occurred, and when murders of doctors and bodyguards were added to the means of protest. To some extent, OR sought to get beyond forms of moderate protest like sit-ins that had a respectable niche in American politics but did not always achieve immediately desired results; by provoking passage of the Clinic Act, with President Clinton's comment in signing it, that "as a nation we must remain committed to the rule of law," it came close to narrowing the means available to protesters.[41] Public recoil was just as evident when pro-choice women attempted to block bridges or tunnels or disrupt traffic to the inconvenience of uninvolved travelers. Some kinds of civil disobedience had gained acceptance as part of democratic politics, but there were lines that, according to widely held views, should not be transgressed.

Even as controversy over abortion led some commentators to comb through previous radical movements, with particular praise of the "underground railroad," few came to unqualified praise of William Lloyd Garrison. Willke's misgivings were not unusual. Some critics of OR actually preferred the example of the English reformer William Wilberforce, who worked in Parliament for over two decades to end slavery "legally, peacefully, noncoercively" and without the slaughter brought on by civil war in the United States.[42] It was hard either to imagine emancipation without Garrison or to ignore his divisive or perfectionist convictions—until his often-criticized, fiery pledge to be uncompromising, immoderate, unequivocating, a pledge said to have killed dialogue, was reprinted in an unlikely location, *First Things*, a journal by and for prominent intellectuals, some of whom had abandoned the left in the 1960s over its immoderation, its chilling effect on reasoned, respectful discourse, and especially religious discourse, in what it called the "public square." Its editor, Richard John Neuhaus, was a former Lutheran clergyman converted to Catholic priest and an antiwar liberal and civil rights champion whose course had been profoundly shaken by *Roe v. Wade*.[43] Indeed, the issue of abortion may be said to have angered him as slavery had aroused Garrison.

In November 1996, with a divisiveness comparable to Garrison's, *First Things* opened a long-enduring breach within conservatism by publishing a symposium entitled "The End of Democracy?" The furor was not a surprise. It had been predicted in editorial meetings, and Neuhaus in an introduction admitted the essays might be viewed as "irresponsibly alarmist."[44] The essays focused on recent court decisions concerning abortions, doctor-assisted suicides, same-sex marriages, and other issues considered vital to traditional religious teachings and to the views of life held by large numbers of citizens. The court decisions, it was argued, showed that American democracy was well on its way to being replaced by a "regime" in which unelected judges ruled without any popular mandate on issues of fundamental importance. One essay after another called for resistance, civil disobedience, or revolution.

It was hard to apply the notion of civil disobedience to abortions. Women had disobeyed the law when they had abortions as had doctors, of whatever level of competence, when they performed them. So how to break the law now? What examples from the past were relevant? Interspersed with the essays appeared classic statements on civil disobedience by Martin Luther King, Jr., and Dietrich Bonhoeffer (though both recognize limits set by divinely imposed expectations of obedience), and one essay was fully devoted to the 1995 encyclical of Pope John Paul II, "The Gospel of Life," calling for conscientious objection to civil law that violates moral truth. To predictable charges of extremism Neuhaus answered, "We do not believe the Pope is an alarmist." And there in the end appeared "Garrison on Proclaiming Moral Truths," a statement much criticized by scholars for decades until champions of the civil rights revolution began to read the Boston abolitionist with new appreciation: "Tell a man whose house is on fire, to give a moderate alarm; tell him to moderately rescue his wife from the hands of the ravisher; tell the mother to gradually extricate her babe from the fire into which it has fallen—but urge me not to use moderation in a cause like the present" (42). In a curious way the symposiasts, in denouncing the assumption of unwarranted power by Supreme Court and other federal justices in decisions that violated traditional conceptions of life and morality upheld by Catholicism, evangelicalism, and orthodox Judaism presented their position as a modern example of traditions of intransigent opposition.

Almost immediately, the symposium's editors were corrected by its only contributor with judicial experience, Robert Bork, expressing a wish that the editors had not preceded his essay with comments questioning the legitimacy of the "regime."[45] The magazine received letters of resignation from at least four of its editorial consultants, who objected to inflammatory, anti-American rhetoric in the style of 1960s radicalism.[46] Other conservative writers, though agreeing with criticisms of some judicial decisions, had no patience for the talk about insurrection. Norman Podhoretz, the editor of *Commentary*, called Neuhaus's posture "reminiscent of 'the extremist hysteria of the old counterculture of the 60's' which had driven both of us out of the left in the first place."[47] In the January issue of *First Things* Neuhaus wrote a long clarification regretting the resignations and insisting that he and the other editors had been misunderstood. It is doubtful that many readers found matters clarified. The crisis was still attributed to unelected judges who had a "problem" with religion and refused to base their decisions on moral law or the will of the people rather than their own opinions. "If, as we hope, we are not on the way to the end of democracy, the judiciary will restrain itself, or it will be restrained." How and by whom? He referred ominously to the "specter of violent revolution" as militia men trained in the Idaho woods, accompanied by caution that "the delusions of weekend revolutionaries should not set the boundaries of political change." Neuhaus denied that the symposium writers had issued a call to civil disobedience, at least not following the organized model associated with the civil rights movement and Martin Luther King, Jr. This was puzzling. Perhaps he backed off too far, inasmuch as organized civil disobedience remained common at clinics associated with the medical procedure under protest.

Critics sometimes noted with irony that Bork flirted with civil disobedience and even came close to advocating it. He spoke hypothetically of a public official defying a Supreme Court decision. That disobedience was linked with contempt for the student left and feminism and gratitude to the marines and the University of Chicago for correcting his own youthful errors.[48] In 1996 Bork wrote a best-selling book, *Slouching Towards Gomorrah*, a jeremiad on the hedonistic immorality of contemporary American life and near destruction of the moral foundations of American society, both of which he blamed on the student culture of the 1960s, particularly SDS's onslaught against traditional authority and radical feminism's antagonism to the family, and on the failure of liberal institutions to stand up to these obnoxious forces. Other targets were the diminished influence of traditional religious institutions and, unsurprisingly, the poorly reasoned opinions of judges, of which the most ridiculous to Bork, and hateful to other *First Things* voices, appeared in the Supreme Court's decision in *Planned Parenthood v. Casey*, a case that afforded an opportunity to overrule *Roe* (as Chief Justice Rehnquist urged) and reject its mistaken reliance on a "right of privacy." Instead, three of the majority justices spoke of a right to "personal dignity and autonomy" that was essential to "personhood." "At the heart of liberty," they continued, "is the right to define one's own concept of existence, of meaning, of the universe, and of the mystery of human life."[49] It is true that the *Casey* majority expressed much concern for the welfare of pregnant women and none for fetuses before they are viable. But it may also be true, though perhaps unintended, that the rhetoric of "personhood" could encourage new perspectives on many kinds of disabilities including deafness, with which this book started, and Down syndrome, for which pregnant women, their partners, and physicians frequently screen.[50] New perspectives could mean new expressions of civil disobedience.

To the theme of merciful respect for all human life that the *First Things* writers had publicized and the attacks on feminism and hedonism that energized his book, Bork added specific denunciation of assisted suicide, which Dr. Jack Kevorkian had turned into a well-publicized expression of civil disobedience. Dr. K. acknowledged assisting in 130 deaths, some of them in the back of his van, sometimes videotaping the use of a device he had invented to allow a patient to perform the termination of his or her own life. After escaping punishment in four trials (juries often refused to convict him), he was found guilty of second-degree murder in 1999 and eventually served eight years in prison before promising never to engage in another suicide. Bork puzzled over Kevorkian's high public approval, especially since some of his patients were not close to death (obviously many wished to make the decision while they retained control). The doctor had many critics, too. In speeches and interviews Kevorkian compared himself to Thoreau,[51] and after his death in 2011, some praised his actions as classic cases of civil disobedience raising discussion of unjust laws that restricted human dignity; others called the same actions murders, violations of religious and philosophical principle, an "abhorrent perversion" of that honored tradition.[52]

Civil disobedience was not initially an important factor in decisions whether to cease feeding comatose patients in a persistent vegetative state. Before the 1980s the law, medical practice, and even religious doctrine had not really been tested as they were in the case of Nancy Cruzan, a young Missouri woman injured in a car crash in 1983.[53] She had suffered permanent brain damage from lack of oxygen; her life was sustained intravenously for several months and thereafter via a feeding tube directly into her stomach. Four years later, her family, accepting the fact that she would not get better, asked the rehabilitative center to unhook the tube. It refused, largely over liability issues, and her putative welfare became a legal dispute in which the state supreme court overruled lower courts by a 4–3 vote and required "clear and convincing evidence" that refusal of further medical treatment was what Nancy herself would have wanted. For her family this was six years after her irreversible coma had begun. In June 1990 a highly divided U.S. Supreme Court did little to clarify the matter except to agree that Nancy's own wishes should determine whether the feeding tube could be withdrawn. Five months later, three of Nancy's friends testified to conversations in which she had said that she would never want to live "like a vegetable" (a topic under discussion because of cases in the news), the state dropped out of the issue, and the feeding tube was removed, giving her about two weeks to die—but not without a last-minute intervention by Randall Terry and other OR veterans who converged on Missouri, staged a sit-in in Attorney General William Webster's office, and attempted to enter the rehabilitation center and reinsert the tube on their own. Describing their campaign as "anti-euthanasia," they carried signs reading "HOW WOULD YOU LIKE TO BE STARVED TO DEATH?" In the rehabilitation center they employed "the tactics of civil disobedience" when their progress was blocked, falling on their knees, flourishing Bibles and rosaries, and praying loudly. The family observed that their harassers were only interested in press coverage. One of these OR activists, the one designated to "drop a tube" down Nancy's throat, told an author reporting on the event that "it has to do with life." She had a child with Down syndrome. "It doesn't matter whether you are talking about an unborn child or a person like Nancy. I believe that even people in that situation are valuable. When we take care of them, *we* become more compassionate caring for them."[54]

Humanitarian concern for the disabled had a long history, and some scholars have said that among all the minorities pressing for civil rights after the 1960s "Americans—or at least their government leaders—[saw] disabled Americans as the most deserving." Their inclusion in "the minority rights revolution was ... remarkably easy and appropriate."[55] But it was never unopposed. It took sit-ins in Washington in the 1930s to force consideration of the "handicapped" for Works Progress Administration jobs. With protests by returning World War II veterans, it became increasingly evident that humanitarian concern for the disabled was being transposed into movements by the disabled themselves to win their own struggle for independent living. As their status changed from beneficiaries to lobbyists to citizen activists, public reaction was mixed, but they often gained the feelings of achievement through struggle characteristic of a civil rights movement. An article published by the Institute on Community Integration at the University of Minnesota calls attention to political action and voter participation by persons with developmental disabilities and adds that others have participated in politics by means of direct action and civil disobedience. It sets these actions in the context of a long American tradition from the Boston Tea Party through to the lunch counter sit-ins of the 1960s and more recently to demonstrations by people with disabilities protesting inaccessible city buses.

> Direct action can include a wide range of activities. It can include holding a protest rally outside the state capitol while the state legislature is in session. Self-advocates have conducted protests that disrupted public hearings that were stacked toward supporting institutionalization. Some self-advocates have participated in national protests to close institutions and provide community services that support people to remain in the community or move to the community. Others have been known to chain themselves to the White House gates to make a point.

These self-advocates have also blocked traffic or held sit-ins at government offices, braving the risk of getting arrested. These kinds of direct action may make observers angry or uncomfortable, but "people with intellectual and other developmental disabilities have the right to stand up and fight for their rights in the way that they see fit."[56]

Politicians may have disabilities, and they are apt to have family members with disabilities, as do voting constituents. There may be controversies about the costliness of care and change, but they have generally been less bitter than those aroused by movements for equal opportunity and rights for women or gays. One significant exception occurred in spring 2005 in the case of Not Dead Yet, a disability rights organization engaged exclusively with end-of-life issues, when it became entangled in a great political drama surrounding Terri Schiavo, a woman who had been in a vegetative state for fifteen years. The cause of her collapse, like everything else in her case, has been disputed but appeared to be related to dieting. She and her husband were awarded a substantial malpractice judgment. Though at first working cooperatively, her husband Michael, generally supported in the Florida court system, and her parents became bitter antagonists over his opposition as her guardian to continuing nutrition (her feeding tube was removed on several occasions and then replaced) and over her treatment for possible medical conditions, indeed, whether she truly was in a vegetative condition. The spectacle was further complicated by interventions by Florida's legislature, Governor Jeb Bush, the U.S.

Senate, and President George W. Bush. The U.S. Supreme Court declined to intervene four times. Television shows such as *Oprah* and *Hannity & Colmes* gave moral and medical experts highly public occasions to comment on Terri's condition. Radio personality Glenn Beck reported more than $6 million in pledges to induce Michael Schiavo to remove himself from Terri's case.

The context linking the case to the civil disobedience tradition, as well as to partisan conflict in the state and national legislatures, was the contest of pro-life movements with advocates in Florida, a state with many retirees, of a "right to die." Terri's parents appointed Randall Terry as her spokesman in 2003, and he was able to visit Terri and report on her condition. "I want to live," he reported hearing her try to scream out.[57]

The feeding tube was removed on March 18, and Terri Schiavo died in Pinellas Park, Florida, in a hospice on a dead-end street on March 31. This was one instance where civil disobedience was noisy but futile. Governor Bush, vilified by the crowd for not intervening, went on CNN to explain that he could not violate a court order. The parents had requested the crowd to be calm and not to break the law. On one occasion her father was prevented from seeing Terri when the police had locked the entrance because of the crowd's anger and unruliness. Terri's brother pleaded with men who were denouncing the police as "Gestapo": "You are not speaking for my family. . . . We are not going to solve the problem today by getting arrested." Protesters clogged the street; on Easter Sunday eight people got out of their wheelchairs, lay down beside them, blocking the driveway, and showed their support for Terri by chanting "We're not dead yet!" There were also protesters against the protesters, saying that they didn't want to live in a fascist theocracy and noting that they recognized faces from OR actions at abortion clinics. Of course, they had been there, too.[58]

Civil disobedience, like Joe Hill, never died. Despite rumors of its demise after 1968, it persisted in the antinuclear movements of the 1970s; it benefited from a much-publicized "resurrection" in the anti-apartheid demonstrations of the 1980s; and subsequently there were new manifestations in religious anti-abortion movements, soon to be counterbalanced by new feminist movements for whom abortion rights were essential to women's liberation. The sense of tradition remained strong throughout. In 1992, for example, Patricia Ireland, as president of the National Organization for Women, and five other feminist leaders engaged in an "illegal speakout" in front of the White house, where stationary speeches are prohibited, in a demonstration of outrage against the *Casey* decision (which they disliked as intensely as did Bork) and other threats to abortion rights. They placed their action "in the tradition of Margaret Sanger, arrested for distributing birth control, Susan B. Anthony, arrested for voting, and Rosa Parks, arrested for refusing to give up her seat in the front of the bus," as they employed nonviolent civil disobedience ("NVCD," as they called it), ignored police warnings, and were carted off in a van.[59]

At a remove from the issue of abortion, subsequent years brought repeated instances of civil disobedience carried out in courteous cooperation with authorities and without risk of violent confrontation or legal penalty. Often these events occurred at colleges and universities. Consider the ritual summarized in a 1985 news story that I quote in its entirety:

> Five State University of New York students and one alumna who occupied the business office of the university's Albany headquarters in April have been convicted of trespassing, fined $250 each, and told to refrain from similar protests for one year.
>
> The six were arrested during a protest opposing the university's $14.2 million in investments in companies doing business with South Africa.
>
> Albany judge Thomas Keegan also gave them suspended sentences of 12 to 15 days in jail.
>
> Quoting Henry David Thoreau on civil disobedience, he commended the students, dubbed the "SUNY 6," for their efforts and noted that people were obligated to pay a legal price for their moral actions.[60]

For years a number of colleges encouraged and sponsored student involvement in civil disobedience at Fort Benning, Georgia, where college officials, clergy, peace activists and celebrities from the entertainment world protested U.S. training of Latin American police and military forces accused of torture and murder in the repression of democratic movements. In 2000 Father Lawrence Biondi, S.J., the president of my university, joined with Martin Sheen, well known for playing a U.S. president on television, as the "two presidents" marched at the head of 3,600 protesters who "crossed the line" and entered the fort in an act of civil disobedience. Often the issues in student protests concerned tuition raises, or shortfalls in state funding, but some appealed for diversity in student admission and course content—the kinds of issues that SDS ideology had generally ignored. Students at the SUNY campus at Geneseo, for example, held a sit-in at the administration building one afternoon in 1992 in what reporters called "an exceedingly civil example of civil disobedience." The college president, Carol C. Harter, gave her approval of the action, which was directed against state budget cuts, and conducted a news conference with sit-in leaders. Some donned neckties and dressed conservatively. (They had that in common with John Lewis's Nashvillians.) "Be careful," demonstrators were told over a public address system. "We don't want to break anything. That would just make things worse." Some students found this all "too passive" and urged a "more traditional" sit-in, and six of them were arrested on disorderly conduct charges. But even these militants behaved within constraints. Detained briefly when they attempted to block doors, they were released without substantial punishment. Harter told reporters that "she personally experienced campus upheaval in the 1960's," and she was glad this one was peaceful: "Heat with no light doesn't make a lot of sense to me."[61] Nationally, attempts to revive or create a new SDS devolved into disputes over the Weather faction's creativity or irresponsibility.

The new civility was not restricted to educational venues. Huge protests at New York police headquarters in March and April 1999 over the police shooting of Amadou Diallo, a young unarmed Guinean street vendor, led to 1,700 arrests. Shock and anger reverberated throughout the city and nation, much of it directed at New York Mayor Rudolph Giuliani and a pattern of police violence against blacks. Nevertheless, the police, demonstrators, and their attorneys saw advantages in proceeding with advance negotiations, cooperation, and restraint. The arrests took on the "velvet rope" qualities familiar from the anti-apartheid protests. Reporters noted "the cordial choreography" of street theater that has come to define many demonstrations, with protesters and police officers acting "more like co-stars than adversaries." The cordiality contrasted with the ugliness of the shooting, and the "choreography" of the event presented a dramatic contrast to the struggles of many civil rights or antiwar demonstrations in previous decades.[62] Consider this dialogue in one report:

POLICEMAN to Priest: "Father, I can't arrest you unless you actually block the door."
PRIEST, moving forward: "Is this O.K.?"
POLICEMAN: "Yeah, that's good."

"O.K., Father, now you're under arrest."

ANOTHER CLERGYMAN, observing: "A whole new twist to the meaning of 'civil' disobedience."[63]

There were two Gulf wars in this period. The first came in response to Iraq's invasion of Kuwait and was not extremely controversial. After an initial wave of protests, the United States led a U.N.-backed coalition that succeeded in driving Saddam Hussein and the Iraqis back without facing significant opposition on the battlefield or on the home front. In the judgment of Barbara Epstein, who writes both as a peace scholar and activist, "It is probably fair to describe the Gulf War as the worst defeat that the U.S. peace movement has suffered since the late 1940s, when public support for Cold War policies was created, and the peace movement of the time was successfully labeled as un- or anti-American."[64] She attributes the "defeat" to a plethora of disunited groups. But the war, after all, was victorious, brief, and relatively free of casualties, though subsequent illnesses were attributed to exposure to chemicals. The second Gulf War, a decade later, would be longer and more divisive.

In fall 2001, the United States and its allies responded to the 9/11 attacks on New York and Washington by bombing and invading Afghanistan, where the Taliban government had permitted the training of terrorists. Antiwar demonstrations drew thousands of participants around the world and in American cities and college towns. As the U.S. government sought United Nations support and assembled a coalition of allies to extend its "war on terror" into Iraq, protests grew larger and angrier. Justifications for the invasion—that the Iraqi government was developing weapons of mass destruction, that it had hosted the schemers behind the 9/11 attacks on American cities, and that there was an international obligation to liberate a united people from the dictator Saddam Hussein—were spurious. Americans were never given understanding of what motivated the suicide bombers on 9/11. Unlike the first Gulf War, the second (or the "war on terror") aroused protests, some of them on an international scale and with hundreds of thousands of participants, in every year of its duration.[65] Demonstrators introduced impressive and dramatic forms of protest, some solemn, others raucous: the die-ins (mentioned in chapter 1), columns of flag-draped cardboard coffins, women dancing with mock missiles attached to their hips, often including civil disobedience.

In highly significant ways this war differed from the precedents of intervention in Vietnam and Southeast Asia. Although military action was authorized by Congress, there was at all times significant popular opposition; the cost was never made public and openly funded; and there was no draft, no draft cards and therefore no college careers interrupted involuntarily by lotteries or quotas, no draft evasion. The war was fought by all-volunteer armed forces, drawn in part by need for the job and benefits, and joined by armed forces assembled and paid by American corporations. Though the patriotism of those who fought was seldom questioned, so was the fact that they were less economically privileged than those who stayed stateside and supported or opposed the war. Overseas, they were often surrounded by populaces who wanted them gone and toward whom they sometimes reacted terribly. Victory for the United States and its allies, though seldom in grave doubt, was difficult to define or achieve. There was much talk of an "exit strategy" amid comparisons with the "quagmire" in Vietnam. There were few pitched battles against a visible enemy. Casualty rates were high. Antiwar protest recurred on campuses and in city centers, though it is uncertain what effect it had on public opinion. Some protest tactics were creative and moving, but no demonstrations resembled the Oakland troop trains, Sheep Meadow, or the Pentagon. In fact, journalists reported from the onset of war that some antiwar activists were pushing the movement away from "wild-eyed" tactics and toward "civil" demonstrations. Even among the 75,000 who signed a civil disobedience pledge ("the Iraq Pledge of Resistance"), many were determined not to do anything that would look unpatriotic, disturb mainstream opinion, show disrespect to the military (as during Vietnam days), or "cast the movement in a bad light." Others countered that "if we're about to start slaughtering thousands of innocent civilians, you should be inconvenienced in any way possible if it makes you feel the suffering of those people."[66]

With no draft to incite opposition, administration policy sought to keep evidence of death out of the public eye—no media coverage of caskets, no presidential appearances at funerals. An important antiwar protest was led by Cindy Sheehan, the mother of a slain serviceman, Casey, who was killed in a guerilla attack five days after landing in Iraq. She mobilized others in despair and defiance over the president's failure to speak with her. This was especially true of an encampment in August 2005 on the road leading to the ranch house Bush had converted into his Texas White House. Sheehan was joined by veterans of Vietnam protest, politicians, actors, performers, including Joan Baez, who had marched with Dr. King and Cesar Chavez and had been jailed with her mother and sister for interfering with troops leaving Oakland years before. Sheehan was arrested and served time, but the president could not get rid of her; she was arrested again at the White House and again, by now identified by the press as "Peace Mom," with three other women seeking to deliver a petition at the U.S. mission to the United Nations. She became a living symbol of resistance to President Bush's war, reviled by some, often compared by herself and admirers to Rosa Parks.

There were other confrontations at the White House, but college administrations for the most part were not viewed as they once had been as colluding with the administration and its policies. There were many indications that the antiwar movement (there was one) was reluctant from the start to follow old scripts, and even as a public still terrified by the 9/11 attacks withdrew much of its support for a seemingly interminable war, the tactics of protest often were accused of offering hope to the enemy.[67] As Melvin Small, a historian of previous peace movements, summarized early in the war, "in terms of numbers" the movement this time had been "wildly effective, . . . lots of people on the streets and lots of media coverage." But it was ineffective in other ways. "Our administration didn't seem to care about many people in the streets. . . . And it's very difficult to get people to oppose war when they can see their heroic boys and girls fighting for the U.S. on 24-hour television." A teacher of peace and conflict studies at Berkeley, Michael Negler, pointed out, however, "In nonviolence, we don't always judge by immediate results." He added, "Nonviolence is confident it will have positive effects down the line."[68]

Civil disobedience in the late twentieth and early twenty-first century addressed issues and familiarized measures that predecessor movements seldom anticipated. No recent issue has been debated more insistently within the historical framework of civil disobedience than advocacy of same-sex marriage in New Paltz, New York, San Francisco, and across the nation. A *New York Times* columnist compared getting a marriage license to sitting in at a lunch counter. An *Arizona Republic* columnist compared acts of city officials and clergy to freedom rides, draft card burning, and Gandhi's Salt March. The commentator Andrew Sullivan was "moved beyond words by the sight of gay couples taking their lives and rights into their own hands and getting civil marriage licenses," but he cautioned that everyone involved must follow the precedents of "legitimate civil disobedi-ence: violating the law in order to be arrested" while being prepared to accept penalties without "blatant disrespect" for the rule of law. Congressman Barney Frank, among a few others who favored same-sex marriage, rejected the headlong resort to civil disobedience and advised working instead for change through democratic politics.[69] It was not clear that civil disobedience in local confrontations could achieve wider-scale democratic change.

Advocates of civil disobedience were experimenting with new measures. At the outset of this book I noted the Ruckus Society's "high tech" preparation for the 2000 Republican National Convention. A colorful and well-organized website traces the Ruckus Society's origins to "the forest defense movement" in 1995 and a decision to broaden its response to "the increasing impact of the corporate globalization of all forms of life on this planet." It developed week-long training programs after Greenpeace had to cut its programs. It sponsored a wide range of projects concerning migrant labor, Native Americans, and many concerned with environmental issues. Almost all featured civil disobedience actions carried out by well-trained volunteers, most recently the 2011 "Tar Sands Action" and opposi-tion to the Keystone XL pipeline, which led to 1,252 arrests for sit-ins at the White House.[70] Despite the news media's sensationalized treatment, the training programs and the execution were fully within the tradition and its progenitors.

There has probably been no previous time when information about nonviolent civil disobedience has been so readily available. The Ruckus Society's website includes manuals on direct action (most of which require no skill at climbing scaffolds), along with a list of possible partner organi-zations and principles for democratic organizing. Martin Oppenheimer's *A Manual for Direct Action* (1965) is still serviceable, and it is more than updated by James Tracy's *The Civil Disobedience Handbook* (2011) and supplemented with Mark Kurlansky's *Nonviolence* (2006), with its own useful bibliographies. In addition, guides to action can be found at websites of the Fellowship of Reconciliation, Peaceful Uprising, Act Up, Guerilla Girls, and Code Pink, among other organizations. In contrast to the times of bus boycotts and lunch counter sit-ins, any literate person with Internet access will have an easy time in gaining information and advice. Some of these groups are said to be more theatrical than their forebears, but there have often been elements of playacting in shows of disobedient civility.

Think of the Smith sisters, for example, or Parker Pillsbury. Radical feminists introduced theatricality early in the twentieth century, and some dramatic activists could still be taking some of their cues from Jerry Rubin and Abby Hoffman.

The Ruckus Society played a major role in demonstrations at the December 1999 World Trade Organization meeting in Seattle that were notable for their flexibility and mobility as well as the costumes and pageantry of protesters. They were also notable for creation of a coalition of environmentalists, unionists, and young radicals with an anti-capitalist focus not associated with civil disobedience since the 1930s and raising hopes, or fears, as the historian Michael Kazin suggested, of reviving "the anticorporate insurgency of the 1890s." (Those who envisioned a rising international anti-capitalist movement took notice as well of American campus protests in support of improved economic conditions for campus employees.)[71] The dramatic events in Seattle were prologue to further disruptions at conferences of the World Bank, the International Monetary Fund, and other financial meetings in Vienna, Washington, Genoa, Prague, and cities around the world. At some of these events a "black bloc" of anarchists, estimated at 100 out of 40,000 demonstrators in Seattle, seized much attention with property destruction and open conflict with police. At anti-globalization confrontations in Europe, not organized by Ruckus, reporters again distinguished a small, defiant "black bloc" from a vast majority of protesters who were "determinedly pacifist and nonviolent" and dedicated to civil disobedience.[72] Drawing a line between civil-respectable and violent-illegitimate forms of protest has been a recurrent issue in the discourse of civil disobedience from Operation Rescue to stealth attacks by animal rights activists and ecoterrorists to Philip Berrigan's attempt to damage navigational equipment by squirting his blood on board a missile-launching naval destroyer.[73] At the global economic summits and U.S. political conventions the lines may be hard to draw as different groups demonstrate in the same streets, but destructive, covert acts may well clarify and enhance the legitimacy of nonviolent public demonstrations. A survey of philosophical thinking about civil disobedience points out that as civil disobedience remains "a vibrant part of liberal democracies," significant issues that philosophers need to address include "how this practice may be distinguished from more radical forms of protest and how this practice should be treated by the law."[74] Similar questions have arisen in contemporary history, too—does civil disobedience discourage other

forms of political activity? has it encouraged violence and intransigence?—
and these deserve further exploration.[75]

Afterword: The Present and Future of Civil Disobedience

Every day's newspaper includes an example of someone invoking a right
of civil disobedience. If I review here recent instances of so-called civil
disobedience—from Alabama's chief justice defying a court order to remove
a Ten Commandments monument from his courtroom to journalist Judith
Miller refusing to disclose her confidential sources, and from occupations of
public squares in protest against inequality to the "No Papers, No Fear"
busload of undocumented immigrants dramatizing their cause at the 2012
Democratic Party convention—most are likely soon-to-be-forgotten
episodes in a passing cavalcade. But a longer-term perspective unites them.
In St. Louis the head of a teachers' union defended a strike in violation of
state law: "I go back to the basis on which this country was founded. It's
called civil disobedience."[76] That is an oversimplification, of course, but it
reflects a long history. We have observed an evolving, self-conscious tradition of individuals and movements, usually nonviolent, protesting, inter
alia, unfair taxation, Indian removal, slavery, unpopular wars, saloons, deprivation of the rights of women and labor, racial segregation, nuclear energy,
threats to the environment, and legalized abortions. The tradition has not
lacked intellectual and theological justification, nor has it been free of critics
with differing perspectives on public order. The tradition has its heroes and
villains, moments honored and vilified. Generally it has been respectful of
public order, but with significant exceptions, especially in recent decades.

Acts of civil disobedience will almost certainly continue, and many
citizens accept their ubiquity as inevitable and even as a reasonably good
thing. Since current attitudes and policy were established in a turbulent era
of the recent past, more public discussion, making more distinctions and
facing hard questions about law breaking, civil liberties, and legal penalties,
would be beneficial. At present, it is almost breathtaking when a conservative critic like Roger Kimball denounces civil disobedience as a "license for
lawlessness" passed down from the 1960s under the guise of moral rectitude.[77] His view provides a reminder of a conservative tradition that
regarded a controlling power in the state as a prerequisite for civil liberty.
We have seen, moreover, that Gandhi and other great exponents of civil
disobedience championed respect for law. But have recent practitioners
discarded that principle?

During the Occupy movement's encampments and street protests in November 2011 it became clear how widespread knowledge had become of the philosophy and techniques of nonviolent civil disobedience. When the University of California at Berkeley's chancellor justified police violence against protesters by stating that linking arms and forming a human chain is "not non-violent civil disobedience," almost immediately defenders of the protests posted a collection of photos—Burmese monks, Martin Luther King, Jr., and civil rights marchers, Barack Obama and members of his administration, English nuclear disarmament marchers in 1983, gay rights advocates, professors and unionists—all with interlocked arms, each above the ironic caption, "this is not non-violent disobedience." When a Berkeley English professor held out her arms to be arrested, she was instead grabbed by her hair and yanked to the ground. The issue was not the alleged violence of linked arms; nor was it, as the chancellor implied, a refusal "to engage in truly non-violent civil disobedience and to accept the consequences of their decisions." The issue, in the view of supporters of the protest, was simply "disobedience."[78] In fairness, it should be noted that Berkeley did in previous months have protesters clamoring for a third-world-style revolution, calling through a bullhorn, "This isn't your sixties Berkeley sit-in," and throwing cement planters and flaming torches at the chancellor's house. Emphasis on non-violent civil disobedience was not pointless.[79]

At the University of California at Davis, in a scene widely viewed on television and the Internet, police repeatedly and almost nonchalantly doused seated students with pepper spray. The demonstrators, even as they were sprayed, maintained a nonresistant composure that was remarkably disciplined. But if the student protestors' discipline was unmistakable, as composer and professor Bob Ostertag wrote, something else had changed: "Throughout my life I have seen, and sometimes participated in, peaceful civil disobedience in which sitting and linking arms was understood by citizens as a posture that indicates, in the clearest possible way available, protesters' intent to be non-violent." Training manuals had long taught that "sitting and linking arms is the best way to de-escalate any confrontation between police and people exercising their first amendment right to public speech." The police "universally" understood this gesture and knew how to respond when protesters declined to disperse of their own accord. To Ostertag this had become so familiar, "so routine that I have often wondered if this form of protest had become so scripted as to have lost most of its meaning." No longer. As he expressed concern about "a radical departure from the way police have handled protest in this country for half a century,"[80] he was also reaffirming the etiquette of civil disobedience that we have observed in a range of demonstrations on campuses and public squares across the nation.

In an international perspective the "radical departure" might not appear so shocking. To the list of manuals and guides to civil disobedience might be added the compendious works of an American theorist, Gene Sharp, who had been jailed as a conscientious objector during the Korean War, an Oxford Ph.D. and prolific writer whose vision has consistently been based on the writings of Gandhi and focused on liberation movements around the world.[81] He has pursued voluminously Richard Gregg's interest in jiu-jitsu and Krishnalal Shridharani's in civilian nonviolent defense against tyranny and aggression. Amid the excitement of the 2011 "Arab Spring" a front-page article in the New York Times acclaimed Sharp for having created the "Playbook Used in a Revolution," and other papers called him "the 83 Year Old Who Toppled Egypt." Unsurprisingly, Arab commentators found that offensive, and Sharp himself made no such claim. But it is clear that his work has had extensive influence in the Baltic nations, Inner Asia, Southeast Asia, the former Yugoslavia, and elsewhere, and he has made materials widely available on how citizens' movements can undermine oppressive rulers by nonviolent action.[82] Sharp's work has also laid a basis for an emerging field of scholarship on "civil resistance." In what has emerged as an important subject of transnational history, the Indian overthrow of the Raj, which depended in Sharp's analysis less on religious principles aimed at "conversion" of the opposition than on disciplined, nonviolent, military-style tactics, is credited with inspiring Philip Randolph's and Martin Luther King's campaigns in the United States, and in subsequent decades the experience of successful liberation movements has been studied and modified in other nations.[83] The importance of this field and the persistence of nonviolent uprisings in other lands have not yet eclipsed the continuing Americanness of the nation's tradition of civil disobedience, but they may well enrich our understanding of it.

NOTES

CHAPTER 1 **The Drama of Civil Disobedience**

1 Sharon Barnartt and Richard Scotch, *Disability Protests: Contentious Politics, 1970–1999* (Washington, D.C.: Gallaudet University Press, 2002), 21.

2 I. King Jordan, "Deaf President Now (DPN): The Protest Heard around the World in 1988 Continues to Change the World," address to National Press Club, May 9, 2006, at http://president.gallaudet.edu/x3144.xml (retrieved Nov. 14, 2006). For other references to King and Selma, see "Notable Quotes [Kathy Karcher]," http://pr.gallaudet.edu/dpn/viewpoints/own_words/quotes.html; Susan Kinzie, "New Gallaudet President Met with Protest," *Washington Post*, May 2, 2006; "At Gallaudet, a Turn Inward Opens New Worlds," April 30, 2006, National Public Radio, transcribed at http://npr.org/templates/story/story.php?storyID=5369960; and with a less favorable recollection of the 1960s, Jonathan V. Last, "Gallaudet Protests Revive Bad Old Days: It's 1968 All Over Again at University for the Deaf," at http://www.cbsnews.com/stories/2006/10/26/opinion/main2125873.html. Besides gallaudet.com, the best sources on Gallaudet and the DPN movement are the many articles archived at washingtonpost.com and John B. Christiansen and Sharon N. Barnartt, *Deaf President Now!: The 1988 Revolution at Gallaudet University* (Washington, D.C.: Gallaudet University Press, 2002).

3 "In Their Own Words: Tim Rarus" (Gallaudet Public Relations Department, 1997) at http://pr.gallaudet.edu/dpn/viewpoints/own_words/rarus.html. The importance of working together, despite differences in the deaf community, was also stressed by student leader Jerry Covell.

4 Gallaudet Protests: Updates from Kendall Green, http://www.elisawrites.com/?p=315; also at elisa abenchuchan weblog at http://www.xanga.com/elisa_abenchuchan?nextdate=10%2f27%2f2006+14%3a33%3a24.843&direction=n.

5 Susan Kinzie, Nelson Hernandez, and David Farenthold, "Gallaudet Board Ousts Fernandes," *Washington Post*, Oct. 30, 2006. For a range of comments on the effigy

315

burnings, see http://www.insidehighered.com/news/2006/10/30/gallaudet; http://www.ridorlive.com/?m=200610, Oct. 31, 2006.

6 Public statements and releases are collected at http://www.gallaudet.edu/x3430.xml. Useful overviews in the public press included Diana Jean Schemo, "Protests Shut University for Deaf a Second Day," "At University for Deaf, Protesters Press Broader Demands," and "At Gallaudet, Trustees Relent on Leadership," *New York Times*, Oct. 13, 30, 31, 2006; and many articles in the *Washington Post*, including Susan Kinzie, Nelson Hernandez, and David Fahrenthold, "Gallaudet Board Ousts Fernandes," Oct. 30, 2006. There was also rich, ever-changing documentation in the many blogs through which students and alumni communicated throughout these events. See Mark Glaser, "Gallaudet University Protests Gain Global Audience," *Mediashift*, Oct. 17, 2006, at http://www.pbs.org/mediashift/2006/10/online_organizinggallaudet_uni.html; Joseph Shapiro, "Blogs Capture, Amplify Gallaudet Protest," and Ben Brusevold-Newman, "Blogging the Gallaudet Protest," at http://www.npr.org/templates/story/story.php?storyId=6382419; and an open letter disputing NPR coverage at http://danielgreene.com/2006/10/26/open-letter-to-npr-re-blogs-capture-amplify-gallaudet-protest/.

7 Brian Riley, "Justice for Gallaudet," Oct. 17, 2006, at Gallaudet Protest Legal Issues, http://gpli.blogspot.com/; comments posted in response to Kinzie et al., "Gallaudet Students Arrested," at washingtonpost.com, Oct. 14, 2006, at http://www.washingtonpost.com/ac2/wp-dyn/comments/display?contentID=AR2006101300570; Elisa Abenchuchan's weblog, Oct. 19, at http://www.xanga.com/elisa_abenchuchan?nextdate=10%2f20%2f2006+12%3a33%3a0.760&direction=n; Joey Schumacher, comment on Glaser, "Gallaudet University Protests," *Mediashift*.

8 Jane Hurst, "On Nonviolence and Civil Disobedience," Inside Gallaudet, Oct. 19, 2006, at http://news.gallaudet.edu/?id=9583; "Guest blog: Why I Did Not Support the Gallaudet Protest," *Takoma Silver Springs Voice*, Oct. 30, 2006, at http://www.takoma.com/ed_blog/2006/10/letter_why_i_did_not_support_t.html; and "Jane Sings," http://www.janehurst.com/pages/1/index.htm. In her analysis, "the protest was fueled by the threat to Deaf culture that has been posed by advances in technology which are giving individuals more choice about whether they want to live in that small community or whether they want to take on the wider world, which includes a lot of hearing people. Cultures under pressure have historically reacted in ways that are aggressive and/or self destructive, and I think we saw that this year at Gallaudet" ("Why I Did Not Support").

9 Ridor, Oct. 14, 2006, at http://www.ridorlive.com/?m=20061014.; Oct. 23 at http://www.ridorlive.com/?m=200610&paged=8. For a picture of Ricky D. Taylor (Ridor) in a Superman tee shirt with "ASL" embazoned on his chest, see his blog for Nov. 18 at http://www.ridorlive.com/?m=200611&paged=2.

10 Ridor, "My Views," *RidorLive*, Oct. 23, 2006, at http://www.ridorlive.com/?m=200610&paged=8.

11 Ridor and others did criticize Hurst's competence in ASL, which for them was a key sign of how well the university was serving the deaf community.

12 See http://en.wikipedia.org/wiki/Civil_disobedience (retrieved Jan. 18, 2007).

13 Mohandas K. Gandhi, *Collected Works* (1908), 7:217, as quoted in A. L. Herman, "Satyagraha: A New Indian Word for Some Old Ways of Western Thinking," *Philosophy East and West* 19:2 (April 1969): 135.

14 Mary King, *Mahatma Gandhi and Martin Luther King, Jr.: The Power of Nonviolent Action* (Paris: UNESCO, 1999), 21, 527.

15 "Long Island Teens Give Up Cars in Gas Protest" (audio), NPR Morning Edition, June 5, 2008, at http://www.npr.org/templates/story/story.php?storyId=91181145.

16 Mark Edmundson, "2003: The Third Annual Year in Ideas; Civil Disobedience against Affirmative Action," *New York Times*, Dec. 14, 2003.

17 See James Tracy, ed., *The Civil Disobedience Handbook: A Brief History and Practical Advice for the Politically Disenchanted* (San Francisco: Manic D., 2002), 68.

18 King, *Mahatma Gandhi and Martin Luther King*, 527.

19 Mary King, *Freedom Song: A Personal Story of the 1960s Civil Rights Movement* (New York: William Morrow, 1987), 48, 279.

20 "Randolph Tells Philosophy behind March, Movement," *Chicago Defender*, June 19, 1943, p. 13.

21 See his exchange with Sen. Wayne Morse, *Congressional Record*, 80th Cong., 2d Sess., 1948, vol. 94 (April 12), 4313.

22 Andrew W. McTheonia, Jr., "Civil Resistance or Holy Obedience? Reflections from within a Community of Resistance," *Washington and Lee Law Review* 48:1 (Winter 1991): 15–39. See also Ralph W. Conant, *The Prospects for Revolution: A Study of Riots, Civil Disobedience, and Insurrection in Contemporary America* (New York: Harper and Row, 1971), 20–21.

23 OED online edition, s.v. "civil," 3c, under the "strife" that occurs among fellow citizens or within one community. The defects in this definition are obvious. Howard Zinn, ed., *The Higher Law: Thoreau on Civil Disobedience and Reform* (Princeton: Princeton University Press, 1973), xlv.

24 http://mlk-kpp01.stanford.edu/index.php/resources/article/annotated_letter_from_birmingham.

25 Gene Sharp, *Waging Nonviolent Struggle* (Boston: Porter Sargent, 2005), 390–91.

26 See "What Made the Protest So Successful?" at http://pr.gallaudet.edu/dpn/issues/THEWEEK/whysuccess.htm.

27 Oct. 29, 2006. Quoted by David Bar-Tzur, "Unity for Gallaudet Movement, 2006," http://www.theinterpretersfriend.com/pd/fernandes-gallaudet.html (retrieved March 24, 2008).

28 See DeafDC.com blog after announcement of Davila's appointment, Dec. 12, 2006, at http://www.deafdc.com/blog/chris-and-allison-kaftan/2006–12–10/davila-chosen-as-gallaudet-interim-president/ (retrieved March 25, 2006). *RidorLive* blogs are now inaccessible. But see his comments at "The Countdown to

Resurrection, Jan.–March 2008," http://countdown2resurrection.wordpress.com/2008/01/ (retrieved March 24, 2008).

29 Casey Nelson Blake, *Beloved Community: The Cultural Criticism of Randolph Bourne, Van Wyck Brooks, Waldo Frank, and Lewis Mumford* (Chapel Hill: University of North Carolina Press, 1990); Kenneth L. Smith and Ira G. Zepp, Jr., "Martin Luther King's Vision of the Beloved Community," *Christian Century*, April 3, 1974, pp. 361–63.

30 Charles R. DiSalvo, "Abortion and Consensus: The Futility of Speech, the Power of Disobedience," *Washington and Lee Law Review* 48:1 (Winter 1991): 228–29.

31 Jonathan V. Last, "Gallaudet Protests Revive Bad Old Days: It's 1968 All Over Again at University for the Deaf," Oct. 26, 2006, CBS News at http://www.cbsnews.com/stories/2006/10/26/opinion/main2125873.shtml. This article appeared originally in the *Weekly Standard* and was reprinted in the *Philadelphia Inquirer* and other news sources.

32 Susan Kinzie, "A Year Later, Gallaudet Faces Challenging Future," *Washington Post*, Oct. 30, 2007.

33 The highly influential image of "moral jiu-jitsu," originated in Richard B. Gregg's *The Power of Non-Violence* (2d ed., Nyack, N.Y.: Fellowship of Reconciliation, 1959), and is discussed in chapter 7 below.

34 See Gallaudet Protest Legal Issues at http://gpli.blogspot.com/.

35 Todd Gitlin, *The Whole World Is Watching: Mass Media in the Making and Unmaking of the New Left* (Berkeley: University of California Press, 1980), unravels how media exposure shaped the movement. Dellinger says he may have been the source of the phrase, which bolstered morale of demonstrators and gave warning to police. See David Dellinger, *From Yale to Jail: The Life Story of a Moral Dissenter* (Marion, S.D.: Rose Hill, 1996), 329–30.

36 Iver Peterson, "Conservation and Tourist Interests at Odds in Dispute at Yellowstone," *New York Times*, Aug. 5, 1985.

37 Evelyn Nieves, "Freshwater Journal: Sitting in a Redwood Tree, Making a Statement," *New York Times*, Aug. 26, 2002. See also the Earth First! press release "Pacific Lumber Goes After Remedy's Home: Tree Jerry and Other Tree-Sitters," March 20, 2003, at http://www.mindfully.org/Heritage/2003/Pacific-Lumber-Headwaters20mar03.htm (retrieved Oct. 8, 2008).

38 Amy Elisa Keith and Stephen M. Silverman, "Daryl Hannah Speaks from Jail Cell," People.com, June 14, 2006, at http://www.people.com/people/article/0,,1203672,00.html (retrieved Dec. 1, 2011).

39 Kate Zernike, "Threats and Responses: Dissent; Disagreements about Civil Disobedience Divide America's Antiwar Movement," *New York Times*, March 19, 2003. Zernike wrote other articles on these splits.

40 Michael Bess, *Choices Under Fire: Moral Dimensions of World War II* (New York: Alfred A. Knopf, 2006); Bess, "Deep Evil and Deep Good: The Concept of Human Nature Confronts the Holocaust," *Yale Review* 94 (2006): 44–69.

41 Bess (*Choices*, 128) attributes this term to René Girard.

42 Hannah Arendt, "Civil Disobedience," *New Yorker* (Sept.12, 1970), reprinted in her *Crises of the Republic* (New York: Harcourt Brace Jovanovich, 1972), 96.

43 "Blessed are the Meek: The Roots of Christian Nonviolence," *Fellowship* 66 (July–Aug. 2000), 14–15 (reprinted from *Fellowship*, May 1967).

44 *Los Angeles Times* reports by Nicholas Riccardi in *Valley News* (N.H.), Aug. 11, 2000, p. B2.

45 Arendt, *Crises of the Republic*, 83.

46 *New York Times*, Jan. 1, 1997 (barstool rebels); May 10, 1997 (Berrigan); Sept. 8, 1999 (bioengineered corn); *St. Louis Post-Dispatch*, Sept. 5, 1999 (Washington Monument); Oct. 28, 1999 (razor blades).

47 See, e.g., James J. Lopach and Jean A. Luckowski, "Uncivil Disobedience: Violating the Rules for Breaking the Law," *Educationnext* 4:2 (Spring 2005), at http://educationnext.org.

CHAPTER 2 A Heritage of Civilly Disobedient Acts

1 Daniel Berrigan, *The Trial of the Catonsville Nine* (Boston: Beacon Press, 1970).

2 Alfred F. Young, *The Shoemaker and the Tea Party: Memory and the American Revolution* (Boston: Beacon Press, 1999), x.

3 John W. Whitehead, "Civil Disobedience and Operation Rescue: A Historical and Theoretical Analysis," *Washington and Lee Law Review* 48:1 (Winter 1991): 77–78, 121. On Whitehead's 1960s "antiestablishment" movement-culture background, see Jeffrey Toobin, *A Vast Conspiracy: The Real Story of the Sex Scandal That Nearly Brought Down a President* (New York: Simon and Schuster, 2000), ch. 8.

4 Adams is quoted in Young, *Shoemaker*, 101–2.

5 George Bancroft, *History of the United States from the Discovery of the American Continent*, vol. 6 (Boston: Little, Brown, 1854), 484.

6 Ibid., 486.

7 Young, *Shoemaker*, 101.

8 William G. McLoughlin, "Massive Civil Disobedience as a Baptist Tactic in 1773," *American Quarterly* 21:4 (1969): 710.

9 Danny Cevallos, "Civil Disobedience," in F. Clark Power et al., *Moral Education: A Handbook*, 2 vols. (Westport, Conn.: Praeger, 2008), 1:84–85. Cevallos calls the Boston tea protests "arguably riotous" and thus somewhat distinct from his other examples.

10 L. F. Rushbrook Williams, "Indian Unrest and American Opinion," *Asiatic Review*, July 1930, p. 491, cited in Tom Weber, "Gandhi's Salt March as Living Sermon," *Gandhi Marj* online at http://www.transnational.org/SAJT/forum/Nonviolence/2001/Weber_SaltMarch.html (Jan. 14, 2009).

11 Eric H. Erikson, *Gandhi's Truth: On the Origins of Militant Nonviolence* (New York: W. W. Norton, 1969), 447–48; S. Sividas, "Retold, in a Hurry" (review of Anil

Dharker, *The Romance of Salt*), *The Hindu*, Sept. 4, 2005. There are many tellings of this episode.

12 LNCDAMS, Bulletin No. 1, "Civil Disobedience Is Catching On," June 4, 1948 (copies in Swarthmore College Peace Collection).

13 See, e.g., "Love, Law, and Civil Disobedience" (1961) and "Address to the American Jewish Committee" (1965) in David R. Weber, ed., *Civil Disobedience in America: A Documentary History* (Ithaca: Cornell University Press, 1978), 217, 220.

14 Described in Young, *Shoemaker*, 201–2. For the official statement, see Old South Meetinghouse, "Free Programs for Boston Public Schools," at http://www.oldsouthmeetinghouse.org/osmh_123456789files/freeprogramsbostonpublic-schools.aspx (retrieved Jan. 14, 2009).

15 The movement first came to my view in *St. Louis Post-Dispatch*, Feb. 28, 2009, p. A7. For overviews of its spread and charges of right-wing financing, see Reihan Salam, "The Santelli Conspiracy?" *The Atlantic*, online at http://politics.theatlantic.com/2009/03/the_santelli_conspiracy.php (retrieved March 2, 2009). That article did point out, "Lest we forget, the original Boston Tea Party was also a carefully orchestrated media event that used high-flown rhetoric to oppose a tax measure that many cool-headed observers considered entirely innocuous." In a burgeoning literature on the tea party revival, these historical analyses are valuable: Woden Teachout, "The Tea Party in Politics: Why the Event in Boston Harbor Keeps on Appealing to Conservatives," History News Network, June 29, 2009, at http://hnn.us/articles/94858.html; and especially Jill Lepore, *The Whites of Their Eyes: The Tea Party's Revolution and the Battle over American History* (Princeton: Public Square, 2010).

16 Isaac Backus, *An Appeal to the Public for Religious Liberty* (1773), in *Isaac Backus on Church, State, and Calvinism: Pamphlets, 1754–1789*, ed. William G. McLoughlin (Cambridge: Harvard University Press, 1968), 321.

17 Weber, ed., *Civil Disobedience in America*, 36–38; Harrop Freeman, "A Remonstrance for Conscience," *University of Pennsylvania Law Review* 106:6 (1958): 806–8.

18 Backus, *Appeal*, 338–39.

19 L. Kinvin Wroth, "The Rev. Nathaniel Green and the Tax Assessors: Passive Resistance in Eighteenth-Century Massachusetts," *New-England Galaxy* 9:2 (1967): 15–21; William G. McLoughlin, *New England Dissent, 1630–1833: The Baptists and the Separation of Church and State*, 2 vols. (Cambridge: Harvard University Press, 1971), 1:515–21. Backus is quoted on the "check to oppression" (p. 20); McLoughlin on the "turning point," which also entailed a decline in status for the clergy (p. 520).

20 On the bitterly contested "Ashfield Law," see William G. McLoughlin, *Isaac Backus and the American Pietistic Tradition* (Boston: Little, Brown, 1967), 113–19.

21 So says McLoughlin, "Massive Civil Disobedience," 714, and on the 1771 plea, 723. A more detailed account of the king's intervention in the so-called Ashfield case

and its potential for alienating Baptists from their countrymen in revolutionary times may be found in McLoughlin, *New England Dissent*, 516–46.

22 Backus, *Appeal*, 309.

23 Elder Ebenezer Smith, quoted in McLoughlin, "Massive Civil Disobedience," 711.

24 See McLoughlin's excellent account of "the Baptists' dilemma—the conflict of patriotism and pietism, the Christian dichotomy of being in the world but not of it"—in *New England Dissent*, 569–70ff.

25 McLoughlin, ed., *Backus on Church, State, and Calvinism*, 13.

26 Mcloughlin, *Backus and the American Pietistic Tradition*, 198.

27 Backus, *Appeal*, 339–40.

28 L. Kinvin Wroth and Hiller B. Zobel, eds., *Legal Papers of John Adams*, vol. 2, cases 31–62 (Cambridge: Harvard University Press, 1965), 32–47 (on Locke see 41, 44).

29 Noted in McLoughlin, *New England Dissent*, 520n.

30 Bernard Bailyn, ed., *Pamphlets of the American Revolution, 1750–1776* (Cambridge: Harvard University Press, 1965), 1:203–47 (Adams quoted at 209).

31 Ibid., 236–37.

32 Ibid., 209.

33 *The Federalist* (New York: Modern Library, 1951), 91.

34 Albert Furtwangler, *The Authority of Publius: A Reading of the Federalist Papers* (Ithaca: Cornell University Press, 1983), 32–39. If anything, for propagandistic purposes Publius may have toned down concern to compel obedience.

35 Max Farrand, ed., *The Records of the Federal Convention of 1787*, rev. ed., 4 vols. (New Haven: Yale University Press, 1966; 1st pub., 1911), 3:106–7.

36 James Madison, *Notes of Debates in the Federal Convention of 1787*, ed. Adrienne Koch (Athens: Ohio University Press, 1966), 320–22. Emphasis added. The convention at this point accepted, without dissent, this language: "that a Republican form of government shall be guaranteed to each state and that each state shall be protected against foreign and domestic violence." Later the wording was changed to provide for protection against domestic violence "on application of the legislature, or of the executive (when the legislature cannot be convened)."

37 Madison, *Notes*, 321.

38 Herbert Storing, the Anti-Federalists' most careful student, concludes that their greatest strength and weakness was that they "could neither fully reject nor fully accept the leading principles of the Constitution." *The Complete Anti-Federalist*, 7 vols. (Chicago: University of Chicago Press, 1981), 1:6.

39 Jonathan Elliot, *Debates in the Several State Conventions on the Adoption of the Federal Constitution*, 2d ed., 5 vols. (New York: Burt Franklin, 1974; 1st pub., 1861–63), 2:208.

40 Storing, *Complete Anti-Federalist*, 2.8.93, 2.9.24, 2.9.48, 2.9.50, 2.9.110 (in Storing's pagination the first digit identifies the volume, the second a document, the third a page). See Elliot, *Debates*, 2:193–94, n. 73.

41 Elliot, *Debates*, 2:9, 426–29; "Winthrop's Speech to the General Court, July 3, 1645," *The Puritans: A Sourcebook of Their Writings*, ed. Perry Miller and Thomas H. Johnson (New York: Harper Torchbooks, 1963), 205–7.

42 Edward S. Corwin, *The "Higher Law" Background of American Constitutional Law* (Ithaca: Cornell University Press, 1955; 1st pub., 1928–29), 85. The framers could have found similar language in Locke, but with greater emphasis on the reserved liberties of society and less on the supremacy of government. That even some revolutionaries who despised Blackstone were compelled to accept his view of sovereignty is shown in Morton J. Horwitz, *The Transformation of American Law, 1780–1860* (Cambridge: Harvard University Press, 1977), 17–20.

43 Madison, *Notes*, 90.

44 Elliot, *Debates*, 2:426.

45 Ibid., 2:9, 62; 3:37, 294. Note also Washington's letter of transmittal: "Individuals entering into society, must give up a share of liberty to preserve the rest"; similarly, it was "obviously impracticable" to secure the sovereignty of each state in every particular while providing for "the interest and safety of all." Thus Washington (or his ghostwriter Gouverneur Morris) hoped for "a spirit of amity, and of mutual deference and concession." Farrand, *Records*, 2:666–67.

46 John P. Kaminski and Gaspare J. Saladino, eds., *The Documentary History of the Ratification of the Constitution*, vol. 13: *Commentaries on the Constitution Public and Private*, vol. 1 (Madison: State Historical Society of Wisconsin, 1981), 81. On Jefferson's contempt for Blackstone and the "toryism" that lawyers derived from the *Commentaries*, see Leonard W. Levy, *Jefferson and Civil Liberties: The Darker Side* (Cambridge: Harvard University Press, 1963), 143, 151.

47 Mary K. Bonsteel Tachau, "The Whiskey Rebellion in Kentucky: A Forgotten Episode of Civil Disobedience," *Journal of the Early Republic* 2 (Fall 1980): 239–59. A more recent study makes no claim for civil disobedience, instead treating these events as "the single largest example of armed resistance to a law of the United States between the ratification of the Constitution and the Civil War." See Thomas P. Slaughter, *The Whiskey Rebellion: Frontier Epilogue to the American Revolution* (New York: Oxford, 1986).

48 Peter Gay, *The Cultivation of Hatred* (New York: W. W. Norton, 1993), ch. 3.

49 Thomas Paine, *The Rights of Man*, as quoted in Daniel T. Rodgers, *Contested Truths: Keywords in American Politics since Independence* (New York: Basic Books, 1987), 57.

50 For President Jackson's proclamation to the citizens of South Carolina, Dec. 10, 1832, see James D. Richardson, comp., *A Compilation of the Messages and Papers of the Presidents*, vol. 3 (New York: Bureau of National Literature, 1897), esp. 1205, 1216–17.

51 For Jackson's message to Congress, Jan. 16, 1833, see ibid., 1173–95 (quotations at 1184–87).

52 *The Papers of Andrew Jackson*, vol. 4: *1816–1820*, ed. Harold D. Moser, David R. Hoth, and George H. Hoemann (Knoxville: University of Tennessee Press,1994), 93–98.

53 Althea Bass, *Cherokee Messenger* (Norman: University of Oklahoma Press, 1996).

54 See, e.g., George E. Tinker, "Missions and Missionaries," in Frederick E. Hoxie, ed., *Encyclopedia of North American Indians* (Boston: Houghton Mifflin, 1996), 383.

55 Quoted from the record of *Worcester v. Georgia*, 31 U.S. (5 Pet.) at 523.

56 William G. McLoughlin, *Cherokees and Missionaries, 1789–1839* (New Haven: Yale University Press, 1984), 256–58. See also McLoughlin, *Cherokee Renascence in the New Republic* (Princeton: Princeton University Press, 1986), 442–43.

57 See Jeremiah Evarts, *Cherokee Removal: The "William Penn" Essays and Other Writings*, ed. Francis Paul Prucha (Knoxville: University of Tennessee Press, 1981).

58 McLoughlin, *Cherokees and Missionaries*, 258.

59 George R. Gilmer, *Georgians: Memoirs of the First Settlers* (1855), 304, quoted in McLoughlin, *Cherokees and Missionaries*, 260.

60 Jack Frederick Kilpatrick and Anna Gritts Kilpatrick, eds., *New Echota Letters: Contributions of Samuel A. Worcester to the Cherokee Phoenix* (Dallas: Southern Methodist University Press, 1968), 111.

61 Ibid., 109. Quite apart from constitutional issues, the fact that arrests, marches, and chainings took place without warrants or legal process drew strong criticism in the religious periodicals. See Mary Hershberger, "Anticipating Abolition: The Struggle against Indian Removal in the 1830s," *Journal of American History* 86 (1999): 31.

62 Bass, *Cherokee Messenger*, 144.

63 Kilpatrick and Kilpatrick, *New Echota Letters*, 110.

64 Ibid., 123. All emphases in original.

65 McLoughlin, "Civil Disobedience and Evangelism among the Missionaries to the Cherokees," *Journal of Presbyterian History* 51:2 (1973), quotations at 126–29.

66 Ibid., 124, 126.

67 Quoted in William G. McLoughlin, *Champions of the Cherokees: Evan and John B. Jones* (Princeton: Princeton University Press, 1990), 125. A good overview of Boudinot's life and thought: Theda Perdue, ed., *Cherokee Editor: The Writings of Elias Boudinot* (Athens: University of Georgia Press, 1983).

68 Quoted in McLoughlin, *Cherokees and Missionaries*, 257.

69 See Alisse Portnoy, *Their Right to Speak: Women's Activism in the Indian and Slave Debates* (Cambridge: Harvard University Press, 2005), 50–51.

70 Kilpatrick and Kilpatrick, *New Echota Letters*, 110.

71 Ibid., 115.

72 Evarts to Worcester, Feb. 1, 1831, and Worcester to David Greene, June 29, 1831, quoted in McLoughlin, *Cherokees and Missionaries*, 259, 262–63.

73 Gilmer, *Georgians*, as quoted in McLoughlin, *Cherokees and Missionaries*, 263.

74 Jill Norgren, "The Cherokee Nation Cases of the 1830s," *Journal of Supreme Court History* (1994): 71.

75 Jeremiah Evarts to John Ross, July 1830, quoted in Grace Steele Woodward, *The Cherokees* (Norman: University of Oklahoma Press, 1963), 163.

76 Joseph C. Burke, "The Cherokee Cases: A Study in Law, Politics, and Morality," *Stanford Law Review* 21:3 (1969): 509.

77 *Cherokee Nation v. State of Georgia*, 30 U.S. (5 Peters), 17 (1830).

78 Burke, "Cherokee Cases," 517. The other justice was Smith Thompson.

79 Hershberger, "Anticipating Abolition," 31.

80 Joseph Tracy, *History of the American Board of Commissioners for Foreign Missions*, 2d ed. (New York: M. W. Dodd, 1842), 254; Bass, *Cherokee Messenger*, 153–54.

81 31 U.S. (6 Peters) 597 (1832).

82 *Worcester v. Georgia* at 562.

83 Ibid., 595–96.

84 Ibid., 520, 562.

85 Edwin A. Miles, "After John Marshall's Decision: *Worcester v. Georgia* and the Nullification Crisis," *Journal of Southern History* 39:4 (Nov. 1973): 529. This article is the most valuable guide to the issues discussed in the following paragraphs.

86 Quoted in Tracy, *History*, 267.

87 Newspapers surveyed in Charles Warren, *The Supreme Court in United States History*, vol. 2: *1821–1855* (Boston: Little, Brown, 1923) (Google Books), 227–28.

88 Warren, *Supreme Court*, 234.

89 It is a hard story to unravel, and one that is easy to get wrong, as in this account by the famous historian of the Supreme Court, Charles Warren: Georgia officials recognized that after taking a stand for "the supremacy of the National authority" vis-à-vis South Carolina, President Jackson could no longer "countenance disobedience to the mandates of the National Court in any other state." The president was reported as saying he would enforce whatever the Supreme Court ordered in "the *Cherokee Case*," and journalists predicted that Georgia would find a way to avoid "direct collision" with the president. "This prophecy was soon fulfilled; for the Governor of Georgia, influenced by the President's determined stand … , finally issued a pardon to the missionaries upon their withdrawal of their suit; and thus the crisis in the history of the Court was averted." Warren, *Supreme Court*, 236. Jackson kept his intentions unclear, Georgia held to its own consideration, and the crisis ("final" or not) was not averted simply by the pardons. By far the most authoritative account of the last act of this drama is Miles, "After John Marshall's Decision," 519–44.

90 Quoted in Miles, 525.

91 Ibid., 529, 530, 539.

92 Ibid., 535.

93 Ibid., 540.

94 This account follows Tracy, *History*, 266–67, 280–82, with additional information from Miles, "After John Marshall's Decision," 539–41.

95 Kilpatrick and Kilpatrick, *New Echota Letters*, 126–28.

96 According to Tim Alan Garrison: "In several decisions in the latter half of the twentieth century the Supreme Court revived Marshall's assertion that the Native American tribes possess an inherent form of national sovereignty and the right of self-determination. From that point forward the Worcester decision became the Indian nations' most powerful weapon against state and local encroachments on their tribal powers." See his "Worcester v. Georgia (1832)," *New Georgia Encyclopedia* at http://www.georgiaencyclopedia.org/nge/Article.jsp?id=h–2720. See also his *The Legal Ideology of Removal: The Southern Judiciary and the Sovereignty of Native American Nations* (Athens: University of Georgia Press, 2002). In a widely used reader for undergraduate courses Theda Perdue and Michael D. Green make a similar point. Having "languished for nearly a century and a half," the *Worcester* decision became after World War II "one of the cornerstones of federal Indian law." Marshall's opinion furnished arguments tribes used "to reaffirm their sovereign status." Especially important was "the doctrine of retained sovereignty—the idea that a nation retains all those attributes of sovereignty it does not voluntarily surrender." *The Cherokee Removal: A Brief History with Documents* (Boston: Bedford, 1995), 69.

97 Tracy, *History*, 300.

98 McLoughlin, *Champions of the Cherokees*, 131. For reflections on the "desertion" charge, see Rennard Strickland and William M. Strickland, "A Tale of Two Marshalls: Reflections on Indian Law and Policy, The Cherokee Cases, and the Cruel Irony of Supreme Court Victories," *Oklahoma Law Review* 47 (Spring 1994): 116.

99 For one account, see Woodward, *Cherokees*, 225.

100 McLoughlin, "Civil Disobedience and Evangelism," 134–37. Butrick's diary is a featured source at several Trail of Tears sites. In Oklahoma, both Butrick and Worcester opposed an American Board proposal to exclude Cherokee slaveholders from fellowship. McLoughlin, *After the Trail of Tears*, 138–39.

101 Francis Paul Prucha, "Andrew Jackson's Indian Policy: A Reassessment," *Journal of American History* 56 (1969), as reprinted in Albert Hurtado and Peter Iverson, eds., *Major Problems in American Indian History* (Lexington, Mass.: D. C. Heath, 1994), 211–19, quotations at 216. Prucha refers to it as "less-than-disinterested" (219).

102 McLoughlin, *Cherokees and Missionaries*, 259. McLoughlin calls this ethnocentric stance "one of the low points in Indian mission history."

103 Walter H. Conser, Jr., "John Ross and the Cherokee Resistance Campaign, 1833–1838," *Journal of Southern History* 44 (May 1978): 191; McLoughlin, *Champions of the Cherokees*, 170.

104 "Facing History and Ourselves," online at http://www.facing.org/. See also Michael Bess, *Choices Under Fire: Moral Dimensions of World War II* (New York: Alfred A. Knopf, 2006); and George Cotkin, "History's Moral Turn," *Journal of the History of Ideas* 69:1 (2008), and succeeding symposium, pp. 293–331.

CHAPTER 3 **Slavery and Disobedience**

1 Walter Johnson, *Soul by Soul: Life Inside the Antebellum Slave Market* (Cambridge: Harvard University Press, 1999), 5–7.

2 Francis Jackson Garrison, *William Lloyd Garrison, 1805–1879: The Story of His Life Told by His Children* (New York: Century, 1885), 2:145–53.

3 See Mary Hershberger, "Anticipating Abolition: The Struggle against Indian Removal in the 1830s," *Journal of American History* 86:1 (June 1999): 35–39.

4 Catharine E. Beecher, *Educational Reminiscences and Suggestions* (New York: J. B. Ford, 1874), 62–65.

5 Quoted in Alisse Theodore Portnoy, " 'Female Petitioners Can Lawfully Be Heard': Negotiating Female Decorum, United States Politics, and Political Agency, 1829–1831," *Journal of the Early Republic* 23 (2003): 573–610, quotation at 589. See also, *Their Right to Speak*, 49–50.

6 A few years later she entertained the Adventist (Millerite) belief that "the destruction of the world" would precede the millennium and occur in 1843. Marshall Foletta, "Angelina Grimké: Asceticism, Millenarianism, and Reform," *New England Quarterly* 30:2 (June 2007): 212. She well deserved the term "religious virtuoso" that Robert Abzug introduced for her and many contemporaries. See *Cosmos Crumbling: American Reform and the Religious Imagination* (New York: Oxford, 1994).

7 Foletta, 196–97, is very useful on this spiritual itinerary. He corrects other biographers who seek more continuity from her experiences and observations of slavery.

8 See quotations in Hershberger, 34. On Beecher's breakdown and future role, see Kathryn Kish Sklar, *Catharine Beecher: A Study in American Domesticity* (W. W. Norton, 1976), 94–96, 132–37. For a unit of well-chosen excerpts from Beecher's *Essay on Slavery and Abolitionism, with Reference to the Duty of American Females* (1837) and Grimké's *Letters to Catharine E. Beecher, in Reply to an Essay on Slavery and Abolitionism* (1838), see Mason I. Lowance, *A House Divided: The Antebellum Slavery Debates in America, 1776–1865* (Princeton: Princeton University Press, 2003), 404–17. These appear together with essays by Sarah Grimké, Theodore Dwight Weld, and Angelina's appeal to Southern women, which is about to be discussed.

9 Gilbert Hobbs Barnes, *The Anti-Slavery Impulse, 1830–1840* (New York: Harcourt Brace, 1964; 1st pub., 1933), 103.

10 See my review essay, "Scripture and Slaughter: The Civil War as a Theological and Moral Crisis," *Modern Intellectual History* 6:1 (2009): 207–21.

11 Angelina E. Grimké, *Appeal to the Christian Women of the South* (New York: American Anti-Slavery Society, 1836), online at http://www.iath.virginia.edu/utc/abolitn/abesaegat.html, p. 3 (subsequent pages in text). Her sister Sarah M. Grimké also made a forceful statement of the man-thing distinction in *An Epistle to the Clergy of the Southern States* (New York, 1836), online at http://antislavery.eserver.org/religious/grimkeepistle/grimkeepistle.html.

12 Grimké's consultation of authorities distances her from the self-reliant assumption that the Bible is simple to read and interpret that Mark Noll attributes to her sister Sarah Grimké and other contemporaries (*America's God*, 383). Besides the Bible itself, Angelina Grimké's guides were a contemporary English author Thomas Hartwell Horne and the eighteenth-century French Benedictine abbot Augustin Calmet, whose commentaries were still in use. After an extensive quotation from Calmet on the rights of female servants, Grimké asked, "Are the rights of female slaves at the South thus secured?" No, they were all illegally held in bondage according to Hebrew law (pp. 8–9).

13 For her changing mood at this time, see Marshall Foletta, "Angelina Grimké, Asceticism, Millenarianism, and Reform," *New England Quarterly* 80:2 (2007): 197–98. Also valuable: Kathryn Kish Sklar, "'The Throne of My Heart': Religion, Oratory, and the Transatlantic Community in Angelina Grimké's Launching of Women's Rights, 1828–1838," in Sklar and James Brewer Stewart, eds., *Women's Rights and Transatlantic Antislavery in the Era of Emancipation* (New Haven: Yale University Press, 2007), 211–41.

14 *An Appeal to the Women of the Nominally Free States, Issued by an Antislavery Convention of American Women* (New York: William S. Dorr, 1837); Portnoy, *Their Right to Speak*, 162; JeanFagan Yellin, "Doing It Herself: *Uncle Tom's Cabin* and Woman's Role in the Slavery Crisis," in Eric J. Sundquist, ed., *New Essays on Uncle Tom's Cabin* (Cambridge: Cambridge University Press, 1986), 85–90.

15 Thavolia Glymph, *Out of the House of Bondage: The Transformation of the Plantation Household* (New York: Cambridge University Press, 2008), 6. This study focuses on the Civil War and postwar periods.

16 Betty L. Fladeland, "Grimké, Sarah Moore, . . . and Angelina Emily," in *Notable American Women, 1607–1850*, ed. Edward T. James et al. (Cambridge; Belknap Press of Harvard University Press, 1971), 2:97–99.

17 Frederick Douglass, *My Bondage and My Freedom* (1855), in *Autobiographies* (New York: Library of America, 1994), 216–18.

18 Harriet Jacobs, *Incidents in the Life of a Slave Girl*, ed. Jean Fagan Yellin (Cambridge: Harvard University Press, 1987), 72–73.

19 I draw this figure from Elizabeth Fox-Genovese, but I don't think the estimate is controversial. *Within the Plantation Household: Black and White Women of the Old South* (Chapel Hill: University of North Carolina Press, 1988), 156, 295.

20 Samuel Eliot Morison and Henry Steele Commager, *Growth of the American Republic* (New York: Oxford University Press, 1950), 1:537, 539.

21 Letter to Harvey Wish, quoted in Peter Novick, *That Noble Dream: The "Objectivity Question" and the American Historical Profession* (Cambridge: Cambridge University Press, 350, n. 46.

22 Editions from 1940 and 1956 are cited in Joseph Boskin, *Sambo: The Rise and Demise of an American Jester* (New York: Oxford University Press, 1986), 118–19. Also see David Brion Davis, "Slavery and the Post–World War II Historians"

(1974), reprinted in his *From Homicide to Slavery: Studies in American Culture* (New York: Oxford University Press, 1986), 187–206.

23 Raymond A. Bauer and Alice H. Bauer, "Day to Day Resistance to Slavery," *Journal of Negro History* 27:4 (1942): 388–419.

24 Kenneth M. Stampp, *The Peculiar Institution: Slavery in the Ante-Bellum South* (New York: Vintage, 1956), 140, 148.

25 Eugene D. Genovese, "Rebelliousness and Docility in the Negro Slave: A Critique of the Elkins Thesis," in John Bracey, August Meier, and Elliot Rudwick, eds., *American Slavery: The Question of Resistance*, 100.

26 Steven Hahn, *A Nation under Our Feet: Black Political Struggles in the Rural South from Slavery to the Great Migration* (Cambridge: Harvard University Press, 2003), 64–96, quotation at 68.

27 C. Peter Ripley et al., *The Black Abolitionist Papers*, 5 vols. (Chapel Hill: University of North Carolina Press, 1985–92) (hereafter cited as *BAP*), 3:336, 403–10.

28 Herbert Aptheker, *Abolitionism: A Revolutionary Movement* (Boston: Twayne, 1989), 170–71.

29 This account is based on these important works: Robin Blackburn, *The Overthrow of Colonial Slavery, 1776–1848* (London: Verso, 1988), 432–33, 527; Seymour Drescher, *Abolition: A History of Slavery and Antislavery* (Cambridge: Cambridge University Press, 2009), 259–64; and David Brion Davis, *Inhuman Bondage: The Rise and Fall of Slavery in the New World* (New York: Oxford University Press, 2006), 218–21.

30 See Blackburn, *Overthrow*, 526–57. "Antislavery breakthroughs were made … under the pressure of revolutionary or proto-revolutionary events, and the actuality or threat of slave resistance." And again: "The progress of abolition crucially depended on black witness, on slave resistance, and on the 'Black Jacobin' breakthrough of the 1790s."

31 The terminology made it sound as though slave property had been "repossessed by an unseen soul." Johnson, *Soul by Soul*, 204.

32 James W. C. Pennington, *The Fugitive Blacksmith* (London, 1949) as quoted in Johnson, *Soul by Soul*, epigraph, 19, 28, 218—a book that beautifully explores Pennington's key insight.

33 Probably any powerful literary autobiography borders on fiction. Douglass clearly altered fundamental statements about his memories of his parents from one version of his autobiography to another. See Peter Walker, *Moral Choices: Memory, Desire, and Imagination in Nineteenth-Century American Abolition* (Baton Rouge: Louisiana State University Press, 1978), 249–55. Jacobs's *Incidents* was long classified as fiction (she published it as narrative of escape, *Linda*) after first relating the key events in very different terms in her first publication, a letter to a newspaper published in 1853. The story she told there was not about her own suffering but about a woman she called "my younger sister," sold at the age of fourteen to a lecher, a "monster," a member of Congress, who forced her into sexual submission

by jailing and threatening to sell her mother, and who then, after his victim reached twenty-one, sent her and her two children ("who bore too strong a resemblance to him") off to be sold while he took possession of a new fourteen-year-old concubine. See A Fugitive Slave [Harriet Jacobs], "Letter from a Fugitive Slave," *New York Daily Tribune*, June 21, 1853, Documenting the American South, at http://docsouth.unc.edu/jacobs/support16.html. Significant controversy now surrounds the major claim in *Incidents* that she overcame all her owner's stratagems of sexual conquest. See Elizabeth Fox-Genovese, *Within the Plantation Household: Black and White Women of the Old South* (Chapel Hill: University of North Carolina Press, 1988), 392, 462. On the other hand, Jean Fagan Yellin has authenticated so many facts of the author's identity that the book can no longer be dismissed, as it famously once was, as historically uninformative.

34 Davis, *Inhuman Bondage*, 178–79; "At the Heart of Slavery," in Davis, *In the Image of God: Religion, Moral Values, and Our Heritage of Slavery* (New Haven: Yale University Press, 2001), 124–36. See also Douglass, *Autobiographies*, 282–87.

35 Fox-Genovese, *Within the Plantation Household*, 375.

36 See Anita Goldman, "Harriet Jacobs, Henry Thoreau, and the Character of Disobedience," in Deborah M. Garfield and Rafia Zafar, eds., *Harriet Jacobs and Incidents in the Life of a Slave Girl* (Cambridge: Cambridge University Press, 1996), 233–50.

37 Jacobs, *Incidents*, 151, 200; Jean Fagan Yellin, *Harriet Jacobs: A Life* (New York: Basic Books, 2004), 62–79. An excellent source on the chronology of events in the lives of Jacobs and her family: Jean Fagan Yellin, ed., *The Harriet Jacobs Family Papers*, 2 vols. (Chapel Hill: University of North Carolina Press, 2008), 1:xlix–lxxxi.

38 Douglass, *Autobiographies*, 303–24, 338–63, 643–48. In an 1881 retelling of his life he revealed that he had carried identification papers borrowed from a free black sailor.

39 Ibid., 376–78, 699–701.

40 Yellin, *Harriet Jacobs*, 68.

41 *BAP*, 4:350. For blacks' use of the term "self-emancipated," see ibid., 2:69. Like many others, Loguen was self-named—his slave name had been Jarm Logue. His mother had been kidnapped as a child in Ohio, enslaved, and given a slave name. His father was one of her "demi-civilized" owners. *The Rev. J. W. Loguen, as a Slave and a Freeman* (New York: Negro Universities Press, 1968; 1st pub., 1859), 12–15.

42 The woman's movement would demonstrate this point again after the Civil War, often drawing parallels between the tactics of its members and the "wild, unaccountable things" done by abolitionists. See Elizabeth Cady Stanton's comments in *Revolution*, Jan. 29, 1869, p. 48. For suffragists' criticism of Loguen for not including women in demands for suffrage, see *Revolution*, Oct. 22, 1868, p. 96.

43 Benjamin Quarles, *Black Abolitionists* (New York: Oxford University Press, 1969), viii–ix, 18.

44 Jane H. Pease and William H. Pease, *They Who Would Be Free: Blacks' Search for Freedom, 1830–1861* (Urbana: University of Illinois Press, 1990), vii, 1, 3. This work first appeared in 1974. The Peases had already written scathingly of white abolitionists' ambivalence on racial issues, and they had spoken of controversy over black nationalism in 1968 as the recurrence of a 100-year-old debate. See their "Antislavery Ambivalence: Immediatism, Expediency, Race," *American Quarterly* 17 (Winter 1965): 682–95. Their article, "Black Power—The Debate in 1840," *Phylon* 29 (Spring 1968): 19–26, struck a very different tone from *They Who Would Be Free*. It accepted uncritically assertions about "white domination" and prejudice. While noting disagreements among black abolitionists, in this article the Peases held to the abstraction of "the white antislavery movement" (21).

45 *BAP*, 3:24.

46 A recent, thoughtful survey of historical writing on black abolitionists concludes that even as "the field explodes with new books" and "fresh insights," no "new synthesis of the abolition movement" has emerged to "explore the place and the extent of African Americans in the movement." Manisha Sinha, "Coming of Age: The Historiography of Black Abolitionism," in *Prophets of Protest: Reconsidering the History of American Abolitionism*, ed. Timothy Patrick McCarthy and John Stauffer (New York: New Press, 2006), 23–38 (quotation at 37).

47 James Oliver Horton and Lois Horton, *In Hope of Liberty: Culture, Community, and Protest among Northern Free Blacks, 1700–1860* (New York: Oxford University Press, 1997), 236.

48 Patrick Rael, *Black Identity and Black Protest in the Antebellum North* (Chapel Hill: University of North Carolina Press, 2002), 49–53.

49 "Zillah" to "A Friend," *Liberator*, June 30, 1832, in Black Abolitionist Papers, 1830–1865, 17 reels (New York: Microfilming Corporation of America, 1981–83; Ann Arbor: University Microfilms International, 1984) (hereafter cited as BAP [microfilm]), reel 1: 198A.

50 BAP (microfilm), reel 4: 485–490A. Pennington, reacting to the *Latimer* decision (1842), took his text from Isaiah 28:8, the same text on covenants with death and agreements with hell adopted by William Lloyd Garrison to describe the Constitution in reaction to the *Burns* case (1851), also calling for the return of a fugitive to slavery.

51 See, e.g., Samuel E. Cornish's editorials against assemblages of illiterate men who might, in the context of a trial of "Negro Catchers," lose "self-government and become mere subjects of passion." *Colored American*, April 15, 29, 1837, in BAP (microfilm), reel 2: 28B, 39B.

52 James D. Richardson, comp., *A Compilation of the Messages and Papers of the Presidents* (New York: Bureau of National Literature, 1897), 3:1218, 1184–88.

53 Ibid., 1187.

54 "By 1840, some 93 per cent of the northern free Negro population lived in states which completely or practically excluded them from the right to vote." Leon

Litwack, *North of Slavery: The Negro in the Free States, 1790–1860* (Chicago: University of Chicago Press, 1961), 75.

55 Along with many other community studies of segregation and discrimination, see James Oliver Horton and Lois E. Horton, *Black Bostonians: Family Life and Community Struggle in the Antebellum North* (New York: Holmes and Meier, 1879), 68–79.

56 *BAP*, 4:256–57.

57 *BAP*, 3:6; 4:155.

58 *African Repository*, March 1853, in BAP (microfilm), reel 8: 147B.

59 Uriah Boston to Frederick Douglass, April 1855, in *BAP*, 4:279.

60 *BAP*, 3:112, 115, 254–55; 4:153, 260; 5:335, 386. They did not mention Jackson's concerns about slave rebelliousness or invasions from Jamaica.

61 *BAP*, 3:159–60. On contradictory views of the flag, which Maya Angelou has called a "symbol of hypocrisy and hope," see my essay, "Harriet Jacobs and the 'Dear Old Flag,'" *African American Review* 42:3–4 (2008): 596–98.

62 Quotations from Samuel Ringgold Ward and H. Ford Douglas in *BAP*, 4:49, 74. According to Wilson Jeremiah Moses, *Alexander Crummel: A Study of Civilization and Its Discontent* (New York: Oxford University Press, 1989), despite scholarly emphasis on African and folk traditions, "it was from the English/American literary and intellectual traditions that the literate classes of black Americans derived their conceptions of what black culture ought, ideally, to become" (9).

63 For examples, see BAP (microfilm), reel 5: 401B, 401AB, reel 6: 731A, 818B; Samuel Ringgold Ward, *Autobiography of a Fugitive Negro* (London: John Snow, 1855), 123. A probing investigation of links between lineage and rights is Werner Sollors, *Beyond Ethnicity: Consent and Descent in American Culture* (New York: Oxford University Press, 1988).

64 Charles Caples to *Liberator*, Sept. 6, 1834, in BAP (microfilm), reel 1: 523A.

65 Pease and Pease, *They Who Would Be Free*, 3–16.

66 See William Whipper in *BAP*, 3:120–22.

67 On receptiveness to socialization as a sign of merit in Jacksonian political society, see the interpretation in David Brion Davis, ed., *Antebellum American Culture* (Lexington, Mass.: D. C. Heath, 1979).

68 Vincent Harding, *There Is a River: The Black Struggle for Freedom in America* (New York: Harcourt Brace Jovanovich, 1981), 200. This account of black culture stresses a "Great Tradition" including recurrent instances of "civil disobedience" throughout the antebellum era; while it may sometimes exaggerate the extent of radicalism, it points out connections overlooked in other works.

69 Douglass, *Autobiographies*, 398.

70 *David Walker's Appeal to the Coloured Citizens of the World* (1829), ed. Peter P. Hinks (University Park: Pennsylvania State University Press, 2000).

71 Douglass, *Autobiographies*, 393–98. While emphasizing his personal role, Douglass acknowledges "the intervention of the people" as well as legislative threats. In fact

other abolitionists, white as well as black, participated in the ride-in campaigns. See Carlton Mabee, *Black Freedom: The Nonviolent Abolitionists from 1830 through the Civil War* (London: Macmillan, 1970), 98–126.

72 *BAP*, 4:230–32.

73 R. J. M. Blackett, *Beating against the Barriers: Biographical Essays in Nineteenth-Century Afro-American History* (Baton Rouge: Louisiana State University Press, 1986), 60–62.

74 *BAP*, 3:369.

75 *BAP*, 4:187–88.

76 *BAP*, 3:48.

77 *BAP*, 4:341–42. The incident may have occurred in Philadelphia, if at all. See ibid., 345. For similar accounts by the light-complexioned Brown set in Cleveland and on Lake Cayuga, see Mabee, *Black Freedom*, 96–97.

78 *Liberator* (1849), quoted in Mabee, *Black Freedom*, 96.

79 William H. Pease and Jane H. Pease, eds., *The Antislavery Argument* (Indianapolis: Bobbs-Merrill, 1965), 65–71, 192–96. According to Drescher, *Abolition*, 304, the AASS soon exceeded British precedents for publishing and organizing.

80 Tunde Adeleke, "Afro-Americans and Moral Suasion: The Debate in the 1830's," *Journal of Negro History* 83 (Spring 1998): 127–142, quoted at 127.

81 *BAP*, 3:244.

82 *BAP*, 3:182. As an abolitionist Wright was eloquent on the power of racial prejudice to keep even nominally free people segregated and enslaved. Ibid., 183–87; Davis, *Inhuman Bondage*, 48–49.

83 *BAP*, 3:248–49.

84 *BAP*, 3:238, 303.

85 *BAP*, 3:283–85. For blacks' appreciation of Garrison's acceptance of their beliefs and acts of self-protection, see Horton and Horton, *In Hope of Liberty*, 240.

86 *BAP*, 3:357. The editors identify Sidney as "most likely" Garnet.

87 Quoted in Pease and Pease, *They Who Would Be Free*, 235–36.

88 *BAP*, 3:403–10. On John Brown's subsidizing publication, see Hannah Geffert, "Regional Black Involvement in John Brown's Raid on Harpers Ferry," in McCarthy and Stauffer, eds., *Prophets of Protest*, 168.

89 Quoted in Harding, *There Is a River*, 151.

90 *BAP*, 3:168–69.

91 Harding, *There Is a River*, 121. The 1835 Philadelphia convention resolved: "That our duty to God, and to the principles of human rights, so far exceeds our allegiance to those [laws] that return the slave again to his master . . . that we recommend our people to peaceably bear the punishment those [laws] inflict, rather than aid in returning their brethren again to slavery."

92 *BAP*, 3:81; 4:64, 227.

93 *BAP*, 4:367.

94 *BAP*, 4:51. Ward was author of *Autobiography of a Fugitive Negro: His Anti-slavery Labours in the United States, Canada and England* (London: John Snow, 1855).

95 *BAP*, 4:357.

96 Thomas P. Slaughter, *Bloody Dawn: The Christiana Riot and Racial Violence in the Antebellum North* (New York: Oxford University Press, 1991), quotations at 49, 57.

97 Ibid., xi–xii; David Brion Davis, "Life and Death in Slavery," *New York Review of Books*, Jan. 30, 1992, p. 9.

98 Garnet's revolutionary expressions were balanced by his commitment in 1859 to church-based oversight of social improvement. He declined to support John Brown because the time was not right for insurrection. See William H. Pease and Jane H. Pease, *Bound with Them in Chains* (Westport, Conn.: Greenwood, 1972), 169, 181.

99 *BAP*, 3:397–401. Detroit's blacks, like those in other cities, had secret organizations to assist fugitives, though much about them remains hard to determine. See David Katzman, *Before the Ghetto: Black Detroit in the Nineteenth Century* (Urbana: University of Illinois Press, 1973), 40–41. Blacks sometimes cautioned slaves about "misinterpretations of the rights of property. ... Were you better informed, you would not scruple to break your master's locks and take all their money." Philip S. Foner and George E. Walker, eds., *Proceedings of the Black State Conventions, 1840–1865*, 2 vols. (Philadelphia: Temple University Press, 1979), 1:45.

100 *BAP*, 5:89.

101 *BAP*, 5:93–94.

102 *BAP*, 4: 364.

103 *BAP*, 4:348–50. Carol M. Hunter, *To Set the Captives Free: Reverend Jermain Wesley Loguen and the Struggle for Freedom in Central New York, 1835–1872* (New York: Garland, 1993), 218–23, sets this controversy in the context of revivalism.

104 See esp. David Brion Davis, *The Problem of Slavery in the Age of Revolution, 1770–1823* (Ithaca: Cornell University Press, 1975), 523–56. Just before the Christiana riot Parker and the slaveholder argued over what the Bible said about slavery. See W. U. Hensel, *The Christiana Riot and the Treason Trials of 1851* (Lancaster, Pa.: New Era, 1911), 108.

105 *BAP*, 4:87–88; and *Rev. Jermain W. Loguen, as a Slave and as a Freeman*, 435–37.

106 *BAP*, 5:59.

107 "Gandhi often said that if cowardice is the only alternative to violence, it is better to fight. He made this statement conscious of the fact that there is always another alternative: no individual or group need submit to any wrong, nor need they use violence to right the wrong; there is the way of nonviolent resistance." See Martin Luther King, Jr., "Pilgrimage to Nonviolence," in Alice and Staughton Lynd, eds., *Nonviolence in America: A Documentary History* (Maryknoll, N.Y.: Orbis, 1995), 217.

108 Gandhi's view, as he sometimes explained it, resembled the Calvinist distinction between those who eschew sin because of its penalties and those with deeper motivations. See *Gandhi, An Autobiography: The Story of My Experiments with Truth* (Boston: Beacon Press, 1957), 470.

109 In the legal aftermath of the Christiana tragedy, those who sought to play a conciliatory role and refused to aid the posse were in fact indicted for treason. Hensel, *Christiana Riot*, 57–58.

CHAPTER 4 Conflicts of Law in the Age of Reform

1 Henry D. Thoreau, "Resistance to Civil Government," in *Reform Papers*, ed. Wendell Glick (Princeton: Princeton University Press, 1973), 65.

2 *Abraham Lincoln: His Speeches and Writings*, ed. Roy P. Basler (Cleveland: World, 1946), 80–81.

3 Howard Zinn, *A People's History of the United States*, 3d ed. (New York: Harper Collins, 2003); McElroy, "Henry David Thoreau and 'Civil Disobedience,'" *Freedom Daily*, July 25, 2005, at http://www.fff.org/freedom/fd0503e.asp; Gay, "Law, Order, and Enlightenment," in Eugene V. Rostow, ed., *Is Law Dead?* (New York: Simon and Schuster, 1971), 30; Walzer, *Obligations* (Cambridge: Harvard University Press, 1970), 6.

4 Howard Taubman, "On Stage, Thoreau Speaks to Us Today," *New York Times*, Dec. 23, 1970.

5 On the title as determined by the Center for Editions of American Authors, see *Reform Papers*, ed. Glick, 313–15, 320–21. That determination is questioned in Thomas Woodson, "The Title and Text of Thoreau's 'Civil Disobedience,'" *Bulletin of Research in the Humanities* 81 (1978): 103–12. See also Daniel Walker Howe, "The Constructed Self against the State," in *Making the American Self: Jonathan Edwards to Abraham Lincoln* (Cambridge: Harvard University Press, 1997), 235–55. Howe warns that "much of what 'everyone knows' about it [Thoreau's essay] is not true" (236).

6 Thoreau, "Resistance," 79.

7 McLoughlin, *New England Dissent*, 2:1261; Lawrence Rosenwald, "The Theory, Practice and Influence of Thoreau's Civil Disobedience," from William Cain, ed., *The Oxford Historical Companion to Thoreau*, online at http://thoreau.eserver. org/theory.html#n4 (retrieved Feb. 16, 2010), n. 4.

8 Rosenwald, "Theory, Practice and Influence," para. 31.

9 Thoreau, "Resistance," 84.

10 Rosenwald, "Theory, Practice and Influence," para. 33.

11 Howe, *Making the American Self*, 237–41.

12 Thoreau, *A Week on the Concord and Merrimack Rivers* (New York: Library of America, 1985), 108–9. On the foundation of civil disobedience, see Richard E. Cauger, "The Anti-Historical Bias of Thoreau's 'A Week,'" *Encounter* 34 (Winter 1973): 2, 14. The two-week trip was taken in 1839; the book was finished at Walden Pond in 1847 and published in 1849.

13 Susan Ford Wiltshire, "Antigone's Disobedience," *Arethusa* 9:1 (1976): 29–36, quoting Bernard Knox, *The Heroic Temper* (1964).

14 On the importance of conscience to Thoreau, see Howe, *Making the American Self*, 249.

15 See Anita Goldman's essay, "Harriet Jacobs, Henry Thoreau, and the Character of Disobedience," in *Harriet Jacobs and* Incidents in the life of a Slave Girl, ed. Garfield and Zafar, 243–46.

16 Robert D. Richardson, Jr., *Henry Thoreau: A Life of the Mind* (Berkeley and Los Angeles: University of California Press, 1986), 176, 178; Raymond Adams, "Thoreau's Sources for 'Resistance to Civil Government,'" *Studies in Philology* 42 (1945): 651–53; Daniel Walker Howe, *The Unitarian Conscience: Harvard Moral Philosophy, 1805–1861* (Cambridge: Harvard University Press, 1970), 65–66; Howe, *Making the American Self*, 244–45, 249. On aid to fugitives, see *Walden*, chapter on "Visitors"; Gary Collinson, *Shadrach Minkins: From Fugitive Slave to Citizen* (Cambridge: Harvard University Press, 1997), 157–58; Sandra Harbert Petrulionis, *To Set This World Right: The Antislavery Movement in Thoreau's Concord* (Ithaca: Cornell University Press, 2006), 92–95.

17 Adams, "Thoreau's Sources," 649–50.

18 I have discussed this movement extensively in *Radical Abolitionism: Anarchy and the Government of God in Antislavery Thought* (Ithaca: Cornell University Press, 1973), 55–91, and in *Childhood, Marriage, and Reform: Henry Clarke Wright, 1797–1870* (Chicago: University of Chicago Press, 1980), 38–40, 51–52.

19 Perry, *Radical Abolitionism*, 143–44. The community demonstrated some conflict between immediate reform activities and the ultimate regeneration of society.

20 Ibid., 78–79.

21 Odell Shepard, ed., *The Journals of Bronson Alcott* (Boston: Little, Brown, 1938), 136.

22 *Liberator*, Jan. 27, 1843, p. 4, quoted extensively in Carl Watner, "Those 'Impossible Citizens': Civil Resistants in Nineteenth Century New England," *Journal of Libertarian Studies* 3 (1979): 176–77.

23 Watner, "Those 'Impossible Citizens,'" 178.

24 Ibid., 178–80; Clara Endicott Sears, *Bronson Alcott's Fruitlands* (Boston: Houghton Mifflin, 1915), 53–67.

25 Parker Pillsbury, *Acts of the Anti-Slavery Apostles* (Boston: Cupples, Upham, 1884).

26 Ibid., 123–26. For a very similar account, see Sandra Opdycke, "Foster, Stephen Symonds," *American National Biography Online* at http://www.anb.org/articles/15/15-00238.html (accessed Feb. 22, 2013).

27 See my *Childhood, Marriage, and Reform*, 43.

28 Carleton Mabee, *Black Freedom: The Nonviolent Abolitionists from 1830 through the Civil War* (Toronto: Macmillan, 1970), 205–15.

29 Pillsbury, *Acts of the Anti-Slavery Apostles*, 130–45.

30 For a letter from Foster on these hardships, see ibid., 281–82. Foster recognized that his sufferings were nothing compared with those of the slaves. "I can endure the *prison*, but save me from the *plantation*." An important come-outer was Thomas Parnell Beach, who spent three months in a Newburyport jail on a complaint brought by Quakers. With the aid of friends he published a newspaper, "A Voice from Jail," condemning slavery and the churches and extolling the God-given power of speech. See Pillsbury, 320, and my *Radical Abolitionism*, 108–9.

31 Pillsbury, *Acts of the Anti-Slavery Apostles*, 144–46. Spelled *Harper's* in original.

32 Ibid., 157–58.

33 Ibid., 486, 481. He does mention her later contributions to women's rights.

34 Ibid., 147.

35 Julie Roy Jeffrey, *The Great Silent Army of Abolitionism: Ordinary Women in the Antislavery Movement* (Chapel Hill: University of North Carolina Press, 1998), 146, 151–52, 260, n. 29.

36 *Boston Courier*, June 15, 1846, as reprinted in Gary Scharnhorst, " 'Conflict of Laws': A Lost Essay by Henry Thoreau," *New England Quarterly* 61:4 (1988): 569–71. The attribution to Thoreau is almost certainly erroneous.

37 John H. Schroeder, *Mr. Polk's War: American Opposition and Dissent, 1846–1848* (Madison: University of Wisconsin Press, 1973), 99, 105.

38 Robert W. Johannsen concluded that "the public remained largely indifferent" to abolitionist views on the war, "if indeed people knew of them at all." Furthermore, the "number of Americans who reconciled the war with the duties and responsi-bilities of citizens in a republic . . . outweighed those on the other side." *To the Halls of the Montezumas: The Mexican War in the American Imagination* (New York: Oxford University Press, 1985), 275, 287.

39 Abiel Abbott, March 11, 1845, in *The Boisterous Sea of Liberty: A Documentary History of America from Discovery through the Civil War*, ed. David Brion Davis and Steven Mintz (Oxford: Oxford University Press, 1998), 411.

40 Thoreau, "Resistance," 63, 65, 70, 73.

41 Thoreau generalized reasons for his disobedience well beyond the war. "It is for no particular item in the tax-bill that I refuse to pay it. I simply wish to refuse alle-giance to the State, to withdraw and stand aloof from it effectually" (ibid., 84).

42 Wayland is described in these terms by William G. McLoughlin in indicating that Baptists were no longer dissenters but established participants in northern middle-class religious life (*New England Dissent*, 2:1274). See also Daniel Walker Howe, *What God Hath Wrought: The Transformation of America, 1815–1848* (New York: Oxford University Press, 2007), 288–89.

43 See David R. Weber, ed., *Civil Disobedience in America: A Documentary History* (Ithaca: Cornell University Press, 1978), 83–84.

44 Francis Wayland, *The Limitations of Human Responsibility* (Boston: Gould, Kendall and Lincoln, 1838), 103.

45 Ibid., 178–79, 189–81, 183, 185. Also: "Every man must give account of *himself* before God" (188).

46 Ibid., 118.

47 James O. Murray, *Francis Wayland* (Boston: Houghton Mifflin, 1891), 141–43.

48 Quoted in Francis Wayland, Jr., and H. L. Wayland, *A Memoir of the Life and Labors of Francis Wayland* (New York: Sheldon, 1867), 2:332. On Wayland's evolving views, see Edward H. Madden, *Civil Disobedience and Moral Law in Nineteenth-Century American Philosophy* (Seattle: University of Washington Press, 1968), 30–43.

49 Julie Roy Jeffrey has shown how central women were to the Underground Railroad (*Great Silent Army*, 175–88). For a dramatic example of cooperation between antislavery women and a black vigilance committee, see K. K. Sklar, *Florence Kelley and the Nation's Work* (New Haven: Yale University Press, 1995), 23–25.

50 Child's work was published in 1860 by the American Anti-Slavery Society: Lydia Maria Child, *The Duty of Disobedience to the Fugitive Slave Law* (Boston: American Anti-Slavery Society, 1860). On the mounting cry for civil disobedience, see H. Robert Baker, *The Rescue of Joshua Glover: A Fugitive Slave, the Constitution, and the Coming of the Civil War* (Athens: Ohio University Press, 2006), 52–53, 205, n. 101.

51 *Ex parte Bushnell*, discussed in Robert Cover, *Justice Accused: Antislavery and the Judicial Process* (New Haven: Yale University Press, 1975), 216, 255–56.

52 Black Abolitionist Papers (microfilm), 4: 485–490A. Pennington was reacting to the *Latimer* case.

53 According to one careful historian: "Every effort by northerners to include some security for free blacks, particularly the trial by jury and habeas corpus, was defeated. . . . Every guarantee, every security in the new law was for the 'rights' of slave catchers." Thomas D. Morris, *Free Men All: The Personal Liberty Laws of the North, 1780–1861* (Baltimore: Johns Hopkins University Press, 1974), 146–47. On the Fugitive Slave Law of 1850 generally, see this work and Stanley W. Campbell, *The Slave Catchers: Enforcement of the Fugitive Slave Law, 1850–1860* (Chapel Hill: University of North Carolina Press, 1970).

54 John Weiss, *Life and Correspondence of Theodore Parker* (New York, 1864), 2:101.

55 Samuel Willard, *The Grand Issue: An Ethico-Political Tract* (Boston, 1851); Nathaniel Hall, *The Limits of Civil Obedience* (1851), both excerpted in Weber, *Civil Disobedience in America;* and J. G. Forman, *The Christian Martyrs; or, The Conditions of Obedience to the Civil Government* (Boston: W. Crosby and H. P. Nichols, 1851), 31. This stance of disobedience with submission would be consistent with the prescription of a conservative theologian like Charles Hodge (see below), at least on refusing to join a posse but probably not on sheltering and assisting a fugitive.

56 See Douglas C. Stange, "From Treason to Antislavery Patriotism: Unitarian Conservatives and the Fugitive Slave Law," *Harvard Library Bulletin* 25 (1977): 479–81.

57 Albert J. Von Frank, *The Trials of Anthony Burns: Freedom and Slavery in Emerson's Boston* (Cambridge: Harvard University Press, 1998), 31–32.

58 May and Parker quoted in Weiss, *Life*, 1:117–23.

59 Parker quoted in Von Frank, *Trials*, 60.

60 See the Records of the Anti-Man-Hunting League, 1846–1882, Massachusetts Historical Society, Boston. The key figure was the physician Henry Ingersoll Bowditch; there were about eighty members, and according to Bowditch they always drilled with "merriment."

61 *Life and Correspondence of Henry Ingersoll Bowditch*, ed. Vincent Yardley Ingersoll, 2 vols. (Boston: Houghton Mifflin, 1902), 1:207–8.

62 Weber, ed., *Civil Disobedience*, 127.

63 Glyndon G. Van Deusen, *William Henry Seward* (New York: Oxford University Press, 1967), 123. For a valuable account of Seward's speech and events leading up to it, see Jane H. Pease, "The Road to the Higher Law," *New York History* 40 (1959): 117–36.

64 Van Deusen, *William Henry Seward*, 131.

65 Rodgers, *Contested Truths*, 135. The denunciation Seward faced was presented as exemplifying the "labyrinths of error" a politician opens "when he acknowledges a higher law than the constitution." Such a "fanatical declamation . . . must end in the annihilation of all government, all law, all rights. . . . Anarchy and bloodshed; the law of the strong arm; the law of the sword; the Lynch law, and kindred enormities, are the sequence of a doctrine like this." *Washington (D.C.) Republic*, quoted disapprovingly in William Hosmer, *The Higher Law, in Its Relations to Civil Governments: With Particular Reference to Slavery, and the Fugitive Slave Law* (New York: Negro Universities Press, 1969; 1st pub. 1852), 15.

66 Among studies of reform, Robert Abzug's *Cosmos Crumbling: American Reform and the Religious Imagination* (New York: Oxford University Press, 1984) is especially sensitive to the importance of "sacred order."

67 See quotations in Elizabeth Fox-Genovese and Eugene D. Genovese, *The Mind of the Master Class: History and Faith in the Southern Slaveholders' Worldview* (New York: Cambridge University Press, 2005), 499–504.

68 Hosmer, *Higher Law*, 56, 124. These formulations are repeated throughout the book.

69 See Russell D. Parker, "The Philosophy of Charles G. Finney: Higher Law and Revivalism," *Ohio History* 82 (1998): 147–48. Discovery of the radical antebellum holiness movement has been important to recent critics of conservativism within Pentecostal movements, especially Donald Dayton. See his *Discovering an Evangelical Heritage* (New York: Harper and Row, 1976); "The Holiness Churches: A Significant Ethical Tradition," *Christian Century*, Feb. 26, 1975, 197–201; and other essays.

70 Theodore Davenport Bacon, *Leonard Bacon: A Statesman in the Church*, ed. Benjamin W. Bacon (New Haven: Yale University Press, 1931), 344–45.

71 See Moses Stuart, *Conscience and the Constitution, with Remarks on the Recent Speech of the Hon. Daniel Webster in the Senate of the United States on the Subject of Slavery* (Boston: Crocker and Brewster, 1850), 60–62. His moral position shows absolute indifference to the enslaved population: "I may think that Virginia, for example, does a moral wrong by her slavery laws; but it is clearly no political wrong done to others. The matter belongs to her alone, not to her neighbors" (60).

72 E. N. Elliott, ed., *Cotton Is King, and Pro-Slavery Arguments* (Augusta, Ga.: Pritchard, Abbott, and Loomis, 1860), esp. 819, 822, 837, 838.

73 *Systematic Theology*, 3 vols. (Grand Rapids: Eerdmans, 1981), 3:356–60.

74 Alasdair MacIntyre, *After Virtue: A Study in Moral Theory* (Notre Dame, Ind.: University of Notre Dame Press, 1984); "Are There Any Natural Rights?" Charles F. Adams Lecture (Brunswick, Maine: Bowdoin College, 1983).

75 Cf. discussions of *Ableman v. Booth* in Baker, *Rescue of Joshua Glover*, 154–55; and Cover, *Justice Accused*, 186–87.

76 On the "tragedy," see chapter 3. For the trial, in which the presiding judge charged that treason referred to something more than armed resistance to law enforcement, see W. U. Hensel, *The Christiana Riot and the Treason Trials of 1851: An Historical Sketch* (Lancaster, Pa.: New Era, 1911), 86–88. The case and the general issue are discussed in Cover, *Justice Accused*, 215.

77 On the vilification of Massachusetts Chief Justice Lemuel Shaw, see Cover, *Justice Accused*, 250.

78 Ibid., 197–99, 209, 217.

79 For the address, see Jacob R. Shipherd, comp., *History of the Oberlin-Wellington Rescue* (1859; New York: Negro Universities Press, 1969), 175–78; Nat Brandt, *The Town That Started the Civil War* (Syracuse: Syracuse University Press, 1990), 186–89. The sentence was $100, twenty days, and the costs of prosecution. The twenty-eight days already spent in jail were not counted against the sentence.

80 Shipherd, comp., *History of the Oberlin-Wellington Rescue*, 3, 45–46. The rescuers were released in a bargain arranged with the slave hunters who had been incarcerated elsewhere in Ohio. Crowds then celebrated the "signal triumph of the Higher Lawites" (265).

81 Albert Gallatin Riddle, *The Life of Benjamin F. Wade* (Cleveland: William W. Williams, 1886), 118. See also his *Recollections of War Times: Reminiscences of Men and Events in Washington, 1860–1865* (New York: G. P. Putnam's Sons, 1895).

82 Most of these facts are recited in any life of Brown. On his identification with Cromwell, see David S. Reynolds, *John Brown, Abolitionist: The Man Who Killed Slavery, Sparked the Civil War, and Seeded Civil Rights* (New York: Vintage, 2006), 164–66, 274; on his service in the Underground Railroad, see Bordewich, *Bound for Canaan*, 414–26; and on the possible finding of insanity, see James McPherson, "Days of Wrath," *New York Review of Books*, May 12, 2005, p. 15.

83 See these works of Stanley Harrold: *The Abolitionists and the South, 1831–1861* (Lexington: University Press of Kentucky, 1995); *Subversives: Antislavery Community*

in Washington, D.C., 1828–1865 (Baton Rouge: Louisiana State University Press, 2003); *Border War: Fighting over Slavery before the Civil War* (Chapel Hill: University of North Carolina Press, 2010).

84 Quoted in Reynolds, *John Brown*, 342, 492. The latter quotation is taken from an 1881 speech at Storer College in Harpers Ferry.

85 John Brown, Last Address to the Virginia Court, Nov. 2, 1859, and Henry Wise, Message to the Virginia Legislature, Dec. 5, 1859, in Jonathan Earle, ed., *John Brown's Raid on Harpers Ferry: A Brief History with Documents* (Boston: Bedford, 2008), 87, 124.

86 Reynolds, *John Brown*, 366–67, 402; "Concord and Captain John Brown," *Concord Magazine* ("ezine"), March–April 2001, at http://www.concordma.com/magazine/marapr01/johnbrownthoreau.html (retrieved April 21, 2010). Reynolds, with little patience for "ambivalent" attitudes toward Brown (499), applauds the contribution of literary transcendentalism, rather than organized antislavery, in upholding his reputation. Emerson might seem especially marginal to nonresistance were it not for his praise of "the dogma of no-government and non-resistance" as a uniquely American idea (see my *Boats against the Current: American Culture between Revolution and Modernity, 1820–1860* [New York: Oxford University Press, 1993], 127).

87 Reynolds, *John Brown*, 347.

88 Quoted by Jonathan Cohen in "The Ayers Issue," *Inside Higher Education*, Oct. 14, 2008, online at http://www.insidehighered.com/news/2008/10/14/ayers.

89 "Homegrown Terrorist," a review of Reynolds, who uses the same term to describe Brown (438), *New Republic*, Oct. 24, 2005, p. 23. Though historians' reviews tended to be critical, some well-known authors actually fault Reynolds for giving too much credence to the "terrorist" label. See Barbara Ehrenreich's review in *New York Times Book Review*, April 17, 2005, and Christopher Hitchens's in *Atlantic*, May 2005.

90 Reynolds, *John Brown*, 506. Cf. Eric Foner's review of Reynolds's book in *Los Angeles Times Book Review*, May 1, 2005.

CHAPTER 5 "Wild, Unaccountable Things"

1 *An Account of the Proceedings on the Trial of Susan B. Anthony on the Charge of Illegal Voting, . . .* (Rochester, N.Y., 1874), 81–85. Alternative versions online at the Elizabeth Cady Stanton and Susan B. Anthony Papers Project at http://ecssba.rutgers.edu/docs/sbatrial.html (retrieved May 25, 2010).

2 On these subjects, including other peace sects, see Peter Brock, *Pacifism in the United States: From the Colonial Era to the First World War* (Princeton: Princeton University Press, 1968), esp. pt. 4.

3 Quoted in Staughton Lynd and Helen Lynd, eds., *Nonviolence in America: A Documentary History* (Maryknoll, N.Y.: Orbis, 1995), 38–41.

4 I have found only two significant articles, cited below at n. 62, where one might expect the law journals to overflow, on the Supreme Court test case of woman

suffrage, *Minor v. Happersett* (1875). The pioneering work of Ellen DuBois is cited below. The filmmaker Ken Burns said on-camera that shortly before making the documentary film *Not for Ourselves Alone: The Story of Elizabeth Cady Stanton and Susan B. Anthony* (PBS, 2000) he had never heard of Stanton.

5 In 1853 a woman who dressed as a man, and thus as an eligible citizen, in order to vote in Cincinnati received a twenty-day sentence. It is not clear, however, whether such cross-dressing was intended as civil disobedience or simple deception. For this and a reported instance in New York in the same year, see Nancy Isenberg, *Sex and Citizenship in Antebellum America* (Chapel Hill: University of North Carolina Press, 1998), 48, n. 224.

6 Stanton, "Address to the Legislature of New York," at http://www.nps.gov/wori/historyculture/address-to-the-new-york-legislature–1854.htm. See also Harriet H. Robinson, *Massachusetts in the Woman Suffrage Movement* (Boston: Roberts Brothers, 1881), 232–35. Since taxes were at issue, perhaps, Phillips appeared less concerned about property restrictions: the constitution "only recognizes sentient, tax-paying beings," or should only do so (235).

7 For historians, the issue of a long-term perspective on blacks' struggle for civil rights has been the focus of important discussion, even contention, since Jacqueline Dowd Hall's 2005 presidential address to the Organization of American Historians, "The Long Civil Rights Movement and the Political Uses of the Past," *Journal of American History* 91 (2005): 1233–63. Though agreeing that the established or "classic" narrative framework, 1955–1965, is too confined, some have questioned the somewhat extended alternatives reaching back to the 1930s or World War I. See Eric Arnesen, "Reconsidering the 'Long Civil Rights Movement,'" *Historically Speaking* 10:2 (April 2009), 32. Perhaps, however, we can extend the time frame even further to the "black abolitionists' challenges to the Fugitive Slave Act and the evils of chattel slavery," as Vincent Harding showed in *There Is a River: The Black Struggle for Freedom in America*, and even consider women's parallel struggle, too.

8 See Margaret Washington, *Sojourner Truth's America* (Urbana: University of Illinois Press, 2009), 325–26; Patricia A. Schechter, *Ida B. Wells-Barnett and American Reform, 1880–1930* (Chapel Hill: University of North Carolina Press, 2001), 43–44, 71–72.

9 Tera W. Hunter, *To 'Joy My Freedom: Southern Black Women's Lives and Labors after the Civil War* (Cambridge: Harvard University Press, 1997), 99.

10 Roger A. Fischer, "A Pioneer Protest: The New Orleans Street-Car Controversy of 1867," *Journal of Negro History* 53 (1968): 210–33.

11 Marjorie M. Norris, "An Early Instance of Nonviolence: The Louisville Demonstrations of 1870–1871," *Journal of Southern History* 32 (1966): 487–504 (quotation at 504).

12 109 U.S. 3 (1883). On the test cases, see Alan F. Westin, "Ride-In!" *American Heritage* 13:5 (Aug. 1962): 58–64.

13   163 U.S. 537 (1896), available at http://www.law.cornell.edu/supct/html/historics/ USSC_CR_0163_0537_ZO.html. Ferguson was the Louisiana judge against whose decision the appeal was made. Among scholarly studies, most recent is Williamjames Hull Hoffer, *Plessy v. Ferguson: Race and Inequality in Jim Crow America* (Lawrence: University of Kansas Press, 2012).

14   These cases are discussed in many works, including Hyman and Wiecek, *Equal Justice under Law*, 497–502; and Barbara Young Welke, *Recasting American Liberty: Gender, Race, Law, and the Railroad Revolution, 1865–1920* (New York: Cambridge University Press, 2001), 341–63.

15   Cf. the different but compatible emphases of Ellen Dubois, "Women's Rights and Abolition: The Nature of the Connection," and Blanche Glassman Hersh, "'Am I Not a Woman and a Sister?': Abolitionist Beginnings of Nineteenth-Century Feminism," in Lewis Perry and Michael Fellman, eds., *Antislavery Reconsidered: New Perspectives on the Abolitionists* (Baton Rouge: Louisiana State University Press, 1979), 238–83.

16   Anthony did urge Jermain W. Loguen and an association of blacks demanding the suffrage to extend their demand to black women, who suffered grievances "a thousand fold greater than those of colored men." *Revolution*, Oct. 22, 1868, p. [1]. On the effort of at least a few women's rights activists to place black women "at the center of the movement's concerns," see Ellen DuBois, *Woman Suffrage and Women's Rights* (New York: New York University Press, 1998), 92–93.

17   Benjamin Quarles, "Frederick Douglass and the Woman's Rights Movement," *Journal of Negro History* 25 (1940): 35; Angela G. Ray, "The Rhetorical Ritual of Citizenship: Women's Voting as Public Performance, 1868–1875," *Quarterly Journal of Speech* 93 (2007): 4.

18   Susan B. Anthony, reply to Frederick Douglass at American Equal Rights Association meetings, in *Revolution*, May 20, 1969, p. 306.

19   *Revolution*, Jan. 29, 1868, p. 51. For more on the alliance with Train, see Ellen Carol DuBois, *Feminism and Suffrage: The Emergence of an Independent Women's Movement in America, 1848–1869* (Ithaca: Cornell University Press, 1978), 93–104.

20   On Garrisonian commitment to a "broad coalition" and the opposition of third-party abolitionists like Stanton, see Aileen S. Kraditor, *Means and Ends in American Abolitionism: Garrison and His Critics on Strategy and Tactics, 1834–1850* (New York: Pantheon, 1969), 158 and passim. For reconsideration of these issues, see Bruce Laurie, "Putting Politics Back In: Rethinking the Problem of Political Abolitionism," in *William Lloyd Garrison at Two Hundred: History, Legacy, Memory* (New Haven: Yale University Press, 2008), 77–92. The woman's suffrage conventions faced the eccentricity issue in a manner reminiscent of the abolitionists, as when a mad woman rose to speak, police started to take her away, she said she had not elected this ruler, and the audience appreciated her reply and let her speak. See *Revolution*, May 20, 1869, p. 313.

21   *Revolution*, Jan. 29, 1869, p. 48.

22 Cf. *Revolution*, June 18, 1868, p. 374: "Did Charles Remond ever refuse to extend the right hand of fellowship to an earnest worker in the Anti-Slavery cause, because he was not in favor of the enfranchisement of woman?" This is one of many examples of the same point drawn from antislavery history to defend association with Train. Here the cause of black women is said to have been abandoned by abolitionists and championed by feminists.

23 Stanton's remarks have much in common with 1960s justifications of abolitionists as agitators who had no obligation to work though decorous and conventional methods. The problem with that view is that it seemingly justifies *any* wild agitation. For a more considered view of the way in which even agitators must have a strategy and weigh different tactics, cf. Kraditor, *Means and Ends*.

24 *Revolution*, Nov. 26, 1868, p. 328. For debate over abolitionist principles and Train at the convention of the American Equal Rights Association, including Stephen Foster and Frederick Douglass, see ibid., May 20, 1869.

25 *Revolution*, April 21, 1870, p. 24.

26 *Revolution*, July 22, 1869, p. 41.

27 A. G. Riddle, "The Right of Women to Exercise the Elective Franchise, under the Fourteenth Article of the Constitution" (Washington, D.C.: Judd and Detweiler, 1871), 13.

28 *Revolution*, April 27, 1871, n.p.

29 *Bradwell*: 83 U.S. 130 (1873). *Minor*: 88 U.S. 162 (1875). Quotation from Belva Lockwood, Annual Report at NWSA meeting, 1876, *History of Woman Suffrage*, ed. Elizabeth Cady Stanton, et al., 6 vols. (New York: Fowler and Wells, 1881–1922), 3:6.

30 On the justification of civil disobedience as a means of enlightening public opinion (in this case, with reference to the Fourteenth Amendment), see Arendt, *Crises of the Republic*, 81. On the uses of losing cases for advancing discussion and understanding, with reference to Anthony and the New Departurists, see Jules Lobel, *Success without Victory: Lost Legal Battles and the Long Road to Justice in America* (New York: New York University Press, 2003), ch. 4.

31 "Women Who Voted, 1868 to 1873—Sorted Chronologically," Stanton and Anthony Papers Online at http://ecssba.rutgers.edu/resources/voterspr.html (retrieved May 6, 2010).

32 *Scott v. Sandford*, 60 U.S. 393 at 403.

33 Susan B. Anthony, "Is it a Crime for a Citizen of the United States to Vote?" at http://www.law.umkc.edu/faculty/projects/ftrials/anthony/anthonyaddress.html [unpaginated].

34 *Scott v. Sandford* at 421.

35 Ibid., at 426.

36 She attributes this view to Attorney General Edward Bates as well as senators and judges who have cited the same "monarchical idea" in opposition to the rights of American women ("Is It a Crime," n.p.).

37 "Is It a Crime," n.p.

38 Ibid. She quotes a letter to her from Benjamin F. Butler: "I do not believe anybody in Congress doubts that the Constitution authorizes the right of women to vote, precisely as it authorizes trial by jury and many other like rights guaranteed to citizens."

39 Linda G. Ford, *Iron-Jawed Angels: The Suffrage Militancy of the National Woman's Party, 1912–1920* (Lanham, Md.: University Press of America, 1991), 21; Doris Stevens, *Jailed for Freedom: The Story of the Militant Suffragist Movement* (New York: Schocken, 1976; 1st pub., 1920), 3.

40 *Revolution*, Aug. 6, 1868, p. 71.

41 *Revolution*, May 7, 1868, p. 281. See also April 30, p. 7, for survival of the scene in Topeka without being demoralized.

42 They could argue that women originally had the franchise in that state and it had been withdrawn without their consent. *Revolution*, Sept. 10, 1868, p. 162. On the voting, Nov. 12, 1868, p. [1]; Nov. 19, 1868, p. 307. The next year 214 came forward: Nov. 18, 1869, p. 314. Other comments on Vineland: July 8, 1869, p. 9, 11; Aug. 26, 1869, p. 113; Nov. 3, 1870, pp. 278–79. For another instance, see Nov. 19, 1868, pp. 308–9.

43 *Revolution*, Sept. 24, 1868, pp. 180–81; Oct. 1, 1868, pp. 195–96; Oct. 15, 1868, pp. 236–37.

44 *Revolution*, April 29, 1869, p. 263; April 20, 1871, n.p.; April 27, 1871, n.p. Other examples, see May 27, 1869, p. 327 (Elizabethtown, N.J., voters).

45 *Revolution*, Dec. 23, 1869, p. 395; Jan. 20, 1870, pp. 38–39.

46 *Revolution*, Nov. 11, 1869, p. 300. For other instances, see Nov. 25, 1869, p. 327; April 13, 1871, n.p. For an instance of South Carolina black registrars allowing black women to vote, see April 20, 1871, n.p.

47 Cf. Basch, who says "hundreds" (p. 57), and Leslie Friedman Goldstein, who says 150 in "a widespread campaign of mild civil disobedience." *The Constitutional Rights of Women* (Madison: University of Wisconsin Press, 1979), 73.

48 *Revolution*, Oct. 21, 1869, p. 234.

49 *Revolution*, Nov. 18, 1869, p. 314. The charge of theatricality recurs in criticisms of civil disobedience. It is raised by critics who prefer either political education or violent "militancy." National Woman's Party agitation, as we will see, welcomed such criticism and accentuated the theatricality of confrontation.

50 *Revolution*, March 17, 1870, p. 171.

51 *Revolution*, May 19, 1870, pp. 305–6.

52 *Revolution*, Jan. 26, 1871, n.p.

53 A. G. Riddle, "The Right of Women to Exercise the Elective Franchise under the Fourteenth Article of the Constitution," speech delivered at a Suffrage Convention in Washington, Jan. 11, 1871, and argument delivered to the Judiciary Committee (Washington: Judd and Detweiler, 1871). Also see *Revolution*,

April 27, 1871, n.p. This speech also includes news of Washington women, E. D. E. N. Southworth, Grace Greenwood, et al., seeking to register, accompanied by Frederick Douglass.

54 Published with *Sarah E. Webster v. The Judges of Election* (Washington, D.C.: Judd and Detweiler, 1871).

55 *Revolution,* May 11, 1871, n.p.

56 *Suffrage Conferred by the Fourteenth Amendment: Woman's Suffrage: Sara J. Spencer vs. the Board of Registration, and Sarah E. Webster vs. the Judges of Election, Argument of the Counsel for the Plaintiffs, with the Opinions of the Court* (Washington, D.C.: Judd and Detweiler, 1871).

57 "A Note About This Volume," *An Account of the Proceedings in the Trial of Susan B. Anthony, on the Charge of Illegal Voting, at the Presidential Election in Nov., 1872,* in *Women in America from Colonial Times to the Twentieth Century,* ed. Leon Stein and Annette K. Baxter (New York: Arno Press, 1974; 1st pub., 1874).

58 For a valuable account of the trial, see Kathleen Barry, *Susan B. Anthony: A Biography of a Singular Feminist* (New York: New York University Press, 1988), 248–274.

59 *Account of the Proceedings,* 83–84.

60 Ibid., Appendix, 160–61. See also on tax resistance, speech of Matilda Gage, ibid., 182–83.

61 According to one version of the story, she refused to pay, but her highly sympathetic attorney, Henry Rogers Selden, paid it because he "could not see a lady" he "respected put in jail." Thereby he closed off any opportunity to appeal the case. See "Western New York Suffragists: Biographies and Images" at http://www.winningthevote.org/F-HRSelden.html.

62 Norma Basch, "Reconstructing Female Citizenship: *Minor v. Happersett,*" in Donald G. Nieman, ed., *The Constitution, Law, and American Life: Critical Aspects of the Nineteenth-Century Experience* (Athens: University of Georgia Press, 1992), 52–66. Also see Angela G. Ray and Cindy Koenig Richards, "Inventing Citizens, Imagining Gender Justice: The Suffrage Rhetoric of Virginia and Francis Minor," *Quarterly Journal of Speech* 93 (2007): 375–402.

63 Waite noted that no state, at the time he wrote, had accorded women the suffrage when admitted, and this had never been raised as an argument against admission. Goldstein, *Constitutional Rights,* 81–82.

64 Basch, "Reconstructing," 61.

65 Francis Minor did not give up. See his "Woman's Legal Right to the Ballot: an Argument in Support of)," *The Forum,* Dec. 1886, pp. 351–60, on the oddity in naturalization cases that mothers could transmit to their sons rights that they did not possess.

66 See, e.g., *Revolution,* July 30, 1868, p. 59.

67 *Revolution*, June 25, 1868, p. 394.

68 Copy of letter to Internal Revenue collector in *Revolution*, June 17, 1869, p. [1].

69 *Revolution*, June 25, 1869, p. 393. See also an essay on "Woman as a Tax-Payer," Oct. 14, 1869, p. 229.

70 *Revolution*, April 9, 1868, p. 210.

71 *George W. Wheeler v. Sarah E. Wall*, 6 Allen, Massachusetts Reports 558; William I. Bowditch, *Taxation of Women in Massachusetts* (Cambridge: John Wilson, 1875), 33 and passim.

72 Andrea Moore Kerr, *Lucy Stone: Speaking Out for Equality* (New Brunswick: Rutgers University Press, 1992), 103.

73 For the best account, see Dorothy Sterling, *Ahead of Her Time: Abby Kelley and the Politics of Antislavery* (New York: W. W. Norton, 1991), 367–72. *Woman's Journal* covered these events closely from 1872 on.

74 Emily Sampson, *With Her Own Eyes: The Story of Julia Smith, Her Life, and Her Bible* (Knoxville: University of Tennessee Press, 2006), 117–18.

75 Julia E. Smith, comp., *Abby Smith and Her Cows, with a Report of the Law Case Decided Contrary to Law* (Hartford: [American Publishing Co.], 1877), 10, 14, 27. Hereafter cited as *ASHC*. I have used a facsimile edition published by Arno Press in 1972, but I have examined the original work as noted below (n. 103).

76 *ASHC*, 9, 14, 17.

77 Pamela Cartledge, "Seven Cows on the Auction Block: Abby and Julia Smith's Fight for Enfranchisement of Women," *Connecticut Historical Bulletin* 52:1 (1987): n. 19, finds this hard to verify or disprove.

78 *ASHC*, 14, 36.

79 See *ASHC*, 23, 63, on "the redeemed eight." According to Cartledge's account (25), they bought back six. She cites Elizabeth G. Speare, "Abby, Julia, and the Cows," *American Heritage* 8 (June 1954), although Speare in fact says that "the Smiths' agent bought back four of the cows but was obliged to sacrifice the others" (55). That might be a possible reading of *ASHC*, 14. By the account in Kathleen L. Housley, *The Letter Kills but the Spirit Gives Life: The Smiths—Abolitionists, Suffragists, Bible Translators* (Glastonbury, Conn.: Historical Society, 1993), the other three were "apparently not sold but were returned to the Smiths" (150). Julia's description of the picture of the cows says that "three have since been disposed of" (*ASHC*, frontispiece, [5]).

80 *ASHC*, 68, 70–73.

81 *ASHC*, 14. From *Springfield Republican*, Jan. 6, 1874.

82 *ASHC*, 54. From *Woman's Journal*, June 26, 1875.

83 Thoreau, "Resistance," 89–90.

84 "This is a bit of Defoe's English, ladies and gentlemen." *Springfield Republican*, quoted in *ASHC*, 13. Abby and correspondent of *Boston Post* in *ASHC*, 26. On Julia's "artless simplicity" according to *Woman's Journal*, see *ASHC*, 44.

85 One interviewer pointed out that the inclusion of the cows in the circle of friendship was "a serious rather than a jocular matter." Though they may have been Abby's property legally, they were Julia's pets emotionally. As Abby made public, they responded when Julia called their names, followed her in single file, and could be milked only if she stood where they could see her. She pleaded with the heartless tax collector to leave two together so that one would not be alone and bereft. A remarkable passage on the pathos of their lives links the sale of the cows with deaths in the family (and perhaps with the sisters' childlessness): "She [Julia] says now she can no more have the comfort of raising a fine calf, now and then, from the dread of following it to the sign-post to see it sacrificed." *ASHC*, 15, 21, 13, 26, 36, 22, 40.

86 Richard B. Gregg, *Power of Nonviolence* (discussed previously in chapter 1 and more extensively in chapter 7). Gregg stresses the importance of onlookers. The Smiths drew national attention to their moral fight.

87 This is Lucy Stone's report. *ASHC*, 56. *Woman's Journal*, July 10, 1875.

88 *Boston Journal*, Feb. 20, 1874, quoted in *ASHC*, 30.

89 *Woman's Journal*, March 13, 1886, p. 85.

90 "The Misses Smith Interviewed by Dr. C. C. Dills," *Hartford Daily Times*, Jan. 22, 1874, in *ASHC*, 21.

91 Housley, *Letter Kills*, 140.

92 Ibid., 136. This is the best source on the family's pre–Civil War life and antislavery activity.

93 *ASHC*, 57, 66. Letter from Abby H. Smith and Sister to the *Winsted Press*, Feb. 3, 1876.

94 *ASHC*, 57, 66, from the *People*, Aug. 15, 1875. The Bible was advertised on the end papers of *ASHC*.

95 Sampson, *With Her Own Eyes*, 135–36.

96 *ASHC*, Introduction, p. 7. Cf. the sisters' account of the speech on the wagon, 34.

97 Glastonbury officials learned to resent their depiction as predatory bumpkins in scores of news stories. Through it all, the sisters maintained control over their own "story." In a way, they show us only as much as they want to. A key to Julia's storytelling is reticence and selective revelation. A key to her effectiveness as a protester/propagandist is the dramatic sense of privacy invaded by government, trust violated by neighbors, and fame coming unsought.

98 Elizabeth Cady Stanton et al., eds., *History of Woman Suffrage*, 3:72, 98–99. The larger work in 6 vols. was compiled in 1881–1922 and is now available online in various formats.

99 Linda K. Kerber, *No Constitutional Right to Be Ladies: Women and the Obligations of Citizenship* (New York: Hill and Wang, 1980), 112–23. Kerber's criticism of the Smiths is not harsh; in fact, she is more critical of the continuing permeation of tax law with imagery of heterosexual households—which the Smiths did not have.

100 *New York Tribune*, April 24, 1876, in *ASHC*, 70.

101 *Woman's Journal*, Nov. 4, 1876, in *ASHC*, 74.

102 "The Misses Smith Interviewed," *ASHC*, 21.

103 I have examined a copy at the American Antiquarian Society.

104 The third case was decided in their favor to the extent that their land could not be taken, though other personal property (including cows) could be and was.

105 Sampson, *With Her Own Eyes*, 69.

106 At Julia's instruction, after her death her body was brought back to Glastonbury and buried under a stone carrying the name she owned as a single woman and located, in birth order, between her sisters Laurilla and Abby.

107 The best statement of this critique is Carolyn C. Jones, "Dollars and Selves: Women's Tax Criticism and Resistance in the 1870s," *University of Illinois Law Review* (1994), which quotes the critic of the Smiths (from *Woman's Journal* 5 [1874]: 130) at 280, n. 74. Jones also quotes Mary Ryan's *Woman in Public: Between Banners and Ballots, 1825–1880* (Baltimore: Johns Hopkins University Press, 1990), 155, on a general shift in thinking after the Civil War in which individuals "began to call themselves not citizens but taxpayers and intimated that they were linked to the commonweal by a private monetary function."

108 *ASHC*, 60.

109 Many agreed that propertied women ought to have the vote, but they held that those with none needed it more so that they could vote out the grog shops and avoid getting beaten and saddled with the town's debt (*ASHC*, 11, 42). Officials and husbands are described as hesitant to offend a voter.

110 Rogers M. Smith, *Civic Ideals: Conflicting Visions of Citizenship in U.S. History* (New Haven: Yale University Press, 1997), 388. The author was A. A. Sargent.

111 See "The Suffrage Cause and Bryn Mawr—The British Lecturers," at http://www.brynmawr.edu/library/exhibits/suffrage/speakers3.html.

112 Article entitled "Deeds Better than Words," Oct. 26, 1906, on *Clio Talks Back* blog of International Museum of Women, at http://www.imow.org/community/blog/viewEntry?id=34.

113 See Ford, *Iron-Jawed Angels*, 15–59, quotations at 29, 31, 33, 58.

114 See Katherine H. Adams and Michael L. Keene, *Alice Paul and the American Suffrage Campaign* (Urbana: University of Illinois Press, 2008), xvi, 347.

115 Even their intramural opponents who virtually detested them recognized this point. See *Woman Citizen*, Nov. 24, 1917, arguing that the administration should give only "light punishment" to unpatriotic banners and desist from "excessive severity" in enforcing traffic laws. The goal was not to play into the pickets' hand.

116 Mary Beard's phrase, as quoted in Ford, *Iron-Jawed Angels*, 63.

117 Ibid., 230–38. All told, Ford says about 2,000 stood on Woman's Party picket lines, about 500 were arrested, and 168 went to prison (7).

118 Doris Stevens, *Jailed for Freedom: The Story of the Militant American Suffragist Movement* (New York: Schocken, 1976; 1st pub., 1920), 330–35.

119   The Court of Appeals for the District of Columbia ruled that picketing the White House was not an unlawful kind of assembly unless the gathering was for an unlawful purpose. This decision set a precedent for many other protesters over subsequent decades. See Ernest A. Lotito, "Picketing of the White House Old but Aimless Practice," *Washington Post*, Oct. 17, 1963, at http://www.prop1.org/history/1776plus/631017.htm.

120   Nancy F. Cott, *The Grounding of Modern Feminism* (New Haven: Yale University Press, 1987), 62.

121   Inez Haynes Irwin, *The Story of Alice Paul and the National Woman's Party* (Fairfax, Va.: Denlinger, 1977; 1st pub., 1964), 198–429, provides a detailed, chronological account of the picketing campaign and the participants' experiences with no reference to chaining. Sherna Berger Gluck's *From Parlor to Prison: Five American Suffragists Talk about Their Lives* (New York: Monthly Review, 1985) provides oral histories of suffragists that ought to include references to any chaining if it occurred. But see Eric Foner's assertion in *The Story of American Freedom* (New York: W. W. Norton, 1998), that "Paul . . . with a group of followers chained herself to the White House fence" (171).

122   Lotito, "Picketing"; Scott H. Bennett, *Radical Pacifism: The War Resisters League and Gandhian Nonviolence in America, 1915–1963* (Syracuse: Syracuse University Press, 2003), 179.

123   The reference was to Hazel Hunkins Hallinan. *Bangor Daily News*, Aug. 26, 1977, p. 4, at http://news.google.com/newspapers (retrieved May 20, 2010). There is no reference to chains, locks, or gates in a nearly contemporaneous article by a *Washington Post* writer, based on an interview with Hallinan. See Katherine Conger Kane, "Hazel Hunkins Hallinan, A Survivor of That Sturdy Band," *Modesto Bee*, Aug. 24, 1977, at http://news.google.com/newspapers?nid=1948&dat=19770824&id=6YQ5AAAAIBAJ&sjid=k38FAAAAIBAJ&pg=4512,2732658.

124   See news release "Six Chained to White House Gate over DADT Arrested" at LGBT POV, http:www.lgbt.pv.com/2010/04 (retrieved May 21, 2010).

125   See, e.g., *Woman Citizen*, June 30, 1917; July 7, 1917, p. 100.

126   *Woman Citizen*, Nov. 17, 1917. Quotations are from a summary of Catt's remarks.

127   Cf. Anne Firor Scott and Andrew MacKay Scott, *One Half the People: The Fight for Woman Suffrage* (Urbana: University of Illinois Press, 1982): "Probably the militant tactics did more good than harm. Nervousness about what the radical women might do next encouraged both congress and the president to make concessions and to embrace the more conservative suffragists as the lesser evil" (41). See also Christine A. Lunardini, *From Equal Suffrage to Equal Rights: Alice Paul and the National Woman's Party, 1910–1928* (New York: New York University Press, 1986), 148–49. For a more critical appraisal, see Eleanor Flexner and Ellen Fitzpatrick, *Century of Struggle: The Woman's Rights Movement in the United States*, enl. ed. (Cambridge: Harvard University Press, 1996), 279–80.

128   Ford, *Iron-Jawed Angels*, 7, 255, 246.

CHAPTER 6 **Beyond Submissiveness**

Epigraphs: *Let Something Good Be Said:* Speeches and *Writings of Frances Willard,* ed. Carolyn De Swarte Gifford and Amy R. Slagell (Urbana: University of Illinois Press, 2007), 24; oral history interview, April 29, May 7, 1959, University of Michigan–Wayne State Institute of Labor and Industrial Relations, quoted by David Brody, "Workplace Contractualism in Comparative Perspective," *Industrial Democracy in America: The Ambiguous Promise,* ed. Nelson Lichtenstein and Howell John Harris (New York: Cambridge University Press, 1996), 204.

1 Henrietta Rose, *Nora Wilmot: A Tale of Temperance and Woman's Rights* (Columbus: Osgood and Pearce, 1858), 166–208. Jed Dannenbaum discusses the novel in "The Origins of Temperance Activism and Militancy among American Women," *Journal of Social History* 15 (1981): 242.

2 *Revolution,* Feb. 25, 1869, p. 124; April 15, 1869, p. 233.

3 Norman H. Clark, *Deliver Us from Evil: An Interpretation of American Prohibition* (New York: W. W. Norton, 1976), 71; Jack S. Blocker, Jr., *American Temperance Movements: Cycles of Reform* (Boston: Twayne, 1989), 63.

4 Review of Jack S. Blocker, Jr., *"Give to the Winds Thy Fears": The Women's Temperance Crusade, 1873–1874* (Westport, Conn.: Greenwood, 1985), in *Journal of Interdisciplinary History* 18 (1988): 550.

5 W. H. Davis, ed., *The Temperance Reform and Its Great Reformers* (New York [and seven other cities]: Nelson and Phillips, 1878), 272.

6 Jed Dannenbaum, *Drink and Disorder: Temperance Reform in Cincinnati from the Washington Revival to the WCTU* (Urbana: University of Illinois Press, 1984), 218, 223. This book is much broader in coverage than its title indicates.

7 Miriam M. Cole, "The New Temperance Movement," *Woman's Journal,* Feb. 21, 1974; Stanton et al., eds., *History of Woman Suffrage,* vol. 3: *1876–1885,* 500–501. The editors add to Cole's remarks their own repugnance at the "desecration of womanhood" when appeals were made to rum sellers in saloons and on thoroughfares instead of to elected officials in halls of legislation.

8 W. F. Crispin, "Woman Suffrage and Temperance in Ohio," *Woman's Journal,* Feb. 28, 1874, p. 66.

9 "My Vote Is My Prayer," *Woman's Journal,* March 7, 1874; E. Winell, "Woman Suffrage and Temperance," *Woman's Journal,* April 18, 1974. Jane Grey Swisshelm urged suffragists not to dismiss "the Woman's war on liquor-selling," see *Woman's Journal,* April 4, 1874. She, too, noted the practical answer to the argument against voting that women will suffer by contact with rude men. She predicted a turn toward suffragism but did not dismiss what was occurring.

10 "The Women's War in Cleveland," *Woman's Journal,* April 18, 1874. Valuable discussions of suffragism and the temperance crusade include Jack S. Blocker, Jr., "Separate Paths: Suffragists and the Women's Temperance Crusade," *Signs* 10 (1985): 450–76, and esp. Ruth Bordin, *Woman and Temperance: The Search for Power and Liberty* (Philadelphia: Temple University Press, 1981).

11 J. T. Sunderland, "The Woman's Crusade," *Woman's Journal,* May 30, 1874, p. 170.

12 Alexander Keyssar, *The Right to Vote: The Contested History of Democracy in the United States* (New York: Basic Books, 2000), 186–87.

13 Daniel Okrent, *Last Call: The Rise and Fall of Prohibition* (New York: Scribner, 2010), 18.

14 *Let Something Good Be Said*, ed. Gifford and Slagell, 24.

15 Jack S. Blocker, Jr., *Retreat from Reform: The Prohibition Movement in the United States, 1880–1913* (Westport, Conn.: Greenwood, 1976), 136.

16 Fran Grace, *Carry A. Nation: Retelling the Life* (Bloomington: Indiana University Press, 2001), 139; Robert Smith Bader, "Mrs. Nation," *Kansas History* 7 (1985): 261.

17 See my *Radical Abolitionism*, chs. 7, 9; Hal D. Sears, *The Sex Radicals: Free Love in High Victorian America* (Lawrence, Kans.: Regents Press), 3–28.

18 Sears, *Sex Radicals*, 172–77.

19 Helen Lefkowitz Horowitz, *Rereading Sex: Battles over Sexual Knowledge and Suppression in Nineteenth-Century America* (New York: Vintage, 2003), 347.

20 Ibid., 375. See also Andrea Tone, *Devices and Desires: A History of Contraceptives in America* (New York: Hill and Wang, 2001).

21 John H. Houchin, *Censorship of the American Theatre in the Twentieth Century* (Cambridge: Cambridge University Press, 2003), 52–57; Sears, *Sex Radicals*, 264–66.

22 For a brief, balanced account, see Geoffrey Blodgett's in *Notable American Women*, 3:652–55.

23 Full title: *Cupid's Yokes, or, The Binding Forces of Conjugal Life: An Essay to Consider Some Moral and Physiological Phases of Love and Marriage, Wherein Is Asserted the Natural Right and Necessity of Sexual Self-Government* (Princeton, Mass.: Cooperative Publishing, 1876).

24 Martin Henry Blatt, *Free Love and Anarchism: The Biography of Ezra Heywood* (Urbana: University of Illinois Press, 1989), quotation at 105.

25 Sears, *Sex Radicals*, 172, 180–82.

26 Ibid., 74–80.

27 Ibid., 110–12. Besides an interrupted sentence of several years at hard labor, Harman had been beset with legal threats and charges for most of a decade.

28 Ibid., 263–65.

29 Quotations in ibid., 264–65.

30 Ibid., 79.

31 Ibid., 81–86.

32 Ibid., 91–96.

33 See Morgan Edwards, "Neither Bombs nor Ballots: *Liberty* and the Strategy of Anarchism," in *Benjamin R. Tucker and the Champions of Liberty: A Centenary Anthology*, ed. Michael E. Coughlin, Charles H. Hamilton, and Mark A. Sullivan (St. Paul: Michael E. Coughlin, 1986), 72.

34 Tucker, "The Power of Passive Resistance," *Liberty*, Oct. 4, 1884, reprinted in *Instead of a Book by a Man Too Busy to Write One: A Fragmentary Exposition of Philosophical Anarchism* (New York: Haskell House, 1969; 1st pub., 1897), 411–13.

35 Wendy McElroy, *The Debates of* Liberty: *An Overview of Individualist Anarchism, 1881–1908* (Lanham, Md.: Lexington, 2003), 160.

36 Sears, *Sex Radicals,* 250–51; Martin Blatt, "Ezra Heywood and Benjamin R. Tucker," *Benjamin R. Tucker and the Champions of Liberty,* 40–41. Tucker stepped in as a temporary editor of the *Word* during Heywood's first stint in jail. But the gains from publishing the "O'Neill Letter" over again because it was bound to lure Comstock's reaction were at least questionable. Tucker published a translation of Tolstoy's controversial "The Kreutzer Sonata," but the effectiveness was not clear.

37 Mary Alden Hopkins, "Birth Control and Public Morals: An Interview with Anthony Comstock," *Harper's Weekly* (May 22, 1915), Humanities and Social Sciences Online at H-net, Michigan State University, 1998, at http://www.expo98.msu.edu/people/comstock.htm (retrieved June 16, 2010).

38 On Margaret Sanger's indictment, flight, and return; William Sanger's jail sentence; shifts in public interest from obscenity to women's role in society; and tense relations with Emma Goldman in a context of revolutionary violence, see Ellen Chesler, *Woman of Valor: Margaret Sanger and the Birth Control Movement in America* (New York: Anchor, 1992), 103–27. On Goldman's decision to speak on birth control as a gesture of support for William Sanger, with the expectation of arrest, and criticism of Margaret Sanger's failure to support Ben Reitman, see, e.g., *Living My Life* (New York: Penguin, 2006), 313, 321–22, 333. She was also jailed in Missouri for opposition to World War I conscription.

39 Paul Frederick Brissenden, *The I.W.W.: A Study of American Syndicalism* (New York: Columbia University Press, 1918), 261.

40 Review from the *Survey* (June 1913), in Joyce L. Kornbluh, ed., *Rebel Voices: An I.W.W. Anthology* (Ann Arbor: University of Michigan Press, 1964), 214.

41 Elizabeth Gurley Flynn, "The Truth about the Paterson Strike," in Kornbluh, ed., *Rebel Voices,* 217–18.

42 For the songs and much about his death, see ibid., 126–57. I have quoted briefly from John Dos Passos, *1919,* in *U.S.A.* (New York: Library of America, 1996), 717–18, and Henry F. May, *The End of American Innocence* (New York: Alfred A. Knopf, 1959), 178.

43 Words by Alfred Hayes, music by Earl Robinson. For lyrics, see Ronald D. Cohen and Dave Samuelson, "Songs for Political Action," Bear Family Records BCD 15720 JL, 1996, p. 72 (2005). This was said to be Sheehan's favorite song.

44 Upton Sinclair, "To Frank Tannenbaum in Prison," *International Socialist Review* 14 (June 1914): 756; Emma Goldman, *Living My Life,* vol. 2 (New York: Alfred A. Knopf, 1931), ch. 40. On the church invasions, see *New York Times,* March 12–28, 1914; Max Eastman, "The Tannenbaum Crime," *The Masses,* May 1914. On Tannenbaum's life, see "Introduction: Frank Tannenbaum (1893–1969)," in *The Future of Democracy in Latin America: Essays by Frank Tannenbaum,* ed. Joseph Maier and Richard W. Weatherhead (New York: Alfred A. Knopf, 1974), 3–41;

Charles A. Hale, "Frank Tannenbaum and the Mexican Revolution," *Hispanic American Historical Review* 75:2 (May 1995): 215–46.

45 Flynn, "Truth about the Paterson Strike," 218.

46 It is important not to underestimate the transformative importance of the IWW. Flynn reported this "method of conducting strikes" as so successful that the United Mine Workers had adopted IWW practices, "and in Michigan they are holding women's meetings, children's meetings, mass picketings, and mass parades, such as never characterized an American Federation of Labor strike before" ("Truth about the Paterson Strike," 219–20).

47 Roger N. Baldwin, "Free Speech Fights of the I.W.W.," in "I.W.W.: Twenty-Five Years of Industrial Unionism" (pamphlet, Chicago: IWW, 1930), unpaginated.

48 "The Victory in New Jersey" (New York: ACLU, 1928).

49 Melvyn Dubofsky, *We Shall Be All: A History of the Industrial Workers of the World* (Chicago: Quadrangle, 1969), 173; Kornbluh, *Rebel Voices*, 94.

50 Baldwin, "Free Speech Fights."

51 "The I.W.W. in Theory and Practice," 5th rev. ed. (Chicago, n.d. [ca. 1937]), 53.

52 See Dubofsky, *We Shall Be All*, 196–97.

53 Baldwin, "Free Speech Fights," [2].

54 "One Big Union of All Workers," 5th rev. ed. (Chicago: IWW, 1957), 29–30.

55 "Speech to the IWW in 1905," online at "The Lucy Parsons Project," at http://www.lucyparsonsproject.org/writings/speech_to_iww.html. The historian of American socialism William Loren Katz indicates that these words "presage the 'sit-in' strikes of the 1930s, the anti-war movement of the 1960s." On the GE strike and later sit-downs linked to Parsons, see "The Gandhi Strike," at http://home-front.homestead.com/gandhi_strike.html (retrieved July, 14, 2010).

56 Frederick S. Boyd, "The General Strike in the Silk Industry," *The Pageant of the Paterson Strike* (New York: Success Press, 1913), quoted in a National Park Service study guide at http://www.nps.gov/history/nr/twhp/wwwlps/lessons/102paterson/102facts2.htm (retrieved July 13, 2010).

57 The best study of this idea as adopted in the IWW is Salvatore Salerno, *Red November, Black November: Culture and Community in the Industrial Workers of the World* (Albany: State University of New York Press, 1989). For a clear presenta-tion of uses of the "folded arms" image in France, by a former Wobbly and sojourner in other labor and revolutionary movements, see Albert Weisbord, "French Syndicalism," from *The Conquest of Power: Liberalism, Anarchism, Syndicalism, Socialism, Fascism, and Communism* (1937), ch. 14, at http://www.weisbord.org/conquest14.htm.

58 Nunzio Pernicone, *Italian Anarchism, 1864–1892*, at http://www.revolutionbythe-book.akpress.org/italian-anarchism–1864%E2%80%931892-%E2%80%94-book-excerpt.

59 See Reg Groves, "Folded Arms!" *Labour Monthly* (May 1930), reprinted at http://www.marxists.org/history/etol/writers/groves/1930/05/arms.htm.

60 Robert Rives La Monte in *International Socialist Review* (1912): 212. See also André Tridon, *The New Unionism* (New York: B. W. Huebsch, 1913), 21, 29.

61 Howard Zinn, *A People's History of the United States* (New York: Harper and Row, 1980), 324.

62 Ibid., 390. In a telefilm version of the *People's History*, entitled "The People Speak: Democracy is Not a Spectator Sport," Marisa Tomei conveys the spontaneous words of a participant remembering the General Motors sit-down.

63 "Sit-Down Strikes during 1936," *Monthly Labor Review* (May 1937): 1233–35. There are excellent surveys going back to Walter Galenson, *The CIO Challenge to the AFL* (1960), and including Robert Zeiger, *The CIO, 1935–1955* (1995). The sense of unquenchable labor conflict as perceived at the time is recaptured in Jeremy Brecher, *Strike!*, rev. ed. (Cambridge, Mass.: South End, 1997), 159ff.

64 Sidney Fine, *Sit-Down: The General Motors Strike of 1936–1937* (Ann Arbor: University of Michigan Press, 1969), 122.

65 Michael Torigian, "The Occupation of the Factories: Paris 1936, Flint 1937," *Comparative Studies in Society and History* 41 (April 1999): 330–33.

66 "Sitdown," *Nation* (Dec. 5, 1936), 652–54. The phrase "folded arms" recurred in the abundant news coverage of the sit-downs.

67 *NLRB v. Jones & Laughlin Steel Corp.*, 301 U.S. 1 (1937).

68 *NLRB v. Fansteel Metallurgical Corp.*, 306 U.S. 240 (1939). For thoughtful exploration of these issues, see Jim Pope, "Worker Lawmaking, Sit-Down Strikes, and the Shaping of American Industrial Relations, 1935–1958," *Law and History Review* 24 (2006), online at http://www.historycooperative.org/journals/lhr/24.1/pope.html.

69 Ibid., paras. 69–71, citing A. F. Whitney, "Thinking Clearly on Property Rights," *Railroad Trainman*, March 1937, pp. 136–37; Staughton Lynd, "Communal Rights," *Texas Law Review* 62 (1984): 1417, 1423–24.

70 Pope, "Worker Lawmaking," paras. 75–77, conflating UAW local newspapers and "pointers" to organizers; and other labor publications, 1937.

71 Ibid., paras. 39–40.

72 Ibid., paras. 96–98.

73 Ibid., para. 35.

74 Torigian says of the American occupations (and the French), unlike the Italian, that they "posed no challenge to the existing order, respected private property (which was violated only in the name of a higher property right to one's jobs), avoided violence, and focused on social-economic demands entirely compatible with a market economy" ("Occupation of the Factories," 332).

75 His protest was specifically against wartime policies imposing unionization in a business not closely related to the military effort and with considerable turnover of employees. For a contemporary account, see "U.S. at War: Seizure!" *Time*, May 8, 1944, online at http://www.time.com/time/magazine/article/0,9171,933315,00.html (retrieved July 29, 2010).

76 See Eleanor Fowler, quoted by Carrie A. Foster in *The Women and the Warriors: The U.S. Section of the Women's International League for Peace and Freedom, 1915–1946* (Syracuse: Syracuse University Press, 1995), 245. Fowler was labor secretary of WILPF. See also *Time*, Dec. 14, 1936, online. "The Berkie," a huge factory, was never unionized.

77 A. J. Muste, "Sit-Downs and Lie-Downs," in *The Essays of A. J. Muste*, ed. Nat Hentoff (Indianapolis: Bobbs-Merrill, 1967), 203–6.

CHAPTER 7 Adapting a Philosophy of Nonviolence

1 Not often quoted, this introduction was broadcast on NPR's *Morning Edition*, Aug. 28, 2003, and is archived at the National Public Radio website, NPR.org.

2 Martin Luther King, Jr., *Stride Toward Freedom: The Montgomery Story* (New York: Harper & Row, 1964; 1st pub., 1958), ix, 72–88.

3 For the best introduction to this long story, see Charles Chatfield, ed., *The Americanization of Gandhi: Images of the Mahatma* (New York: Garland, 1976).

4 Gregg to Sayre, Sept. 9, 1960, "Gregg, Richard 1946–1969 folder," John Nevin Sayre Papers, Series A, American Correspondence, Box 6, DG 117 (hereafter Sayre Papers), Swarthmore College Peace Collection (hereafter SCPC).

5 Gregg to Sayre, Feb. 14, 1961, Sayre Papers. The book cited was *Mathematics for the Million* (1937) by a noted popularizer, Lancelot [not Lionel] Hogben. The "travels" of ideas, particularly the idea of nonviolence, was a recurrent theme. He told Sayre (Sept. 23, 1960) that he had written a special introduction on this theme for a new Indian edition of the *Power of Nonviolence*. Several years later he quoted Alfred North Whitehead's *Adventures of Ideas* (1963) on how long it takes for ideas to be translated into action (Dec. 6, 1963).

6 Krishnalal Shridharani, *War without Violence* (Canton, Maine: Greenleaf, 2003), 1. This is a recent offprint version of the 1962 edition. (Hereafter *WWV*, 1962 ed.)

7 A prize-winning essay in Gandhi's weekly newspaper in 1908 identified three saintly precursors of passive resistance: Jesus, St. Stephen, and Henry David Thoreau. Gandhi himself, in the same year, also praised Thoreau's fearless devotion to principle and added three additional exemplars of the courageous defiance of social convention that he urged Indians to emulate: Luther, Galileo, and Columbus. See A. L. Herman, "*Satyagraha:* A New Indian Word for Some Old Ways of Western Thinking," *Philosophy East and West* 19:2 (April 1969): 127–28, 135–36. Also useful: George Hendrick, "The Influence of Thoreau's 'Civil Disobedience' on Gandhi's *Satyagraha*," *New England Quarterly* 29 (1956): 462–71.

8 *Indian Opinion*, Sept. 7, 1907 (two articles), Sept. 14, 1907, Oct. 5, 1907, in *Collected Works of Mahatma Gandhi* (1907), quoted in Herman, "*Satyagraha*," 135–36.

9 Dennis Dalton, *Mahatma Gandhi: Nonviolent Power in Action* (New York: Columbia University Press, 1993), 13.

10 Ibid., 14–15; Herman, "*Satyagraha*," 123–27 (quoting letter to P. Kadanda Rao). In my view, Herman goes too far in arguing that satyagraha is *entirely* western in origin, whereas Dalton is more persuasive in noting both what Gandhi made of Thoreau (17–18) and the undeniable strands of Indian influence, not to mention what he learned in London and South Africa.

11 A descendant of one founder—William Lloyd Garrison—Villard sat with a copy of the first issue of the *Non-Resistant* before him and quoted it at length. See Krishnalal Shridharani, *War without Violence: A Study of Gandhi's Method and Its Accomplishments* (New York: Harcourt, Brace, 1939) (hereafter *WWV*, 1939 ed.), xix–xx.

12 Useful guides to this prehistory are Vijay Prashad, "The Influence of Gandhi on the American Non Violence Movement," *Little India Online*, March 2002, http://www.littleindia.com/India/march02/ahimsa.htm; Richard G. Fox, "Passage from India," in *Between Resistance and Revolution: Cultural Politics and Social Protest*, ed. Richard G Fox and Orin Starn (New Brunswick, N.J.: Rutgers University Press, 1997), 65–82; and Sudarshan Kapur, *Raising up a Prophet: The African-American Encounter with Gandhi* (Boston: Beacon Press, 1992).

13 Richard B. Gregg, *The Power of Non-Violence* (Philadelphia, London: J. B. Lippincott, 1934) (hereafter cited as *PNV*, 1934 ed.), 54. The hyphen was dropped in later editions.

14 This phrase is used in analysis of Gregg's text to be found in Charles Chatfield, *For Peace and Justice: Pacifism in America, 1919–1941* (Knoxville: University of Tennessee Press, 1971), 207. Gregg served on the War Labor Board during World War I (Fox, "Passage from India," 75).

15 Mildred B. Young, "Richard B. Gregg, In Memoriam," *Friends Journal*, May 15, 1974, p. 303.

16 Chatfield, *For Peace and Justice*, 204. See also the obituary by John M. Swomley, Jr., in *Fellowship* 40:4 (April 1974): 23.

17 He was not a Quaker, though frequently mistaken for one (see, e.g., Kapur, *Raising up a Prophet*, 47). According to Charles Barker, he was not a churchgoer. See Barker's introduction to Richard B. Gregg, "Psychology and Strategy," in *The Psychology and Strategy of Gandhi's Nonresistance* (New York: Garland, 1972), 8.

18 See Gregg to Mary Van Kleeck, Russell Sage Foundation, March 17, 1936, DGA, Box 506, SCPC; Gregg to Sayre, Feb. 23, 1933, Sayre Papers. See also *National Cyclopedia of American Biography* (1921; digitized 2010), s.v. "Valentine"; and Elisabeth Israels Perry, *Belle Moskowitz: Feminine Politics and the Exercise of Power in the Age of Alfred E. Smith* (New York: Oxford University Press, 1987), 90.

19 See, e.g., Stuart B. Hill, "Companion Plants," http://eap.mcgill.ca/publications/EAP55.htm (retrieved May 23, 2012).

20 Joint letter to "Friends all over the world," April 1956, SCPC; "Bapu" to Gregg, May 17, 1935, Comprehensive Site, Gandhian Institute, at http://mkgandhi.org/letters/richardcook/main.htm.

21 Joint letter, April 1956. He had used her gardens for his experiments in biodynamic gardening (Helen Philbrick and Richard B. Gregg, *Companion Plants and How to Use Them* [Old Greenwich, Conn.: Devin-Adair, 1966], iv, viii, xiii).

22 As noted above, he visited India for three months in 1913. The visit had nothing to do with Gandhi, who in fact still resided in South Africa. His principal visit, which began in 1925, was very much intended as one of learning and participation in the Gandhian movement. Gregg returned to India with his first wife (Gandhi called them Govind and Radha) for six weeks in March–April 1930. He attended a World Pacifists' meeting in India in December 1949, two years after India's independence and one after Gandhi's death. On the fifth visit in 1956, he and his new wife Evelyn stayed two years, teaching, living for long periods in a small village and in the populous capital, inspecting agricultural life from fertile Kerala to the arid plateau and Simla Hills in the north, taking stock of India's development and enjoying the status of old friends.

23 Quotation from *Indian Review* (Feb. 1934) in correspondence of Gandhi with Richard Gregg, Comprehensive Site, Gandhian Institute, at http://mkgandhi.org/letters/richardcook/main.htm. Except as noted otherwise, I rely on this source for most information on Gregg's time in India and his friendship with Gandhi.

24 "I lived entirely in Indian houses, wore Indian clothes, ate Indian food, read Indian literature, learned as much of the languages as I could, and tried to absorb Indian ways" (*Indian Review*, Feb. 1934, quoted at Comprehensive Site, ibid.).

25 He used his experience in Kotgarh as the basis of a historical example in *Power of Nonviolence* (1959 ed.), 21–22.

26 Richard Gregg, *Economics of Khaddar* (Madras: S. Ganesan, 1928), 224. For Gregg's continuing loyalty to the constructive program after Indian independence and Gandhi's death, see Richard B. Gregg, *A Philosophy of Indian Economic Development* (Ahmedabad: Navajivan, 1958).

27 Gregg's purchase of a secondhand typewriter led to some admonitions from Gandhi. Much of their correspondence focused on vegetarianism. They wrote about authors whom they both admired, such as the vegetarian John Harvey Kellogg. Gregg tried to teach Gandhi about vitamins, about eating fresh fruit, about the Bates method for curing bad eyesight. Gandhi arranged for Gregg to have an operation on his piles once he gave up on a vegetarian cure. Later they corresponded about hopes that vegetarian dietetics might cure Mrs. Gregg's mental disorder. Gandhi joked that people might regard them as "cranks," but Gregg shows much less openness to that idea.

28 Other committee members included Caroline Urie, Alfred G. Baker Lewis, and Robert Newton. For relevant correspondence and information compiled, see the folder "Pamphlet (proposed) on nonviolence in strikes, etc.," Gregg Papers, CDG-A 506, SCPC. On his explanation for traveling to England, see Gregg to Devere Allen, July 3, 1936.

29 Richard B. Gregg, *The Power of Nonviolence* (Nyack: Fellowship of Reconciliation, 1959) (hereafter cited as *PNV*, 1959 ed.), 51.

30 Chatfield makes a similar criticism in *For Peace and Justice*, 205.

31 *PNV*, 1959 ed., 49.

32 The term was borrowed approvingly from W. H. H. Rivers.

33 Chatfield, *For Peace and Justice*, 203–12, is acute on the assumption of the plasticity of human nature in Gregg's work.

34 *PNV*, 1934 ed., 137–38.

35 Ibid., 139, 225.

36 Chatfield, ed., *Americanization*, 679. Besides Chatfield's exposition of Gregg's accomplishment, a good overview is found in Joseph Kip Kosek, *Acts of Conscience: Christian Nonviolence and Modern American Democracy* (New York: Columbia University Press, 2009), 85–111.

37 "They should strive for such details even as clean bodies, clean houses, clean streets, clean talk" (102).

38 Gregg distinguished civil disobedience from anarchy—which paid no regard to existing law and order. It was instead the violation of "a specific law which seems repugnant to the dignity of universal law" and willingly goes to jail or accepts whatever punishment comes. See, for example, his "draft of a brief statement on Civil Disobedience," Feb. 23, 1961, intended for distribution to students and other protesters (SCPC).

39 *PNV*, 1934 ed., 147, 149.

40 Ibid., 177, 179, 185ff.

41 Taylor Branch, *Parting the Waters: America in the King Years, 1954–1963* (New York: Simon and Schuster, 1988), 171; Farmer, *Lay Bare My Heart*, quoted in Kapur, *Raising Up a Prophet*, 121.

42 Fox, "Passage from India," 78.

43 Mary King, *Mahatma Gandhi and Martin Luther King*, 507.

44 *WWV*, 1939 ed., xxiii–xxv.

45 Smiley, "A Pebble Thrown into the Pond," *Fellowship*, June 1989, quoted in Mary King, *Mahatma Gandhi and Martin Luther King*, 123–24.

46 Krishnalal Shridharani, *My India, My America* (New York: Duell, Sloan and Pearce, 1941), 72. This work is the best source on his life, and I follow it except as otherwise noted.

47 He thanked Robert M. MacIver, Robert S. Lynd, and six other professors in his acknowledgments. He thanks Lynd, in addition, for serving as a check on his judgments on American culture by going over his chapter on that subject (*WWV*, 1939 ed., vii, 297).

48 *Warning to the West* (New York: Duell, Sloan and Pearce, 1942); *The Mahatma and the World* (New York: Duell, Sloan and Pearce, 1946).

49 For a tribute and summary of his life, see Tushar Bhatt, "A Forgotten Gujarati Gem: Krishnalal Shridharani," Jan. 1, 2010, at http://tusharbhattsgujarat.blogspot.com/2010/01/tushar-bhatts-gujarat-tushar-bhatts_01.html.

50 *WWV*, 1939 ed., xxxiii–xxxv; *My India*, 33–43.

51 Branch, *Parting the Waters*, 171, no citation. On cigar smoking, see the account of Richard G. Fox, who sent an associate to interview Shridharani's wife ("Passage from India," 79, 80 n. 6). In *My India* Shridharani describes a number of pleasant encounters (dancing, for example) with young women that could hardly have occurred in India. But these would not qualify as "woman chasing." These matters would not matter very much if Branch's fine book were not so widely read.

52 Shridharani, *My India*, 375–76.

53 Krishnalal Shridharani, *WWV*, 1962 ed., 247. His American memoir indicates no particular curiosity about this subject except, almost in passing, when he criticizes pacifists for an "atomistic approach" to social problems (*My India*, 278–80).

54 *WWV*, 1939 ed., xxxv–xxxvi.

55 Ibid., 43.

56 Ibid., 301, 308.

57 *PNV*, 1934 ed., 118; 1960 ed., 95 (taken from *Atlantic Monthly*, Aug. 1928).

58 Delivered to an assembly of the entire university at Stanford in 1906; published in *McClure's* and elsewhere in 1910.

59 *WWV*, 1939 ed., xxxvi, 154, 276, 286.

60 Louis Menand, *The Metaphysical Club: A Story of Ideas in America* (New York: Farrar, Straus and Giroux, 2001), 440–41.

61 Menand (ibid., 441) places Martin Luther King entirely outside the pragmatic tradition he described, but the point may need more thought.

62 *WWV*, 1962 ed., 39–42. The best known of these accounts were Negley Farson's in the *Chicago Daily News*. Reports like these became familiar in the United States later on, but without many stories of armed officers declining to do their "duty."

63 Negley Farson, "The Terror in India" (1930), reprinted in Chatfield, ed., *Americanization*, 257–58. For analysis of these reports and reactions to attempted British censorship, see Manoranjan Jha, "Civil Disobedience, American Opinion and the British," *Journal of Indian History* 56:3 (1978): 558–60.

64 On the use of "nonresistance" in the 1930s, see, e.g., Villard in his preface to Shridharani's book, where he wrote of Jesus's nonresistance as "the most dangerous resistance." Justus Ebert, among others, wrote of the "passive resistance" employed by the IWW: "The I.W.W. is charged with violence. The violence that the I.W.W. commits is the violence of passive resistance. It is the violence of removing hands from the machinery of production and stopping the employer's profits" (*The I.W.W, in Theory and Practice* [Chicago, 1921], 52).

65 Gregg is criticized in particular on this point in James F. Childress, "Nonviolent Resistance and Direct Action: A Bibliographical Essay," *Journal of Religion* 52:4 (Oct. 1972): 392–93.

66 Clarence Marsh Case, *Non-Violent Coercion: A Study of Methods of Social Pressure* (New York: Century, 1923).

67 Ibid., 295–319, quotations at 296–301, 319.

68 Ibid., 395, 402–3, 414.

69 The circumstances are well described in Kosek, *Acts of Conscience*, 91–92.

70 *PNV*, 1959 ed., 164, 187 n. 15.

71 *PNV*, 1934 ed., 146–47.

72 *PNV*, 1959 ed., 51.

73 *WWV*, 1962 ed.

74 In a thoughtful book on Richard Gregg and FOR, Joseph Kip Kosek refers to the 1930s as the "Gandhian moment" (*Acts of Conscience*, 86–87). That was a time when consciousness of Gandhi in popular culture was strong. I use the term for the period after the Montgomery boycott when the applicability of Gandhian principles in American life was widely, if temporarily, discussed. See, for example, Chester Bowles, "What Negroes Can Learn from Gandhi," *Saturday Evening Post*, March 1, 1958, pp. 19–21, 87–89.

75 Quotation from 1941 (probably from *My India*) in Vijay Prashad, "PropaGandhi Ahimsa in Black America: The Influence of Gandhi on the American Non Violence Movement," *Little India*, March 2005, at http://www.electricprint.com/academic/department/AandL/AAS/ANNOUNCE/vra/king/phil_gandhi_black.html (retrieved June 1, 2012).

76 Howard Kester to Richard Gregg, July 28, 1937, Southern Tenant Farmers' Union Papers, 1934–1970, microfilm at Kent Library, Southeast Missouri State University; Louis Cantor, *A Prologue to the Protest Movement: The Missouri Sharecropper Roadside Demonstration of 1939* (Durham: Duke University Press, 1969), 60–61. I can find no corroboration for what would have been the remarkable participation of the radical Caribbean historian C. L. R. James in 1941 as a lecturer and pamphleteer for striking sharecroppers in southern Missouri, where "in anticipation of tactics used in the 1960s civil rights movement, James urged Blacks to enter segregated restaurants, 'ordering, for instance, some coffee,' launching a sit-down and campaigning around the issue." Paul Dorn, "A Controversial Caribbean: C. L. R. James," at http://www.runmuki.com/paul/CLR_James.html, citing *Encyclopedia of the American Left*, 387.

77 See Richard M. Dalfiume, "The 'Forgotten Years' of the Negro Revolution," *Journal of American History* 55 (1968): 90–106; Robert Korstad and Nelson Lichtenstein, "Opportunities Found and Lost: Labor, Radicals, and the Early Civil Rights Movement," *Journal of American History* 75 (1988): 786–811.

78 John D'Emilio, *Lost Prophet: The Life and Times of Bayard Rustin* (New York: Free Press, 2003), 46–47, 83–85.

79 Pauli Murray, *The Autobiography of a Black Activist, Feminist, Lawyer, Priest, and Poet* (Knoxville: University of Tennessee Press, 1989), 130–49. First published as *A Song in a Weary Throat: An American Pilgrimage* (1987).

80 Paul R. Dekar, "The *Harlem Ashram*, 1940–1947: Gandhian Satyagraha in the United States" (unpub. paper), online at http://www.peacehost.net/HarlemAshram/dekar.htm; Glenda Elizabeth Gilmore, *Defying Dixie: The Radical Roots of Civil Rights, 1919–1950* (New York: W. W. Norton, 2008), 386.

81 Murray, *Autobiography*, 147.

82 Ibid., 198–209; Scott Berg, "Before the Marches," *Washington Post*, Feb. 16, 2001, p. WE34.

83 Murray, *Autobiography*, 201.

84 Gilmore, *Defying Dixie*, 385–6.

85 Kapur, *Raising Up a Prophet;* Gerald Horne, *The End of Empires: African Americans and India* (Philadelphia: Temple University Press, 2008); King, *Stride Toward Freedom*, 78.

86 See generally Paula F. Pfeffer, *A. Philip Randolph, Pioneer of the Civil Rights Movement* (Baton Rouge: Louisiana State University Press, 1990); and Paula F. Pfeffer, "Randolph, Asa Philip," *American National Biography Online*, at http://www.anb.org/articles/15/15–01101.html; accessed Feb. 26, 2013.

87 David Kennedy, *Freedom from Fear: The American People in Depression and War, 1929–1945* (New York: Oxford University Press, 1999), 766–68; Joseph Lash, *Eleanor and Franklin: The Story of Their Relationship, Based on Eleanor Roosevelt's Private Papers* (New York: W. W. Norton, 1971), 534–35.

88 See Scott H. Bennett, *Radical Pacifism: The War Resisters League and Gandhian Nonviolence in America, 1915–1963* (Syracuse: Syracuse University Press, 2003), 134–72.

89 Pfeffer, *A. Philip Randolph*, 140; Jervis Anderson, *A. Philip Randolph: A Biographical Portrait* (New York: Harcourt Brace Jovanovich, 1973), 276; Laurence S. Wittner, *Rebels against War: The American Peace Movement, 1933–1983* (Philadelphia: Temple University Press, 1984), 185–86.

90 Pfeffer, *A. Philip Randolph*, 140, 147, 167.

91 Ibid., 153–54; James Tracy, *Direct Action: Radical Pacifism from the Union Eight to the Chicago Seven* (Chicago: University of Chicago Press, 1996), 64.

92 Joan V. Bondurant, *Conquest of Violence: The Gandhian Philosophy of Conflict* (Berkeley: University of California Press, 1965), 220–21. Gregg's view of a just settlement is discussed above. For Shridharani, see *WWV*, 1962 ed., 22–23.

93 Cong. Record, vol. 94, 80th Cong., 2d Sess., Senate, April 12, 1948, 4312–13.

94 Ibid., 4313–14.

95 Anderson, *A. Philip Randolph*, 105–8. Anderson's biography is based in part on interviews with Randolph.

96 Quoted in Tracy, *Direct Action*, 10.

97 Quoted in ibid., 2.

98 See David Dellinger, *From Yale to Jail: The Story of a Moral Dissenter* (Marion. S.D.: Rose Hill, 1996).

99 For a blogger's view that there were no draft dodgers or draft resisters, see James David Pearce, "No Draft Dodgers in WWII" (2000) at http://pages.prodigy.net/jabeckpearce/poor_town/tales/draftdodgers.htm (retrieved Nov. 10, 2010).

100   Key figures would prominently include Bayard Rustin, Homer Jack, David Dellinger, Staughton Lynd, James Peck, Glenn Smiley, George Houser, with significant guidance from the "greyheads," particularly A. J. Muste, referenced by an aging Richard Gregg above.

101   On communities, see Tracy, *Direct Action*, 80–81. Many links between World War II draft resisters and protests against nuclear testing, tax resistance, and opposition to Jim Crow can be traced in the "Roster of Freedom Riders" in Raymond Arsenault, *Freedom Riders: 1961 and the Struggle for Racial Justice* (New York: Oxford University Press, 2006), 533–87.

102   See Arthur Waskow, *From Race Riot to Sit-In: 1919 and the 1960s* (Garden City: Anchor, 1966), 225, an early study of sit-ins and changing meanings of "creative disorder."

CHAPTER 8 **The Civil Rights Revolution**

1   Julius Lester, "To Recapture the Dream," *Liberation* (1969), reprinted in Alexander Bloom and Wini Breines, eds., *"Takin' It to the Streets": A Sixties Reader* (New York: Oxford University Press, 1995), 631–36.

2   Mary King, *Mahatma Gandhi and Martin Luther King*, 121.

3   Anthony Lewis and the *New York Times*, eds., *Portrait of a Decade: The Second American Revolution* (New York: Bantam, 1965), 37–59.

4   *New York Times*, Feb. 23, 1946, quoted in August Meier and Elliott Rudwick, *CORE: A Study in the Civil Rights Movement* (Urbana: University of Illinois Press, 1975), 35.

5   Jerome A. Ennels and Wesley Phillips Newton, "Maxwell Air Force Base and Gunter Annex," *Encyclopedia of Alabama*, updated 2009, online at http://www.encyclopediaofalabama.org/face/Article.jsp?id=h–1337 (retrieved Jan. 2, 2010).

6   Barbara Ransby, *Ella Baker and the Black Freedom Movement: A Radical Democratic Vision* (Chapel Hill: University of North Carolina Press, 2003), 142.

7   John Egerton, *Speak Now against the Day: The Generation before the Civil Rights Movement in the South* (New York: Alfred A. Knopf, 1994), 620.

8   King, *Stride Toward Freedom*, 31.

9   Quoted in David J. Garrow, *Bearing the Cross: Martin Luther King, Jr., and the Southern Christian Leadership Conference* (New York: Harper Collins, 2004), 12.

10   See ibid., 11–21; Taylor Branch, *Parting the Waters: America in the King Years, 1954–1963* (New York: Simon and Schuster, 1988), 128–30.

11   Branch, *Parting the Waters*, 138–41; King, *Stride Toward Freedom*, 46–48.

12   Lewis, ed., *Portrait of a Decade*, 61.

13   The work of J. Mills Thornton III valuably establishes the local political context. For an overview, see "Montgomery, Ala., Bus Boycott," *Encyclopedia of African-American Culture and History*, 2d ed., ed. Colin A. Palmer (Detroit: Macmillan Reference, 2006), 4:1471–74. See also his *Dividing Lines: Municipal Politics and the Struggle for Civil Rights in Montgomery, Birmingham, and Selma* (Birmingham: University of Alabama Press, 2002).

14   Garrow, *Bearing the Cross*, 62; Mary King, *Mahatma Gandhi*, 118–19.

15 D'Emilio, *Lost Prophet*, 227.

16 The best account of King's "resident Gandhian tutors": Mary King, *Mahatma Gandhi*, 118–226.

17 See Gene Sharp, *Waging Nonviolent Struggle: Twentieth Century Practice and Twenty-First Century Potential* (Boston: Porter Sargent, 2005), 56–58, and *The Methods of Nonviolent Action* (Boston: Porter Sargent, 1973), 219–35.

18 See her obituary, *New York Times*, Oct. 25, 2005.

19 King, *Stride Toward Freedom*, 29.

20 That is the word used by Paula Giddings, *When and Where I Enter: The Impact of Black Women on Race and Sex in America* (New York: Bantam, 1985), 264.

21 Louis Lomax, *The Negro Revolt* (New York: Signet, 1962), 92, as quoted in Giddings, *When and Where I Enter*, 261–62. Another example of exaggeration: "There are very few people who can say their actions and conduct changed the face of the nation. . . . and Rosa Parks is one of those individuals." John Conyers quoted in *New York Times* obituary, Oct. 25, 2005.

22 "Rosa Parks: An Early Interview" (1956), in Fred D. Gray, et al., *The Children Coming On: A Retrospective of the Montgomery Bus Boycott* (Montgomery: Black Belt Press, 1998), 91.

23 Interview of Rosa Parks by John H. Britton for the Civil Rights Documentation Project, Sept. 28, 1967, as quoted in a revisionist blog: Prison Culture (pseud.), "Rosa Parks: Criminal Legal Reformer and Practitioner of Transformative Justice," at http://www.usprisonculture.com/blog/2010/12/24/rosa-parks-criminal-legal-reformer-practitioner-of-transformative-justice (retrieved May 30, 2012).

24 Michael Janofsky, "Thousands Gather at the Capitol to Remember a Hero," *New York Times*, Oct. 31, 2005, as quoted in Jeanne Theoharis, "'A Life History of Being Rebellious': The Radicalism of Rosa Parks," in *Want to Start A Revolution? Radical Women in the Black Freedom Struggle*, ed. David F. Gore, Jeanne Theoharis, and Komozi Woodard (New York: New York University Press, 2009), 115–37.

25 Garrow, *Bearing the Cross*, 59.

26 They are identified in David J. Garrow, ed., *The Montgomery Bus Boycott and the Women Who Started It: The Memoir of Jo Ann Gibson Robinson* (Knoxville: University of Tennesse Press, 1987), 136–37. One of them, Claudette Colvin, eventually got some publicity in her own right. See Margot Adler, "Before Rosa Parks, There Was Claudette Colvin," at http://www.npr.org/templates/story/story.php?storyId=101719889 (retrieved Dec. 28, 2010).

27 *Browder v. Gayle*, 142 F. Supp. 707—Dist. Court, MD Alabama 1956. The district court's 2–1 decision was affirmed by the U.S. Supreme Court, *per curiam*, at *Gayle v. Browder*, 352 U.S. 903 (1956). Aurelia Browder was a seamstress, a widow, and mother of six children. William A. Gayle was mayor of Montgomery.

28 The suggestions appear in *Stride Toward Freedom*, 144–45. No churches or organizations in the white community took any similar responsibility; the city

commission vowed to stand forever "like a rock, against social equality, inter-marriage, and mixing of the races under God's creation and plan."

29 Theoharis, " 'Life History,' " 137; Douglas Brinkley, *Rosa Parks* (New York: Penguin, 2000), 175–76.

30 Quoted in Theoharis, " 'Life History,' " 128.

31 See Rustin, "Even in the Face of Death" (1957), in Devon W. Carrado and Donald Weise, eds., *Time on Two Crosses: The Collected Writings of Bayard Rustin* (San Francisco: Cleis, 2003), 102, 106.

32 In interviews Ella Baker agreed that "the genesis of the idea for SCLC started in the minds of people in the North, not in Montgomery." Besides Baker herself, she identified the project's initiators as Rustin and a lawyer named Stanley Levison, in whose kitchen "it was designed," and who became a major influence on King. See Garrow, *Bearing the Cross*, 644–45, and for a similar account, Carrado and Weise, eds., *Time on Two Crosses*, xxiv.

33 On the shift in focus from nonviolent direct action to voter registration, see Adam Fairclough, *Martin Luther King, Jr.* (Athens: University of Georgia Press, 1995), 53. For Baker, it was not so abrupt a shift (Ransby, *Ella Baker*, 183).

34 Garrow, *Bearing the Cross*, 85–86.

35 Epilogue, Gray et al., *Children Coming On*, 243.

36 King, *Stride Toward Freedom*, 114–16. David Garrow has suggested that, while the passage has not received much scholarly attention, it may lead to understanding of King's personal transformation in Montgomery. See his "King's Plagiarism: Imitation, Insecurity, and Transformation," *Journal of American History* 78:1 (1991): 91–2.

37 George Barrett wrote of King's "fusion of Christianity, Hegelianism, and Gandhism" and his introduction of Hegel's philosophy as giving "the Negro a new awareness (and therefore a new strength)." He added, "Many admit they don't always understand his words, but as one of his own congregation put it, 'we sure get the force of his meaning.' " Lewis, ed., *Portrait of a Decade*, 68, 70.

38 Rustin quoted in Gray et al, *Children Coming On*, 343; Baker quoted in Garrow, *Bearing the Cross*, 625.

39 One exception is Mills Thornton, whose *Dividing Lines* approaches the story not through King or the boycotters but through the political context in which events erupted.

40 See Garrow, *Bearing the Cross*, 111–12, 650. See also Garrow, "King's Plagiarism," and "The Intellectual Development of Martin Luther King, Jr., Influences and Commentaries," *Union Seminary Quarterly Review* 40 (1986): 5–20.

41 King, *Stride Toward Freedom*, 36, 73, 188.

42 Ibid., 193–94.

43 Ibid., 191, 197. The effectiveness of *Stride Toward Freedom* as a primer on nonvio-lence may be questionable. In 1969 I watched a procession of students who were striking their classes, including mine, as they marched toward what turned out to

be, as predicted, a "trashing" of bank windows in a nearby shopping plaza. One good and likable student waved to me as he marched along, took *Stride Toward Freedom* from his pocket, held it up, and shouted appreciatively, "Great book, Dr. Perry!"

44 Thornton reminds readers of the importance of the injunction in ending segregation on the buses, but the boycott "began the process of moving the civil rights movement out of the courtroom by demonstrating that ordinary African Americans possessed the power to control their own destiny" ("Montgomery, Ala., Bus Boycott," 1473).

45 I have a copy of the comic, which can be found online. On its publication and influence, see William Vance Trollinger, "Prescient Pacifists" (book review), *Christian Century*, Jan. 12, 2010; Kosek, *Acts of Conscience*, 320–21; David L. Lewis, *King: A Critical Biography* (Baltimore: Pelican, 1971), 113; John Lewis, *Walking in the Wind: A Memoir of the Movement* (San Diego: Harvest, 1999), 48, 72, 74, 91; Taylor Nix, "Remembering Martin Luther King and The Montgomery Story Comic Book," Urban Book Store, Jan. 18, 2010, at http://theubs.com/features/themontstory.php (retrieved Jan. 10, 2011). For distribution of a new Arabic translation before the Tahrir Square revolution, see "Amid Revolution, Arab Cartoonists Draw Attention to Their Cause," *Washington Post*, March 7, 2011.

46 Jim Schlosser, "The Story of the Greensboro Sit-Ins," *Greensboro News and Record*, 1998, online at "Greensboro Sit-Ins, Launch of a Civil Rights Movement," http://www.sitins.com/story.shtml (retrieved Jan. 22, 2011); UPI story in Lewis, ed., *Portrait of a Decade*, 72. Important accounts include: Miles Wolff, *Lunch at the 5 and 10* (Chicago: Ivan Dee, 1990) and William H. Chafe, *Civilities and Civil Rights: Greensboro, North Carolina, and the Black Struggle for Freedom* (New York: Oxford University Press, 1980). For a reliable overview of the civil rights struggle, see Harvard Sitkoff, *The Struggle for Black Equality, 1954–1992* (New York: Hill and Wang, 1993). There is no reason to quibble about "firstness," since the term was new and James Farmer, who had been active in similar movements since the 1940s, enthusiastically introduced a website on Greensboro and its legacy "Greensboro Sit-Ins" (above). But there were well-known sit-ins in St. Louis in the late 1940s and in Wichita and Oklahoma City in the late 1950s. The sociologist Aldon Morris found sit-ins in sixteen southern cities between 1957 and 1960. See *The Origins of the Civil Rights Movement: Black Communities Organizing for Change* (New York: Free Press, 1984), 189, 202–5. What was "new," perhaps, was *student* sit-ins.

47 See the account of a leading historian of the great movement that followed: Clayborne Carson, *In Struggle: SNCC and the Black Awakening of the 1960s* (Cambridge: Harvard University Press, 1995), 9.

48 For the context of their decision, see Chafe, *Civilities*, 71–83.

49 Chafe, *Civilities*, 85 (quotation).

50 Carson, *In Struggle*, 11; Chafe, *Civilities*, quoted at 98.

51 "Needed: A 'Just and Honorable' Answer," *Greensboro Daily News*, Feb. 8. 1960, p. A6, online at "Greensboro Sit-Ins."

52 See Branch, *Parting the Waters*, 280–83.

53 Wesley C. Hogan, *Many Minds, One Heart: SNCC's Dream for a New America* (Chapel Hill: University of North Carolina Press, 2007), 26.

54 Hogan (299–300) quotes Kelly Miller Smith: when the "courageous young college students sometimes speak as if there were no background to their thrust, old-timers in Nashville quickly remind them that, in their own way, oppressed Nashvillians have always struggled to erase the shame of their city."

55 Quoted in Hogan, *Many Minds*, 27.

56 Halberstam, *The Children* (New York: Fawcett, 1998), 28.

57 Lewis, *Walking*, 111.

58 Quoted by Halberstam, *Children*, 200, from the *British Weekly*, March 23, 1961.

59 Two good accounts: Halberstam, *Children*, 188–207; Paul K. Conkin, *Gone with the Ivy: A Biography of Vanderbilt University* (Knoxville: University of Tennessee Press, 1985), 447–48, 546–80.

60 Lewis, *Walking*, 106–7.

61 Sitkoff, *Struggle*, 83.

62 Branch, *Parting the Waters*, 291; Carson, *In Struggle*, 22–24. These accounts reject later revisionist accounts exaggerating animosity to King at this time.

63 Carson, *In Struggle*, 28.

64 *Morgan v. Commonwealth of Virginia*, 328 U.S. 373 (1946). For a succinct statement of the background, see Ferrisburg State University, "Jim Crow," Question of the Month, Dec. 2007, at http://www.ferris.edu/jimcrow/question/dec07/.

65 Raymond Arsenault, *Freedom Riders: 1961 and the Struggle for Racial Justice* (New York: Oxford University Press, 2006), 22.

66 Meier and Rudwick, *CORE*, 38.

67 *Boynton v. Virginia*, 364 U.S. 454 (1960). Bruce Boynton, a Howard University law student, had been found guilty of refusing to leave his stool in the whites-only dining area of a Richmond Trailways terminal. In a way, this was a solo freedom ride. Marshall was lead attorney, Hugo Black wrote the decision, and the case was decided under the Interstate Commerce Act rather than as a constitutional issue.

68 Arsenault, *Freedom Riders*, 94–95.

69 See the invaluable rosters of freedom riders in ibid., 533–86.

70 I follow Arsenault, ch. 4 (quotations, 160–61), as more recent than Branch, *Parting the Waters*, but the gory events remain essentially the same.

71 Quoted in Arsenault, *Freedom Riders*, 165.

72 Quoted in Sitkoff, *Struggle*, 95.

73 Arsenault, *Freedom Riders*, 148, 233. No freedom riders, however, abandoned their nonviolent code.

74 On such doubts about nonviolence by James Forman and Stokely Carmichael, see Lewis, *Walking*, 177–78.

75 Lewis, *Walking*, 163; Branch, *Parting the Waters*, 462.

76 Timothy B. Tyson, *Radio Free Dixie: Robert F. Williams and the Roots of Black Power* (Chapel Hill: University of North Carolina Press, 1999), 246–47. For thoughtful appraisals of the episode, see Lewis, *Walking*, 164; Branch, *Parting the Waters*, 466–67.

77 See ch.7 of Lewis, *King*, 140–70. Also, more briefly, ibid., 184–86. On publicity, which was her department at SNCC, see Mary King, *Freedom Song*, 157, 428.

78 Branch, *Parting the Waters*, 738–44.

79 Ibid., 770; Gregory (with Robert Lipsyte), *Nigger* (New York: Simon and Schuster, 1964), 178–80.

80 Garrow, *Bearing the Cross*, 265–67; Rustin, "Preamble to the March on Washington," in Carbado and Weise, eds., *Time on Two Crosses*, 112–15.

81 Lewis, ed., *Portrait of a Decade*, 217.

82 Widely available, as at Martin Luther King online, http://www.mlkonline.net/dream.html.

83 For the original draft and subsequent fracas, see Lewis, *Walking*, 216–30. For analysis and context, cf. Eric J. Sundquist, *King's Dream* (New Haven: Yale University Press, 2009), 42ff. For an early perception that Lewis's speech aroused such alarm because of its frank criticism of the federal government as well as southern racist institutions, see Howard Zinn, *SNCC: The New Abolitionists* (Boston: Beacon Press, 1964), 190–91.

84 Carson, *In Struggle*, 95.

85 John Lewis, *Walking*, 387.

86 Meier and Rudwick, *CORE*, 408.

87 Essays in *Liberation*, Sept. 1959, Oct 1959; reprinted in *Southern Patriot* 18:11 (Jan. 1960). See the excellent analysis in Tyson, *Radio Free Dixie*, 213–19.

88 Hogan, *Many Minds*, 162; Elizabeth Sutherland, *Letters from Mississippi* (1965), quoted in Mary King, *Freedom Song*, 373–74. On SNCC's internal debate, see Doug McAdam, *Freedom Summer* (New York: Oxford University Press, 1988), 122–23 (though he uses the misleading heading "The Abandonment of Nonviolence").

89 Taylor Branch, *At Canaan's Edge: America in the King Years, 1965–68* (New York: Simon and Schuster, 2006), 477, 483–92.

90 Garrow, *Bearing the Cross*, 485.

91 David Lewis, *King*, 312; Branch, *At Canaan's Edge*, 471–73.

92 See Arnold Rampersad, *Jackie Robinson: A Biography* (New York: Ballantine, 1997).

CHAPTER 9 The Sixties and the Great Tradition of Social Protest

1 Douglas T. Miller, *On Our Own: Americans in the Sixties* (Lexington, Mass.: D. C. Heath, 1996), 182; James Miller, *"Democracy Is in the Streets": From Port Huron to the Siege of Chicago* (New York: Simon and Schuster, 1987), 48.

2 Miller, "*Democracy*," 44, 48.

3 George Cotkin, *Existential America* (Baltimore: Johns Hopkins University Press, 2003), 242–45. See reference to Kaufmann in Miller, "*Democracy*," 44.

4 I have used the 1964 printed version of the *Port Huron Statement*. See pp. 3, 8–9, 36.

5 See Casey Hayden in Alexander Bloom and Wini Breines, eds., *"Takin' It to the Streets": A Sixties Reader* (New York: Oxford University Press, 1995), 83.

6 See Terry H. Anderson's perceptive *The Movement and the Sixties* (New York: Oxford University Press, 1995).

7 Quoted in Robert Cohen, *Freedom's Orator: Mario Savio and the Radical Legacy of the 1960s* (New York: Oxford University Press, 2009), 6, 41.

8 Cohen, *Freedom's Orator*, 41, 43–44; Jo Freeman, "From Freedom Now! to Free Speech: The FSM's Roots in the Bay Area Civil Rights Movement," in Robert Cohen and Reginald E. Zelnik, eds., *The Free Speech Movement: Reflections on Berkeley in the 1960s* (Berkeley: University of California Press, 2002), 73–79.

9 Of many accounts of these events, most recent is Cohen, *Freedom's Orator*, 75–97.

10 Margot Adler, "My Life in the FSM: Memories of a Freshman," in Cohen and Zelnick, eds., *Free Speech Movement*, 116.

11 Bloom and Breines, *"Takin' It to the Streets*," 112.

12 This account follows Michael Rossman, *The Wedding within the War* (Garden City: Doubleday, 1971).

13 Bloom & Breines, *"Takin' It to the Streets*," 115; Adler, "My Life in the FSM," 116.

14 Cohen, *Freedom's Orator*, 100–101.

15 Obituary, *New York Times*, Nov. 8, 1996; text in Cohen, *Freedom's Orator*, 326–32.

16 Cohen and Zelnick, eds., *Free Speech Movement*, 122.

17 Ibid., 384.

18 Most got off lightly, but the leaders received jail sentences and probation agreements forbidding illegal actions. Cohen, *Freedom's Orator*, 243.

19 E.g., CBS's "The Berkeley Rebels" (1965), which may still be viewed at "The Free Speech Movement," at http://www.lib.berkeley.edu/MRC/FSM.html (retrieved March 31, 2012).

20 "The 'Rossman Report': A Memoir of Making History," in Cohen and Zelnick, eds., *Free Speech Movement*, 189–214. For a more personal, passionate expression of the "They take away everything" theme, see Rossman's "The Birth of the Free Speech Movement," *Wedding*, 92–120.

21 Cohen, *Freedom's Orator*, 140–41; David A. Hollinger, "A View from the Margins," in Cohen and Zelnick, eds., *Free Speech Movement*, 184. To Hollinger this trait was exceptional.

22 Harold Taylor, review of Rossman's *On Learning and Social Change* (New York: Random House, 1972) in *Change* 4:9 (1972): 56–58. Also see Rossman's thoughtful remarks "The FSM and Education" in "Looking Back at the Free Speech Movement [1974]" at http://www.fsm-a.org/stacks/lookingback%281974%29.html (retrieved April 5, 2011).

23 Rossman, *Wedding*, 122; Adler, "My Life in the FSM," 120.

24 David Lance Goines, "The Filthy Speech Movement," in his *The Free Speech Movement: Coming of Age in the 1960s* (Ten Speed Press, 1993), chap. 50, revised for electronic presentation, 1999, at http://texts.cdlib.org/view?docId=kt687004sg &query=&brand=calisphere. Schorer is quoted at 494–95. On faculty reaction to the "filthy speech" crisis, see Reginald E. Zelnick, "On the Side of the Angels: The Berkeley Faculty and the FSM," Cohen and Zelnick, eds., *Free Speech Movement*, 320–22.

25 Cohen, *Freedom's Orator*, 233–38.

26 Jerry Rubin, *Do It!: Scenarios of the Revolution* (New York: Simon and Schuster, 1970), 4, 109–12.

27 Quoted in Cohen, *Freedom's Orator*, 222.

28 Rossman, "The Fourth Night of Cambodia," *Wedding*, 8–12.

29 William Scranton et al., *Report of the President's Commission on Campus Unrest* (Washington D.C.: Government Printing Office, 1970), 25–28. William Scranton was governor of Pennsylvania, 1963–67.

30 See Hugh Davis Graham, "On Riots and Riot Commissions: Civil Disorders in the 1960s," *Public Historian* 2:4 (1980): 22–23.

31 Rossman, "A Violence Sequence," *Wedding*, 208–22.

32 Rossman, "New York: The War Is Over," *Wedding*, 222–32.

33 Staughton Lynd, "Radical Politics and Nonviolent Revolution," *Liberation* 11:2 (April 1966): 13–19. This speech was delivered at rallies in Chicago and Madison, Wisc.

34 See Steve Batterson, *Steven Smale: The Mathematician Who Broke the Dimension Barrier* (Providence, R.I.: American Mathematical Society, 2000), 98–104; "Some Autobiographical Notes," in F. Cucker and R. Wong, eds., *The Collected Papers of Steven Smale* (Singapore: World Scientific, 2000), vol. 1, pt. 3, pp. 469–79, at http:// ebooks.worldscinet.com/ISBN/9789812792815/toc.shtml (retrieved March 31, 2012).

35 I follow Batterson, *Steven Smale*, 107–23. Rubin's *Do It!* is influential but not reliable.

36 For a thoughtful study of the VDC and review of scholarly literature on its effectiveness, see Gerard J. De Groot, "The Limits of Moral Protest and Participatory Democracy: The Vietnam Day Committee," *Pacific Historical Review* 64:1 (1995): 95–119.

37 Wilmer J. Young, "A Testimony for Radical Peace Action," Pendle Hill Pamphlet 118 (Wallingford, Pa., 1961).

38 See Paul Goodman's remembrance of his son Matthew at Bronx Science in *New Reformation* (Oakland: PM Press, 2010; 1st pub., 1970), 161.

39 For the letter and the context of events, see online: "Conelrad Adjacent," posted Jan. 16, 2011, at http://conelrad.blogspot.com/2011/01/eleanor-roosevelts-snippy-letter-to.html (retrieved March 31, 2012).

40 Charles DeBenedetti (with assisting author Charles Chatfield), *An American Ordeal: The Antiwar Movement of the Vietnam Era* (Syracuse: Syracuse University Press, 1990), 50; PBS, "People and Events: Operation Alert" in "Race for the Superbomb," http://www.pbs.org/wgbh/amex/bomb/peopleevents/pandeAMEX64.html (retrieved June 11, 2012).

41 Amy Swerdlow, *Women Strike for Peace: Traditional Motherhood and Radical Politics in the 1960s* (Chicago: University of Chicago Press, 1993), 16–19, 138.

42 Ibid., 134–35.

43 Ibid., 178–81, 211–27.

44 Norman Mailer, *The Armies of the Night* (New York: Plume 1994; 1st pub., 1968), 271.

45 Lawrence S. Wittner, *Rebels against War: The American Peace Movement, 1933–1983* (Philadelphia: Temple University Press, 1984), 267, quoting *Fellowship*, May 1, 1960, and *American Sociological Review* 27 (Oct. 1962): 658, 665.

46 For a good, clear summary, see Wikipedia, s.v. "Selective Service System," sec. 1, "History," online at http://en.wikipedia.org/wiki/Selective_Service_System#History (retrieved March 31, 2012).

47 Mel Piehl, *Breaking Bread: The Catholic Worker and the Origin of Catholic Radicalism in America* (Philadelphia: Temple University Press, 1982), 231; Murray Polner and Jim O'Grady, *Disarmed and Dangerous, The Radical Lives and Times of Daniel and Philip Berrigan* (New York: Basic Books, 1997), 126; DeBenedetti, *American Ordeal*, 96. Estimate found in Wikipedia, s.v. "Draft Card Burning" citing Sherry Gershon Gottlieb, *Hell No We Won't Go: Resisting the Draft during the Vietnam War* (New York: Viking, 1991), 173.

48 Paul Goodman, "We Won't Go," *New York Review of Books*, May 18, 1967, June 29, 1967.

49 David Maraniss, *They Marched into Sunlight: War and Peace, Vietnam and America, October 1967* (New York: Simon and Schuster, 2003), 456.

50 Mailer, *Armies of the Night*, 69–79.

51 Ibid., 225, 232, 260–61, 266, 275, 279.

52 Robert S. McNamara, *In Retrospect: The Tragedy and Lessons of Vietnam* (New York: Random House, 1995), 305.

53 Adam Garfinkle, *Telltale Hearts: The Origins and Impact of the Vietnam Antiwar Movement* (New York: St. Martin's Press, 1995), 302.

54 Jesse Kindig, "Draft Resistance in the Vietnam Era," in "Antiwar and Radical History Project—Pacific Northwest," online at http://depts.washington.edu/antiwar/ (retrieved May 9, 2011), citing Laurence M. Baskir and William A. Strauss, *Chance and Circumstance: The Draft, the War, and the Vietnam Generation* (New York: Alfred A. Knopf, 1978), 69. See also Sherry Gershon Gottlieb, *Hell No, We Won't Go! Resisting the Draft during the Vietnam War* (New York: Viking, 1991), and David Cortright, *Soldiers in Revolt* (Garden City: Anchor, 1975).

55 DeBenedetti, *American Ordeal*, 375.

56 Ben Welter, "The Big Lake One," March 27, 2008, http://blogs2.startribune.com/blogs/oldnews/archives/6 (retrieved May 15, 2011). See also http://www.selective-service.org/barry-bondhus-case.htm (retrieved May 15, 2011).

57 Francine du Plessix Gray, "The Ultra-Resistance: on the Trial of the Milwaukee 14," *New York Review of Books*, Sept. 25, 1969, with follow-up letter, "Moral Choice," by John H. Fried, Oct. 9, 1969.

58 Garry Wills, *Certain Trumpets: The Call of Leaders* (New York: Simon and Schuster, 1994), 263–64; Anne Klejment, "War Resistance and Property Destruction: The Catonsville Nine Draft Board Raid and Catholic Worker Pacifism," in *Revolution of the Heart: Essays on the Catholic Workers*, ed. Patrick Coy (Philadelphia: New Society, 1988).

59 Murray Polner and Jim O'Grady, *Disarmed and Dangerous: The Radical Lives and Times of Daniel and Philip Berrigan* (New York: Basic Books, 1997), 122–32.

60 Ibid., 123–26; Piehl, *Breaking Bread*, 232–33.

61 William Stringfellow, "The Death of Roger La Porte," *Catholic Worker*, Nov. 1966, p. 1.

62 Lynd, "Radical Politics," 14.

63 Polner and O'Grady, *Disarmed and Dangerous*, 176–92, 196–201. These events are recounted in a number of other studies.

64 See "First Lecture," in William Sloane Coffin, Jr., and Morris L. Leibman, *Civil Disobedience: Aid or Hindrance to Justice?* (Washington: American Enterprise Institute, 1972), 5. On the fugitives: Polner and O'Grady, *Disarmed and Dangerous*, 215.

65 Polner and O'Grady, *Disarmed and Dangerous*, 190–92; Karl Meyer quoted (1957) in "A Radical Takes Root," *University of Chicago Magazine* 93:4 (April 2001); Daniel Berrigan, *Portraits of Those I Love* (New York: Crossroad, 1982), 88. Also see generally Klejment, "War Resistance and Property Destruction."

66 Staughton Lynd, "Letter from Jail: Telling Right from Wrong," *Liberation* 13:7 (Dec. 1968), 12–13.

67 See his impressive memoir, Terry Sullivan, "The Movement" (Denver: Christian Radical Press, 2006), available online at http://www.angelfire.com/un/crp/pdf-htm/move.html (retrieved June 6, 2012).

68 Bernardine Dohrn, Billy Ayers, Jeff Jones, and Celia Sojourn, "Prairie Fire: The Politics of Revolutionary Anti-Imperialism: the Political Statement of the Weather Underground" (San Francisco: Communications, 1974). Now an expensive collectible, it is available online at: www.usasurvival.org/docs/Prairie-fire.pdf (retrieved June 6, 2012).

69 Ibid., 6–7, 13–14, 21, 24.

70 On basic details, a valuable early work is Ron Jacobs, *The Way the Wind Blew: A History of the Weather Underground* (London: Verso, 1997). There is a renaissance of serious studies, including most recently Dan Berger, *Outlaws of America* (2005); Jeremy Varon, *Bringing the War Home* (2004), in addition to many memoirs.

71 At Mennonite colleges opposition to the Vietnam War was "public and fervent," according to Valarie Ziegler's paper on John Howard Yoder at Mid-America History Conference, Memphis, 2003. But Donald W. Dayton has characterized the 1960s in evangelical colleges as a time of escape and avoidance (*Discovering an Evangelical Heritage* [New York: Harper and Row, 1976]). For conversations in Parchman between midwestern evangelicals and northeastern nonreligious freedom riders, see *The Political Autobiography of Charles A. Haynie: A Memoir of the New Left* (Knoxville: University of Tennessee Press, 2009), 4, 48–50.

72 Frank Rich, "Off the Town after the Riot," *Harvard Crimson*, April 20, 1970.

73 "Education: New Campus Mood: From Rage to Reform," *Time*, Nov. 30, 1970. The book in question: Charles A. Reich, *The Greening of America* (New York: Random House, 1970).

74 Noam Chomsky, "Mayday: The Case for Civil Disobedience," *New York Review of Books*, June 17, 1971, at http://www.chomsky.info/articles/19710617.htm (retrieved July3, 2011).

75 Reprinted in Hannah Arendt, *Crises of the Republic* (New York: Harcourt Brace Jovanovich, 1972), 96.

76 Christian Bay, "Civil Disobedience," *International Encyclopedia of the Social Sciences*, 17 vols. (New York: Crowell Collier and Macmillan, 1968), 2:473–87.

77 Graham Hughes, "Civil Disobedience and the Political Question Doctrine," *New York University Law Review* (March 1968), as quoted in Arendt, *Crises*, 100.

78 Quoted in William Safire, ed., *Safire's Political Dictionary* (New York: Random House, 1978), 120.

79 Andrew Greeley, "The Berrigans—Phrenetic?" *Holy Cross Quarterly* 4:1 (Jan. 1971): 15–19.

80 Herbert J. Storing, "The Case against Civil Disobedience," in Hugo Adam Bedau, ed., *Civil Disobedience in Focus* (London: Routledge, 1991), 86, 94. First published in Robert A. Goldwin, ed., *On Civil Disobedience: Essays Old and New* (Chicago: Rand McNally, 1969).

81 Abe Fortas, *Concerning Dissent and Civil Disobedience* (New York: New American Library, 1968); William O. Douglas, *Points of Rebellion* (New York: Random House, 1970).

82 Mulford Q. Sibley, "On Political Obligation and Civil Disobedience," in Michael P. Smith and Kenneth L. Deutsch, eds., *Political Obligation and Civil Disobedience* (New York: Thomas Y. Crowell, 1972), 21. This essay originally appeared in *Journal of the Minnesota Academy of Science* (1965).

83 Jack P. Greene, ed., *Encyclopedia of American Political History* (1984), s.v. "Civil Disobedience."

84 See S. Jonathan Bass, *Blessed Are the Peacemakers: Martin Luther King Jr., Eight White Religious Leaders, and the "Letter from Birmingham Jail"* (Baton Rouge: Louisiana State University Press, 2001). For a 2011 interdenominational expression of repentance that "some of us have not progressed far enough beyond the initial message from the Birmingham clergy," see "Ministers Answer King's Letter

from Birmingham Jail," at http://www.pres-outlook.com/news-and-analysis/ 1-news-a-analysis/11013-ministers-answer-kings-letter-from-birmingham-jail. html (retrieved June 6, 2012).

85 See John P. Diggins, *Up from Communism: Conservative Odysseys in American Intellectual History* (New York: Harper Torchbooks, 1977), 362, 446; Will Herberg, " 'Civil Rights' and Violence: Who Are the Guilty Ones?" *National Review*, Sept. 7, 1965, pp. 769–770. For the views of another *NR* regular, see Ernest van den Haag, *Political Violence and Civil Disobedience* (New York: Harper and Row, 1972).

86 Michael Walzer et al., "Civil Disobedience and 'Resistance,' " *Dissent* 15:1 (Jan./Feb., 1968): 13–15.

87 Ibid., 16–18.

88 Ibid., 19–21.

89 Ibid., 21–23.

90 Ibid., 23–25.

91 Storing, "Case against Civil Disobedience," in Bedau, ed., *Civil Disobedience in Context*, 87.

92 Eugene V. Rostow, ed., *Is Law Dead?*, symposium of the Association of the Bar of the City of New York (New York: Touchstone, 1971), 51–53.

93 In *Brown v. Louisiana*, 383 U.S. 131 (1966) the convictions of CORE members seeking to integrate a public library in Louisiana were set aside. In *Walker et al. v. City of Birmingham*, 388 U.S. 307 (1967) the U.S. Supreme Court sustained the convictions of Martin Luther King, Jr., and other clergy for violating a Birmingham city ordinance and Alabama state court restraining order. The majority (Stewart, joined by White, Harlan, Clark, and Black) cited precedents concerning anti-strike injunctions. Justices Warren, Douglas, Brennan, and Fortas in dissent raised First Amendment issues. King and seven other black ministers were sent to jail, where he wrote his famous letter. Fortas, *Concerning Dissent*, 14–17, 35.

94 President Kennedy, radio address to the nation, Sept. 30, 1962. American RadioWorks (American Public Media), online at http://soundlearning.publicradio. org/subjects/history_civics/whitehouse_on_civilrights/Transcript_%20JFK%20 Addresses%20Nation%20Pre.pdf.

95 Fortas, *Concerning Dissent*, 35.

96 Martin Oppenheimer and George Lakey, *A Manual for Direct Action* (Chicago: Quadrangle, 1964).

97 Howard Zinn, *Disobedience and Democracy: Nine Fallacies on Law and Order* (New York: Random House, 1968), 16.

98 *St. Louis Post-Dispatch*, Feb. 11, 2000; Lisa Belkin, "Doesn't Anybody Know How to Be a Fugitive Anymore?" *New York Times Magazine*, April 30, 2000, pp. 60–65.

99 Jon Wiener, "Give Peace a Chance," *Nation*, Oct. 20, 1997. On the Civil Obedience Act, see "The Civil Rights Act of 1968," in Bernard Schwartz, ed., *Statutory History of the United States: Civil Rights* (New York: Chelsea House, 1970), 2:1629–1837, esp. 1654–56.

100 There is surprisingly little about his life before Spelman in his autobiography, *You Can't Stay Neutral on a Moving Train* (Boston: Beacon Press, 1994). He discussed his many courtroom appearances at pp. 159–62. Details of his life were reviewed in his appearance in the Camden 28 courtroom: http://www.pbs.org/pov/camden28/special_zinn_02.php (retrieved June 20, 2011).

101 Zinn, *Disobedience and Democracy*, 121.

102 For a helpful overview, see Kimberley Brownlee, "Civil Disobedience," in *Stanford Encyclopedia of Philosophy*, at http://plato.stanford.edu/entries/civil-disobedience/ (2009).

103 Patricia Roberts Harris, "Comment" on Eugene V. Rostow, "The Rightful Limits of Freedom," in Rostow, ed., *Is Law Dead?* 103–9. One of Arendt's aims in *Crises* was to refute various writers who had stressed the duty of civil disobedients to go to jail. For conservative critics of "resistance" who accord legitimacy to some forms of "disobedience," see the comments by Lewis Feuer and Irving Kristol in Bedau, ed., *Civil Disobedience*, 204–5, 208–9. For an argument that rejected Fortas's position yet still tried to "limit" disobedience in several ways (to passive, noninjurious acts, preferably not involving property damage, on serious issues), see Lawrence R. Velvel, *Undeclared War and Civil Disobedience: The American System in Crisis* (New York: Dunellen/Lawyers' Committee on American Policy towards Vietnam), 193–214.

104 "Religious Obedience and Civil Disobedience: A Policy Statement of the National Council of Churches of Christ in the United States of America, Adopted by the General Board, Jan. 7, 1968," in Smith and Deutsch, eds., *Political Obligation*, 66–72. For conflicting views of such guidelines, see Guenter Lewy, *Peace and Revolution: The Moral Crisis of American Pacifism* (Grand Rapids: Eerdmans, 1988); and William Robert Miller, *Nonviolence: A Christian Interpretation* (New York: Schocken, 1966), 202–14.

CHAPTER 10 The Day of the Demonstrations Isn't Over

1 Storing, "Case against Civil Disobedience," in Bedau, ed., *Civil Disobedience in Context*, 85.

2 See, e.g., "Social Change-In," *AARP Bulletin*, July–Aug. 2010, p. 47.

3 Taylor Branch, *At Canaan's Edge: America in the King Years, 1965–68* (New York: Simon and Schuster, 2006), 635. For a long-term perspective, see Lucy G. Barber, *Marching on Washington: The Forging of an American Political Tradition* (Berkeley: University of California Press, 2002).

4 http://www.4president.org/speeches/carter1976acceptance.htm.

5 Samuel Lovejoy, "Somebody's Got to Do It," *Time It Was: American Stories from the Sixties*, ed. Karen Manners Smith and Tim Koster (Upper Saddle River, N.J.: Pearson Prentice-Hall, 2008), 415–32; Robert Surbrug, Jr., *Beyond Vietnam: The Politics of Protest in Massachusetts, 1974–1990* (Amherst: University of Massachusetts Press, 2009), 20–48, esp. 42–43.

6 Barbara Epstein, *Political Protest and Cultural Revolution: Nonviolent Direct Action in the 1970s and 1980s* (Berkeley: University of California Press, 1991), 88.

7 For these events, see *New York Times*, Aug. 5, 1985; Sept. 15, 1985.

8 Todd Gitlin, "Divestment Stirs a New Generation," *Nation*, May 18, 1985, pp. 585–87. Further arrests occurred, notably at Wesleyan, on a national day of protest, Oct. 11, 1985. See *Nashville Tennessean*, Oct. 12, 1985.

9 "Conservative Students Plan Drive against Investments in Russia," *Chronicle of Higher Education*, June 26, 1985, p. 26.

10 Iver Peterson, "Conservation and Tourist Interests at Odds in Dispute at Yellowstone," *New York Times*, Aug. 7, 1985.

11 Eric Eckholm, "Fight on Animal Experiments Gains Intensity on Many Fronts," *New York Times*, May 7, 1985.

12 Channel 9 (WWOR-TV), 10 o'clock news, Jan. 1, 1992.

13 William Safire, "On Language," *New York Times Magazine*, Sept. 15, 1985.

14 Gitlin, "Divestment," 586; *New York Times*, Feb. 8, 1985; *Wall Street Journal*, July 5, 1985. On NOW see "Friends Smeal, Goldsmith Contend for Presidency of NOW," *Houston Chronicle*, Aug. 26, 1985, sec. 12:2.

15 *New York Times*, Feb. 8, 1985.

16 *New York Times*, June 25, 1985.

17 Gandhi, *Autobiography*, 470; Miller, *Nonviolence*, 74–75.

18 Quoted in Branch, *Canaan's Edge*, 744.

19 "Anti-Abortion Protests," *Washington Post*, June 21, 1978.

20 Peter Carlson, "'Please Don't Kill Your Baby,'" *Post Sunday Magazine*, March 20, 1988, pp. 24ff.

21 Gina Kolata, "Nomadic Group of Anti-Abortionists Uses New Tactics to Make Its Mark," *New York Times*, March 24, 1992. Marty contrasted the Lambs to Operation Rescue, a "rough" outfit "whose only purpose is to make us angry." But the separation between them was not so clear. On the Lambs' association with murder, see David Samuels, "The Making of a Fugitive," *New York Times Magazine*, March 21, 1999. On violence and murder in the "abortion wars," a growing list of studies includes: Eyal Press, *Absolute Convictions: My Father, a City, and the Conflict That Divided America* (New York: Henry Holt, 2006), Jon Wells, *Sniper: The True Story of Anti-Abortion Killer James Kopp* (Missasauga, Ont.: Wiley, 2008), and James Risen and Judy Thomas, *Wrath of Angels: The American Abortion War* (New York: Basic Books, 1998).

22 Ari L. Goldman, "Evangelical Group Sets Prayer Protest of Federal Policies," *New York Times*, May 25, 1985. *Sojourners* has continued to publish and sustain the zeal of "liberal" or "progressive" Christians committed to the causes of justice and peace and to the sanctity of life—which motivates them to oppose most abortions without seeking to criminalize them. See Jim Wallis, "Make Way for Pro-Life Democrats," *Sojourners* 33:6 (June 2004): 5.

23 See James Barron, "Violence Increases against Abortion Clinics," *New York Times*, Nov. 5, 1984; Joseph Scheidler, *Closed: 99 Ways to Close the Abortion Clinics* (San Francisco: Ignatius, 1985).

24 See the long article by Linda Witt, "Man with a Mission—Joe Scheidler Pulls No Punches in His Crusade against Abortion," *Chicago Tribune*, Aug. 11, 1985, reprinted in Eric Zornie, "Will Abortion Protesters Be as Good as Their Lawsuit Claims They Are?" *Chicago Tribune*, Oct. 2, 2007, online at http://blogs.chicagotribune.com/news_columnists_ezorn/2007/10/will-abortion-p.html   (retrieved June 9, 2012).

25 Kirk Johnson, "Connecticut Abortion Protesters Clog Jails," *New York Times*, June 21, 1989; Tamar Lewin, "With Thin Staff and Thick Debt, Anti-Abortion Group Faces Struggle," ibid., June 11, 1990,; Dan Barry, "Icon for Abortion Protesters Is Looking for a Second Act," ibid., Nov. 20, 2001; Catherine S. Manegold, "Abortion Foes See Tactics Backfire in New York," ibid., July 19, 1992.

26 Barry, "Icon"; Jay Rogers, "Looking Back at the 1980s: America's #1 Social Issue," (Dec. 1989), at http://www.forerunner.com/forerunner/X0416 Americas1Social_Is.html (retrieved Aug. 26, 2011).

27 Ronald Smothers, "Atlanta Protests Prove Magnet for Abortion Foes," *New York Times*, Aug. 13, 1988; Julian Bond, "Dr. King's Unwelcome Heirs," ibid., Nov. 2, 1988.

28 Catherine S. Manegold, "Protests in Buffalo Fade into a Footnote to Abortion," *New York Times*, May 3, 1992.

29 Sharon Erickson Nepstad, *Religion and War Resistance in the Plowshares Movement* (Cambridge: Cambridge University Press, 2008), 107.

30 The jury awarded, by a 9–3 vote, $8.2 million, little of which was successfully collected. "February 8, 1991: Lovejoy Surgicenter v. Portland, Oregon Prolifers," online at Randy Alcorn's website: http://www.epm.org/resources/2010/Jan/20/february–8–1991-lovejoy-surgicenter-v-portland/ (retrieved Jan. 21, 2010).

31 *Clinic Blockades:* Hearing Before the Subcommittee on Crime and Criminal Justice, Committee on the Judiciary, H.R. 102d Cong., 2d Sess., May 6, 1902, p. 21. The congressman was Mel Levine of California.

32 Ibid., 139.

33 Ibid., 140, 167.

34 Michael Bray in ibid., 170.

35 Cynthia Gorney, *Articles of Faith: A Frontline History of the Abortion Wars* (New York: Simon and Schuster, 1998), 246–47. No reference was made to Virginia Minor's defense of her right to vote, launched in the same building.

36 Ronald Reagan, *Abortion and the Conscience of the Nation* (Nashville: Thomas Nelson, 1984), 34. The parallel may be overdrawn. A "Human Life" Bill, which Reagan praises (p. 30), was introduced by Senator Jesse Helms, not the most ardent champion of racial equality.

37 J. C. Willke, M.D., *Abortion and Slavery: History Repeats* (Cincinnati: Hayes, 1984), 34, 66, 69. His principal source on antislavery: Dumond, *Antislavery* (1961). A

more successful study of parallels was Mary Meehan, "Lessons from the Anti-Slavery Movement," *Human Life Review* (Summer 1999, revised 2004), at http://www.meehanreports.com/abolition.html.

38 Larry Gara's *The Liberty Line: The Legend of the Underground Railroad* first appeared in 1961. Gara himself had been imprisoned for three years as a draft resister and protested against racial segregation in prison during World War II.

39 Tim Stafford, "In Reluctant Praise of Extremism," and Paul Brenton, "Casualties of the Abortion Wars," *Christianity Today*, 36:12 (Oct. 26, 1992): 18–24. See also Stafford's *Shaking the System: What I Learned from the Great American Reform Movements* (Downers Grove, Ill.: InterVarsity, 2007). For praise of Barry Goldwater's declaration that "extremism in defense of liberty is no vice" from a Georgia champion of the "Abortion Abolition Movement," see Neil Horsley, "Notes of Interest," at http://christiangallery.com/sept943.html (retrieved Dec. 16, 2004). Horsley credited the slogan to Karl Hess. It is doubtful that Hess, who attributed the quotation to Harry Jaffa and ultimately Cicero and moved far to the left of Goldwater, would have welcomed the salute.

40 Bruce Ledewitz, "Perspectives on the Law of the American Sit-In," *Whittier Law Review* 16 (1995): 501–2, 525–27.

41 "Remarks by the President at Signing of 'Freedom of Access to Clinic Entrances Act,'" online at http://clinton6.nara.gov/1994/05/1994–05–26-presidents-remarks-at-clinic-access-bill-signing.html.

42 For a critique of OR's claim that parallels with the abolitionists justified civil disobedience, making its own claim that William Wilberforce's example was truer to Scripture than the American abolitionists, see David Hagopian, "The Rhetoric of Rescue," *Antithesis* 1:4 (July–Aug. 1990), at http://www.reformed.org/webfiles/antithesis/index.html. For another anti-abortion admirer of Wilberforce, Rep. Christopher Smith, see "Single-Minded Crusader Who Is Blocking Dues to U.N.," *New York Times*, Nov. 15, 1999.

43 In 1970 Neuhaus was identified as active in SANE, Clergy and Laymen Concerned about Vietnam, among other liberal movements, pastor of a Lutheran church in Bedford-Stuyvesant, and a delegate to the 1968 Democratic Convention in Chicago where he was "arrested in a protest against the denial of civil liberties." He had also been arrested twice during "actions for racial justice." Peter L. Berger and Richard J. Neuhaus, *Movement and Revolution* (Garden City: Anchor, 1970). In this work he took seriously the prospect of revolutionary change. There was of course no mention of abortion.

44 "The End of Democracy? The Judicial Usurpation of Politics," *First Things* 67 (Nov. 1996). On the editorial meetings, see Damon Linker, *The Theocons: Secular America under Siege* (New York: Anchor, 2007), ch. 3. The breach "was never fully healed," wrote John Podhoretz in *Commentary* at the time of Neuhaus's death (http://richardjneuhaus.blogspot.com/).

45 Correspondence, *First Things*, Jan. 1997.

46 The four: Peter Berger, Midge Decter, Walter Berns, and Gertrude Himmelfarb. See their contributions to a subsequent symposium, "On the Future of Conservatism," *Commentary* 103 (Feb. 1997). In that symposium William Kristol suggested it would have been more constructive to cite the coalition builder Abraham Lincoln rather than the "fiery" words of Garrison.

47 Ibid. Podhoretz noted that Neuhaus was now denying that "the symposium said what so many of us understood it as saying. . . . It is a wonder to me that my old friend Richard Neuhaus has forgotten what we learned while fighting those wars as comrades-in-arms against the radicalism we had both formerly espoused."

48 Robert Bork, *Slouching Towards Gomorrah: Modern Liberalism and American Decline* (New York: HarperCollins, 1996), 32.

49 *Planned Parenthood of Southeastern Pa. v. Casey*, 505 U.S. 833 (1992) 505 U.S. 833. For Bork's comments, see *Slouching Towards Gomorrah*, 103, 111.

50 The possibility stands out today in the discussion of the rights of "persons" in Justice Stevens's concurring opinion. In legal precedent the idea of "personhood" has application only "postnatally"; and "a developing organism that is not yet a 'person'" does not have what is sometimes described as a "right to life" or presumably the other rights associated with "personhood" cited by the majority in this decision. "This has been and, by the Court's holding today, remains, a fundamental premise of our constitutional law governing reproductive autonomy." *Planned Parenthood v. Casey*, 914. To be clear, Stevens discusses the rights of mothers but does not bring up rights for children, once born.

51 See, e.g., Jack Kevorkian, "Kevorkian and the Ninth Amendment," transcribed speech at Kutztown University, Sept. 2009, online at www.pasocsociety.org/article3-kevorkian (retrieved May 15, 1212).

52 See, e.g., *New York Times*, letters, April 19 and 22, 2011.

53 The equally well-known case of Karen Quinlan was decided by the New Jersey Supreme Court in 1976. After her respirator was removed, she lived ten more years in a vegetative state.

54 Marilyn Webb, *The Good Death: The New American Search to Reshape the End of Life* (New York: Bantam, 1999).

55 John D. Skrentny, *The Minority Rights Revolution* (Cambridge: Harvard University Press, 2002), 274.

56 Mary F. Hayden, "Civil Rights, Civil Protest, Civil Disobedience: Using Direct Action to Change Society," Institute on Community Integration, at http://ici.umn.edu. An excellent Wikipedia article (yes, I know teachers often disallow such citations) on the "disability rights movement" includes scores of references to activists, lawsuits, legislative campaigns, civil disobedience demonstrations, and judicial rulings on the rights and duties of protesters.

57 The dispute between husband and parents, the intervention of politicians, the role of pro-life lawyers and the ACLU, and the complex stages of decision making in

the Florida courts were widely reported. It remains hard to determine "Terri's truth," amid all the conflict and grandstanding.

58 The occasion inspired vivid reporting. See Rick Lyman, "Protesters with Hearts on Sleeves and Anger on Signs," *New York Times*, March 28, 2005; and Manuel Roig-Franzia, "Schiavo 'Is Failing,' Her Father Says," *Washington Post*, March 29, 2005.

59 *National NOW Times*, Aug. 1992, pp. 1, 4.

60 *Chronicle of Higher Education*, Sept. 4, 1985, p.26. In mentioning Thoreau, the judge reminds us how little political etiquette has to do with historical fact. He might more fittingly have mentioned a conventional moralist like Francis Wayland.

61 See *Universitas* 27:2 (Winter–Spring 2001): 6–11; *New York Times*, Feb. 21, 1992.

62 Dan Barry, "Civil Disobedience, Negotiated: Arresting Choreography," *New York Times*, March 28, 1999, sec. 4, p. 1.

63 Metropolitan Diary, *New York Times*, April 12, 1999.

64 Barbara Epstein, "The Antiwar Movement during the Gulf War," *Social Justice* 19:1 (1992): 115–37.

65 See the impressive compilations: http://en.wikipedia.org/wiki/Protests_against_ the_invasion_of_Afghanistan; and http://en.wikipedia.org/wiki/Protests_ against_the_Iraq_War.

66 Kate Zernike, "Disagreements about Civil Disobedience Divide America's Antiwar Movement," *New York Times*, March 19, 2003, A20; Kate Zernike and Dean E. Murray, "Antiwar Movement Morphs from Wild-Eyed to Civil," ibid., March 29, 2003, B1; Frank Davies (Knight Ridder), "Anti-war Activists Regroup, Try Variety of Tactics," *St. Louis Post-Dispatch*, March 28, 2003.

67 Jennifer Kerr (Associated Press), "Sheehan Arrested during Anti-War Protest," *New York Times*, Sept. 26, 2005; Karen Houppert, "Cindy Sheehan, Mother of a Movement?" *Nation*, June 12, 2006, pp. 11–16; Anemona Hartocollis, "War Opponents Are Convicted in U.N. Protest," *New York Times*, Dec. 12, 2006.

68 Evelyn Nieves, "Antiwar Groups Shifting Their Focus on Bush," *Washington Post*, April 14, 2003.

69 Frank Rich, "A Gay Marriage War in the Making," *New York Times*, Feb. 28, 2004; O. Ricardo Pimental, "Gays' Civil Disobedience Is Lesson Worth Copying," *Arizona Republic*, Feb. 22, 2004; "Rep. Frank Opposes Gay Marriage Effort," CNN. com, Feb. 19, 2004; Andrew Sullivan, "The Rule of Law," The Daily Dish, Andrewsullivan.com (retrieved March 3, 2004).

70 See the website at www.ruckus.org. For an earlier, more radical manual from Earth First!, see *Earth First! Direct Action Manual*, 1st ed., at http://issuu.com/ conflictgypsy/docs/efdirectactionmanual?mode=window&viewMode=double Page, 160 pp. (retrieved June 11, 2012).

71 Michael Kazin, "Saying No to W.T.O.," *New York Times*, Dec. 5, 1999; Emma Bircham and John Charlton, eds., *Anti-Capitalism: A Guide to the Movement* (London: Bookmarks, 2001), 72–73. For an extensive, fair-minded account of the

demonstrations, see Kit Oldham, "WTO Meeting and Protests in Seattle (1999)," two parts, at http://www.historylink.org/index.cfm?DisplayPage=output. cfm&file_id=9213 (retrieved June 11, 2012).

72 See, e.g., Alessandra Stanley and David E. Sanger, "Italian Protester Is Killed by Police at Genoa Meeting," *New York Times*, July 21, 2001; John Tagliabue, "The Protesters: With Eye on Unequal World Wealth, Young Europeans Converge on Genoa," ibid., July 22, 2001.

73 *New York Times*, May 10, 1997. The seventy-three-year-old Berrigan estimated that he had spent seven and one-half years in jail since joining civil rights marchers in Selma, Alabama, in 1961. Among other examples, probably few would give the sanction of civil disobedience to protesters who chopped down genetically engineered corn at the University of Maine in 1999, fewer still to those who burned down a ski lodge and chairlifts in Vail, Colorado, and almost none to whoever sent letters booby-trapped with razor blades to university scientists (*New York Times*, Sept. 8, 1999; *Post-Dispatch*, Oct. 28, 1999; *Nashville Tennessean*, Oct. 23, 1998.) The most extreme measures, firebombs and explosives, associated with animal rights, are not usually thought of as civil disobedience, but they have had success in causing universities and laboratories to regulate their own practices.

74 Kimberley Brownlee, "Civil Disobedience," *Stanford Encyclopedia of Philosophy*, at http://plato.stanford.edu/entries/civil-disobedience/. On environmental and animal-rights protests, she cites the work of Daniel Markovits, "Democratic Disobedience," in *Yale Law Journal* 114 (2005): 1897–1952.

75 Studies of anti-nuclear protests, like Epstein's *Political Protest* and Surbrug's *Beyond Vietnam*, explore the former question, and studies of the anti-abortion movement, like Ledewitz, "Perspectives on the Law of the American Sit-In," raise the latter one.

76 Mary Armstrong, AFT local 420 President, quoted in *Southeast Missourian*, Jan. 7, 2005 at http://www.semissourian.com/story/153813.html (retrieved June 10, 2012).

77 Roger Kimball, *The Long March: How the Cultural Revolution of the 1960s Changed America* (San Francisco: Encounter, 2001), 131.

78 See Robert J. Birgenau, "Message to the Campus Community about 'Occupy Cal,'" at http://newscenter.berkeley.edu/2011/11/10/message-to-the-campus-community-about-occupy-cal/; [Micha Lazarus], Nov. 11, 2011, Not Non-Violent Civil Disobedience, at budgetcrisis.Berkeley.edu; Angus Johnson, "On Margo Bennett, 'Linked Arms,' and Police Violence at the University of California," at http://studentactivism.net/2011/11/14/on-margo-bennett/. Birgenau later apologized to the community. See http://www.dailycal.org/2011/11/22/birgeneau-apologizes-for-police-response-to-occupy-cal/.

79 Tad Friend, "Protest Studies: The State Is Broke, and Berkeley Is in Revolt," *New Yorker*, Jan. 4, 2010, pp. 22–28.

80 Ostertag, "The Militarization of Campus Police," *Huffington Post*, Nov. 19, 2011, at http://www.huffingtonpost.com/mobileweb/bob-ostertag/uc-davis-protest_b_1103039.html.

81 Sharp's works include *The Politics of Nonviolent Action* (Boston: Porter Sargent, 1973), now available in three overlapping volumes, and *Waging Nonviolent Struggle: 20th Century Practice and 21st Century Potential* (Boston: Porter Sargent, 2005). His ninety-three-page guide to liberation from oppressive rule, "From Dictatorship to Democracy," initially published in Bangkok, is available online (4th ed., East Boston, Mass.: Albert Einstein Institution, 1910) in twenty-four languages.

82 Sheryl Gay Stolberg, "Shy U.S. Intellectual Created Playbook Used in a Revolution," *New York Times*, Feb. 16, 2011; Susan P. Jacobs, "Gene Sharp, The 83 Year Old Who Toppled Egypt," *Daily Beast*, Feb. 14, 2011, at http://thedailybeast.com/articles/2011/02/14; As'ad AbuKhalil, "Gene Sharp: The New York Times Story of the Origins of the Tunisian and Egyptian Uprisings," Feb. 14, 2011, Angry Arab News Service, at http://angryarab.blogspot.com/2011/02 (retrieved June 10, 2012).

83 See the major collection of twenty-two essays by participants in the Oxford University project on civil resistance: Adam Roberts and Timothy Garton Ash, eds., *Civil Resistance and Power Politics: The Experience of Non-Violent Action from Gandhi to the Present* (New York: Oxford University Press, 2009). Sharp's work is set in historiographical context in an initial essay by April Carter. See also the thoughtful review by Brian Urquhart, "Revolution without Violence?" *New York Review of Books*, March 10, 2011, pp. 37–40. For another study's broad conclusion that nonviolent uprisings are more likely than violent ones to be successful and to lead to democratic government, see Erica Chenoweth, "Give Peaceful Resistance a Chance," *New York Times*, op-ed page, March 10, 2011; and Maria Stephan and Erica Chenoweth, "Why Civil Resistance Works: The Strategic Logic of Nonviolent Conflict," *International Security* 33:1 (2008): 7–44.

INDEX

Abalone Alliance, 286

Abby Smith and Her Cows (Smith), 144–49

Abenchuchan, Elisa, 5–6

Abernathy, Ralph, 217, 226

Abolitionism: and aid to fugitive slaves, 88–92, 100, 101, 110–15, 121–22, 123, 126, 132, 333n99; black abolitionists, 72, 76–93, 132, 205, 330n44, 330n46, 341n7, 343n22; in Britain, 85; and Civil War, 127; compared with anti-abortion movement, 2, 14, 288, 296–98, 377n42; compared with woman suffrage, 2, 170, 329n42, 342n20; critiques of, 109, 110, 113; dramatic forms of protest by, 19; factors supporting, 328n30; and Garrisonian nonresistance, 85–87, 92, 100–103, 105, 114, 198, 200, 297, 298, 299; and higher law, 115–19, 121–24, 155, 332n91; and Mexican War, 107–8; and moral suasion, 84–86, 101; in northern New England, 103–6; precedents for, 2–3, 23; and religious arguments against slavery, 63–67, 73, 87, 90–92; and right of self-defense and violent resistance, 86–93; and "speak-ins"/church invasions, 104–5; and Underground Railroad, 2, 76, 90, 122, 205, 265, 295, 296, 297, 337n49; violence against abolitionists,

104–6; women in, 62–69, 105–6, 147, 343n22; and women's rights, 130–32. *See also* Slavery; *and specific abolitionists*

Abortion and abortion rights, 289–91, 298, 299, 300, 304–5. *See also* Anti-abortion movement

Abortion and the Conscience of the Nation (Reagan), 296

Abzug, Robert, 326n6, 338n66

Acts of the Anti-Slavery Apostles (Pillsbury), 103–6

Act Up, 293, 310

Adamic, Louis, 176, 189

Adams, John, 27–28, 31, 34

Adams, John Quincy, 50

Adams, Samuel, 25

Adeleke, Tunde, 85

Adler, Margot, 251–53

Affirmative action, 11

Afghanistan, 292, 307

Agape and Eros (Nygren), 224

Agnew, Spiro, 257, 282

AIDS epidemic, 269, 293

Alabama State University, 228

Albany, Ga., 238

Alcoholism. *See* Temperance movement

Alcorn, Randy, 295

Alcott, A. Bronson, 100, 102–3

Alsop, Stewart, 274

2, 15, 232, 269; of King, 14–15, 219, 238, 279; and labor movement, 168–69; of missionaries to Georgia Cherokees, 45–49, 51–55; of racial segregation protesters, 129, 130, 202–3, 216, 232, 246; of Ruckus Society members, 310; of Cindy Sheehan, 309; of Shridharani, 194; of Smith sisters for tax resistance, 145; of student protesters, 253, 254, 257, 281, 305, 306, 368n18; in temperance movement, 159, 162; of Thoreau, 20, 32, 94–95, 96, 97, 184, 253; and treason charges, 209; of Vietnam War protesters, 265–70; for violations of Fugitive Slave Law, 14, 89–90, 121–22, 126, 141; of woman suffragists, 126, 133, 134, 140–41, 150–52, 154, 155, 305
Arsenault, Raymond, 233
Assisted suicide, 298, 301–2
Atomic weapons. *See* Nuclear armament and nuclear testing
Audience of civil disobedience, 17–20
Augustine, Saint, 280
Autobiography (Gandhi), 184–85
Avery, Sewell, 24, 178

Backus, Isaac, 30–34, 47
Bacon, Leonard, 117–18
Baez, Joan, 169, 253, 270, 309
Bailyn, Bernard, 35
Baker, Ella, 215, 225, 231, 364nn32-33
Baker, Russell, 240
Baldwin, Roger, 170–72
Ballou, Adin, 100, 101
Bancroft, George, 27, 28, 80
Baptists, ix, 2, 14, 30–35, 44, 58, 88, 96, 108–9, 336n42
Barker, Charles, 356n17
Basch, Norma, 141, 142, 344n47
Baseball, 246
Bates, Edward, 343n36
Battle of New Orleans, 81
Beach, Thomas Parnell, 336n30
Beck, Glenn, 304
Beecher, Catharine, 60–63, 67
Beecher, Rev. Charles, 111, 114, 297

Beecher, Harriet, 61
Beecher, Henry Ward, 164
Bellows, Henry W., 113
Bennett, D. M., 166
Berger, Peter, 378n46
Bergman, Walter, 234
Berkeley. *See* University of California at Berkeley
Berns, Walter, 378n46
Berrigan, Daniel and Philip, 24, 25, 268–69, 295, 311, 380n73
Berry, Mary, 287
Bible translation, 147, 148–49
Biblical arguments. *See* Religious justification of civil disobedience
Bigelow, Albert, 234
Biondi, Rev. Lawrence, S. J., 305
Birmingham, Ala., civil rights campaign, 234–35, 238–40, 246, 275
Birth control, 163, 164, 167, 305, 352n38
Black, Hugo, 366n67, 373n93
Black Abolitionist Papers, 77
Black Americans: as abolitionists, 72, 76–93, 132, 205, 330n44, 330n46, 341n7; in American Revolution, 81; antebellum northern blacks, 79–83, 93, 337n53; and black culture, 331n62, 331n68; in Civil War, 92; disfranchisement of, 116, 249, 330–31n54; education of, 83–84; stereotypes of, 69–71, 76, 131; urban migration of, 202, 221; and woman suffrage, 342n16, 343n22. *See also* Civil rights movement; Integration; Reconstruction amendments; Segregation; Slavery; Voting rights; *and headings beginning with* Slave
"Black bloc," 311
Black Laws, 117
Blackmun, Harry, 292
Black nationalism, 330n44
Black Panthers, 271
Black Power, 243, 245
Blackstone, William, 38, 322n42, 322n46
Bond, Julian, 294
Bondhus, Barry, 266